THE CHOREOGRAPHIC ART

THE CHOREOGRAPHIC ART

An Outline of its Principles and Craft

by

PEGGY VAN PRAAGH

AND

PETER BRINSON

WITH A FOREWORD BY

CYRIL BEAUMONT

SEVENTY-THREE PHOTOGRAPHS AND
11 DRAWINGS BY ROBERT BRUCE CHURCH

ADAM & CHARLES BLACK
LONDON

PRINTED IN GREAT BRITAIN
BY R. AND R. CLARK LTD., EDINBURGH

DEDICATED TO

THE CHOREOGRAPHERS OF

THE FUTURE

FOREWORD
BY CYRIL BEAUMONT

FIFTY years ago, the word choreography would have evoked small response; but during that period a public for Ballet has grown up, and an examination of Ballet's components is no longer confined in its interest to members of the profession.

The present volume therefore appears at an appropriate moment. It is the product of a collaboration extending over some six years and is concerned with the choreographic art. It is not a practical manual on how to compose ballets and dances, but a detailed examination of the manifold problems that confront the choreographer. It is a pioneer work on a very difficult subject; and it is apposite to consider first the qualifications of the two authors.

Peggy van Praagh has an honoured place in the history of British Ballet: a pupil of Margaret Craske, in 1938 she was a principal dancer in Tudor's London Ballet, and in 1941 joined the Sadler's Wells Ballet as solo dancer. When the Sadler's Wells Theatre Ballet was formed in 1946, Miss van Praagh was appointed its ballet mistress, and from 1952 to 1955, under Dame Ninette de Valois, was its assistant director. She has worked under many choreographers, created a number of roles in Tudor's repertory, and has staged ballets in Canada, Munich and Copenhagen. She is now artistic director of The Australian Ballet.

Peter Brinson is a product of Oxford University, where he took First Class Honours in Modern Greats after the war and started to earn his living as a writer. He was Director of Research, Film Centre, from 1948 to 1953. Having long had an interest in Ballet, in 1955 he founded at Oxford the first university extension courses dealing with its history and with the principles of Choreography, and five years later was invited to undertake similar work for Cambridge University. He has contributed articles on Ballet to leading periodicals and was for a time deputy ballet critic to the *Sunday Times* and ballet critic to *The Queen*. In 1960 he was awarded a Research Fellowship by the Council of Europe to study and report upon the European Archives of Classical Ballet. This enabled him to examine, often with his co-author, the theatre collections in ten

vii

European capitals. Miss van Praagh also visited New York three times and spent a fortnight in Moscow to study the Bolshoi Theatre Ballet and to survey material in the State Theatrical Collections. Thus every effort has been made to gather material on the chosen subject.

The joint authorship of the book is unusual, being the views of a dancer and producer having all the practical details of staging and reproducing a ballet at her finger-tips, fused with the historical knowledge and critical approach of a university lecturer and writer.

Turning to the book proper, the first thing that impresses one is the well-ordered plan. After a succinct analysis of the meaning and purpose of choreography and the training and qualities essential to the dancer aspiring to become a choreographer, the authors survey the origin and main currents of choreography from the sixteenth century to the present day, not only in relation to Europe, but also viewing its development in the United States of America and Soviet Russia.

Having provided the reader with a basic knowledge of choreography in times past, the authors approach the core and prime purpose of their book, which is a careful and detailed examination of the role of the choreographer and the manifold difficulties, practical and theoretical, direct and indirect, artistic and technical, which confront him in his onerous task.

We begin with a consideration of the various types of ballet composition and the search for a theme, weighing the possible advantages and disadvantages of different examples. We pass to the choreographer's collaborators: the artistic director, the composer of the music, the designer of the settings and costumes, and the contribution which each can make to the achievement of a successful entity. Then is discussed the choreographer's material—the bodies of trained dancers and the vocabularies of diverse languages of dance, which he may draw upon for inspiration or mould to some new conception of his own.

Finally, we come to the point at which the roles are cast, the dances allotted, soli and ensembles worked out, and climaxes inserted to achieve vital *coups de théâtre*, followed by the devising of links and endings to unite the whole. Now we see the work transferred from studio to theatre stage, and when the ballet has been rehearsed with full orchestra and attained its first performance, the question arises, how can the work be preserved in all its original freshness, without

loss of technical detail and quality of performance? This perhaps is
the crowning problem. Once the cast is changed, it is difficult for a
newcomer to match the creator of a role, because he or she has not
shared with the choreographer 'the agony and the ecstasy' which
attend all creative work. The newcomer receives the words, so to
speak, of the play, but not the accents which first made them live.

The book concludes with an admirable series of appendices. Here
the serious reader may study with profit typical examples of ballet
scenarii ranging from the eighteenth century to our own times, and
some examples of working notes of a choreographer's collaborators;
moreover, with an eye to the future, there are sections comprising
suggested courses of training for choreographers and for ballet critics.
Certainly this country, which under Dame Ninette de Valois, Dame
Marie Rambert, Sir Frederick Ashton and their collaborators, has
built up internationally admired organisations in a little over thirty
years, should establish a School of Choreography. Here, aspirants
would learn the rudiments of their craft, and, as they progressed,
receive inspiration and more advanced instruction from master
choreographers, whose accumulated wisdom would then be passed
on instead of perishing with them.

The study of choreography in all its manifold aspects presents a
formidable task, for it is a vast and intricate subject. This work is
well planned, well written, and forms a notable contribution to the
literature of the Dance. For the serious student of ballet history there
is an admirable epitome of a wide range of material; while the
would-be choreographer will find within a great well of practical
instruction and counsel, derived from actual experience, than which
there is no better teacher.

It is a real pleasure to recommend this book. As a broadly based
introduction to the choreographic art, the first of its kind, it will
remain, I feel confident, a standard work of reference, guidance, and
inspiration.

ACKNOWLEDGMENTS

IN the six years it has taken to write this book we have visited, singly
or together, all the principal countries where classical ballet flourishes,
and received endless kindness and help from people and institutions
all over the world.

Our principal thanks must go to Mr. Cyril Beaumont, O.B.E.,
Miss Mary Skeaping, M.B.E., and Mr. Ivor Guest. Mr. Beaumont
and Miss Skeaping read the entire manuscript; Mr. Guest read the
historical section and gave us much help with illustrations. All three
placed their wide knowledge at our disposal and were generous
beyond measure with time, criticism and suggestions. Mr. Beaumont
also wrote our foreword, corrected proofs, helped us with illustrations and allowed us to quote extensively in Appendix II from *A
Ballet called Giselle* and *A Ballet called Swan Lake*. He gave us, in fact,
the benefit of a life's work devoted to ballet. This has received
already an international recognition of greater substance, but no less
warmth, than ours. The homes of classical ballet, France and Italy,
honour him respectively as a Chevalier of the Légion d'Honneur
and Knight Officer of the Order of Merit. In Britain, where the
Order of the British Empire recognises his contribution towards
the foundation and development of our national ballet, he is
honoured equally by both its great teaching organisations. Chairman
of the Imperial Society of Teachers of Dancing and of its Cecchetti
Society Branch, he received the Imperial Award of the I.S.T.D. in
1961 and the Queen Elizabeth II Coronation Award of the Royal
Academy of Dancing in 1962. We owe a very great deal, too, to our
staff without whom the book could not have been produced, principally Margaret Moores, the book's secretary throughout the six years
of its creation; also her assistants, Jennifer Bungey and Kate Vischer;
and Vera Brinson, who was our administrative assistant, read the
proofs and compiled the formidable index.

Besides these we are deeply indebted—

in the *United Kingdom* to:
Dame Ninette de Valois and Dame Marie Rambert for helpful discussions and advice: Miss Kathleen Gordon, Director of the Royal

Academy of Dancing, Miss Ursula Moreton, Ballet Principal of the Royal Ballet School, and Miss Dinah Watkins of the Royal Academy for permission to study and use material from the course on the theory and practice of ballet production sponsored by the Academy's Production Club; the choreographers Sir Frederick Ashton, Miss Andrée Howard, Mr. Jack Carter, Mr. John Cranko, Mr. Peter Darrell, Mr. Kenneth MacMillan and Mr. Norman Morrice for useful discussions and, often, for permission to quote from their writings or their private note books; Mr. Werdon Anglin for reading the proofs and much useful criticism; Mr. Leon Arnold for advice on the cue sheet and lighting notes in Plate XXVI; Mr. William Beresford and the press staff of the Royal Opera House, Covent Garden, for help and interest far beyond the obligations of their office; Dr. William Cole, F.R.A.M., and Mr. Michael Moores for advice and musical criticism; Miss Margaret Dale for permission to quote from one of her television camera scripts at Appendix VII; Mr. Michael ffoulkes for help with research; Mr. Ifan Kyrle Fletcher for advice on sources and theatre collections all over Europe; Miss Eleanor Fox for translating Russian material and for advice on Soviet sources; Dr. V. France for advice and much helpful criticism of the sections devoted to the ballet of Imperial Russia, Diaghilev and the Soviet Union; Mr. Victor Glasstone for the loan of reference material; Mr. Nigel Gosling and Mr. Kenneth Rowell for advice and criticism of the sections on stage design and costume; Miss Jane Holland for the use of her library; Miss Mona Inglesby for permission to reproduce the Stepanoff notation in Plate XXXV; the Hon. Eveleigh Leith and the Royal Ballet Benevolent Fund for the loan of photographs; Mr. Duncan Melvin and, in particular, the theatrical managements of Mr. Peter Daubeny and Mr. Leon Hepner for generous help in seeing foreign companies visiting London; Mr. Johaar Mosaval and Mr. Garth Welch for being patient models for our illustrations; Mr. George Nash of the Victoria and Albert Museum for help in research; Mr. Roy Round for lending his skill and photographic talent to the thankless task of recording documents; the late Mr. Cyril Swinson for the wise guidance which writers hope for, but do not always receive, from their publishers and without whose encouragement this book would never have been written; Miss Joan Wildeblood for advice on period movement and manners; Mr. G. B. L. Wilson and Penguin Books Ltd. for permission to base Appendix X on their famous *Dictionary of Ballet*; Mr. Michael Wood, General Manager of the Royal Ballet, for smoothing our path and easing our passage through innumerable doors; the photographers, acknowledged on the plates, who often went to immense trouble on our behalf; the Trustees of the Chatsworth Settlement for permission to reproduce Plate I(a) from the Devonshire Collection, Chatsworth; Messrs. Putnam & Co. for permission to reproduce Appendix IV from Alexandre Benois' *Reminiscences of the Russian Ballet*; Hinrichsen Edition Ltd., for Plate XXIII(a) reproduced from Lionel Bradley's *Sixteen Years of Ballet Rambert*; John Cranko, Mr. & Mrs. Rudolf Benesh and Messrs. A. & C. Black, Ltd., for permission to reproduce the example of Benesh notation at Plate XXXIV; Miss Dorothy Curchin for secretarial assistance; Messrs. Constable & Co. Ltd., publishers, for permission to quote from *Fokine: Memoirs of a Ballet Master* by Vitale Fokine and Anatole Chujoy; the Editor of the *Sunday Times* for permission to quote from Mr. John Cranko's article on *The Prince of the Pagodas*;

in the *United States of America* to:
the choreographers, Miss Agnes de Mille and Mr. Jerome Robbins, for giving time to answer questions, and Miss de Mille for allowing us to reproduce her original notes from *Rodeo* at Plate XXXIX; Miss Ann Hutchinson for help in searching out photographs and for advice on sources; Mr. Walter Terry for much time spent in criticising and revising the section on American choreography in Chapter VIII; Miss Ann Hutchinson and the Dance Notation Bureau, New York, for permission to reproduce the example of Labanotation at Plate XXXIV; Miss Betty Cage for help in obtaining photographs; Messrs. Little, Brown & Co., publishers, for permission to quote from *Fokine: Memoirs of a Ballet Master* by Vitale Fokine and Anatole Chujoy;

in the *Union of Soviet Socialist Republics* to:
Mr. Yuri Bakhrushin, director of the great museum which bears his name, for help in obtaining photographs, for material generously sent to us and for useful conversations; Mr. M. Gorbunov, Rector of the Lunacharsky State Theatrical Institute, Moscow, for permission to quote from the report by Mr. A. V. Shatin to the all-union choreographic conference, 1960, and for other material about his Institute; Mrs. Nina Karasyova and Mrs. Natalie Roslavleva for answering endless questions by letter and in person and for much

personal kindness, and Mrs. Roslavleva for reading and criticising our views on Soviet choreography in Chapter IX; Mr. A. V. Shatin, Dean of the Lunacharsky Institute, for time generously given to discussion and answering questions;

in *Austria* to:
Dr. Franz Hadamowsky, Professor Dr. Heinz Kindermann and Miss Derra de Moroda for help and guidance in studying the rich theatre collections of Vienna; Herr Direktor Ernst Schneider for help in studying the impressive technical facilities backstage at the Vienna Opera House;

in *Denmark* to:
Mr. & Mrs. Allan Fridericia and Mr. Svend Kragh-Jacobsen for the use of their personal libraries and for conversations, help and advice covering not only Bournonville and the Danish ballet, but ballet in many aspects and countries; Mrs. Karen Neiiendam for allowing and encouraging our studies at her Teaterhistorisk Museum, Copenhagen;

in *France* to:
Madame Irène Lidova for criticising our views on French ballet in Chapter IX, for endless help in obtaining photographs and for continual guidance through the range of ballet in France; M. André Ménetrat for help during our studies at the library of the Paris Opéra; M. Milorad Miskovitch for many valuable conversations; M. Pierre Rhallys for permission to quote the scenario of his ballet *Prométhée* at Appendix III; M. André Veinstein and Mlle Marie-Françoise Christout for much kindness during visits to the great library of the Arsenal in Paris; Messrs. Hachette, Arts du Monde, Paris, for permission to reproduce eight photographs in M. Boris Kochno's personal collection from his book, *Le Ballet*; Les Editions du Rocher for permission to reprint the scenario of *Parade* from *Scenario Théâtre de Poche* by Jean Cocteau.

in *Germany* to:
Mr. Richard Adama of Hanover and Mr. Erich Walter of Wuppertal for valuable conversations and help; Professor Dr. Rolf Badenhausen, Professor of Theatre Science in the University of Cologne, and Herr Helmut Grosse for giving us the freedom of the Univer-

sity's great theatre collection at Schloss Wahn, Cologne, and to Mr. Hugo Delavalle for much kindness during the same visit; Dr. Gunter Schöne and Dr. Vriesen for equally helping us to study the treasures of the Clara Ziegler Theatre Museum, Munich;

in *Holland* to:
Mr. J. G. F. Boon, Mr. Hans Reeser and Mr. Ben Albach for help and kindness in researches respectively at the University Library and the Theatre Museum, Amsterdam; the Director and staff of the Theatre Museum, Amsterdam, for the drawing at Plate IV(a) and help in research;

in *Italy* to:
Avv. Stefano Rosso-Mazzinghi of the Cini Foundation, Venice, and Dr. Stefano Vitadini, Director of the Museum and Livia Simoni Library, La Scala, Milan, and Signor Ercoli Ghia for help and kindness during researches at their institutions;

in *Poland* to:
Professor Dr. Stanisława Sawicka, Director of the Warsaw University Library, for help in obtaining the photographs of costume designs for Jason and Medea in Plate III, and Madame Irena Turska for a copy of her *Jean Georges Noverre: Teoria i Praktyka Tańca*;

in *Sweden* to:
Professor Agne Beijer and Mrs. G. Kalderen for kindness and help during studies in the Drottningholm Theatre Museum; Herr Per Bjurström for the same assistance in the National Museum, Stockholm, and for the help of his book, *Giacomo Torelli and Baroque Stage Design*; Miss Erica Heinze-Dorman for patience and help in translating from Swedish originals; the Librarian and staff of the Royal Library, Stockholm, for guidance in their valuable records of seventeenth- and eighteenth-century ballet; and Miss Mary Skeaping, M.B.E., then Director of the Royal Swedish Ballet, and Mr. Caj Selling for many kindnesses during research in Stockholm.

Many others, too, were generous with time, kindness and information. We owe them thanks for their confidence as well as their help. Whatever merit our book possesses we share with those we have consulted; its faults are ours alone.

CONTENTS

CONTENTS

ILLUSTRATIONS

The Choreographic Picture

BETWEEN PAGES 276 AND 277

xxi

PART I

THE CHOREOGRAPHER

CHAPTER I

PROLOGUE

DANCING is a language whose words are movements of the body. Choreography is the art of assembling movements creatively so that they have meaning, style and form.

It was not always so. At first choreography meant the writing down of dance steps. This was how Noverre described it. During the nineteenth century it came to mean the invention of new steps and the assembly of old ones. But choreography cannot stand alone. Today the term often implies more. It can include the production and staging of a ballet as well as the invention of characters and movements.

Five and a half centuries ago Domenico of Piacenza became the first known dancing master to record the creation of dances. Others have developed what he began. In particular, the books of five masters—Weaver[1] of England, Noverre of France, Blasis of Italy, Bournonville of Denmark and Fokine of Russia—provide a foundation for the theoretical study of choreography.

All these masters saw their art as the union of dance with music and mime, stage design and costumes to tell a story or create a mood. This union is the essence of the art of ballet, the art of choreography.

The art of ballet, therefore, is the perfect theatrical blending of four component arts; drama, music, design and dance. Dance is only one art among four. Yet so often today is the choreographer, who creates the dances, called upon to provide the story, select the music and designs, and produce the finished work that the distinction between the arts of 'choreography' and 'ballet' has become blurred. Because of this and because choreography is *so* dependent on its allied arts we have followed in this book the sequence of a ballet's creation. The choreographer occupies the centre of our stage, but the composer, designer and writer have their place. The problems of each can be seen in relation to the whole.

There are as many languages of dancing as there are languages of

[1] John Weaver (1673–1760); Jean Georges Noverre (1727–1810); Carlo Blasis (1797–1878); August Bournonville (1805–1879); Michel Fokine (1880–1942).

words. Some, like Spanish dance, correspond to national frontiers. Others cross frontiers and become international. Classical ballet is an international language whose local accents reflect the physiques, temperaments and traditions of the countries in which it has settled. Thus today there are French, Italian, Danish, Russian and British schools of ballet.

In this book we try to point the general from the particular. The particular is British since we are British. Being British, we restrict ourselves to classical choreography. 'Modern', 'central European' and similar styles of dancing have little place in the British theatre scene. They enter our story only to show their influence on the classical idiom.

Being young our British School is more homogeneous than its ancestors in France, Italy, Denmark and Russia, but lacks their strong traditions. Our approach to choreography has had to be equally homogeneous, leaning on the foreign past.

In one sense, however, we have had little help from the past or from abroad. Weaver and Noverre, Blasis, Bournonville, Fokine, and others less famous, wrote only about their own choreography. They did not examine very thoroughly the theory and practice of other choreographers. Or if they did they kept their conclusions to themselves.

We are not choreographers, although we are theatre people, trained in the classical ballet. Hence we have tried to see classical choreography as a whole. From the experience of many choreographers and the recorded views of a few, who speak for themselves as often as possible in the chapters which follow, we have attempted notes on the theory and practice of their art as a preparation for further study.

CHAPTER II

THE CHOREOGRAPHER

'YOU see,' said Diaghilev in 1915, 'given the talent, one can make a choreographer in no time.'[1] He spoke of Massine. The talent was there and Diaghilev was a superb teacher. But when talent is not there no-one can create an artist. In this sense choreographers are born, not made.

The choreographer is a dancer whose emotions, mind and physique give him the power to translate life into dance images. He can 'explain Things conceived in the Mind, by the *Gestures* and *Motions* of the Body'.[2]

Such a person will be sensitive by nature to visual impressions. He will be perceptive and observant of the world around him, retaining the image of what he sees. To a sensitive eye he will add a sensitive ear and exceptional feeling for music.

He need not have a powerful intellect in the academic sense, but his mind will be alert and keenly intelligent. Not only will he feel visually; he will think visually. He will have the gift of leadership, the ability to inspire other dancers. Like a good officer in the army he will be adept at 'man management'. 'He must know what a dancer can do, what is easy, what is difficult, and what is impossible, so that he can get as much as possible out of his dancers without demanding the impossible of them'.[3]

His physique will be that of a dancer. He will be lively in mind and alert in his body. He need not be a great performer, but he must be able to feel physically the movements he invents for his dancers. Unlike a dancer he may not be interpretative. He is the one who combines his natural gifts with his training to create what the dancer interprets. When he creates he should feel, like Dauberval, that 'it is not enough for me to please the eye. I wish to interest the heart.'[4]

[1] S. L. Grigoriev, *The Diaghilev Ballet 1909–1929*, p. 108, (Constable London, 1953).
[2] John Weaver, *Essay towards an History of Dancing* (London, 1712).
[3] Niels Bjørn Larsen, *A Ballet is Created*; programme of the Royal Danish Theatre, May 1960.
[4] Quoted by Blasis, *Traité de la danse* (Milan, 1820).

Therefore, choreography charges steps, movements and patterns with thoughts and emotions so that spectators are stirred as by a painting or a poem. The choreographer sculpts thought and feeling into movement.

This is more than arranging steps. Every good teacher arranges steps daily in class out of the vocabulary built up since Beauchamps established the five positions in the seventeenth century. It is more than technical facility in devising new movements and patterns on stage; or the ability to charm and astonish onlookers. There are dozens of competent dance arrangers who do this every night in the theatre and in film and television studios. They are the journalists of the choreographic world.

The choreographer must be concerned with deeper things. What he creates is the dance element of ballet. This dance element can be in any style—expressionist, perhaps, or in the Kathak style of north India. In this book, as we have said, we deal only with the style of the classical *danse d'école* evolved in Europe, and known also as 'academic', 'operatic dancing' or 'classical' ballet.

Behind the choreographer of the academic style today lies a vocabulary of steps compiled over three centuries. His grammar of movement is descended from the social dancing of ordinary people, adapted for the theatre by hundreds of choreographers in thousands of ballets. His traditions are those of the world of ballet and its companies. He inherits the influence and traditions of the related arts of music, painting, sculpture and literature. In the classroom he meets the dancers who will be his masters and servants, his material and inspiration.

How can the young choreographer acquire all this knowledge and use it? How can he find among traditional sources of inspiration the means of reaching a contemporary audience? How can he choose his themes, where find his collaborators, how use his dancers?

The choreographer must be trained first as a dancer. He must have passed through the *danse d'école* and learned a dancer's craft on stage as an ordinary member of a ballet company. He must have absorbed a classical dancer's sense of discipline and the long classical tradition which a great ballet company carries forward.

'Classical ballet teaches basic movement. It develops strength, speed, suppleness, lightness, in fact all possible qualities of movement. It is most important for a choreographer to have felt this training all through his body.

'There is, in classical ballet, only one way to achieve this training. . . . Through training in class, complete submission to classical discipline, you acquire strong sensations of dancing. You acquire the discipline of eye and arm and leg. You acquire the basic line which is the other great gift of classical training. . . .

'In the training of a dancer, more than in any other art, the character is revealed. . . . Bit by bit you see a dancer who wants to do things in his own way. You begin to try to find out why, and gradually you will find out. . . . You find, in fact, that he will make a choreographer.'[1]

This passage, by one of the greatest educators of choreographic talent, emphasises the essential foundation of the choreographer's training. He must be steeped in dancing. He need not be a great dancer. He need not complete, even, a dancer's career before becoming a choreographer. But he must know what it is like to be a dancer. A few, like Nijinsky, begin choreography after great dancing success. Some, like Balanchine and Tudor, develop as choreographers soon after leaving school and dance on stage very little. Many, like Fokine, and especially Massine, combine dancing with choreography for a major part of their careers.

Among pupils at ballet school and dancers in a company a few appear with the urge and ability to create movement in their own way. These are the future choreographers. A major ballet company probably finds two or three with real talent in a decade. Apart from the brief efforts of Nijinsky and the launching of Lifar, Diaghilev developed only three—Massine, Nijinska and Balanchine—in the twenty years of his company. Fokine was already formed when he and Diaghilev began to work together.

Like other artistic talents, choreographic talent usually reveals itself young and must be carefully nurtured. Noverre, Viganò, Perrot, Petipa and Fokine were all young when they produced their first ballets even though their maturest work was not created until they were over thirty and had made their mark as dancers.

Today it is rare for choreographers to continue long as dancers. Demands upon dancers and choreographers are heavier than they were in other centuries, so specialisation must start earlier. The moment at which it starts will vary with the individual, but as soon as choreographic talent reveals itself certain additions should be made

[1] Marie Rambert, 'The Education of a Choreographer', from *The Ballet in Britain* (Oxford University Press, 1962).

to the aspiring choreographer's dance training.

Besides daily classes in classical technique he or she should be given additional musical education, beyond what he acquires as a dancer. It is only in this century that choreographers no longer have to play a musical instrument in the course of their work. Previously they played the violin for their classes and rehearsals. It is still desirable to play an instrument. Certainly they should be able to read a score and understand the fundamentals of musical construction and harmony. The musical director of the school or company should be able to guide them in this.

The student choreographer should study painting and sculpture historically and aesthetically. To train the mind, he ought to read widely and acquire a taste for literature. A good grounding in these subjects should have been given in the ballet school. The teachers responsible should encourage more advanced study and advise how it should be undertaken.

The young person should acquire a practical and theoretical knowledge of choreographic history. Partly this should be absorbed during his study of the *danse d'école*. The teacher in the subject should advise on further researches. At school, his training ought to have included instruction in period and national dances, especially those of his own country. He should understand the importance of these dances in the development of contemporary choreography. He can learn this best through practical experience. His mind, too, should be receptive to new ideas and dance styles other than his own. He should see as many other ballet companies as possible.

He should help himself and seek help from others. He should develop his powers of observation. He should go to concerts and be, like Fokine, a visitor to museums and art galleries. The inspiration of painters and sculptors, past and present, should be added to his knowledge of dancing. Fokine studied Persian miniatures before creating *Schéhérazade*. From Hogarth's cartoons Ninette de Valois drew her groups for *The Rake's Progress*. From a mind receptive to dance styles outside the classical tradition came some of Tudor's dramatic choreography.

By working as a dancer in a theatre with a company, the aspirant choreographer can watch major choreographers of the day, studying their styles, their methods of work and the way they handle dancers. Whatever his own competence as a dancer the environment of school and company will be a vital formative influence. In this environment he will learn (or fail to learn) the proper attitude of an artist to his work.

In the theatre, the choreographer must learn the craft of his trade. He must understand the theatre, theatre lore and the laws of dramatic composition. He must be able to use choreographic conventions so that his development of a theme seems logical and plausible to his audience. He should learn that creative work lies as much in the disposition and selection of these conventions as in original ideas and new movements for his dancers. New movement is not the greatest of a choreographer's needs. Fokine showed that taste, simplicity and dramatic ability are more important. To these he should add judgement. 'Like a sculptor, the choreographer, together with the dancers, forms his positions and groups and links them with steps and movements. In so doing a more beautiful or striking effect than intended is sometimes produced. Here the choreographer must have a quick and sure judgement to know which of these effects to choose.'[1]

Wherever possible a young choreographer should practise choreography in the small ways open to him at school demonstrations and the private occasions of the dancing world. He should not appear as a choreographer before the public too soon. When he does so it should be with small works and a small cast. In small works he can learn to simplify and select, a discipline as vital to the telling of a story as the building of a character and the forming of groups and patterns. If he tries to fill a large canvas too early he may make a blurred impact on his audience through indecisive compositions. The simple things learned on a small stage will provide the basis for the embroidery, the patterns and the masses of dancers who will people his larger canvases later on.

Regional ballet groups, workshop organisations and local ballet societies are useful to meet the first practical needs of young choreographers. These organisations provide dancers, a stage and a sympathetic audience. But they must have firm artistic direction and be as willing to refuse the obviously second rate as they are to encourage the talented. Proper standards are as important in a workshop as in the world outside.

But after the workshop? A young choreographer needs a small professional company for his next ballets. In this field, as in many other ways, the small professional company under sound artistic direction holds a vital place in the national pattern of ballet. The

[1] Niels Bjørn Larsen, *op. cit.*

Ballet Rambert is the supreme example of this in England.

When the young choreographer has passed the test of a small company successfully he is ready for a large stage. In his journey so far he will be lucky if his training for his complex art has been consistent. Many people will help him. Advice will be plentiful, but sporadic. The artistic director of his company will watch over him. In day-to-day matters, however, he will be on his own, working by trial and error.

Nowadays, when there is so heavy a demand for ballet-trained choreographers in the theatre, cinema and television this trial and error is not good enough. There is much to be said for faculties of choreographic training to be established in the principal ballet schools, equivalent to the composition classes provided by musical academies for young composers. In Moscow, of course, such a faculty has existed for many years; details are given at Appendix VIII A. Faculties of choreographic training like this, adapted to British conditions in the way we outline at Appendix VIII B, could provide the guidance a young choregrapher can rarely find in the busy life of a professional company. The special value of such courses would lie in the mental discipline they demand as well as the practical training they would provide in choreographic craft.

Formal training, of course, can never be a substitute for day-to-day experience in the theatre. It can never make a choreographer out of someone who lacks creative talent. Neither teacher nor training can give this vital spark. But every aspirant's progress might be quicker, his mind and talents clearer, and his experience richer from what he could absorb in such training. The training, too, will help the aspirant in his search for a personal idiom. He must discover for himself the original ways in which he will use his qualities and skills to say things worth saying. This is the final test. It is the one the young dancer must face and solve before he is worthy to practise the art of choreography.

PART II

THE CHOREOGRAPHER IN HISTORY

CHAPTER III

SOCIAL BEGINNINGS

ALL arts draw much upon tradition. The first step in understanding them is to understand their past. This is especially true of choreography. No other art is tied to its past in such a degree, because no other art derives so exclusively from one element of society, the court, in such particular social-historical circumstances.

Therefore we must glance at this past. We need only to sketch it to show its influence. Others have written its history.

From prehistory into history dancing fulfilled a basic need in man's emotional nature, embellishing and expressing hopes, fears and wishes. As social organisation developed, and society divided into tribes, nations and classes, so the social function of dancing became more complex. Its language, steps and movements came to mirror not, as once, the conceptions of primitive, classless tribes, but the conceptions of a divided society. Dancing itself became divided.

A principal part of this division remains as folk dance. Its forms are descended directly from primitive, communal dances. The peasant folk dance, in fact, is the foundation upon which all contemporary dancing is built. The other main part became grouped round society's opposite pole, the court. Here lay the centre of social power and sophistication.

By the beginning of the sixteenth century the court dance was far developed. If its steps were not different from the village green, their performance was a world away from peasant manners. Between the sixteenth century and the French Revolution these steps developed heights of refinement and complexity through the court, so that from the court ballet is descended most of the vocabulary of today's classical technique.

The court ballet was one way in which renaissance princes used the arts to reflect in themselves the power and glory of the state. Italy launched the court ballet but theatre archives all over Europe are filled with the records of these magnificent productions.

On Sunday, 29th January, 1617 the young King Louis XIII of France appeared in a *Ballet du Roy*. The nature of the ballet with its 'designs, machines, sets and all the manner of masks' was set down and published the same year. Publication was important so that the magnificence of the entertainment might become known to rival courts.

The occasion was typical of its kind. It was given in a large room with members of the court looking down upon the floor from three sides. Each role was written for a particular nobleman. The characters were symbolic and involved speaking or singing, as well as dancing. The Count de la Roche-Guyon, for example, appeared as a demon of the Hunt. General des Gallères was a demon of madness.

His Majesty took the role of fire. Such casting revealed the propaganda purpose behind the entertainment. Fire cleanses impurities explained the book of the ballet, . . . 'and it is a principle desire of His Majesty to summon all his subjects to their duty, and purge them of all reasons for disobedience. . . . At the same time His Majesty destroys easily those who anger him.'[1]

From such descriptions, but still more from occasional note-books of ballet masters, especially in Italy, we know something of the productions of the period. Virtuoso dancing was a male preserve. Turns, jumps, beaten steps and even *pliés* were practised, but the leg was not yet turned out from the thigh.

At the Royal Library in Stockholm we see the application of this technique in the hand-written note-book of an unnamed teacher of dancing. It was written in Brussels, 1614–1619[2] and is the kind of general note-book teachers still keep. In it, pupils have signed their names to record their classes, as pupils still do. The signatures and notes are a mixture of languages. 'On the 14th of March 1616 I began with Mattheu Boyes of Cologne.' 'This gentleman with his lady began on the 11th November.' Among the signatures are descriptions of ballets, libretti, music and production notes. These make this nameless work one of the first genuine choreographer's note-books.

The term 'ballet' is used to describe not only a complete entertainment, but individual dances, *entrées*, or mimed songs. In a long *Ballet des mineurs des pays*, for instance: 'First enter the miners, dancing their ballet . . .' and 'then return the two wild moors and the two satyrs, each with a lighted torch, and dance a ballet. . . .'

[1] *Discours Au Vray du Ballet dansé par le Roy, Le Dimanche XXIX Jour de Janvier 1617* (Paris, 1617).
[2] We acknowledge the help of Miss Mary Skeaping who drew our attention to this book.

The dance notes concentrate on patterns rather than steps, as one would expect if the performance took place on a floor with most of the audience looking down upon it. The dances appear to be social dances of the period well combined to a climax. Each *entrée* is more complicated than the last, including in one ballet, a series of figures which spell the letters of the alphabet. This was always a popular trick.

Bits of music show airs or musical themes which are repeated and developed as the dances develop. None of the music yet had bars or other punctuation, but, like most dancing masters for many centuries, the anonymous author was a competent musician as well as a teacher and dancer.

Above the music is written sometimes the rank or name of the dancer concerned, 'Ballet de Monseigneur le Prince', or the kind of singer, 'tenor', 'contratenor', 'bass' and so on.

Often the incidents to be declaimed or the announcements to be made in a ballet are jotted down in verse. There are ideas for ballets, like 'Subject for a Ballet of Seven Virtues'; and there are practical production notes: 'How to make grenades which burn in water'. 'How to make fuses.' The seventeenth century was a period in which masques and spectacular ballets of this kind were an item of every festival and a part of every great occasion. Dancing was a necessary social attribute so that dancing masters were essential members of the community. They taught manners and deportment, as well as dancing. Manners were becoming increasingly artificial, so much so that it was hard on occasions to separate them from dancing. Thus we find a dancing master, like de Lauze in France, combining the two in a treatise on dancing and deportment in 1623. Many colleagues did the same. Manners became a 'science of behaviour towards others'.[1]

This link between deportment and dancing has had an important influence on ballet. Elaborate manners were an element of the English court masque under James I. They played an even greater part in the court ballets through which Louis XIV emphasised the divinity of kingship to the world. The title 'Sun King' itself derived from a role Louis danced in Lully's *Ballet de la Nuit* in 1653.

At first, the court ballets of the great king were communal affairs, performed as they always had been by the king and his courtiers,

[1] F. de Lauze, *Apologie de la danse*, 1623, trans. Joan Wildeblood (Frederick Muller, London, 1952).

including women. There was no serious distinction between performers and onlookers, singers or dancers. Being performed in some
large room, and watched from a balcony *above* the performers,
elaborate costume and ground pattern mattered more than steps.

These court ballets reflected many of the principles of the baroque
art of the period. Their themes and presentation fulfilled the same
sort of function as the decorations in a baroque church. They lifted
man out of himself to a world of immortality where the limits
between the possible and the impossible disappeared. They glorified
the monarch, of course. But their choreography still submitted the
part to the whole as baroque art always did. It was a choreography
of the ensemble even when it matched elaborate costumes with
flourishes, embellishments and conceits of arms and legs for individual dancers. Sumptuous, colossal, in every sense royal, the ensemble never over-reached itself. It was ordered, like Versailles,
always by the reason of symmetry and geometry.

Individual technique developed within this framework. The distinction between noble and character roles had been recognised for
many years before Louis XIV first danced in public in 1651. The
noble roles were reserved for the king and the court. The more
virtuoso character roles were performed by professional dancers,
who appeared at the court of Louis XIII about 1630. By the middle
of the seventeenth century these professionals had developed something like a vocabulary of court dancing. In this vocabulary they
combined especially two elements from the court ballet: the steps
of its social dances, and the deportment proper to a courtier.

Gradually, under the influence of royal enthusiasm and the ever-
present need to embellish the fame of the greatest court of the day, the
demands made on performers became infinitely elaborate. The importance of good teaching for the dancers became as urgent as good
dance composition. Louis, therefore, established in 1661 an Académie
Royale de Danse. Eight years later he founded a separate Académie
Royale de Musique. This exists today as the Paris Opéra. When the
withdrawal of the king from dancing heralded the end of the court
ballet it was the professional dancers, and the Académie Royale de
Musique under Lully, which translated the court ballet to the public
theatre where it became opera-ballet.

Under Louis XIV Lully was the great composer of the court and
opera-ballet. His work established a strong musical tradition which
was embellished further in different ways by Jean Philippe Rameau

in the first half of the eighteenth century. Although ballet music has often been despised by later composers, the work of these pioneers established standards which remain a point of reference.

The technique of dancers, trained by the court ballet master Beauchamps, and his successors, had to equal the musical demands of Lully and Rameau. In this training notation proved important. Beauchamps himself was a 'choreographer' in the original sense of the word. He developed a system of writing down steps and dances. To write them down meant, first, that they had to be analysed. The analysis, of course, threw more light on the nature of the steps, and so improved teaching and dancing.

This influence of notation on technique is often overlooked. The most complete early notation system was devised by Raoul Feuillet at the end of the seventeenth century and remained in use for nearly a hundred years. It played its part, without doubt, in the technical advances of the eighteenth century. To it we owe our knowledge of many eighteenth-century dances.

History thus produced the special circumstances from which seventeenth-century Paris gave to the world a new art form. The world can see these origins today in two qualities inseparable from the art. The names of the steps are French wherever ballet is taught; the deportment of dancers in ballet is still essentially aristocratic.

Where the French king led, the courts of Europe followed. Christina of Sweden, the kings of Denmark and Poland, the princes of Germany and Italy, the Holy Roman Emperor, all had their Ballets. Even the taciturn William of Orange, later William III of England, danced in a *Ballet de la Paix* at the Hague in 1668.

In Italy the lyric theatre began to enter public theatres early in the seventeenth century. The move began in Venice in 1637. Consequently the dance became professional in Italy earlier than it did in the rest of Europe. The immediate result was a development of technique beyond what the French had achieved. The brilliance and speed which distinguished the Italian School in the nineteenth century was already an Italian attribute in the seventeenth century, compared with the grace of the French. It was a proper reminder that Italy and France together share the honour of developing ballet as a theatre art.

The more absolute monarchy declined the more ballet turned from the court to public performance. The public had been admitted to court ballet in France even in the time of Louis XIII, but when the

C.A.—2

Académie Royale de Musique gave its first public performance in 1671, court ballet moved formally on to the stage and changed, thereby, its nature. At court, choreography had presented most of its dances in horizontal lines directly forward towards the king with special attention to ground pattern. (Plate II.) It was watched from three sides by an audience whose tiered seats looked down upon the dancers. In the theatre the dance was seen from the front only at eye level. Hence the technique of the dancer became as important as ground pattern. This intensified the dancer's struggle for freedom of movement against the restrictions of costume and moral fashion. Women, who began to appear in ballet during the 1680s, especially demanded freedom from their heavy dresses.

Throughout the eighteenth century costume reforms alternate with technical advances in this way. Dresses were shortened and lightened; panniers, masks, wigs and heeled shoes all disappeared before the French Revolution. *Pirouettes, entrechats, cabrioles, coupés, pas de bourrée* and other steps developed in virtuosity as a result.

The way these steps were performed can be traced in costume designs, which often show gestures, *épaulements* and so on. Technical manuals discuss them with drawings which are sometimes as rich as those in Gregorio Lambranzi's *New and Curious School of Theatrical Dancing.*

Published in Nuremberg in 1716 this work illustrates a remarkable group of character dances in full costume, all of which require a high degree of acting ability as well as technique. The influence of *commedia dell' arte* is strong, the dances being aimed at a less sophisticated public than the court.

Elaborate scenery and stage machinery were principal features of ballet at court and in the theatre. Records in Amsterdam, Milan, Vienna and elsewhere show the huge stage designs which artists like the Bibienas delighted to create from the late seventeenth century onwards. Under their hand whole squares and streets grew up. Great palaces were constructed with statues and colonnades vanishing in perspective. Classical gardens were laid out where the characters could display one formal pose after another.

In the large room where ballets were danced at court the stage design was a permanent construction, different sections being lit for different scenes. Once opera-ballet developed in the theatre scenery could be changed and the stage effects, which mattered so much, were easier to achieve. During the eighteenth century machinery became much more efficient above, below and behind the stage. The Drottningholm Court Theatre near Stockholm still has a machinery of ropes and wheels which has survived from the end of the eighteenth century. This can change seven wings on each side of the stage, a backcloth and flies in ten seconds. A model theatre of the same period in the Amsterdam Theatre museum demonstrates the same achievement, which is faster than most scene changes today.

Such developments helped the success of ballet in the theatre. At first dancing continued to be combined with speech and song in opera-ballet. Gradually words and dance separated. Speech went one way to become opera. Dance went another to become ballet without words, the *ballet d'action*.

The first *ballet d'action* was produced in London on 2nd March, 1717. This date marks the birth of ballet as we know it. Its creator was John Weaver, one of a remarkable group of English dancing masters in London at the beginning of the century. The ballet was *The Loves of Mars and Venus*.

From Weaver's description it seems to have been a kind of dance drama. 'Stage-Dancing,' he wrote, 'was at first design'd for *Imitation*, to explain Things conceiv'd in the Mind, by the Gestures and Motions of the Body, and plainly and intelligibly representing *Actions*, *Manners* and *Passions*.' So, 'without the help of an Interpreter, a Spectator shall at a Distance . . . be capable of understanding the *Subject* of the Story represented. . . .'[1]

The Loves of Mars and Venus was a success. A second ballet was presented the following year. Afterwards, nothing. The *ballet d'action* could not grow in England at a time when the court had ceased to patronise the arts, when censorship of the drama was intensified and Government and Parliament made it clear that in their view the arts were a matter for private interest alone.

Yet the English dancing masters of the early eighteenth century are important. Weaver was a considerable theoretician, as well as a practical man of the theatre. His written work, especially the *Essay towards an History of Dancing*, 1712, and *Anatomical and Mechanical Lectures upon Dancing*, 1721, are original contributions to knowledge which mark the beginning of English dance literature. *The Art of Dancing*, by another member of the group, Kellom Tomlinson, is an important technical manual of the day. Every bit as good as the better known *Le Maître à Danser* by the Frenchman Pierre Rameau,

[1] John Weaver, *Essay towards an History of Dancing*, pp. 160-161 (London, 1712).

it was completed before Rameau's book appeared in Paris in 1725, although Tomlinson could not get his book published in London until 1735.

Long before Weaver, ideas for ballets without words were being discussed. After Weaver ballet masters experimented on stage in different parts of Europe.

Occasionally their experiments were helped by composers of note, even if serious composers generally ignored the ballet. Gluck's *Don Juan* with the choreographer, Angiolini, in Vienna, 1761. and Mozart's *Les Petits Riens* with Noverre in Paris, 1778, are examples of scores which suggested how great the *ballet d'action* could be. More often, ballet music at this time consisted of the 'old trumpery French airs' which Mozart described scornfully to his father from Paris, when writing about his 'friendly act towards Noverre'.

Noverre's *Letters on Ballet and Dancing* summed up the experience of the *ballet d'action* at the time of their publication at Stuttgart in 1760. This is the blueprint for ballet to come; not ballet for the court but ballet for a broader public.

The friend of Voltaire, Diderot and the Encyclopaedists, a follower of Rousseau, Noverre applied to ballet the enlightened ideas of his day. 'Poetry, painting and dancing, Sir, are, or should be, no other than a faithful likeness of beautiful nature.'[1] The words which open the first letter echo Rousseau and anticipate the Romantics.

Noverre made five fundamental propositions. First, all ballets should possess a good plot, which the audience should be able to follow without programme notes.

Second, he emphasised the value of good music and commissioned scores in place of the medley of existing tunes to which the ballets of his time were generally composed.

Third, he insisted that all dancing must be designed to express or assist the development of the theme. All dancers, including the *corps de ballet*, must be expressive and further the plot in all their movements. Choreographers should encourage dancers to interpret roles in their own way. Then the choreographer should mould this interpretation instead of expecting the dancer to copy him exactly.

To help achieve these aims Noverre demanded, fourth, the reform of stage costume, the abolition of the use of masks, and, fifth, the restoration and development of the art of mime.

[1] Noverre, *Letters on Ballet and Dancing*, p. 9 trans. Beaumont (Beaumont, London, 1930).

The abolition of masks, finally achieved in 1773 through a theatrical accident rather than because of Noverre's ideas, implied proper care in casting so that the right dancer might be placed in the right role. Hence Noverre examined and defined the types of dancer useful in ballet. His reforms of costume aimed at historical truth and the proper combination of costumes with each other and with the scenery in a single stage picture, as well as giving greater freedom to the dancers' limbs. Freedom for the limbs encouraged by the costume reforms of Camargo and Sallé, earlier in the century, followed particularly from the introduction of flesh-coloured tights during the 1780s. (Plate III (a), (b) and (c).)

In mime Noverre asked that choreographers and dancers should pay as much attention to acting as they did to executing steps. He advised the study of real people—workmen, tradesmen, soldiers—whose way of movement and behaviour would provide inspiration. Not only the principal dancers, he said, but every member of the corps de ballet should react individually and truthfully to a dramatic situation.

Besides this, the letters laid down the qualifications and training which should be given to a dancer and choreographer. Noverre advised the all-important turn-out of the thigh because it 'gives ease and brilliancy, it invests steps, positions and attitudes with grace', but he did not absolutely demand it. Usually the turn-out achieved was no more than forty-five degrees.

He required a proper general education for his dancers. Artists in so noble an art should be widely read and have inquiring minds. A mere dancer of steps, a technician, is not an artist. 'This art, born of genius and good taste, can become beautiful and varied to an infinite degree', but only if it maintains artistic integrity and unity in all its parts.

Noverre fought a long battle for these principles, not all of which he fulfilled in practice himself. The scenario for his ballet Medea and Jason (Appendix I), has many of the faults of over-elaboration against which he protested in his Letters. It seems clear, too, that whilst he developed a more expressive use of the corps de ballet, dissolving its rigid patterns into more imaginative groups, he did not conceive of dance movement expressive in itself. This had to come with the nineteenth century. Rather his set dances were interspersed with mime scenes, as arias are set in recitatif. Dancing had learnt to 'speak for itself', but in a limited way.

The ballets Noverre produced at Stuttgart, Vienna and Milan established him as the foremost choreographer of Europe. Yet his principal achievement is to have set it all down in writing as guidance for the very different ballet of the future. Through his letters a theory of the *ballet d'action* became widely available. Through the *ballet d'action* the choreographer replaced the writer as the master of the ballet stage. Thus choreographers responsible for the flowering of ballet in the romantic movement grew up under Noverre's influence even when they were not his pupils. And, like the echo of a trumpet far away, Fokine's neo-romantic choreography in the twentieth century recalled the great man's ideals.

CHAPTER IV

ROMANTIC CHOREOGRAPHY

BY the outbreak of the French Revolution the *ballet d'action* was established firmly in public theatres. It had a well-developed vocabulary of steps, technical manuals, and a soundly based theory of production. It possessed teachers, choreographers and dancers able to develop its aristocratic language.

The French Revolution showed for the first time the internal conflicts through which this development takes place. The fundamental conflict lies between the aristocratic origins of the art and the new public which it meets constantly in the theatre. From the court, as we have seen, choreography inherited a formal, aristocratic language of movement. The language was transferred from court to theatre. Since then, historical events, consequent upon the growing wealth of society, have brought this language into conflict with a succession of new ideas from a widening public. As the public has grown the choreographer has been forced to adapt the language of his inheritance, or be rejected by his public.

This conflict provides the dynamo and driving force for the evolution of ballet. Differences of temperament, physical characteristics and historical development cause it to be resolved differently in different countries. Wherever ballet takes root, therefore, it moves forward at a different pace. Hence national ballets at different stages of evolution influence each other, producing further conflicts in a chain reaction. The critical influence of companies upon each other is almost as important to ballet's evolution as the fundamental conflict between its inheritance and changing audience. Choreography needs the stimulus of international exchange.

When both sides of the conflict are evenly balanced the periods of calm set in, even of stagnation, which are a feature of ballet history. When the strength of new ideas overcomes the old ones periods of rapid change develop. The French Revolution and the nineteenth century illustrate this process.

At first sight it appears that the ossified practices of eighteenth-century ballet were destroyed suddenly by the new ideas of the

23

Revolution. In fact, the destruction was gradual. The triumph of new ideas in the Revolution was the end of an ideological struggle which went on for years behind the scenes, even in dance circles. Noverre's demands were one expression of the struggle. Dauberval's *La Fille Mal Gardée* was another.

La Fille Mal Gardée made its debut at the Grand-Théatre, Bordeaux, on 1st July, 1789. Ivor Guest's researches for the version now in the Royal Ballet's repertoire have completed our knowledge of this event.[1]

It was one of the first ballets to break with the formula of gods, goddesses and 'rustics' from which Noverre never escaped. It brought to the stage a village at harvest time peopled with ordinary folk, farmers, a village notary, peasant boys and girls. Its new world, sunlit, gay and alive, announced the realistic face of romantic ballet.

Its original score tells us much about ballet and ballet music at the end of the eighteenth century. The music is an arrangement of tunes, by whom we do not know. It might have been by Dauberval himself, although this is unlikely. All choreographers of this period were musicians able enough to arrange music. There still exist, for example, ballet scores by Gasparo Angiolini, Noverre's great rival, and by Salvatore Viganò, the wonderful choreographer of the pre-romantic period in Milan.

Ballet composition was not regarded very highly at the time, nor was it necessary to have a conductor. The simple dance melodies were directed from the stand of the leading violin. Few choreographers, and even fewer composers and critics, applied Noverre's dictum that 'music is to dancing what words are to music'.[2]

Some of the melodies were borrowed from popular operas and other sources, whenever these suited the action on stage. This habit continued in ballet music throughout the nineteenth century and still, sometimes, recurs. The harmonies were as simple as the melodies. There was little descriptive writing, no *leitmotifs* and no thematic continuity. The music was merely an accompaniment to the action.

The scenery for *La Fille Mal Gardée* was realistic. The costumes already reflected the freedoms we associate with the early nineteenth century. Finally, as if to underline the choreographer's intention to

[1] See Ivor Guest, *La Fille Mal Gardée* (*The Dancing Times*, London, 1960). John Lanchbery and Ivor Guest, The Scores of *La Fille Mal Gardée* in *Theatre Research*, Vol. III, Nos. I and II, 1961.
[2] Noverre, *Letters on Ballet and Music*, p. 60 (Beaumont, London, 1930).

appeal to a wider public, the leader of the harvesters in one of the early performances 'proposed a toast to the Third Estate which was much applauded'.[1] At that time the States General had just declared itself a National Assembly, under pressure from the Third Estate. The Bordeaux theatre of the day was more susceptible to these political events than the theatres of Paris.

We do not know the details of Dauberval's choreography. We do know, however, that all over Europe during these years choreographers were experimenting with new forms. Responding to social change, they were trying to develop their art in directions which satisfied their own inclinations and those of their audiences.

One such choreographer was another Frenchman, Charles Didelot. At the King's Theatre, London, in 1796, he produced an old, and still popular, mythological tale in a new way. *Flore et Zéphire* was one of his greatest works. It introduced the idea of the flying ballet which was so essential a part of early romantic choreography. It had none of the rococo mannerisms and conventions which would have stifled such a story, even in Noverre's hands. It was, instead, a drama of human passion which 'attracted its audiences by the poetical portrayal of earthly experiences'.[2]

These were years when earth took over from Olympus on the ballet stage. Choreographers, especially in France, developed the kind of story which had enjoyed success in Bordeaux. Usually it was a story with a rustic setting, where the characters became entangled in an idealised conflict of good and evil. This theme and treatment, descended from Rousseau's ideal 'state of nature', was the first sign of the romantic movement in ballet.

The other principal theme of the early nineteenth century was of man the heroic, the conqueror of the elements, the master of knowledge. History was the principal source for ballets of this kind. It attracted great and minor choreographers alike.

One of the minor choreographers was Jean Rochefort, premier danseur and ballet master at the Schouwberg, Amsterdam. He left behind a note-book and a list of thirty-two ballets 'comprising the répertoire of M. Rochefort'. They include *Telemachus* (1803) and *Tamerlan en Bajazet* (1810).

The note-book contains details of costumes and scenery, draft

---

[1] Lanchbery and Guest, *op. cit. Theatre Research*, Vol. III, No. I, 1961, and Beaumont, *Complete Book of Ballets*, p. 6 (Putnam, London, 1951).
[2] V. Kamenev, *Anglo-Soviet Journal*, London. Autumn 1959.

scenarii, cast lists and notes on the principal choreographic groups of certain ballets. They give us a picture of a choreographer of the period preparing for rehearsals. First, he assembled and studied all the known historical sources which could provide background and choreographic incident. From this he prepared an outline of the action and the development of the principal characters. Next he chose the cast. Then he drew sketches of key scenes and stage pictures in his note-book. After this he was ready for rehearsal.

Besides his thirty-two ballets Rochefort fulfilled his choreographer's public duties by creating many *pièces d'occasion*. One of these was a *Homage to His Majesty Louis-Napoleon, King of Holland*. Here and in an even more gorgeous production in Milan, by Gaetano Gioja for Napoleon's Viceroy of Italy, we see the old court ballet adapted to serve the new monarchs.

Gioja, *maître de ballet* at La Scala, was a principal choreographer of the day. His production, created at Milan on 24th February, 1810, illustrates the kind of spectacle at which Italian choreographers excelled. The occasion was the return of the Viceroy after the Peace of Vienna the previous year.

In a setting of monumental splendour Gioja disposed two choirs and a company of dancers. Principal among them were Thérèse Coralli and her husband, the twenty-one year old Jean Coralli, future choreographer of *Giselle*. The climax was an elaborate Hymn to Peace, danced and sung, to symbolise Napoleon's dominion.

Italian choreographers developed this spectacular tradition and so made Milan the centre of the heroic *genre* in ballet. The heroic ballet adapted neo-classical principles to choreography. Among painters Blake in England, David and Ingres in France and Italy, Thorvaldsen in Denmark, used neo-classicism to present their heroic view of mankind. Shelley reflected the same approach in poetry, and in Milan, Salvatore Viganò, one of the great choreographers of the age, did the same in ballet.

Viganò called his ballets *coreodramma* to distinguish them from the more usual method of ballet construction in Paris. He rejected French notions of varying mime with set dances and *divertissements* in the development of a story. He preferred instead a union of dance with mime which became dramatic movement set to music. Thus his ballets became dance-dramas.

In many ways Viganò is a paragon among choreographers. The pupil of his father and of Dauberval, he came of a family in which there were so many dancers that when they were touring Europe at the turn of the century the family several times danced all the leading roles of a ballet themselves. He was an excellent dancer and mime, a good composer of music, and a prolific writer. But what distinguished him particularly from most of his contemporaries was his breadth of classical learning and his wide interests. His libretti, with their scholarly footnotes and references to expand an argument or character, show how thoroughly he had studied his subject.

When he succeeded Gioja as *maître de ballet* at La Scala, in 1812, Viganò was known already in most of the great theatres of Europe, including London. We can trace his movements through archives in Milan, Vienna and elsewhere which have drawings of him and of his wife, Maria Medina, recording their appearances.

She was small, plump, not pretty, but voluptuous and expressive in her movements. Sometimes she is shown dancing barefoot in the loose draperies for which she was famous. (Plate III (c).)

His ballets were spectacular, large as life, with huge casts and vast, architectural scenery. The libretto for *Prometheus*, runs to thirty printed pages and six acts. The score had been written by Beethoven, a rare example at that time of a well-known composer writing ballet music. It had no less than forty-three important roles apart from minor characters, cyclops, lords, ladies and a numerous *corps de ballet*.

The greater part of Viganò's forty-odd works explored similar heroic themes in one way or another. Among them were *Othello*, *The Titans*, *Richard Cœur de Lion*, *Joan of Arc*, *Alexander the Great*, *Gli Strelizzi* (about Peter the Great), *Daedalus and Icarus*, and *Coriolanus*, with himself in the title role. The finest of them were produced at Milan. Often they had décor created by Alessandro Sanquirico whose work matched in realism, size and imagination the choreography of Viganò.

These great productions from 1812 until Viganò's death in 1821 made Milan a centre of the ballet world. If, as Garrick said, Noverre was the Shakespeare of the dance, Viganò was its Shelley.

Viganò was one of the first choreographers to distinguish between the choreographic creation of a ballet and its production on stage. He himself was responsible always for both, but he made the distinction in his writing and perhaps in his methods. Thus to some extent he posed the possibility of a producer who was not necessarily also the choreographer.

Conceiving the idea of a ballet to be its most important element he refused to sacrifice dramatic action to virtuosity. To tell his stories he created dance images and characters of exceptional quality and power. To realise them he demanded that his dancers should act their roles in the round every moment they were on stage. Even when they were stilled in statuesque groups and poses inspired by his classical studies the stillness had to be animated by feeling. In other words, the themes and ideas Viganò adopted required not only a new style of choreography, but a new style of acting and dancing.

His search for maximum expression through the simplest means clarified movement and so influenced technique. He gave the *corps de ballet* a new importance by using it creatively to tell the story. Each of its members were made characters in their own right; or the whole *corps* was used in sweeping mass movements to comment on the action and carry forward the drama.

Because of his use of the *corps* Viganò has often been called the choreographer of the ensemble. Yet all the resources of his choreography were directed in fact to one end, the elevation of his hero. In this he remained a true neo-classicist and man of his age. It is this which distinguished in him the neo-classical choreographer from the choreographer of the baroque. In technique neo-classicism clarified the conceits of baroque and rococo. It gave the dancer a clearer, simpler line. In theme it emphasised the individual and prepared the world for the goddess to come, the romantic ballerina.

Viganò's work at Milan was only one expression of the flowering of ballet which followed the French Revolution. Vienna and St. Petersburg, capitals of the Holy Alliance, reflected this no less than the courts of Italy and Germany, and the theatres of Paris and London.

Everywhere choreographers were in demand. They came forward from Italy and especially from France. Auguste and Armand Vestris, Pierre Gardel, Louis Milon, Jean Aumer and, later, Filippo Taglioni, are some of the names which occur most frequently on programmes of the period. None of them could equal Charles Didelot in influence. As Viganò adorned the school of Italy, so Didelot adorned that of France and Russia.

Yet, like Noverre, Didelot's creative life was spent mostly outside France. He took to Russia the grace of the French school, its advanced teaching methods, and his own development of Noverre's *ballet d'action*. This subordinated technique to the demands of theme, as did Viganò. But Didelot made a greater use of dancing than Viganò and ranged more widely in his choice of theme. He emphasised mime, explored the beauty of ground pattern and stage groups, and insisted on the importance of characterisation even in the ensemble. To him the *ballet d'action* must be a unified work of dance, mime and scenic effect. Irascible, excitable and brilliant, his teaching in Russia over nearly three decades till 1836 laid the basis of Russian classical ballet.

Just as choreographers in this period explored new themes in new *genres* for their expanding audience, so they developed virtuosity to give their dances greater brilliance. Costume reforms encouraged this. Choreographers of the revolutionary period and after made great use of Noverre's 'light and simple draperies of contrasting colours, worn in such a manner as to reveal the dancer's figure'.[1] Other reforms initiated before the Revolution also came into general use: the soft heel-less slipper and the *maillot*, or flesh-coloured tights.

Thus the way was clear to freedom of movement for women as it was already for men. Male technique reached a special virtuosity in the early years of the nineteenth century. High jumps, *entrechats*, *pirouettes* and *tours en l'air* were the steps in which men excelled. 'Female dancing was less complicated. It was devoid of great flights and was mostly *terre-à-terre*. The technique of *pirouettes* was undeveloped because of undeveloped dance on *pointes*. Resting on high *demi-pointes* a ballerina stayed on the point of stretched toes only occasionally and for an instant. . . . Equally limited was support in *pas de deux*. A ballerina usually leaned on her partner's hands. He seldom lifted her to the level of his chest, and never threw her up into the air. Great attention was paid to the arms of a ballerina.'[2]

Pirouettes for women became more brilliant the more the ballerina's shoe was perfected during the first three decades of the century. Finally, the support of the shoe enabled her to turn and travel on *pointe*.

This use of the *pointe* is the principal technical innovation of the period. It gave to choreography a new dimension. Yet we cannot say when or how it began. Pushkin's Istomina, the Russian ballerina, perhaps used the *pointe* fleetingly as early as 1819. Certainly it was well known by 1827 when the actor, Jelgerhuis, published his important book on mime and movement in Amsterdam.

This book, *Theoretische Lessen over de Gesticulatie en Mimiek*, uses a form of choreographic notation to indicate stage movement. Its

[1] Noverre, *op. cit.* p. 73.
[2] V. Krasovskaya, *The Russian Ballet Theatre from its Origin to the Middle of the 19th Century* (Moscow, 1959).

lessons, prepared principally for actors, are based on classical ballet and often show dancers on *pointe*. Jelgerhuis analyses contemporary and period movement in great detail so that his book is a valuable indication of what mime probably looked like in the early romantic ballet. It appears to have been emphatic, naturalist, bordering on melodramatic. It had not acquired yet the formality of the classical mime which Petipa used.

The use of the *pointe* may have been developed first in Italy, following the example of acrobats who used it as a trick. An illustration in the Amsterdam Theatre Museum supports this theory (see Plate IV (a)). Four drawings show members of the Köbbler family dancing a *pas de deux* in 1812. The Köbblers were acrobats with a ballet training. In one of the pictures a dancer stands on *pointe*, the working leg perfectly extended *à la seconde*. Of course the drawing may idealise what happened, but it is one of the earliest pictures we know of the use of the *pointe* in a dance.[1]

Technical developments of this kind, combined with shorter, more transparent costumes, emphasised the importance of line in a dancer. Elegant line and good technique depend largely on the turn-out of the thigh. The full turn-out at ninety degrees had been developing slowly from the forty-five degrees more usual in Noverre's time. Now the full turn-out became compulsory.

These technical advances were codified by Carlo Blasis in two important teaching manuals. His *Traité de la danse* appeared first in French at Milan in 1820. This was followed ten years later in London by *The Code of Terpsichore*.

Blasis was an Italian dancer, choreographer and teacher born at Naples in 1797. He studied under Viganò in Milan and assimilated the teaching of Noverre, Dauberval and others. In time, he became *premier danseur* at La Scala and was the choreographer of more than fifty ballets. But his great contribution to choreography lay in his training of classical dancers. This was done in two ways, through his work at the Imperial Academy of Dancing in Milan, and through his books. He became the director of the Academy in 1837 and so trained many of the most famous Italian dancers of the great period of classical dancing later in the century.

Blasis laid the foundations of present-day classical teaching. This teaching is preserved and explained in his books. He extended

[1] See also Walter Terry, *On Pointe* (Dodd, Mead & Co., New York, 1962), for further theories about the introduction of the *pointe*.

Noverre's ideas pedagogically where the choreographers had extended them dramatically.

The range of his vocabulary is smaller than the classical vocabulary today. Blasis fashioned some new steps and developed old ones. But generally he sought to make dancers perfect more in what existed than to train them as instruments for new kinds of movements. This is the difference between teaching then and now. The ideal of perfection in a relatively narrow vocabulary remained a characteristic of all nineteenth-century teaching and choreography.

Blasis recommended the proper ages for children to begin their training. He laid down the routine of *barre* and centre practice. He detailed theories of *port de bras* and line of the body. All this he incorporated into a system of steps and exercises. Variations of his routine are still followed throughout the world.

Thus the technical basis of nineteenth-century choreography was defined by the 1820s. Even as this happened choreography began to feel the influence of a reaction which had set in among thinkers and artists.

The reaction stemmed from the industrial changes accelerated by the Napoleonic Wars. In place of the idyllic relations between man and man which had been the vision of Rousseau and the Enlightenment, there appeared relations of self-interest and 'cash payment'. These commercial relations altered the artist's relations with his public. The old patriarchal relationship of artist and patron died. Instead, the artist had to make his way with new masters who had no taste and regarded him as expendable or, at best, only decoratively useful. To most thinkers and artists the new world turned out to be cold, cruel and philistine.

Poet and painter, architect and choreographer, composer and writer were conscious of the new forces at work. Most could neither analyse them deeply nor understand them. A few realists faced the situation by continuing to depict the world as it was, good and bad. A larger part mingled their observation of the real world with an imaginary world where they could create the freedom and beauty denied them in their new conditions. Many took refuge entirely in this world.

Such a turning away from reality provided an escape for society, disturbed by the forces of industrialism, as much as for the artist.

> 'Beauty is truth, truth beauty'—that is all
> Ye know on earth, and all ye need to know.

Keat's Grecian Urn proclaimed the romantic illusion which comforted the artists and their supporters.

This romantic movement, arising out of the industrial revolution, began to influence ballet during the late 1820s. It developed under the twin influences of neo-classicism and the cult of nature inherited from the eighteenth century. Neo-classicism, once the post-revolutionary confidence had gone out of it, left choreographers with themes in far-away countries and far-away times which had no need to take account of contemporary reality. From the far-away countries it was but a small step to the far-away places of the imagination through which the romantic ballet entered its highest phase in 1832.

The previous year Meyerbeer's opera, *Robert le Diable*, had caused a sensation in Paris with its ballet of ghostly nuns created by the choreographer, Filippo Taglioni. Inspired by this, the tenor in the opera, Adolphe Nourrit, suggested to the opera director, Dr. Véron, the scenario of a new ballet. It was to be based on Nodier's story *Trilby ou le Lutin d'Argaïl*, which he called *La Sylphide*.

Set in Scotland, *La Sylphide's* theme of a supernatural being falling in love with a mortal man on his wedding night, confirmed the ascendancy of the romantic movement in ballet. It had the qualities which already pleased the new audiences of the day—the life of ordinary folk, a strange country and a remote historical period. To this it added a new quality, the remote world of the spirit. James, a mortal man, leaves the peasant world of his farmhouse in Act I to pursue a beautiful imaginary being into the forest of Act II. He finds her, but a spell destroys them both the moment he touches her. The real and the supernatural cannot meet. (Plate IV (b).)

Thus *La Sylphide* translated the romantic illusion into choreographic terms. Ethereality was suggested not only by Didelot's flying wires, but by the use of movement on *pointes*. It was one of the first creative uses of the *pointe* in choreography. Ethereality was conveyed, too, by lighting, décor and a development of costume design for the beings of the other world. It no longer revealed the figure, as the costumes of the earlier period had done. It concealed it in billowing masses of pale material, which reached halfway down the calf and changed the female silhouette. In this costume movement became mysterious and wonderful. The silhouette remains in use today, and has even influenced contemporary fashion through 'the ballerina skirt'. (Illustration 1 and Plate IV (c).)

In this way stage designers set about uniting the real and imaginary worlds within a naturalist framework. The practice of changing scenes in view of the audience was abandoned from 1831 onwards in favour of lowering the curtain between each act. The public was separated finally from the artists. Romantic illusion and theatrical illusion became one.

Gaslight, introduced to the stage of the Paris Opéra in 1822, reinforced the aura of supernatural mystery. Ciceri, designer of *La Sylphide*, *Giselle* and many operas and ballets, made great use of the power it gave to vary illumination. Through new lighting methods and the quality of their stage pictures he and other designers extended the imaginative limits of the proscenium theatre.

Thus Romanticism gave to costume and scene design the same kind of fresh inspiration it gave to choreography. The emotions with which designers charged their work helped to create a unity between music and design, seeing and hearing, place and time such as the eighteenth century had hardly known.

If we compare *La Sylphide* with *Giselle* we can understand more of the way the romantic ballet developed. Nine years separate the two works. The form of both is similar. Each has two acts. The first represents real life; the second is a world of fantasy. But in *Giselle* (Appendix II) man is no longer destroyed in the world of fantasy. The artist now gives him hope. Love is powerful enough to redeem him for his own world.

In construction and technique *Giselle* shows many improvements over *La Sylphide*. The principal roles, especially the role of the ballerina, are more strongly developed dramatically and choreographically. The flying wires, which had played so important a part in the ethereal qualities of Didelot's *Flore et Zéphire*, and then of *La Sylphide*, all but disappear. In *Giselle* they are replaced by the improved technique of the dancers on *pointes*. With *Giselle* the illusion of ethereality becomes an achievement of the dancer not of the machinist.

Giselle became the finest work of French Romantic ballet. This had a unity between theme, music and choreography which can still be the envy of ballet-masters. (Plate V (a).)

The music was descriptive and charged with atmosphere, marking an important development in music for choreography. From then on, music ceased to be merely a rhythmic accompaniment to dancing. It began to contribute to the story on stage.

Adolphe Adam, the composer, made this contribution in several

C.A.—3

ways, most significantly in his use of *leitmotif* and a fugue. His *leit-motifs* depicted the characters of the story with much more effect than Halévy had achieved in 1830 when he introduced the device to ballet music in *Manon Lescaut*.[1] In *Giselle*, the *leitmotifs* are repeated and developed to underline the development of the action.

The fugue in Act II is even more dramatic. Unfortunately, it is cut from most productions of the ballet today.[2] It occurs at the moment when Giselle leads Albrecht to the cross above her grave in an effort to save him from the wilis. The queen of the wilis sends wave after wave of wilis against the cross. Each attack corresponds to a 'voice' in the fugue. The attacks fail. Even the power of the queen herself fails until she draws Giselle away from the cross, and Albrecht follows her.

These musical devices were certainly repeated in the choreography of Perrot and Coralli. Therefore *Giselle* marks the first appearance of choreographic *leitmotif*. The steps of Giselle's gay dance with Albrecht at the beginning of Act I are repeated in today's version, when she goes mad at the end of the act, and again in Act II when she has become a wili. Each time the repetition has a different style and emphasis. But the steps are the same.

All the choreography is imbued with a similar dramatic purpose. Demi-character influences in the steps of Act I suggest the everyday world. A colder, purer classical technique is used for the spirit world of Act II. In both acts the choreographic lines and patterns are typically those of romantic art—gentle curves of elbows, wrists and inclined head, softness everywhere.

The story is told through dancing and short mime sequences in which the *corps de ballet* play as important a role as the principals. The dancing of the principals in Act I uses steps of *batterie* and elevation to suggest the joy of life. The *pas de deux* passages in the same act take the form of dancing together rather than supported movements. Supported lifts and virtuosity for the ballerina were not yet a general rule in *pas de deux*. But we see a beginning of the conception in Act II. Here the story calls for lifts and steps of elevation to give the illusion of flight.

These examples illustrate a particular influence of romanticism

[1] We are indebted for this research to Mr John Lanchbery, principal conductor of the Royal Ballet.
[2] The fugue was reintroduced to West European audiences in 1953 when Mary Skeaping produced *Giselle* for the Royal Swedish Ballet.

upon technique. The romantic movement caused technique to be reapplied. Not only was the dance used to tell a story in pictures; it was used to penetrate into feelings and emotions. So when the ballerina was lifted in the air the lift showed more than her intangibility. It showed her flying away, even drawn away whilst longing to stay in her lover's arms.

Such ideas, of course, had been present in *La Sylphide*. For this the Taglionis, Filippo, choreographer of the ballet, and Marie, the first Sylphide, must be given pioneer credit. But it was Perrot who perfected them through his genius and the unique abilities of Carlotta Grisi, his Giselle.

Coralli, not Perrot, got the credit for *Giselle* in 1841, although Perrot created Grisi's dances. Later Perrot reproduced the ballet in St. Petersburg. This was the version, revised by Petipa in the 1880s, which Nicholas Sergueeff revived for the Paris Opéra in 1924 and for the Vic-Wells Ballet at the Old Vic in 1934.

Only August Bournonville can match Perrot as a creator of the romantic ballet. Both were pupils of Auguste Vestris. Both developed the ideas of Noverre and Dauberval. Both, like Baudelaire the supreme creator of French romantic poetry, were realist in outlook, romantic in imagery and classical in the purity of their technique. In their choreography the twin elements of romantic art are woven together, images drawn from life around them and images drawn from the idealist imagination.

'The dance', wrote Bournonville, 'is beautiful as an art because it seeks its ideal equally in plastic beauty and in lyric and dramatic impressions.

'The beauty it strives to attain is not founded on vague principles of fashion or taste, but on changeless laws of nature. . . .'[1]

In Copenhagen Bournonville created more than fifty ballets and *divertissements* during a long life, which ended in 1879. His principal contribution to the *ballet d'action* lay in the folk *genre*. His ballets brought to the stage fisherfolk from Italy, townsfolk from Flanders, Spaniards, Norwegians, Czechs and Russians, besides a collection of Scandinavian elves and trolls. Each ballet is full of vitality and the inspiration of travels abroad, but never exploits technique as an end in itself.

As dramatist and choreographer Bournonville combined the technique of the school of Vestris with national dances, mime and

[1] A. Bournonville, Foreword to *Études Chorégraphiques* (Copenhagen, 1861).

the temperament and physiques of his Danish dancers. These ideas dominated the Danish ballet for fifty years after his death. His ballets are still the kernel of the Royal Danish repertoire. In the classroom his methods continue to be used by teachers in the Royal Theatre School and other Danish dance studios.

From his book *Études Chorégraphiques*, and from *Bournonville's Trinskole* by Allan Fridericia after Hans Beck, it is clear that Bournonville followed as thorough a system as Blasis. Parts of the *Études* are reproduced in Appendix VIA to illustrate the technical basis of his choreography, and give a glimpse of the methods of the school of Vestris which dominated the romantic ballet.[1]

Line did not occupy the significant place it occupied later in Russian classical teaching. Great emphasis was laid on elevation and *pirouettes*, the latter in many positions and combinations requiring great control. Exercises for elevation were divided into slow and quick (presumably large and small), *batterie* and *ballon*. They started always with frequent repetitions of a very simple movement built into almost choreographic *enchaînements*. Therefore Bournonville's dancers possessed strength and control as well as speed and lightness.

About a dozen of Bournonville's works are still performed by the Royal Danish Ballet. In them we can see something of the style and form of his choreography and the way the dancers' vocabulary was used. Together they comprise a living museum of the romantic ballet.

Bournonville's *Le Conservatoire* remains the purest choreographic expression of the School of Vestris on the stage today. The present one-act version is taken from *Konservatoriet*[2], a two-act work composed by Bournonville in 1849. He intended it as a memorial of his studies under Vestris at the Paris Opéra in the 1820s. What we see now are incidents during a class in Vestris' time. The ballet-master takes the class, playing his violin as all ballet-masters used to do until pianos began to be used for class at the turn of our own century. Everyone is there, from *petit rat* to *étoile*. The care with which the Danes have preserved this choreographic treasure allows us to see the nearest possible representation on stage of the French classical style from which all national schools today are descended.

La Sylphide and *Napoli* illustrate the classical and national elements

[1] See also *Bournonville and Ballet Technique*, by Erik Bruhn and Lilian Moore (Black, 1961) for a further analysis of the Bournonville system.

[2] The full title of the two-act work is *Konservatoriet eller et avisfrieri*. The music is by H. Paulli. The present shortened version was arranged by Harald Lander and Valborg Borchsenius in 1941.

of Bournonville's choreography, his twin worlds of fantasy and reality. *La Sylphide* was produced first in Denmark in 1836. It used Nourrit's story but Bournonville created his own choreography to a Danish score in place of Taglioni's original. Bournonville himself danced the role of James with Lucile Grahn, his pupil, as the Sylphide.

The three-act *Napoli* was created six years later after a visit to Italy. Again Bournonville danced the leading male role. Brilliant in its mime and crowd scenes, filled with dancing and theatrical tricks, it has remained one of the most popular of Danish ballets.

Bournonville seems to have choreographed the leading male roles of his ballets more strongly than the female roles. Probably this was because he was himself a fine male dancer. In his day the School of Vestris emphasised male rather than female virtuosity. It is the men who are given the bravura passages in *La Sylphide* and *Napoli*. The variations for James and the two male soloists in Act I of *La Sylphide*, and the soli in Act II of *Napoli*, are some of the finest variations for men in the classical repertoire.

From his heroines Bournonville expected grace, charm and elegance. In place of virtuoso turns one finds mostly poses on *pointe*, jumps and *batterie*. His *pas de deux*, too, are mostly of a *demi-caractère* nature, helping forward the story. They do not include spectacular lifts nor supported *pirouettes*.

The ensemble dances, as well as the solo variations, show that Bournonville possessed a rich choreographic imagination. The vocabulary of steps was not large, but his imagination, mingling with invention and musicality, found ways for these steps to express the range of human feeling.

Jules Perrot also often took for his heroes men of humble origin. Sometimes, as in *Catarina*, his ballets directly reflected the democratic tendencies of the day by ridiculing the aristocracy. Always his themes combined the real and fantastic elements of romantic thought. The humble heroes, for example, are set against the background of their own surroundings—Gringoire in the crowded streets of *La Esméralda's* Paris; and Matteo the fisherman of *Ondine*.

It was not only the themes which gave Perrot's ballets their wide appeal to the new public of the nineteenth century. As male dancer and choreographer he was the greatest figure of the romantic ballet. While he lacked the good looks expected of a dancer he was a superb exponent of the school of Vestris. His movements had extraordinary harmony, rare grace, elasticity and rhythm. As a mime he was unequalled. In speed and elevation he astonished the eye. 'It is', said Gautier, 'visible music. . . . Perrot the airy! Perrot the sylph, Perrot the male Taglioni!'

As a choreographer Perrot drew upon the same technical vocabulary as Bournonville. But he was more of a poet than the Dane. His imagery was more brilliant, his range wider.

Though a great male dancer, he expressed himself, especially, through his ballerinas. Unlike Bournonville, he gave the bravura passages to women. Hence he played a principal part in elevating the ballerina to her supreme position in nineteenth-century choreography.

To choreography he brought expressive dance images and a development of symphonic form. These gifts were best represented in *Giselle*, *La Esméralda* and the *Pas de Quatre* which he created in London in 1845.

Dancing, he believed, should be expressive in itself. It should be danced action. If virtuosity is used it should be only as an aid to expression. It must never be an end in itself. Hence we find in his choreography as much attention to minor roles as to major ones. Ensembles, *pas de deux* and *soli*, all contribute to the final effect.

His development of symphonic form follows naturally from his search for expression. By 'symphonic form' in choreography we mean more than the orchestration of movement at which Perrot was master. We mean the blending of all the elements of choreography into an harmonious whole to serve a dramatic purpose.

The elements comprise various styles of classical and character dancing, mime and passages of *pas d'action*. These can be used in divertissements and other kinds of ensemble dances, crowd scenes, *soli*, *pas de deux*, *pas de trois* and so on. Better than anyone before him Perrot showed how to balance these elements to express themes in narrative or mood form. Most of his ballets were narratives, but the *Pas de Quatre* was a short ballet of mood. If there was a weakness in this symphonic method it lay not in the choreographic construction but in its musical base. The necessity of really good music for ballet only began to be understood when the romantic ballet was nine-tenths dead.

The romantic ballet, then, represents the collective effort of many choreographers to adapt their aristocratic language to new themes and new audiences. When they were most successful they produced the great works of the period.

Their success can be measured by the extraordinary flowering of ballet as an art throughout Europe and America during the nineteenth century. For the first time the art of choreography captured the public mind. New ballet companies sprang up to supply the demand. They encouraged the local training of dancers and choreographers.

But the greatest dancers continued to come from France and Italy. The Austrian Fanny Elssler and the Dane Lucile Grahn were exceptions among ballerinas of international fame. The big names earned larger sums than ever before. Fanny Cerrito, for example, was paid £200 a month to appear at Covent Garden in 1855. Though this was a large figure at the time it was by no means exceptional.

Ever nomadic, the dance world travelled far and fast. It had need of the wings of sylphs and wilis. On 8th March, 1846, Fanny Elssler found that time would not allow her to fulfil the terms of two contracts. One contract obliged her to remain in Venice until 24th March. Therefore, she wrote to M. Balochino at the Hoftheater, she would not be able to appear in Vienna on 25th March, as agreed by contract with him.

Choreographers travelled as much as their ballerinas. Perrot was ballet-master for long periods in London, Paris, Milan and St. Petersburg, not to mention brief engagements in smaller cities. Arthur Saint-Léon ranged more widely to Lisbon, Madrid, Vienna, Berlin, Rome, St. Petersburg and other centres. No-one, though, could match the Taglioni's, Filippo, creator of *La Sylphide* and his two children Marie and Paul. Over three-quarters of a century these three, their brothers and children, appeared in cities all over Europe and America. The record of their ballets can be traced in archives as far apart as Leningrad, Munich, Naples and New York.

This activity does not mean that choreography always reached a high level of good taste, let alone art. There were choreographers like Voitus van Hamme of Amsterdam, one of the most prolific in ballet history. For forty years into the 1860s he created large-scale spectacular works at the Schowburg and elsewhere. Often his ballets followed the tradition of *commedia dell' arte* with a broad knock-about comedy popular in Holland. Sometimes they were reproductions of successful romantic ballets like *Giselle*. His listed works fill seven pages of the catalogue and much shelf space in the library of Amsterdam University. None of it is remembered on stage today.

Van Hamme was a choreographic journalist. He gave his audience the spectacular element in ballet he knew it liked. In this he anticipated the direction the romantic movement would take. When he borrowed an idea or reproduced a ballet he usually acknowledged the original. Other choreographers were not so honest, since there was no copyright protection, so we find *La Sylphide* and *Giselle* variously appearing in many repertoires, without acknowledgement to the original creators.

About 1855, for example, *La Sylphide* was presented in a Chinese setting by David Costa, an Italian choreographer. He reproduced this version in Italy with Amina Boschetti as the Sylph and himself as James, re-christened Zabi. In 1843, barely two years after its creation in Paris, *Giselle* was presented at La Scala, Milan. The five scenes of the libretto followed the original story but made no acknowledgement to the authors. The characters remained the same, although the action was transferred to Bosnia. Fanny Cerrito danced Giselle to new choreography by Antonio Cortesi, ballet-master at La Scala.

Always, too, we find romantic fantasy balanced by the naturalism of decor and production. Designers and choreographers made great use of mechanical contrivance to strengthen stage illusion. Munich Theatre Museum has a relic of their thoroughness. It is a pair of peacock-coloured wings worn by the Sylph of *La Sylphide*. Perhaps they were worn by Lucile Grahn who died in Munich. The wings are attached to a tiny mechanism which was attached to the costume. A key winds it up so that when the Sylph first appears before the sleeping James her wings move and she 'flies'. In Act II this mechanism was exchanged for the one with which we are more familiar. It allows the Sylph's wings to fall off, first one, then the other, as she dies in James's arms.

Always impressive in output, romantic choreography began to assume new qualities from about the 1850s. Its themes hardened into formulae. Interest centred on how things were said rather than what was said. Virtuosity claimed more and more of the choreographer's attention.

The tendency appeared first in Italy. It was encouraged by the spectacular tradition in Italian ballet and the virtuoso emphasis at the school in Milan. It reflected also the negative elements always present in romantic choreography. None of these elements was so damaging as the emphasis placed upon the ballerina. By elevating the ballerina at the expense of her partner romanticism in the end drained away the drama and emotion it once gave to choreography. Form dominated content so that display became the principal end of dancing.

In matters of display the Italian School surpassed the French. Accordingly, Italian ballerinas became more and more popular in Paris, London and elsewhere at the expense of their French colleagues. This was clear already in 1847. On a day in that year the records at La Scala show pupils of the Academy dancing in one hundred and twenty-nine different theatres of the world.

We must not think, though, that romanticism everywhere eliminated the male dancer, nor that the choreography of the 1860s and 1870s altogether lost the greatness it had enjoyed in the 1840s.

Arthur Saint-Léon represents what is best in the choreography of romanticism's last period. There were many others whose work was stimulated by the extraordinary interest of the public. One of them was Justamant, ballet-master at Lyon.

Justamant made choreographic records of many of the full-length ballets he produced in Paris, London, Lyon and elsewhere. His stories continued the romantic formula. Mortal men fell in love with immortal beings. But the treatment was melodramatic with long mime scenes and 'conversations' in huge productions where the tricks of the machinist were rivalled by the mass movements of a large *corps de ballet*.

Men still took part in these ballets, but the role of the hero and many other leading roles were mimed, not danced. The man's principal function was to support the ballerina and be handsome or wicked as the story required. In the sixties and seventies Justamant does not seem to have used women *en travestie* for male roles, as many choreographers did in France and England at the end of the century. In 1870, for example, Saint-Léon originally made Franz in *Coppélia* a role *en travestie*.

Male virtuosity continued to be required in character dancing. For this purpose a male dancer might be introduced at a particular moment in the ballet, usually to provide a climax or to open a scene. He would appear, dance his variation, and not be seen again. He had nothing to do with the plot and might not even be listed on the programme.

Thus M. Charles was given two variations in Justamant's 'ballet-féerie', *Les Néréides, ou Le Lac enchanté*. These variations illustrate the nature of male dancing at the time and show something of the quality of their uninspired, but thoroughly professional choreographer and producer. The ballet, in two acts and four scenes, was first presented at the Grand-Théâtre, Lyon, on 11th March, 1861.

The variations were part of an Hungarian dance which opened the second scene. Justamant's script calls it a *Pas hongrois* or *Redowa*. The Redowa was popular in romantic choreography and was danced in a rapid 3/4 time. This version by Justamant began with a *pas de cinq* for M. Charles with four *coryphées*. Eight measures before the end of the *pas de cinq* Charles left the stage to prepare for his first solo. This lasted sixteen measures followed by a *pas de quatre* of twenty-four measures for the girls. Then came Charles's major variation. The dance ended with a coda begun by the girls. As they danced M. Charles entered for a brilliant but exhausting *pas de cinq* of thirty-six measures. They finished, all five, with *une pirouette en dedans sur le pied gauche, finir sec et en suite sur les deux pieds*.

Saint-Léon, of course, was a creative choreographer where Justamant was content to follow accepted patterns. *Coppélia*, Saint-Léon's masterpiece, shows him to be also a craftsman who maintained the principles of the *ballet d'action* at a time of general decline. Some of *Coppélia's* continuing popularity is due to an exceptionally good scenario by Nuitter and Saint-Léon from a tale by Hoffmann. Much of it is due to the versatility and virtuosity of Saint-Léon's choreography, especially the national dances of Eastern Europe in whose use he was a master.

National dances have always inspired choreographers. They appealed especially to romantic choreographers because they strengthened the naturalist setting of romantic thought. If a ballet was placed in some foreign country national dances helped to provide the foreign flavour.

Saint-Léon seems to have used such dances mainly for their spectacular element. Although he understood the value of a good story, he understood still more his public's interest in spectacle. Hence he used his dancers' virtuosity to develop spectacle within the framework of the *ballet d'action*. In so doing he became the bridge between the romantic ballet and the great displays of classical virtuosity which Petipa created in St. Petersburg.

Such a changed conception of the *ballet d'action* required a more developed musical base for its choreography. Delibes supplied it. His score is the principal reason for *Coppélia's* long life.

Delibes' scores for *Coppélia* in 1870 and *Sylvia* in 1876 announced the new kind of ballet music which was to be developed in Russia by Tchaikovsky and his successors. The use of *leitmotif* introduced by Adam was continued in these scores, which combined the character of original composition with the needs of the theatre and the ballet stage. They had colour and their own musical validity even while they helped to tell the stories of the ballets and create atmosphere. This was what Tchaikovsky specially admired. Noverre would have been pleased, too, because they were 'to dancing what words are to music'. Even as it died the romantic ballet passed the priceless gift of music to its successors.

In France, so far as one can date any movement in art precisely, *Coppélia* marked the end of the romantic ballet and of the School of Vestris. At its première in the Opéra on 25th May, 1870, the hero, Franz, *en travestie*, danced opposite a French-trained Italian Swanilda. Henceforth the teachings of Blasis more and more replaced the teachings of Vestris in the French capital.

The Emperor Napoleon III and Empress Eugénie were present. Within four months Saint-Léon was dead. On 20th November he was followed to the grave by Giuseppina Bozzacchi, his Swanilda, the little seventeen-year-old dancer who became, like many of her fellow dancers at the Opéra, a victim of the Prussian siege of Paris. Slowly the centres of ballet shifted from Paris and Milan to Milan and St. Petersburg, where choreography was developed in different classical forms.

CHAPTER V

CLASSICAL CHOREOGRAPHY

THE Italian School of Ballet grew in Milan but flowered in St. Petersburg. In the last half of the nineteenth century the virtuosity of its dancers made it the most influential school in Europe. In Russia Italian virtuosity found its most creative expression.

Elsewhere, virtuosity became merely part of spectacular display. In London, for example, Italian and other foreign ballerinas appeared in a succession of gorgeous productions at the Alhambra Theatre from the 1860s onwards. Often the productions were staged by Italian choreographers.

The London press contains vivid descriptions of the brilliant costumes, transformation scenes, storms, earthquakes, menageries of animals and armies of female *corps de ballet* who wheeled and marched and waved their legs across its stage.

In Italy, the spectacular tradition in choreography was encouraged by the vogue of the spectacular ballet. The archives of La Scala, Milan, contain choreographic scripts of large productions by Luigi Manzotti in the seventies, eighties and nineties. Manzotti was a dancer, mime and choreographer who had been born in Milan in 1838 but spent much of his dancing life in Rome. He returned to Milan in 1872 and created his first production at La Scala three years later.

The records of two of his most popular ballets, *Excelsior* and *Amor*, show the large scale on which he worked. *Excelsior* was first produced at La Scala on 11th January, 1881. It had six parts and twelve scenes, thirty-four principal roles and a supporting cast of over three hundred dancers and extras. Many of its novelties and effects were made particularly brilliant by electric light, which was just beginning to be used in the theatre.

Amor, five years later, was equally elaborate. Manzotti called it 'a choreographic poem', but the epic scale of the production makes this claim modest, to say the least. Its two parts and sixteen scenes ranged from the Dawn of the Universe to the Pantheon of the Arts in Greece, the Destruction of Rome, the Battle of Legnano and the

Ultimate Victory of Liberty and Love. Two hundred dancers, two hundred and fifty extras, one ox, two elephants, eighteen horses and 'ten electric light machines' were required for the ballet. Leading the dancers were Emma Palladino, already well known in London through two seasons at the Alhambra Theatre, and Enrico Cecchetti.

The fame of these spectacles at La Scala took them to other theatres in Italy and abroad. *Excelsior* enjoyed a great success at Her Majesty's Theatre, London, in 1885 with Giovannina Limido and Cecchetti in the lead. *Amor* went to the Teatro Costanzi, Rome, in the autumn of 1886, when Cecchetti again partnered Palladino. Indeed, the travels of Manzotti's ballets helped to spread the influence of the Italian School. Among other dancers they took Cecchetti to Russia.

The pages of Manzotti's choreographic scripts are squared as if for mathematics. On each page each of the principal characters is represented by a different coloured circle. Opposite, the action, the lighting and the mimed conversations are described for each dancer or group. Key passages from the score sometimes accompany the descriptions, or the number of counts to a dance is given. Occasionally there are drawings of important scenic effects, groupings of dancers or individual poses. But usually the dancers are just blobs. Their patterns and positions *en masse* were more important to Manzotti than their steps. So the script looks like staff directions for troop movements or the disposition of soldiers for battle.

Clearly, the ballets required little originality in the creation of dances, but plenty in matters of production. They remained ballets, however, not circuses nor pageants. Manzotti applied choreography to two purposes: the representation of patriotic themes, and theatrical effect.

Almost all his themes reflected the new national pride of united Italy. Hence he anticipated, perhaps even influenced, the patriotic and jingo ballets which became popular a few years later in London at the Alhambra and Empire theatres. The theatrical effect was achieved by carefully arranged processions, groups and ensembles as well as spectacular decoration. Interspersed with the groups or dances were explanatory passages of mime to advance the story. For climax he presented his principal dancers in *soli* and *pas de deux*. These exploited the virtuosity of the best Italian-trained male and female artists available to him. 'The lean and lissom *primo ballerino* Signor Enrico Cecchetti', wrote a critic of *Excelsior* in London, 'not only fairly astounds by his wondrous pirouetting, but dances throughout in such finished and graceful style as fairly to conquer the prejudices I have generally entertained against the masculine ballet dancer.'[1]

The same year in which Cecchetti achieved this triumph in London, Virginia Zucchi, another product of the School of Blasis, made her debut at a café-concert in St. Petersburg. Many famous dancers, of course, had appeared in the Russian capital before Zucchi. Most of the great romantic ballerinas danced there, usually with success. But no other debut held quite the significance which this one came to hold.

When Zucchi went to Russia, ballet there appeared to be in decline. Interest had waned after the days of Didelot and high romanticism. In spite of lavish Imperial patronage, aesthetic values and public taste had sunk to a low level. Spectacle was what attracted the audience more than dramatic interest or interpretation. Indeed, the situation seemed more depressing than in Italy or France because the conventions into which ballet had settled everywhere seemed particularly rigid in Russia, supported by the court, and by influential balletomanes. Yet for many years the Imperial Ballet had produced dancers who rivalled the great names of the West.

None, for instance, outshone the fame of Pushkin's Istomina.

> And suddenly a leap: behold she flies
> Like down puffed by Aeolian lips.

From her debut in Didelot's *Acis and Galatos* in 1815 to her retirement in 1836 Istomina's success symbolised the new place of the ballerina on the Russian stage.

The excellence of the Imperial Company which produced such dancers was remarked by Gautier himself in 1858. 'The ballet school provides remarkable solists and *corps de ballet* who have no equals in coordination, precision and speed of movements.'[2] It was the French School of Vestris which he saw. This was still being taught in St. Petersburg in 1885 when Virginia Zucchi arrived from Italy. Its principal exponents were Marius Petipa, a Frenchman, and the Swede, Christian Johansson.

Johansson and Petipa must be counted among the advantages which ballet in Russia possessed at the beginning of the eighties. Johansson had already danced and taught in St. Petersburg for forty

---

[1] *Illustrated Sporting and Dramatic News*, 1st August, 1885.
[2] T. Gautier, *Voyage en Russie* (Paris, 1858).

years. A gifted pupil of Bournonville, and so of the School of Vestris, he, more than anyone, created what came to be called the Russian School of Ballet. He did it by studying Russian performance on stage and Russian teaching methods in the school. These he combined with what he felt to be best from the French and Danish Schools. The result at the beginning of this century was a great flowering of Russian dancers trained in his system. He was Denmark's contribution to the mainstream of the classical dance at the end of the nineteenth century. He personifies the influence which the ballet of one country can exert upon another.

Petipa, confident, ambitious, and trained in the French School, had joined the Imperial Ballet in St. Petersburg as a dancer in 1847: he was fourteen years with the company before being appointed ballet-master in 1862 to succeed Perrot. But it was not until Saint-Léon's final departure in 1869 that he became undisputed choreographer. By then he had worked with and learned much from Perrot and Saint-Léon. In the same period Russian dancers developed their style and technique under the stimulus of foreign choreographers, teachers and dancers.

Like the fairy godmothers at the birth of the Sleeping Beauty the great names of European choreography and teaching thus brought gifts to the young Russian ballet. But Russian ballet, as such, was still half asleep. It was still ballet-in-Russia. The man who roused her for national greatness was Ivan Vsevolojsky, Director of the Imperial Theatre, St. Petersburg, from 1881–1889.

Before Vsevolojsky's appointment Petipa does not seem to have consolidated the striking choreographic qualities which appeared later in *The Sleeping Beauty* and *Swan Lake*. Following Saint-Léon's example he was content, albeit reluctant, to give the public and his superiors the display they wanted, arranged to the insipid music of official composers. Only the circumstances of a court ballet, the grace of the French School, and Petipa's undoubted choreographic talent made these spectacles displays of dancing rather than of scenic effects. Scenic effects were not ignored, of course. Petipa counted on their help and the talents of his ballerinas to give him success.

Bournonville rightly criticised this vulgar departure from the highest principles of the *ballet d'action*. 'I looked in vain for action,' he wrote in his memoirs about a visit in 1874, 'for some dramatic interest, some sanity. Occasionally I was lucky enough to strike a fragment in which reason prevailed (as in M. Petipa's *Don Quixote*, for instance) but the effect was at once dispelled irrevocably by the bravura entries which were greeted with wild enthusiasm by the audience.'

Most of Petipa's work at this time consisted of revivals. He enjoyed some success with *Don Quixote* and even more with *La Bayadère* in 1877. But nothing he did, nor any of the Russian ballerinas he preferred to use, could recall the popularity ballet had once enjoyed under Didelot and Perrot. Vsevolojsky countered the growing isolation of the art with two measures. A short time after the success of her debut in St. Petersburg in 1885 he engaged Virginia Zucchi for the Imperial Theatres. A year later he abolished the post of the official composer of ballet music. These steps allowed new influences to vary the formulae within which ballets were created.

Zucchi was a strong dramatic dancer, a powerful mime and a fiery, rather than a brilliant, technician. All these qualities appeared a revelation to the Russian dancers trained in the grace of the French School. She showed the Russians the blocked point shoes which helped the brilliance of the Italian School in dancing on *pointe*. Her technique, and the technique of the Italians who followed her, brought new teaching methods to the Imperial Schools, supplementing those of Johansson. In this cause she shortened the Russian *tutu* to the length favoured in Italy, giving greater freedom to the legs.

These *tutus* were a development from the romantic ballet skirt, which the dancers' continual struggle for freedom of the limbs had shortened to create a new silhouette. Henceforth, the romantic silhouette and the silhouette of the classical *tutu* became the basic silhouettes of the ballerina's costume. (Illustration 1.)

Among many other Italians who danced in St. Petersburg during the eighties and nineties three, besides Zucchi, were of special importance. Enrico Cecchetti and Carlotta Brianza arrived in 1887, the year of Zucchi's departure. Pierina Legnani, the most successful of all the ballerinas, made her debut in St. Petersburg in 1893.

Like Zucchi, Cecchetti and Brianza were seen first in a *café-concert* in the Livadia Park, where the management were presenting versions of Manzotti's ballets. In fact, Manzotti and the Italians in the Arcadia Theatre, Livadia, proved strong competition to Petipa at the Imperial Theatres.

Cecchetti's success was greater than that of his partner. Just as he had astounded the London public, so he astounded the Russians by

his demonstration of male virtuosity. Almost at once he was engaged
for the Maryinsky, while Brianza had to wait till 1889 for the same
compliment. Following her engagement she created in 1890 the role
of Princess Aurora in the first performance of *The Sleeping Beauty*.

As Cecchetti's technique was studied by Russian male dancers, so
that of Pierina Legnani was studied by the women. She stayed eight
years in St. Petersburg, longer than any other Italian ballerina,
becoming the first *prima ballerina assoluta* in Russian ballet history.

(a)   (b)

I. BASIC FEMALE SILHOUETTE

(a) The Romantic Silhouette showing high-waisted skirt.
(b) The Classical Silhouette showing the *tutu*, a shortened skirt freeing
the legs, lowering the waist-line and altering the silhouette.

Among other things she contributed the trick of thirty-two *fouettés*
to the Russian vocabulary. This was first seen in Ivanov's *The Tulip
of Harlem* at the Maryinsky in 1893. Two years later she repeated it
as Odile in *Swan Lake* with such success that these *fouettés* now symbolise one of the principal technical developments which the Russians
absorbed from the Italians. The development was the use of the head
in *pirouettes* and other turns, the principle of 'spotting' on an object
so that the head is the last part of the body to face the front and the
first to do so again in turning. 'Spotting' prevents dizziness, and lends

C.A.—4

brilliance to a turn. It was the reason (and carefully guarded secret) why the ballerinas of the School of Milan turned so well.

Petipa had not wanted to engage Italian dancers, preferring the Russians he had trained in his French methods. Compelled to use the Italians, he exploited their ability. They extended the range of his choreography; he presented them in the one setting in Europe at the time where their talents could flower most richly.

It is important, therefore, to know more about the technical resources the Italians offered him. What were the methods used in Milan and what did the Italians take with them to St. Petersburg besides the particular tricks for which they are famous?

In the archives of La Scala today, tucked into a folder with other *memorabilia*, is a foolscap exercise book. In the book someone has recorded two groups of ballet classes. Each group represents a series of classes given by a teacher in Milan, six different classes, one for each day of the week. One of the teachers was Cesare Coppini, formerly a principal male dancer at La Scala. He was head of the School at the time these notes were written, and taught the class of perfection. The other was Caterina Beretta, former *prima ballerina* of La Scala, a private teacher at the time of these notes, subsequently head of the School in the early years of this century.

The pupil for whom the exercises were recorded was Pierina Legnani herself. Probably the writing is hers. The date of the notebook is the end of the eighties or the beginning of the nineties.

These exercises, in fact, may be those mentioned by the London critic of *St. Paul's Magazine* on 25th August, 1894. Legnani was then appearing in London during the summer holiday of the Imperial Theatre. 'Pierina Legnani', wrote the critic, 'tells you that the secret of success lies in hard and incessant work. Every day she practises for two hours in the morning, even during her so-called holiday in the autumn. English dancers, as a rule, shirk constant practice as soon as they get over the preliminary stage and begin to do one thing fairly well; they give up the arduous exercises and wish to continue flying before they have thoroughly mastered the art of perfect walking.'

The young Legnani probably made these notes to take with her when she began to visit foreign theatres after her debut at La Scala in 1888. They give us a complete picture of the weekly methods of two teachers in the most advanced class of the most famous ballet school in Europe in the 1880s. This school provided the technical foundation of most European choreography at the time. So we reproduce the notes in full at Appendix VI B.

The classes, of course, were based on Blasis' methods and were for women only. The men were taught separately. The shape of the classes was similar to classes today, except that a particular section was devoted to *pirouettes* in various positions. *Pointe* work, too, was emphasised. *Pointe* shoes seem to have been worn throughout the class, or at least from the beginning of centre practice. The limited range of steps employed by both teachers, the simplicity of the combinations and the emphasis on repetition all confirm the characteristics of nineteenth-century technique and choreography which we have noted elsewhere. The aim was to make a dancer perfect in relatively few steps, rather than to provide the choreographer with material capable of the widest possible range of movement.

The connection between these exercises and those used later in Cecchetti's teaching is clear. Some of the *adages* and *enchaînements* resemble the method handed down by Cecchetti but they have less variety and there is not the daily group of steps in *allegro*. Cecchetti developed these characteristics in his method following his experiences as a teacher in Russia. Legnani's exercises, in other words, provide a link between the method of Blasis and the method of Cecchetti. In particular, they show the nature of the virtuoso brilliance which the Italians gave to the Russian School.

Sometimes the contribution of the School of Milan to the Russian School is underestimated. The Russian School today derives technically from a blend of the French School of Vestris and the Italian School of Blasis with Russian temperament and physique. The Italian contribution in the eighties and nineties was, therefore, essential, first to the best period of Petipa's choreography, then to the development of the Russian School itself at the beginning of this century.

One other contribution was equally essential. If the French and Italians provided Russian ballet with its technical base, the Russians themselves developed its musical base. Glinka had prepared the way already with his ballet scenes in *Ivan Susanin* and *Russlan and Ludmila*, but musical opportunies for ballet were extended enormously when Vsevolojsky abolished the post of official composer of ballet music in 1886. Three years later he was able to commission from Tchaikovsky the score of *The Sleeping Beauty*, which had its first performance in 1890.

'I can never understand', protested Tchaikovsky to Taneiev, another composer, 'why "ballet-music" should be used as a contemptuous epithet. The music of a ballet is not invariably bad—there are good works of this class—Delibes' *Sylvia*, for instance.'[1]

Tchaikovsky had a deep respect for Delibes' music. '*Swan Lake*', he wrote on another occasion, 'is poor stuff compared to *Sylvia*.'[2] What Delibes began, Tchaikovsky continued. Through their joint work the barriers of mediocrity in ballet music began to be broken down.

Petipa respected the composer's talent but hardly allowed him more licence than he allowed the musical hacks usually appointed to turn out tunes for his ballets. Before a note of music for *The Sleeping Beauty* had been composed, Petipa 'planned the ballet in the most minute detail, suggesting not only the rhythm, orchestration, dramatic character and exact length of each number, but even breaking them up into bars. For example, Petipa's notes on the conversation between the King and the Master of Ceremonies in Act I, gave strict instructions for the pattern of the music:

No. 4 the king asks: 'What happened?' Give 4 measures for the question and 4 for the answer . . . 'Where are you taking them?'—4 measures. Answer—'To prison'—4 measures. Question—'What have they done?' —4 measures. Answer—points to knitting needles—4 measures.

Similarly, for the comic dance between Puss-in-Boots and the White Cat in Act III, Petipa suggested:

Repeated mewing, denoting caressing and clawing. For the end— clawing and screaming of the male cat. It should begin 3/4 amoroso, and end in 3/4 with accelerated mewing.[3]

Sometimes Tchaikovsky's personal taste or the dictates of musical pattern and balance led to variations from Petipa's plan. Even so, his versatility and musicianship helped him to fulfil Petipa's demands precisely while still creating fine music. He developed Delibes' use of *leitmotif* and showed a remarkable understanding of the requirements of music for the theatre compared with music for the concert hall.

Tchaikovsky's talent thus made possible a closer collaboration

[1] Modeste Tchaikovsky (edited Newmarch), *The Life and Letters of Peter Ilyich Tchaikovsky*, p. 292 (The Bodley Head, London, 1906).

[2] Modeste Tchaikovsky, *op. cit.* p. 241.

[3] Further details are contained in Lillian Moore's note to Chapter X of her *Russian Ballet Master, The Memoirs of Marius Petipa*, and in Yuri Slonimsky's essay on Marius Petipa in *Dance Index*, Vol. VI, Nos. 5 and 6 translated by Anatole Chujoy.

between composer, choreographer and author at a higher level than had been achieved before. Particularly, he had the ability to express emotion by means of melody and harmony. Emotion, of course, is present in all great music, in Bach and Beethoven as well as in Chopin and Mendelssohn, or any of the so-called Romantic composers. In Tchaikovsky it is particularly noticeable and this is one reason why his music is so suitable for ballet. Choreography is happier musically with something actual than with something implied. Choreographers find it easier to develop a visual scenic melody when the music for their visual pictures is in no doubt about its own intentions.

So it is easy to see why Tchaikovsky's music appeals particularly to lyric choreographers. Delibes displays similar qualities in the second act of *Coppélia*. In the work of both composers movement and emotion—the 'exterior' and 'interior' aspects of the music—are perfectly balanced. Their music, in fact, is not only a part of the choreographic picture but adds a fresh dimension to it. Both also are *dancers'* composers. Their music stimulates dancing by giving dancers a special rhythmic momentum and inspiration.

There can be no doubt that Tchaikovsky's music has helped to preserve Petipa's choreography today. When it was composed it was the principal inspiration of Petipa's greatest works. Neither before nor after did the choreographer match what he created in *The Sleeping Beauty* and *Swan Lake*. The creative collaboration of the two artists worked well because the musical and choreographic methods of classical ballet ran parallel to each other. The operatic structure of the choreography with great solo 'arias' for the ballerina, unknown in Perrot's day, was matched by the musical structure.

Between them Tchaikovsky and Petipa perfected a new style of ballet and choreography—the classical style—to suit the taste of the day and the circumstances of an aristocratic audience. The romantic stories remained but they were transferred mostly to royal surroundings where the luxury of setting could satisfy the public demand for spectacle. To tell the stories in this setting the *danse d'école* was brought to a new peak of perfection. (Plate V (b).)

Not withstanding the help of Tchaikovsky, the Italians and his assistant Lev Ivanov, it took time for Petipa to establish this new choreographic structure. He did so finally through *The Sleeping Beauty* in 1890, *Casse-Noisette* in 1892 and the revival of *Swan Lake* in 1895 after Tchaikovsky's death.

The structure was built to a formula of three or more spectacular acts providing a full evening's entertainment. Nowhere else except in Russia did the custom exist for ballet to be presented alone for a whole evening in this way. In Paris and London, even in the great period of romanticism, ballet supported an opera or a play, perhaps both.

Each act of a Petipa ballet contains numerous *pas d'action*, *pas de caractère* and dances for the *corps de ballet*. The last act ends in a climatic grand *pas de deux* for the ballerina and her partner, followed by a finale. This formula was conventional by the 1890s and became more so until Fokine and others rebelled against it, although it exerts still a powerful influence on creators of ballet today. We see it repeated choreographically in John Cranko's *Prince of the Pagodas*, and musically in Khachaturian's *Spartacus*.

Matching the new structure, the softness, roundness and emotional intensity of the romantic style were replaced with clear, straight symmetry of outline, perfection of form and formal beauty. Romanticism thus became classicism through the transfer of its style from bourgeois Paris to the Russian court, and through the marriage of its French technique with Italian virtuosity.

At the same time it lost the emphasis on content which was a feature of the best romantic work. The search for spectacle, for technical brilliance at the expense of content, dominated the Petipa scenario. Little interested in themes or stories, except as excuses for dancing, undisturbed by the inconsistencies and downright bad taste of the décor, costumes and much of the music of his time, Petipa worked unswervingly through more than fifty full-length ballets in forty years to develop the technique of his dancers in an ever grander choreographic setting.

By such means the classical ballet elevated virtuosity to an end in itself. In particular virtuosity was used to display the ballerina. Thus choreography went full circle from Viganò. No longer was man the conqueror, the god on stage. Now woman was deified, the centre of the universe. Ballet became a vehicle for her talent. Man was her support.

Where the romantic ballet had given the *corps* character and individuality, Petipa used it architecturally and anonymously. The use of the *corps en masse* was developed beyond anything seen before. It dressed the stage as mobile scenery. It performed exits and entrances as endlessly impressive as the slowly moving line of dancers advancing in *arabesque* in *La Bayadère*. It took part in great ensemble dances, for as many as two hundred performers at a time. Its patterns and images had exceptional invention and great beauty. But never were its dancers expected to act or display the emotions of particular people.

Within the setting of the ensemble Petipa's solo dances and *pas de deux* shone like jewels. Their technical brilliance was displayed particularly in *divertissements*, such as the fairy variations in *The Sleeping Beauty*, which exploited the particular qualities of individual dancers. He brought the classical *pas de deux* to perfection, completing its symmetrical structure out of earlier forms, and adapting it, like his solos, to the talents of his dancers. The structure took the form of an opening *pas de deux*, a variation for the man, a variation for the woman and a concluding coda which brought the dance to a climax.

This form appears in all his great ballets, as a grand *pas de deux* for the principal *danseurs nobles* and/or a *demi-caractère pas de deux* for virtuoso dancers. In *The Sleeping Beauty* the final *pas de deux* between Aurora and her prince is the grand *pas de deux* for the noble dancers. That between the Blue Bird and the Princess Florine is the *demi-caractère pas de deux*. Cecchetti was the first Blue Bird. It was his virtuosity which the *pas de deux* principally exploited, showing that Petipa understood the importance of good male dancing. Petipa also understood that his best talent lay in creating dances for women, so he would sketch out the dances for the men leaving the dancers to complete them, often with Johanssen's help. Cecchetti probably created most of the choreography for the Blue Bird himself. Exceptional in its day for its display of male technique, the dance is still one of the great virtuoso *pas de deux* of choreographic art, and one of the few classical *pas de deux* to survive in which male technique equals or exceeds that of the female.

All Petipa's dances added a wealth of steps and poses to the vocabulary of ballet, perfection of finish and new qualities of phrasing. He used space more boldly than his predecessors—horizontally in the ground patterns of his ensemble and other dances; vertically in the flights of elevation which accompanied, especially, his *pas de deux*.

With due care in casting, the technical difficulties of Petipa's best ballets provide a challenge to every ballet company and training for generations of dancers. Hence they are the foundation of the classical repertoire today, honoured alike by artists and public. Since Petipa himself was always unwilling to depart from his original cast it follows that these ballets should be reproduced today with the same qualities in mind. Equally, producers now should be unwilling to give the roles to young dancers who lack the necessary technique.

It could never be said of Petipa's choreography that it was Russian. It was French, performed in the Russian manner. Two further achievements were necessary before a Russian school of ballet could be said formally to exist. Russian dancers had to supersede the Italians in the leadership of the Imperial ballet; and a Russian choreographer had to come forward to develop choreography from the point to which Petipa had brought it. These events both took place before Petipa retired in 1903.

During the nineties Russian dancers, led by Mathilde Kschessinskaya, Nicholas Legat and others, began to surpass the technique of their Italian rivals. In the middle of the same decade, on 27th January, 1895, *Swan Lake* was revived at the Maryinsky Theatre, St. Petersburg. The first and third acts were created by Petipa, the second and fourth acts by Ivanov. The lyrical tenderness of the second and fourth acts did more than provide a suitable contrast between the magical world of the Swan Lake and the hard brilliance of Petipa's royal court. They announced the first Russian choreographer of the classical period.

Lev Ivanov added to all that Petipa had achieved an extra quality of musical expression. With Petipa the choreography was often created in his mind before the music was composed. By detailing tempi and the number of bars required to his composer he could even start work before he heard the music. Music and choreography alike obeyed his will. The choreographic image was largely intellectual.

With Ivanov the choreographic image was emotional, a flowering of the music. He reflected the content of the music in his choreography, as well as its dynamics, so that his dance images and choreographic patterns achieved a depth of feeling foreign to Petipa.

Because of this one may say that the *pas de deux* in the second act of *Swan Lake* between the Swan Queen and Prince Siegfried is the earliest surviving classical *pas de deux* to express the emotion of love in pure movement. Earlier *pas de deux* by Petipa required mime to say 'I love you' because the dance which followed usually expressed little but the virtuoso qualities of the dancers. Ivanov's *pas de deux* required no mime to convey its message. Its movements were visual music, so expressive in themselves that even today this dance remains potentially one of the great choreographic love poems.

Through Ivanov, therefore, the classical ballet of the nineteenth century reached its highest perfection. Under his inspiration choreography began to turn again to the lyrical and romantic. It began to assume the guise of twentieth-century classicism, 'strong and beautiful only by virtue of a romanticism brought under control'.[1]

[1] André Gide, *Pretexts*, edited by Justin O'Brien, (Secker and Warburg, London, 1960).

CHAPTER VI

NEO-ROMANTIC CHOREOGRAPHY

THE best work of Petipa and Ivanov made Russian choreography pre-eminent in grandeur of conception and expression. The achievement was as much Tchaikovsky's as theirs. Without the inspiration of his music, and occasionally the music of younger composers like Glazunov, most choreography at the end of the nineteenth century fell into a well-worn groove. It was stifled by conventions as formal and absurd as those which ruled society outside the theatre walls.

The most pernicious convention was that which demanded the total supremacy of the ballerina on stage. Everything was subordinate to her and, after her, to the particular abilities of the leading dancers. Most ballerinas regarded their roles as existing for them, not they for the roles. Soloists behaved in the same way.

Often these dancers created their own variations from steps they could do well, regardless of character, situation or musical phrasing. This was possible because all variations followed a standard structure, 'roughly as follows:', said Fokine, 'first part, sixteen bars; second part, sixteen bars; then a repetition of the first, another sixteen bars.'[1] Women were expected to end their solos with some sort of fast turn for which the orchestra provided a *tremolo* of appropriate length. Men were supposed to finish with a *pirouette* or *tour en l'air*. Every variation, therefore, became an exhibition in search of applause.

The ballerina and others in dancing roles, including the *corps*, continued to wear conventional classical costume of tights, *tutu* and so on no matter what the story of the ballet or the role they were playing. Jewellery and hair styles were chosen to suit themselves, not the role. Some motif on the costume indicated, perhaps, that the character was Spanish or Polish, rich or poor. That was all. Artists in mime roles and supers in the same ballet, on the other hand, wore costumes proper to setting and character. (Plate V (b).)

With such conventions ruling the stage it was exceptional to find

[1] Fokine and Chujoy, *Fokine, Memoirs of a Ballet Master*, p. 48 (Little, Brown & Company, Boston, U.S.A., 1961).

real lyric or dramatic content in ballet, such as Ivanov and Tchaikovsky gave to *Swan Lake*. Generally there was neither unity of
action nor continuity of music and choreography, no characterisation
and no proper choreographic image. Every ballet unfolded in the
same fixed, illogical manner.

Similar absurdities could be found in the opera and drama of this
period, not only in Russia but all over Europe. Edward Gordon
Craig and George Bernard Shaw, were two of those who carried
forward the attack on convention in the British theatre. In Russian
drama the new approach was reflected in the work of Tchekov,
Stanislavsky, Nemirovich-Danchenko and Gorsky, among others. In
Germany, partly under the influence of Wagnerian music-drama,
Adolph Appia published *Die Musik und die Inscenierung* in 1899. This
became a bible of new ideas about stage decoration and the possibilities of electric light.

We have noted already that electric light was introduced to the
theatre in the late 1870s. Its arrival required new standards of scenery,
costumes and make-up. What might escape notice in the dangerous
days of gas appeared as a serious weakness, even in the dim orange
light of early electric bulbs.

The improved quality of the lighting system, and its mobility on
stage, extended the possibilities of scenic design in two directions of
realism and fantasy. It was seized upon by all the reformers of the
theatre. Light became a painter as evocative as the paint brush. The
stage designer became a lighting expert, often seeing his paint on
canvas as a kind of undercoat for the lights he knew he would throw
on to it. Design became mobile, changing as the plot developed.
Above all, light became one of the principal means of creating mood,
making the switchboard on the prompt side of the stage the nerve
centre of the production.

The possibilities of light and design in ballet attracted the talents
of a group of artists around the magazine *The World of Art*, founded
in St. Petersburg in 1899. *The World of Art* was edited by Serge
Diaghilev and staffed by young, or youngish, painters and writers
such as Alexander Benois, Constantine Korovin, Leon Bakst, Walter
Nouvel and Valentin Serov. Stravinsky called Serov 'the conscience
of our whole circle'.[1] 'Korovin's decors', said Benois, 'amazed us
by their daring approach to the problem [of scenic painting] and,

[1] Igor Stravinsky, 'Memories of the Russian Ballet', *The Observer*, London,
31st August, 1958.

above all, by their high artistic value—the very quality which was so often missing in the elaborate productions of the Imperial stage.'[1]

Presently, the directors of the Imperial Theatres began to invite painters from the group to design for the ballet, instead of always using the official theatre designer. Sometimes the collaborations were painful and short-lived. The group were middle-of-the-road reformers. They criticised academic classicism on the one hand and the treatment of art as subordinate to social purpose on the other. Hence they were less 'dangerous' than other reformers. Even so, their conceptions of ballet and scenic design were radically different from those of Petipa.

These young men were painters before they were scene designers. In their work they were neo-romantics, not classicists influenced by progressive ideas from the studios of Paris. Whether in Benois' aristocratic, restrained pastels, Roehrich's rugged primitiveness or in Bakst's vivid palette (Plate XIII (a)), it was concepts of the easel which they brought to the ballet. In time they revolutionised stage decoration, influencing art and fashion beyond the ballet.

In love with the theatre, they approached the stage as if it were an enormous canvas. Their designs looked like enlargements of easel canvases, producing effects which were homogeneous in a new way. They showed that there was a vital place for the painter in the theatre. Through them painters began to see design for the ballet as Diaghilev saw it, 'the fresco of the contemporary artist'.

Only choreographers could develop choreographic forms to express these and other new ideas. Alexander Gorsky and Michel Fokine became pioneers of a new movement in choreography.

Gorsky demanded greater truth and realism on the ballet stage. He sought it as much by telling the story through acting, as in integrating *corps* and soloists to realise it through dancing. His revival of Minkus' *Don Quixote* at the Maryinsky Theatre, St. Petersburg, in 1902 introduced such ideas to the dancers. The production showed how closely the movement of the painters was linked with the vanguard of choreography, especially in bourgeois Moscow where Gorsky staged his new Quixote before taking it to St. Petersburg.

'Costumes and scenery by the Russian artists, Golovine and Korovin, a riot of colour and temperament, marked the turning point of ballet staging', recorded Tamara Karsavina, who appeared as a very

[1] Alexandre Benois, *Reminiscences of the Russian Ballet*, pp. 196-197 (Putnam, London, 1941).

young Cupid in the garden of Dulcinea. 'Curiously unaware of the new tendencies, conservative within, walled in by the never changing public of balletomanes, our ballet stood bewildered at this breaking away from the stale tradition of quasi-realistic scenery, of accepted canons of costumes. Ballerinas regretted their voluminous tarlatans, starting from the waist-line. The new costumes were cut on different, softer lines. The body, no longer encumbered round the hips, appeared supple and elongated. It was the reform of a dancer's line. It was compulsory that in this ballet everybody should dress their hair in Spanish fashion, smooth with a side parting and 'accroche-cœurs'. It was novel to the eye at first, but not half so strange as it is now to look at the photographs of ballerinas in the costume of Pharaoh's daughter,[1] a lotus flower perched upon hair waved and arranged in the latest fashion.

'Gorsky came from Moscow to produce *Don Quixote*. An entirely new element made itself manifest in his handling of the action; not only did the dancing become an organic part of the plot, but the whole structure of the ballet was dramatised. Hitherto the *corps de ballet*, outside the actual dancing, remained passive. It would come on, execute its item and troop out; it would either remain inactive on the stage or vaguely respond to the acting of the principal personages. Gorsky introduced many little episodes. He worked with each group separately. When all was put together, the main plot developed clearly on the background of manifold life.'[2]

Karsavina thus illustrates Gorsky's important place in the history of Russian ballet. He is a double link between Petipa and Fokine, and Petipa and Soviet ballet. Choreographically, his development of the *corps de ballet* has a significance often underrated in the West. His crowd scene in the first act of *Don Quixote*, for instance, is the forerunner of Fokine's crowd scene in *Petrouchka*. This was the first time since romantic ballet that members of the *corps* were given individual movements and episodes to recreate 'the background of manifold life'.

Within this new atmosphere and under the influence of ideas expressed by Gorsky, *The World of Art* and others, Fokine grew and developed. Ten years Gorsky's junior, he was one of the remarkable group of Russian dancers produced at the turn of the century under the influence of Petipa, Johansson and Cecchetti.

[1] Pharaoh's daughter in *La Fille du Pharaon* by Petipa.
[2] Tamara Karsavina, *Theatre Street*, pp. 130-131 (Heinemann, London, 1930).

Never, indeed, had so much talent been produced by one ballet school before. But having been produced, the talent began to question the restrictions imposed by the Imperial Theatres. Several dancers became actively involved in the strikes and protests surrounding the 1905 revolution, their meetings taking place in Fokine's or Pavlova's apartments.

Even before 1905 Fokine's ideas had been formulated. He was in revolt against a ballet which 'turned its back on life and on all the other arts and shut itself up in a narrow circle of traditions;'[1] he was a disciple of Ivanov and Gorsky; he was in search of an expressiveness and an artistic freedom similar to that which *The World of Art* demanded. Deeply influenced by the lofty, noble qualities of the Romantic ballet he contrasted the expressiveness of its choreography with the 'acrobatics' which flourished at the end of the nineteenth century. Hence the choreographic revolution he initiated became a renaissance of romanticism.

'The ballet should be staged in conformity with the epoch represented', he wrote to the director of the Imperial Theatres in 1904. 'The dance pantomime and gestures should not be of the conventional style . . . but should be of a kind that best fits the style of the period. The costumes also should not be of the established ballet style (short tarlatan tutus) but be consistent with the plot. . . .

'The ballet must be uninterrupted—a complete artistic creation and not a series of separate numbers.

'In the interests of retaining the scenic illusion, the action must not be interrupted with applause and its acknowledgement by the artists.

'The music should not consist of waltzes, polkas and final galops—indispensable in the old ballet—but must express the story of the ballet and, primarily, its emotional content.'[2]

Thus was outlined the choreographic revolution which Fokine effected in the next ten years. These principles were put forward, moreover, *before* the arrival of Isadora Duncan in Russia in 1905. Although many people still maintain today that Fokine's reforms were begun under Duncan's influence Fokine himself, in 1914, explained this error, and the differences between himself and Duncan.

'. . . the new Russian ballet' [i.e. Fokine's ballet], he wrote to

[1] Michel Fokine, letter to *The Times*, 6th July, 1914.
[2] Fokine and Chujoy, *Fokine, Memoirs of a Ballet Master*, p. 72 (Little, Brown & Company, Boston, U.S.A., 1961).

The Times, 'is sharply differentiated by its principles both from the older ballet and from the art of that great dancer. . . . Miss Duncan rejected the ballet and established an entirely opposite form of her own. She introduced natural dancing in which the body of the dancer was liberated, not only from stays and satin slippers, but also from the dance steps of the ballet. She founded her dancing on natural movements and on the most natural of all dance forms, namely, the dancing of the ancient Greeks. The new ballet, which also rejects the conventions of the older ballet, cannot nevertheless be regarded as a follower of Miss Duncan.'[1]

Duncan's visit to Russia roused immense interest. It stimulated, perhaps, a more serious consideration of Fokine's ideas. Nevertheless, the American dancer's greatest influence over classical choreography was felt later, elsewhere than in Russia. We shall consider it in the next chapter and in Chapter XVII.

Of more immediate importance was Fokine's meeting with Benois. This occurred in 1907 during the creation of *Le Pavillon d'Armide* for the Maryinsky Theatre. Through Benois, two movements of artistic reform came together, the movement of painters led by himself and of dancers led by Fokine. Diaghilev united them into a single force, the neo-romantic ballet, presented by the Ballets Russes.

'The performances of *Le Pavillon d'Armide*, *Schéhérazade*, *L'Oiseau de Feu* and *Petrouchka*, shown to Europe between 1909 and 1912, were not ballets in the former, narrow sense of the word; rather, a new form of spectacle based on a rejuvenation of the traditions of the St. Petersburg Ballet. . . . As it was not possible for us to revive our Russian ballet in our own country, we were reviving it, oddly enough, for strangers.'[2]

It is clear now from Fokine's memoirs and other sources that the idea of taking Russian ballet to Paris originated with Benois. It was one way of realising reforms which could not be realised in the stale ballet of the autocracy at home.

In Paris Fokine's neo-romantic ballet perfected its own forms just as the romantic ballet had done in the 1830s. Principally these forms were the dramatic one-act ballet, like *Petrouchka*, and the ballet of mood, like *Les Sylphides*. (Plate VI (a) and VI (b).) But the forms themselves did not originate in Paris, nor even always with the

[1] Letter to *The Times*, 6th July, 1914.
[2] A. Benois, *Reminiscences of the Russian Ballet*, pp. 374-375 (Putnam, London, 1941).

Ballets Russes. Some had been evolved already by Fokine in Russia when he created ballets for private performances outside his official duties. *Les Sylphides*, for example, had first appeared as *Chopiniana* in 1907. It was a suite of national dances, in national costumes created for a charity performance in the Maryinsky. In only one dance, the waltz, did the white Taglioni costume of the Romantic era appear. Yet this was the inspiration for the second version of the ballet a year later at the Maryinsky when it was given with the costumes, music and choreography familiar to us. The ballet, unchanged, was named *Les Sylphides* for the opening performance of the Ballets Russes in Paris on 2nd June, 1909. In the Soviet Union today it is still called *Chopiniana*.

In the same way *Le Carnaval* was first created for a charity performance in St. Petersburg in 1910. It was presented with new scenery in Berlin by the Ballets Russes later the same year.

The one-act form broke decisively with the operatic formula of the classical scenario. It suited better the rich but generally impatient, artistically fickle, audience which was to support the Ballets Russes in Western Europe for the next twenty years. The storyless mood ballet, although descended from storyless *divertissements* like the *Pas de Quatre* of 1845, was essentially new, the first great creation of the Ballets Russes. It expressed, better than the narrative form ever could, the essence of the neo-romanticism of which Fokine, Benois and Bakst were the principal exponents.

Each of Fokine's ballets during the first period of the Ballets Russes, ending in 1914, showed an aspect of neo-romanticism at its best and most creative. Every important ballet—The Polovtsian Dances for *Prince Igor*, *Les Sylphides*, *Carnaval*, *Schéhérazade*, *L'Oiseau de Feu*, *Le Spectre de la Rose*, *Petrouchka* and *Le Coq d'Or*—was different from its fellows. Each represented an individual approach to the problem of composition, a new attempt to bend ballet's aristocratic nature to the demands of a new audience.

All, however, were related through Fokine's handling of theme. Each had a profound theme or mood, treated with the simplicity of great art. In this Fokine made one of his most significant contributions to choreography. Following the tradition of Noverre, Viganò and Perrot he affirmed that choreography could express the most complex emotions, that it need not be confined to the frivolous, the fantastic and the spectacular. Spectacle there was, but it had to arise naturally out of the situation and carry the situation forward. No longer, too, did the scenarist think only in terms of remote royal courts or the strange inhabitants of moonlit forests. Just as fishermen and townsfolk peopled the ballets of Bournonville so the streets of St. Petersburg formed the stage for *Petrouchka*.

Fokine matched this development of theme with a corresponding development of choreographic technique and dance vocabulary. In *Le Spectre de la Rose*, *Prince Igor*, *Le Carnaval* and other works, he created roles for Nijinsky, Bolm and the male *corps de ballet* which restored the male dancer to his proper place in choreography. By depriving the ballerina of her former dominance, he influenced all future choreographic construction and all future choreographers.

Under Petipa the style of *corps de ballet* dances had rarely varied, marvellous though their architecture often was. Under Fokine the *corps* was used to create atmosphere by movements always exactly in accord with period (*Petrouchka*), place (*Prince Igor*) or mood (*Les Sylphides*). Even when, in *Les Sylphides*, *corps* movements were orchestrated in unison, as in Petipa's day, Fokine breathed a deep emotion into the movement and created original, exquisite groupings.

Fokine thus developed the Romantic conception of the *corps de ballet*. He showed how it could become a group of individual beings, or be used collectively. He demanded of his dancers more individuality and expression than they had given ever before. In formal dances he disposed the *corps* in groups and swiftly dissolving patterns, of which he was a master, in place of Petipa's more two-dimensional lines and pictures. In informal scenes, like the street scenes in *Petrouchka*, he introduced apparent improvisation for the ensemble to contrast with the set dances of the soloists.

His dance vocabulary drew upon national dance steps and rhythms to realise the stories from native folk-lore which supplied some of his themes. He gave the Princesses in *L'Oiseau de Feu* a dance of elegant style on half point, and created a robust character dance for the nurse-maids of *Petrouchka*. An earlier choreographer would certainly have put the Princesses into *tutus* and on *pointe*, and given classical steps to the nurse-maids.

In academic steps and poses Fokine introduced a lyrical quality by rounding body lines, softening classical movement and by using off-balance positions such as the arabesques in *Les Sylphides*. His linear curves and use of elevation were reminiscent of Perrot although his groupings and movements—among the most beautiful of choreographic creations—preserved a classical symmetry and balance. Traditional mime was rejected. Theme and emotions, he insisted, should be expressed in movements of the whole body, not just the arms and legs.

This revolution in choreography took place a mere twenty years after the first performance of *The Sleeping Beauty* had crowned Petipa's classicism with glory. It developed the theories put forward to the directorate of the Imperial Theatres in 1904. The theories were enlarged by Fokine on 6th July, 1914, in his letter to *The Times* already quoted. Today this letter provides an unofficial code of five rules for choreographers.

'Not to form combinations of ready-made and established dance-steps, but to create in each case a new form corresponding to the subject, the most expressive form possible for the representation of the period and the character of the nation represented—that is the first rule of the new ballet.

'The second rule is that dancing and mimetic gesture have no meaning in a ballet unless they serve as an expression of its dramatic action, and they must not be used as a mere divertissement or enter-tainment, having no connection with the scheme of the whole ballet.

'The third rule is that the new ballet admits the use of conventional gesture only where it is required by the style of the ballet, and in all other cases endeavours to replace gestures of the hands by mimetic of the whole body. Man can and should be expressive from head to foot.

'The fourth rule is the expressiveness of groups and of the ensemble dancing. In the older ballet the dancers were ranged in groups only for the purpose of ornament, and the ballet master was not concerned with the expression of any sentiment in groups of characters or in ensemble dances. The new ballet, on the other hand, in developing the principle of expressiveness, advances from the expressiveness of the face to the expressiveness of the whole body, and from the expressiveness of the individual body to the expressiveness of a group of bodies and the expressiveness of the combined dancing of a crowd.

'The fifth rule is the alliance of dancing with other arts. The new ballet, refusing to be the slave either of music or of scenic decoration, and recognising the alliance of the arts only on the condition of complete equality, allows perfect freedom both to the scenic artist and to the musician. In contradistinction to the older ballet it does not demand 'ballet music' of the composer as an accompaniment to dancing: it accepts music of every kind, provided only that it is good and expressive. It does not demand of the scenic artist that he should array the ballerinas in short skirts and pink slippers. It does not impose any specific "ballet" conditions on the composer or the decorative artist, but gives complete liberty to their creative powers. . . .'[1] As the initiator and executant of these reforms Fokine became the most inspired and influential choreographer of the first half of the twentieth century.

His greatest successes, however, were achieved with collaborators whose quality matched his own. Fokine recognised this and emphasised the importance of a perfect balance between the component arts of ballet. Bakst and Benois, then Glazunov, Stravinsky, Ravel and others all played their part.

Most significant of all was the collaboration of Fokine with Stravinsky. Here we see the full extent of the revolution represented by the Ballets Russes. It was not just a choreographic revolution, nor a revolution in scenic design, but a profound change in the whole direction of ballet. It rested upon a new conception of music for choreography and a new partnership between composer and choreographer. *Petrouchka* marks at once the most perfect example of this partnership in the Diaghilev Ballet and the most decisive break with the earlier tradition of ballet music.

'From the outset of my activity,' wrote Fokine later, 'I emphasised the total freedom of the composer of the music to express whatever he feels and however he feels it. From the composer I expected a musical pictorialisation. I never specified or even wished to consider the number and kind of measures he needed to accomplish this end. It was on the basis of such principles that the new ballet and the music for it was created. Becoming free, the music grew richer and enriched the dance itself.'[2]

This was precisely how music influenced the choreography in *Petrouchka*, although Fokine felt certain reservations of detail. The role of the composer in this ballet is developed far beyond the position won by Tchaikovsky or even established by Stravinsky himself in *The Firebird*, produced a year earlier. In *Petrouchka* the composer contributes incident, character, psychological interpretation, atmosphere and narrative continuity. He conveys this through a variety of rhythm and sound colour which startled the

[1] M. Fokine, letter to *The Times*, 6th July, 1914.
[2] Fokine and Chujoy, *Fokine, Memoirs of a Ballet Master*, p. 186 (Little, Brown & Company, Boston, U.S.A., 1961).

dancers and musicians when they first heard it and which would have been unacceptable to a choreographer of Tchaikovsky's day.

The scenario of *Petrouchka* achieves exceptional continuity through the device of a plot within a plot. To match this device Stravinsky composed music within music: first national dances and traditional dances, like the dance of the coachmen, rhythmic, well balanced and marvellously enriched with background accompaniment, but never losing its popular quality; second, descriptive music for the principal characters depicting not only their external movements but their internal emotions.

This descriptive music has an atmosphere quite different from the folk atmosphere of the people at the Easter Fair. It can be sensed immediately the showman introduces his puppets. The lively puppet music is followed almost at once by slow, chromatic harmony revealing Petrouchka's inner humanity and longing. In the orchestra the solo piano *is* Petrouchka.

The musical portrait of Petrouchka is enlarged and deepened in his cell. An *arpeggio* in one key is sounded simultaneously with that of another to depict his split personality. Trumpets shriek his frustration. Finally, when Petrouchka is dead and his ghost rises above the booth the same trumpets mock the showman.

The interval of the augmented fourth similarly depicts the Moor's obtuseness and the vanity of his grotesque person. The image is completed for the most part with 'barklike sounds, snarls and bass pizzicato. But what a superbly complete image is thus created in the imagination! What a thrilling experience it is to observe such exactness in the interpretation of the character!'[1]

Full of praise as he is for Stravinsky, Fokine nevertheless pointed out important difficulties in Stravinsky's music from the point of view of ballet. In certain of the ensemble dances, such as the Gypsy Dance, Stravinsky departed from the rhythmic construction necessary to this type of dance. 'The Dance of the Gypsies is not like an authentic gypsy dance because the rhythm, the construction of the phrasing, the introduction of a melody are all without order—as if one gypsy began, then changed her mind; another one started, then also changed her mind.'[2] This criticism emphasises a problem to which we shall return in Chapter XIII.

It was Diaghilev who introduced Stravinsky to Fokine and the other collaborators. Diaghilev, in particular, fulfilled Fokine's fifth

[1] Fokine and Chujoy, *op. cit.* p. 185.   [2] *Ibid.* p. 187.

rule of the new ballet. His personal greatness as an artistic director lay in his ability to select collaborators, draw them together and edit their joint work as a single creation on stage.

To compose and design for ballet therefore became an ambition instead of a drudgery. As in choreography and thematic composition, so in music and design the Ballets Russes broke with the ballet of the nineteenth century while retaining many of its best elements. So great was the change that a ballerina or *premier danseur* of the 1880s could hardly have caught or interpreted (probably would never have understood) the romanticism of *Les Sylphides* or the qualities essential to *Petrouchka*.

To remain new, however, implies the promotion of new talent. In its early days the Ballets Russes, being an extension of *The World of Art*, was a platform for painters, with Fokine dominating the choreographic productions more than Diaghilev. Diaghilev may have been inclined for personal reasons to end this subordination to Fokine. In any case by 1911 Fokine's choreography had been presented exclusively for three seasons running. It was clear that a variety of style was needed, wider even than Fokine could supply, if public interest was to be maintained at its original pitch.

This was a compelling reason for Nijinsky's debut as a choreographer. Diaghilev was well rewarded. *L'Après-midi d'un Faune* announced a new choreographer and a striking choreographic idiom.

CHAPTER VII

NEO-CLASSICAL CHOREOGRAPHY

NIJINSKY created only three ballets in Europe. The first, *L'Après-midi d'un Faune*, appeared in 1912. *Jeux* and *Le Sacre du Printemps* followed in 1913. It has been suggested that signs of his later illness were apparent already in these ballets. In rehearsal he seemed to create his choreography without system or method. The movements he conceived appeared to have less to do with dancing than with a kind of undisciplined eurhythmics which dancers could not remember and found exhausting compared with classical movements.

Fokine claims, too, in his memoirs, that three choreographic ideas, important to the idiom of *L'Après-midi d'un Faune*, appeared first in 'my choreography of the rôle of the Faun in the Venusberg Scene of the opera *Tannhäuser*. This rôle was excellently performed by Nijinsky, and it is small wonder that part of it found its way into his composition.'

The choreography of the Faun in *Tannhäuser* was created by Fokine in 1910 for a charity performance at the Maryinsky. He makes no accusation against Nijinsky. 'Just the contrary: I feel that successful discoveries should enter the life of ballet. Only, when using such a discovery, one should not claim originality.'[1]

It is true, of course, that many successful choreographic creations enter the regular vocabulary of ballet through constant reproduction by dancers. These creations of Fokine, however, are unusually important in this context, because they are fundamental to the style of Nijinsky's ballet. They are, in Fokine's words:

'(1) The entrance of the Faun in a profile position with the palm of the far hand extended flat and turned to the audience, and the other extended back and its back turned to the audience. Almost the entire role of the Faun in *L'Après-midi d'un Faune* is built by Nijinsky on this position.

'(2) In *Tannhäuser* Nijinsky slowly carried the nymph (Karsavina) on to the stage, holding her in such a way that his elbows were

---

[1] Fokine and Chujoy, *op. cit.* p. 208.

pointed in opposite directions. In this ballet Nijinsky carried the scarf in exactly the same position.

'(3) I had the Faun slowly and gradually bend down to kiss the prostrate nymph. The bending was an unusually slow and long drawn-out movement. This moment was transferred to the Nijinsky ballet with some regrettable (from my point of view) changes, by the substitution for the nymph of a piece of cloth.'[1]

In spite of the undoubted difficulties he experienced as a creator, in spite, even, of being less the innovator many people have thought him, Nijinsky is important in choreographic history. *Faune* and *Le Sacre* were considered masterpieces by many artists on both sides of the curtain. *Jeux*, although a failure, introduced to the ballet stage the first contemporary man in contemporary dress, actually, tennis clothes. (Plate VII (a).)

The importance lies not in Nijinsky's choreography, but in the effect his ballets had on public and critical conceptions of choreography. It cannot be shown that Nijinsky influenced any subsequent choreographer. No part of his idiom has entered the classical vocabulary. Nevertheless, he re-emphasised Fokine's teaching that choreography in ballet can explore new movements far outside orthodox classical positions and classical *pas*. Even if his idiom was too chaotic and too lacking in method to influence choreographic language it cleared the air, so to speak. It posed the possibility of fresh directions, other languages. It showed that classically trained dancers could adapt their training to very unclassical movements.

There is no trace of classical line, however free, in Nijinsky's choreography. *L'Après-midi d'un Faune*, inspired by a Greek archaic frieze, was a choreographic incarnation of Bakst's ideas, born during their travels in Greece. By adopting in this ballet a combination of straight lines, sharp angles, static movements and tensions in place of the curvilinear conceptions of Fokine's ballet, Nijinsky broke radically with the dominant style of the Russian neo-Romantic school. In *Le Sacre du Printemps* he introduced primitive and barbaric movements. While painters and sculptors were showing the world new forms and conceptions of beauty, Nijinsky seemed to attempt similar experiments in choreographic sculpture.

Fokine, of course, had done this before him. Fokine had developed the Greek *plastique* more thoroughly than Nijinsky. He had reproduced primitive and barbaric movements of wider range in *The*

[1] *Ibid.*

Polovtsian Dances and other works. But Nijinsky's strange language gave a particular emphasis to these elements in neo-romantic choreography. He seemed to be responding to ideas already put forward by Fokine and recorded later in *The Times*. 'Every form of dancing is good in so far as it expresses the content or subject with which the dance deals; and that form is the most natural which is most suited to the purpose of the dancer. . . .'[1] The response was limited by Nijinsky's defects as a choreographer, his inability to communicate his ideas, his lack of craftsmanship and musical knowledge. Henceforth, however, the straight classical lines of Petipa and the curved lines of Fokine, the shape of the human body itself, were to be bent and made angular by choreographers, each searching to interpret the modern world in their own way.

Stravinsky had cause to complain of Nijinsky's musical deficiencies, but this was not the only reason why his ballet required quantities of rehearsal. His dancers, disciplined in the classical tradition, found it hard to master the new movements he wished to teach them. In *Faune* they had to forget the turn-out of ninety degrees. The ballet was danced 'flat' as on the frieze which inspired it. Feet and legs walked on the same plane in an exact straight line from one side of the stage to the other. This was and remained no more than a choreographic novelty, but it required the dancers to evolve a new placement of the body to maintain balance.

The whole ballet was staged in profile in this way. 'The groups', wrote Fokine, 'are at times very beautiful and exactly reproduce bas-reliefs and paintings on vases. Nijinsky was in a very interesting costume by Leon Bakst: one piece tights covered with cowlike patches, golden horns and a small tail. There never had been such a costume on the stage—half human, half beast. . . .

'There was another peculiarity in *L'Après-midi d'un Faune*. During a strong movement in the music, the nymphs and the Faun stood motionless for a long time. . . . In general, Nijinsky's archaic, angular choreography suits Debussy's music. But I especially approve of his resisting any movement despite the apparent demands of the agitated measures of the music.'[2]

Thus Fokine indicates the interesting elements of *Faune*. Nijinsky himself never left any comment on his work. Unable to analyse or explain in words what he did or why he did it, he could only demon-

---

[1] M. Fokine, letter to *The Times*, 6th July, 1914.
[2] Fokine and Chujoy, *op. cit.* pp. 206 and 209.

strate. No wonder that after one hundred and fifty rehearsals of *Faune*, each dancer reflected perfectly the style of their choreographer!

In *Le Sacre*, Nijinsky followed Stravinsky's music phrase by phrase. Because the primitive ritual inspired him equally with the composer, his choreography evoked the primeval relationship of man to earth, man to the elements, in an extraordinary way. It seemed as if classical ballet had bridged time to join with the beginnings of dancing.

Here, in spite of all the difficulties of its creation, was an epic ballet. It remained in a class by itself until the creation of Antony Tudor's *Dark Elegies* in London in 1937. These ballets, *Le Sacre* and *Dark Elegies*, expressed a whole community, not just an individual. They distilled the essence of a community, rising to epic heights as if impelled by communal emotion. This is why they stand alone. Among other ballets we know, only Nijinska's *Les Noces*, created in Paris in 1923, and Harald Lander's *Qarrtsiluni* (Plate XXIX), created in Copenhagen in 1942, approach this unusual quality.

It seems doubtful if Nijinsky could have developed his ideas much further, even if he had stayed with Diaghilev. His intellectual deficiencies were too great. The break with Diaghilev marks the real end of his creative life. Nothing he did later as dancer or choreographer matched his achievements in the five years between his debut in 1908 and his departure from the Ballets Russes in 1913.

Soon after this upheaval Léonide Massine was brought from Moscow. Four years Nijinsky's junior, his artistic education became a principal charge of Larionov, painter, librettist and producer, under, of course, Diaghilev. A year later, in 1915, Massine was made choreographer to the company.

This appointment completed Diaghilev's artistic ascendancy over his company at the moment when the Russian Revolution cut off its national roots. The Diaghilev Ballet ceased to be Russian and became Franco-Russian, gradually embracing dancers and artists from many nationalities.

After Fokine, Massine has exercised the strongest creative influence over choreography during the first half of the twentieth century. His idiom was already individual and rich in ideas, even in his first works. *Le Soleil de Nuit* was presented in Geneva at the end of 1915; *Las Meniñas* appeared in the Eugenie-Victoria Theatre, San Sebastián, in August, 1915; *Kikimora*, later included in *Contes Russes*, began life the following week in the same theatre.

This early choreography showed the influence which a Moscow training and his own physique would exert upon Massine's style. The Moscow School, always stronger than St. Petersburg in character dancing, now began to impress its traditions on the Diaghilev Ballet through Massine. It meant a change from the predominantly classical style of Fokine to a character and *demi-caractère* style.

Massine did not have the physique to become a classical dancer. Nevertheless, he inherited from Moscow a sound classical training besides the character and *demi-caractère* bias induced by School and physical make-up. As a choreographer, therefore, he used classical movements in a free manner. Sometimes he adapted the steps of national dances. Sometimes he leaned even towards the central European expressionist ideas of Laban. Always his choreographic handwriting was highly individual, but always it was based firmly on classical technique.

Larionov exerted a profound influence upon Massine's early choreography. The modernism of the artist helped to develop the individuality of the choreographer in particular directions. To Larionov, for example, Massine probably owes much of the bizarre quality in the ballets of his first period. And from the artistic education Larionov gave probably comes the angularity, broken lines and irregular groupings which seem to reflect in Massine's choreography certain styles of contemporary painting.

Larionov is important in another respect. From about 1915 into the early 1920s he was an active influence upon Diaghilev's artistic policy. He was librettist, co-producer and choreographic adviser, as well as designer. His relations with the company were closer even than those of Benois or Bakst.

His position emphasised the creative influence of painters upon choreography in this period. First the Diaghilev Ballet, then Rolf de Maré's Ballets Suédois from 1920-1925, embraced the new movement in art, using the best young painters of the day. The decorative success of these companies finally dispelled the unprofitable distinction between painter and stage designer. The nineteenth century separation of stage from studio was over.

Massine's choreography has always reflected strong visual influences. He is a museum man, a gallery man, susceptible to new ideas in art. *Parade* (May, 1917) was the first cubist ballet, cubist in Picasso's décor and costumes, cubist in its dislocation of the dancer's line, cubist in the sounds of Satie's novel score (Appendix III A).

Le Pas d'Acier in 1927 was constructivist, *Ode* in 1928 was abstract. (Plate VII (b).) *Jeux d'enfants* in 1933 was surrealist.

At the same time he has explored new and old sources of inspiration with a curiosity which never seems satisfied. *Contes Russes* (1917) and a new version of *Le Sacre du Printemps* (1920) drew upon Russian folk-lore. *Pulcinella* (1920) used the tradition of *commedia dell' arte*: in this and *Les Femmes de Bonne Humeur* (1917) he developed the humorous character *genre* at which he particularly excels. His greatest work, *Le Tricorne* created in 1919, with decor by Picasso (Plate XIII (b)) brilliantly transposed Andalusian dances into classical choreography. 'It was his complete command of Spanish dancing that amazed me most,' said Karsavina, who created the role of the Miller's Wife in this ballet. 'On the Russian stage we had been used to a ballet in stylisation of Spanish dancing sugary at its best, but this was the very essence of Spanish folk dancing.'[1]

In these ballets Massine initiated every *genre*, except one, which made up his later work. The missing *genre* was the symphonic ballet, developed in the 1930s. His period with Diaghilev up to 1921 may be compared in fertility with Fokine's first period. 'Fokine', wrote Grigoriev, regisseur to the Diaghilev company, 'had introduced new *forms* of dancing, with more complicated movements and grouping, and had established an even balance between the *corps de ballet* and the soloists. Massine, as a next step in the development of choreography, basing himself not on the classical canon direct, but rather on that canon as modified by Fokine, introduced movements more complicated still, and also more mannered and broken up, thus creating his own characteristic style.'[2]

Yet Massine was no more interested in purely academic or virtuoso choreography than Fokine. Seeking inspiration from many sources he added particularly to the classical vocabulary movements adapted from all kinds of national dances. He developed the orchestration of mass movement on stage. He brought to new heights spectacular finales with complicated patterns which built to exciting conclusions. He developed enormously the character ballet and character dancing. 'All ballet', he declared, 'is dramatic, even that erroneously described as symphonic ballet; for that too conforms to the basic form of statement, exposition and denouement.'

Massine's symphonic ballets were the principal new *genre* of the

---

[1] T. Karsavina, *op. cit.* p. 301.
[2] S. L. Grigoriev, *The Diaghilev Ballet*, p. 162 (Constable, London, 1953).

thirties. Only *Symphonie Fantastique*, created to Berlioz's score and scenario in 1936, could be said to follow exactly the 'programme' in the composer's mind. The other three ballets imposed upon the composer's musical thought a subject created by the choreographer. The result was some beautiful choreographic forms to Tchaikovsky's Fifth Symphony in *Les Présages* (1933), Brahms' Fourth Symphony in *Choreartium* (1933) and Beethoven's Seventh Symphony in *Seventh Symphony* (1938). But the validity of using for choreography symphonies existing in their own right (as opposed to symphonic music, like the ballet music of Tchaikovsky or Prokofiev) was left unresolved.

Generally speaking it seems a futile interference with a self-significant work of art to use a symphony as partner to some abstract choreographic illustration. Massine's symphonic ballets, however, were acceptable to many people because they derived their moods from the music, and the interpretation was dramatic, not abstract. There was no movement for the glory of movement, such as Balanchine was already showing at that time in America. Rather, the possibilities of ensemble dancing were explored for a dramatic, even philosophical, purpose. Brooding questions of Life and Death, Destiny and Fate composed the themes, while the choreography expressed in varied ways Massine's delight in mass movement.

In a sense, Bronislava Nijinska, Nijinsky's sister, was Massine's complement. Where he enriched choreography dramatically and in character, she extended the range of classical movement through a neo-classical style which seemed sometimes to continue what her brother never completed.

She was the first classical choreographer to analyse expressionist movement in any profound sense. Her essay, *The School of Movement, a theory of choreography*, which appeared at Kiev in 1920, showed her abilities as a teacher and theorist. Her eight ballets for Diaghilev between 1923 and 1929 demonstrated her theories in practice.

Les Biches, a ballet of manners, presented by Diaghilev at Monte Carlo in 1924, actually attempted a choreographic union of classical and expressionist styles. A *pas seul* for the ballerina Nemchinova used angular novel modern movements for the top of the body, placed upon a foundation of classical leg movements, so that the styles were integrated in a single dancer. Thus did the modern world in truth bend to its will the aristocratic lines of ballet.

Two years later, *Les Noces* developed similar conceptions upon the ensemble. The dancers were used as material to construct a human pyramid and sculptural masses in which arms, legs and heads had roles in the general design. They moved in a strongly rhythmic manner, part geometrical and part architectural.

In later years, Nijinska's choreography became more purely classical, but it was marked always by a strong use of the upper half of the body and by its ingenious use of rhythm. Her style influenced, in particular, Serge Lifar, the dominant choreographer in France during the thirties and early forties. To some extent it influenced also the British choreographers, Ninette de Valois and Frederick Ashton.

Thematically, the Nijinska period was important for developing the one-act mood and narrative ballet in more specific, more economical terms than her predecessors had used. No doubt she was influenced in this direction by Diaghilev's financial difficulties after the box-office failure of *The Sleeping Beauty* in London in 1921.

Massine had made great use of spectacle. Nijinska, and her successor, Balanchine, began to create one-act ballets which jettisoned spectacle. They concentrated only on telling a story or creating a mood. They were spare, taut works of few characters, a small *corps de ballet* and no intermediate dance spectacle. The one-act mood and narrative ballet, in fact, began to develop many of the *genres* we recognise today.

George Balanchine was the last of Diaghilev's choreographers. Whereas the three choreographers of the Diaghilev period before him had all preserved the tradition of the Imperial School, but moulded it to the needs of the Ballets Russes under Diaghilev's influence, Balanchine escaped this influence. He was the one choreographer of the Diaghilev period, after Fokine, to join Diaghilev with ideas already crystallised. The crystallisation had taken place in Leningrad where the Petipa tradition still ruled. There the dominance of tradition had not prevented several young choreographers from experimenting with changes suggested by the revolution. Among these was Kasyan Goleisovsky, one of the most talented and original of Soviet choreographers.

Goleisovsky exerted a strong influence on the young Balanchine. Among his aims in the early twenties appears to have been the achievement of sculptural effects 'for which he was wont almost to denude his dancers of clothing'.[1] He also developed a variety of

[1] S. L. Grigoriev, *op. cit.* p. 203.

forms of choreographic miniature, besides full-length ballets. Several of these miniatures were given at a performance in 1960, which celebrated his fiftieth year in the theatre. Others have been seen at concerts in London and elsewhere. They showed great musicality and a facility in many styles from national dances to an interpretation of Rachmaninov's *Prelude*. In many of them the search for sculptural effect is clear in the poses and *plastique* of the dance.

It may have been through Goleisovsky that Balanchine's own interest in sculptural effect was first roused. The interest was clear in Paris in 1928, when *Apollon-Musagète* linked Stravinsky and Balanchine together for the first time in an artistic collaboration often to be repeated. The music and choreography for this ballet showed a return to classicism, or, rather, the evolution of a neo-classicism in which strict academic steps and lines as exact as Petipa's were blended with bent, turned-in limbs inherited from the 'modern' influences of the moment. All this was presented with clarity and restraint, with beautiful patterns, exciting lifts and an emotional severity serene but cold as the Arctic sky. Especially, the choreographer revealed an unusual feeling for music and an unusual understanding of the possibilities of sculpturing human movement within the limits of classical line.

Sometimes this flair for the composition of movement induced a virtuosity approaching gymnastics. Diaghilev felt obliged to defend his discovery. 'In the plastic efforts of Balanchine in *The Prodigal Son*', he wrote to *The Times* on 13th July, 1929, 'there are far less acrobatics than in the final classical *pas de deux* of *Aurora's Wedding*.' The comparison with Petipa was just. The wheel had turned circle again. The creator of neo-classicism made himself known, acknowledging not Fokine, but Petipa as his guide, with a mission to adapt Petipa's aristocratic classicism to broader tastes.

Diaghilev died suddenly in Venice barely a month after his letter to *The Times*. He left the art of choreography high among the fine arts of the world, securely translated by Fokine from its aristocratic home into the twentieth century. Fokine pursued his own lonely independent path. Three other masters, Massine, Nijinska and Balanchine continued to develop the art in directions already marked out for them. In the wings waited a gifted few who would become the choreographers of national ballets soon to be born.

Diaghilev's legacy, however, did not include a public large enough to support new companies in Europe, America or the British

Commonwealth. The beginnings of such a public were created by Anna Pavlova. Pavlova was important to the art of choreography because she was a great artist who was also the greatest pioneer and propagandist dancing has ever known. She appeared in place after place where ballet had never been seen before. 'Pavlova proved to the world that the ballet dancer could be a completely expressive artist, the equal of a Duse, a Bernhardt, or a Chaliapine.'[1] As such she presented to the world an image of perfect material for the choreographer, the perfect choreographic instrument. By individual example, she elevated choreographic art far above what it had been in the public mind before her time just as the Diaghilev company elevated the art by collective example.

Because of Pavlova's missionary journeys across the world ballet began to flower in America and in remote parts of Britain and the Commonwealth. Dancers in India were inspired to revive ancient forms of their art. Young people everywhere were drawn to the classical dance and the study of choreography. Alicia Markova in England, Frederick Ashton in Ecuador, Robert Helpmann in Australia—these are only three names of British ballet whose careers began through her inspiration. What she started is growing still.

[1] Arnold Haskell, *Ballet*, p. 111 (Penguin, London, 1938).

CHAPTER VIII

CONTEMPORARY CHOREOGRAPHY:
BRITAIN AND AMERICA

(i) BRITAIN

WHY should ballet have taken root in Britain during the thirties when it failed to do so under the inspiration of John Weaver and other dancing masters in the eighteenth century? Why should it have flourished in twentieth-century London when the most brilliant creations of the Romantic Ballet in the nineteenth century left no permanent tradition in the city?

The particular difference between the twentieth century and earlier centuries lies in the raising of public taste by successive education acts from 1870 onwards. The English lyric theatre, deprived of court patronage by the English revolutions of the seventeenth century, could never command continuing public support in England until sections of the middle and working classes embraced it during the 1930s and 1940s. This new audience was stimulated by teachers from Russia and by former members of the Diaghilev and Pavlova companies, who helped to propagate the art of ballet in Britain. The war years scattered their organisations throughout the country, widening the audience more rapidly than would have been possible by other means in so short a time. Public support led subsequently to state support, and court favour for a Royal Ballet in the 1950s. For this achievement the Education Acts of 1870, 1902, 1918 and 1944 must be given as much credit as the pioneer dancers, companies and teaching societies.

Such an historical background profoundly affects the outlook and organisation of ballet in England. 'If one compares the organisation of the Royal Ballet with that of other great state theatres', explained Dame Ninette de Valois to her annual Teachers' Course at the Royal Ballet School in London on 29th July, 1958, 'tremendous differences are immediately disclosed. The court ballets, which grew into the State or National Ballet companies of France, Russia or Denmark, were initiated by the court itself, an exclusive coterie of kings, queens, tsarinas and the like, seeking to provide entertainment for themselves and their guests.

'The English ballet was sponsored by a small civic theatre,[1] which was attempting to provide entertainment for a popular audience, an audience who still remain faithful to our efforts despite the different venue we now inhabit and the very different spectacle of entertainment in dance we now offer. The faithfulness of that audience is one of the most important things to the Royal Ballet and should always be borne in mind.'

Other British companies, growing up in the same way, pioneered alongside the future Royal Ballet. Chief among these was the Ballet Rambert, oldest of British ballet companies and one which has had a profound influence on British choreography. All of these companies had to be self-supporting.

The second great difference, then, between British ballet and the descendants of former court ballets was, and is, financial. Not until the war did the Treasury make any contribution to the arts in Britain. Not until after the war did the Treasury make any substantial move to support the Sadler's Wells Ballet at Covent Garden when that company had become a property of national importance at home and abroad. Even then the grant was made indirectly to the theatre which housed the company, not to the company itself, and the grants were and remain inadequate to the need. They are far less than the grants supporting continental state ballets, provide no security for the Ballet School, little security for the dancers and no retirement pensions.

So British, like similar American, companies of national significance have had to depend for their existence directly on audience support and audience taste, a taste which can be as restricting as it is stimulating. Hence their choreographers have been confronted with the great problem of twentieth-century choreography in a particularly direct form. How to resolve the conflict between ballet's aristocratic vocabulary and the contemporary themes and purpose, which it must express if it is to remain a living art?

Choreographers are engaged with this problem everywhere. It is a condition of their existence in the Soviet Union no less than in Poland, Sweden or France. They have attempted to resolve it

[1] Sponsored by the Vic-Wells theatre organisation under Lilian Baylis, the ballet grew up first in the Old Vic, then in the Sadler's Wells Theatre, whence the company took the name it made famous internationally.

through personal or collective compromises which are reflected in the themes they choose, their methods and their choreographic idiom.

Dame Ninette de Valois was the first choreographer of any importance to face the problem in Britain. The founder of the company which has become the Royal Ballet, she was its foremost choreographer during the thirties. She danced with the Diaghilev company from 1923 until 1926, acquiring there a practical acquaintance with the works of Petipa, Fokine, Nijinsky, Massine, Nijinska and Balanchine. By working with some of these choreographers at different periods of their development she acquired, too, a knowledge of many choreographic styles. Later she assimilated expressionist dance influences current in Germany, especially through the works of Kurt Jooss and Mary Wigman. These influences can be seen in some of her ballets, in the mad scene in *The Rake's Progress* for instance and the ghosts in *The Haunted Ballroom*. And these ballets, together with *Job* and *Checkmate*, reflect similar influences in their style of production.

Among British choreographers de Valois is outstanding as an exponent of the short narrative ballet. Her special inspiration has been the narrative element in British painting. (Plate X.) *The Rake's Progress*, the slighter *The Prospect Before Us* and even *Job*, unique as a *masque* rather than a narrative ballet, are so handled that the choreographic development of their plot and characters are object lessons for any short-story writer. All these works, particularly *The Rake's Progress*, portray the world of real people with a directness exceptional in British ballet. Even the mythical Satan in *Job*, superbly created by Anton Dolin in 1931, is recognisable as a character of our own age.

Checkmate gave other evidence of this contemporary attitude. Of all the de Valois ballets, *Checkmate* bears most distinctly the mark of the thirties. But, perhaps because it trembles on the verge of being a mood ballet, its impact across the footlights is less powerful than *Job* or *The Rake's Progress*. De Valois is not, as Frederick Ashton is, a master of mood.

Nevertheless, *Checkmate* illustrates very well the dual basis of classical technique and folk dance on which the de Valois idiom rests. The clean stabbing *pointe* movements of the red pawns in the opening sequence derive from classical technique. The movements of the black pawns reflect the influence of folk dance. The *pas de basque* is used again and again. There are often thought to be traces of the Morris dance and the sword dance in the pawns' black staves, although de Valois herself says that some of these movements were inspired by a Japanese troupe then appearing in London.

De Valois' treatment of music is definite, often literal. The rhythms are strongly accented, each beat used meticulously, with special attention to phrasing. She handles her narratives equally firmly through an effective use of geometric ground patterns and exceptionally clear choreographic design. Flowing movements, and the emotional or lyric qualities associated with such movement, are absent almost entirely from her work.

In choreographic structure and choice of theme, therefore, de Valois has carried forward the *genre* of dramatic realism initiated by Fokine and continued by Massine. Always her ballets have included strong male roles and made dramatic demands upon the cast. It is these qualities which have been especially valuable to English choreography.

In many ways Sir Frederick Ashton is the complement of de Valois whom he joined permanently at the Sadler's Wells Theatre in 1935. Trained in the Cecchetti method of the *danse d'école*, he was formed as a choreographer principally by Marie Rambert in the late twenties and early thirties. Yet Rambert's contribution could have achieved little without the receptive quality of Ashton's mind and the opportunities de Valois was able to give him. So much has he absorbed from the history of the classical dance that one often seems to see in his work the inspiration of Petipa and Fokine, of Massine and Nijinska.

Ashton, like de Valois, has made great use of the narrative possibilities of ballet. For preference, though, he is a creator of moods rather than a teller of stories. And he has shown a particular concern with the beauty of physical movement, often unconnected with any theme save the theme in the music.

Therefore his choreography seems less directly related to the everyday world than that of de Valois. His journey into ballet has been a search for a personal, almost abstract, conception of 'beauty'. His world is a world of the emotions. Even early effervescent, narrative works like *Rio Grande* and *A Wedding Bouquet*, combining the spoken word with dancing, revealed a quality of emotion which makes the choreography of Ashton poetry to de Valois' prose.

All this sets Ashton's ballets apart from current social happenings.

He is neither 'committed' nor 'engaged'. He is concerned, in his own words, 'with matters of more permanent significance than topical issues'. Yet the thirties and forties found their reflection in him too. *Apparitions*, decorated by Cecil Beaton, *Nocturne*, decorated by Sophie Fedorovitch, and *Horoscope*, which first called attention to the young Michael Somes, were half narrative, half mood ballets. The mood was romantic, mingling nostalgia with a sense of fate and personal tragedy.

Dante Sonata, composed in the first months of war, brought this trend to a conclusion. It signalled the turning-point which the war was to represent in Ashton's choreographic career. Entirely a work of mood, it abandoned all narrative suggestion. Influenced by Jooss's expressionist ideas, it relinquished even traditional ballet costume in favour of bare feet and flowing draperies. Good confronted evil through contrasts of classical and modern movements, white and black costumes. Six years later, when peace had come, *Symphonic Variations* reflected a new world and a new Ashton. Tranquil in the clear space of Sophie Fedorovitch's decor, the ballet had about it the peace of a spring morning. (Plate VIII (a).)

Since those days Ashton has grown in stature and influence. He has become the first choreographer of Britain and one of the first on the world stage. As such he is the founder of British classical choreography, asserting in his manner of work the dominant influence of the choreographer over ballet. 'A choreographer', he once said, 'is responsible not only for the steps of a ballet, but for everything that happens on the stage, the visual moving side of a ballet, the dancing, the expression, the lighting, the production. He need not be a practising musician, but he must have a thorough knowledge and understanding of music.'[1]

Ashton's ballets are now the basis of the modern British repertoire and a training ground for British dancers in the classical technique. His classicism, derived directly from the classical masters, has been developed consistently throughout his professional life. *Les Rendezvous*, his first work for the Sadler's Wells Theatre in 1933, showed his devotion to the beauty of classical dancing at the beginning of his career. He has never wavered from this devotion. The classical vocabulary is his principal inspiration. No other dance idiom has exerted a comparable influence upon him.

His signature in choreography is a lyrical, flowing dance style.

[1] B.B.C., February, 1959.

This began by placing special emphasis on plastic movement for the upper part of the body and now gives a similar attention to movements of the feet and legs. Ashton sculpts these movements with great subtlety and increasing verve. Each develops naturally out of the movement before it, the flow of dancing matched by intricate and beautiful groups.

To perform such choreography requires dance quality, a sense of style and great care in fulfilling the particular characteristics of individual roles. Humour and wit are often present in Ashton's work, although great dramatic roles are rare. *Les Patineurs*, for instance, calls for dance quality in the least member of the *corps de ballet*. It is built on steps of elevation, *fouettés sautés*, *grands jetés en tournant*, and so on. *Les Masques*, a very different type of ballet created for Dame Marie Rambert, was a ballet of classical steps with emphatic stylisation of movements for the top of the body. Like *Les Patineurs*, *La Peri*, *Birthday Offering*, and most Ashton ballets, the right style was essential to its performance.

His ballets are filled with exacting roles for particular dancers. The ballerina and her partner in *Les Rendezvous*, the Blue Boy and Blue Girls in *Les Patineurs*, and the six soloists in *Symphonic Variations* have helped to train two generations of British dancers. The training has been remarkable for its versatility since Ashton's versatility is greater, perhaps, than that of any living choreographer. On the one hand is *Ondine*, narrative in form because only the narrative form can extend to three acts, yet so near to a three-act ballet of mood, if that were possible, that it appears rather a poem in three cantos than a three-act drama. On the other hand is *La Fille mal gardée*, a narrative two-act work of choreographic humour with enormous popular appeal, using the old classical formulae. Beside them lies an amazing variety of output, including works of English wit and humour, like *Façade*, and an exploration of abstract territory which began with *Les Rendezvous* before the abstract *genre* was properly established in the ballet repertoires of Europe and America.

Andrée Howard, trained also in the great forming ground of Madame Rambert's Ballet Club, made her first attempt at choreography in 1933. *Our Lady's Juggler* showed at once an ability to sustain mood and create atmosphere with remarkable economy of movement. This has always been her strength.

In her early days she was influenced by the two senior choreographers of the Ballet Club, Ashton and Antony Tudor, inclining towards Ashton. Like his work, her ballets are marked by lyrical qualities, flow of movement, exquisite taste, deep sensitivity and a restraint which is very English in its understatement. Yet her style and themes have always been personal and original.

She it was in 1947 who created the first British two-act ballet, *The Sailor's Return*. Her love of animals has induced her to portray many animal characters from literature, notably in *Mermaid* (1934) and *Lady into Fox* (1939). These half human, half animal heroines were conveyed through a use of classical movement which was inventive and exceptionally musical. Feeling for music, indeed, is innate in her choreography. Always, she remains faithful to its spirit without becoming the slave of crotchets and quavers.

Many of Howard's best qualities may be seen in *La Fête Étrange*. (Plate XIV (b).) Based on a scenario by Ronald Crichton from a solitary episode in Alain Fournier's novel, *Le Grand Meaulnes*, *La Fête Étrange* was produced for the London Ballet at the Arts Theatre during the time of Dunkirk in 1940. The London Ballet was one of the first small companies to raise the flag of ballet during the war after the great shut-down of theatres in 1939. It seems fitting that in *La Fête Étrange*, this company should have presented the English theatre with a fine choreographic legacy of the war years, heavy with the sadness of the period, yet noble and filled with wonder.

Today, violent emotions parallel the heroism and mourning of the thirties and forties. On both sides of the Atlantic psychology and the psychologist have been summoned to the side of the choreographer. They guide him more openly now than ever they did when innovators such as Antony Tudor and Agnes de Mille made their early experiments with psychology at the Ballet Club at the same time as Andrée Howard.

In this turn towards psychology Kurt Jooss and Martha Graham exerted a strong influence. Jooss, the German expressionist choreographer, worked first in Germany, then in England before and during the war. In *The Green Table* and *The Big City* he presented the social conflicts of the thirties more potently than anyone in the classical idiom. Graham was, and remains, one of the most provocative of America's expressionist choreographers.

The emotional tensions of our era found powerful expression in the work of these two. Then the same image became reflected in the work of more classically trained choreographers such as Tudor, de Mille, Howard and Jerome Robbins. Howard's *The Fugitive*, created for Ballet Rambert in 1944, was a tragedy of real life, 'the more moving', wrote Lionel Bradley, 'because we have been shown the sisterly affection and the awakening of young love which are both rudely shattered by the climax of the action'.[1]

Later, Howard's *A Mirror for Witches* (Appendix III c (iii)) became one of the most interesting ballets of social conflict produced at Covent Garden during the post-war decade. But it was really younger choreographers, like John Cranko and Kenneth MacMillan, who exploited moods of violence most thoroughly. They developed this *genre* from the narrative example of Helpmann's *Miracle in the Gorbals*, *Hamlet* and *Adam Zero*, and from Tudor's extension of the mood ballet into psychology.

Antony Tudor was launched as a choreographer by Madame Rambert in 1931. During the rest of the thirties he realised with increasing success the special dramatic qualities of ballet-making which flowed from her inspiration.

Much influenced by Fokine and by the expressionist work of Kurt Jooss, Tudor developed Fokine's ideas in terms of mood, psychology and character. He examined the emotional stresses in human lives. He was one of the first in British choreography to present living characters, as opposed to types. Their emotional relationships, one with another, provide the substance of his ballets.

Very varied in theme and origin, these ballets are presented through a choreography which is more cerebral than Ashton's. Each work is the result of a search for some style of movement particularly applicable to the subject and the music.

In *Dark Elegies* (1937), about which we spoke in the last chapter, he introduced folk movement because the dancers represented peasants and because he was attracted to folk movement and had studied it. He discarded classical turn-out and *pointes* for his *corps* in this ballet, but retained these technical qualities for his three principal dancers. Thus he used their classical virtuosity to make a dance impact on the audience and to build a mood of emotional tension.

In *Jardin aux Lilas* (1936)—(Plate VIII (b))—where his characters were members of high society, he used a purely classical technique to represent their aristocracy, maintaining at the same time the individual movements and images by which he had come to be known and which he developed into a personal style.

Considering his small output of ballets, Tudor has made an

[1] Lionel Bradley, *Sixteen Years of Ballet Rambert*, p. 22 (London, 1946).

extraordinary impact on both sides of the Atlantic. He was never well known in Britain before he went to America in 1939 yet his ballets maintain their influence here over dancers, critics and choreographers. This impact is due in part to the strong personal style of his choreography, the result of a constant search for original classical movement. But it derives mostly from the contemporary problems which compose his themes and which have helped to bring the art of choreography into closer touch with everyday life. In this lies his principal contribution to the art.

The same contemporary approach appeared in the choreography of Robert Helpmann, when he began to create ballets for the Sadler's Wells company from 1942 onwards. Of all the pre-war and war-time British choreographers these two, Antony Tudor and Robert Helpmann, most directly mirrored the social climate of their period. But whereas Tudor expressed his themes through the emotional conflicts of contemporary people, rarely making a narrative statement, Robert Helpmann commented strongly in narrative form upon the contemporary social scene. The comment was indirect in *Comus* and *Hamlet*, direct in *Miracle in the Gorbals* and *Adam Zero*.

Comus posed again the struggle of good and evil, purity and temptation. *Hamlet*, produced in 1942, found in the mind of a dying man the fevered reflection of a war-torn world. *Miracle in the Gorbals* (1944) depicted the social evils of slum life. *Adam Zero* (1946) commented upon the empty life-span of middle-class man.

Through these ballets Helpmann developed a concept of dance-drama in English choreography. Like Tudor he stressed the use of real characters in ballet. Unlike Tudor his ballets suffered from a poverty of choreographic invention, but they told their story powerfully through realistic mime and dramatic movement. In this sense, Helpmann opened the way for post-war dramatic ballets like Alfred Rodrigues' *Blood Wedding*, Peter Darrell's *The Prisoners* and Norman Morrice's *Two Brothers*.

At a time when the English repertoire of necessity consisted almost entirely of classical ballets, Helpmann nourished an understanding of dramatic values and theatre sense in the dancers of the forties, so maintaining a balance with the past and contributing much to public interest in choreography during the difficult war years. Through his ballets, too, he introduced for the first time to English choreography the idea of using a producer (Michael Benthall) who was other than the choreographer or the artistic director. This important idea, like the conception of dance-drama, has yet to be fully explored.

During and after the war a new generation of English choreographers grew up, facing a world very different from the thirties. Among them was Frank Staff whose fruitful short career left *Peter and the Wolf* and *Czernyana*, full of choreographic wit and character, in the repertoire of Ballet Rambert. The most established of these choreographers now are Walter Gore, John Cranko, Alfred Rodrigues, Kenneth MacMillan and Jack Carter.

Gore, the oldest, seems influenced by Tudor in a style which is marked by strong musicality, sense of rhythm and an original approach to movement. He favours dramatic themes as in *The Night and Silence*, although a sense of comedy has contributed to his reputation. *Simple Symphony* for Rambert in 1944 shows this humour very well. Like Tudor and Andrée Howard, he developed and did much of his best work under Dame Marie's guidance.

John Cranko, Kenneth MacMillan and Alfred Rodrigues, on the other hand, are the first group of British choreographers, other than Ninette de Valois, to have grown up outside the direct influence of Rambert.

Cranko displays a continuing philosophical strain which seems to derive from a personal search for an ideal way of life. His exceptionally creative talent is also his greatest problem. So intense and so often uncontrolled is the flood of choreographic ideas that the ideas seem to become things-in-themselves, undeveloped to proper conclusions. His principal successes lie in the poetic-philosophic field (*Beauty and the Beast* (1949), *Harlequin in April* (1951) (Appendix III c (i)), *The Shadow* (1953), *The Lady and the Fool* (1954), *Antigone*, Plate XVIII (b) (1959)) and in the field of comedy narrative (*Pineapple Poll* (1951), *Bonne-Bouche* (1952)).

In some of these works, especially *The Lady and the Fool* and *Antigone*, he shows an ability to comment with telling effect on contemporary social attitudes. In others, like MacMillan after him, he develops the *genre* of the mood ballet in terms of human psychology, using an idiom which reflects the wide studies of an enquiring mind. *The Prince of the Pagodas*, for example, embraces jazz and jive dancing and the folk dances of Europe, Africa and the East, all disciplined by the classical vocabulary.

MacMillan mingles an equal grasp of the classical vocabulary with intensely contemporary movements and music, often from jazz

sources. *Somnambulism* (1953), his first and one of his most successful
ballets, used the jazz music of Stan Kenton. At that time such music
was something of a novelty in England, let alone in English ballet.

His themes mix fantasy and eccentric comedy with compassion
(like Cranko) for lonely or unhappy people. The choreography is
clear-cut, precise, highly original in construction and very demanding on the dancers. *The Burrow* (1958), exploring the tensions of
persecuted people, reflects these qualities. It may be counted among
the most important English dramatic ballets of the fifties. Yet,
balancing it, is a preoccupation with astringent abstract dancing after
the manner of Balanchine in America, using, as Balanchine often
does, the music of Stravinsky.

Latterly, MacMillan's style has become more lyrical, his themes
more realistic. Ironically, the change began with *Le Baiser de la Fée*
early in 1960 although by the end of that year, when he created *The
Invitation*, he declared himself 'sick to death of fairy stories'.

'I want people to go to the theatre to be moved by something
they can recognise. When I created *Noctambules* [Appendix III c,
(ii)] and earlier ballets I used to think it didn't matter what you
said, but how you said it. I've changed my mind now, so the movements I use are changing too.

'In *The Invitation* the movement is not nearly so broken, angular
or sharp as it used to be, not sharp at all for the principals. There is
an emphasis on the *pas de deux* which I began in *Baiser*. Previously I
haven't paid so much attention to *pas de deux*, probably because I
myself was never a very good partner. I've learned it over the years
and feel now I can express more in *pas de deux* than solos.'[1]

These new lyrical qualities, 'not sharp at all', were developed in
Diversions, a plotless ballet significant for the maturity and firmness
of the idiom. Here the movements have a plastic quality not always
present in the choreographer's earlier work. The line of the body is
used fully, running unbroken time and again through the whole
length of stretched arms, legs and feet. The images flow unhurriedly
one from another. The vocabulary is economical and self-assured.
Even *The Rite of Spring*, later in 1962, makes no return to the sharpness and spikiness of his early movements, however angular its sculptural effects. This is his most important work to date, a ballet of
astonishing invention and musical sensitivity, yet more intellectual
than emotional in its appeal. It assaults the mind rather than the heart,

[1] To Peter Brinson, December, 1960.

exploring a new range of movement and a new idiom, made possible
by the rising standard of dancers trained in the Royal Ballet School.

Cranko's *Antigone* and MacMillan's *The Burrow* and *The Invitation*
were striking additions to the dramatic *genre* when it seemed this
genre was little favoured at Covent Garden. Other exponents of the
genre have been Alfred Rodrigues and three choreographers outside
the Royal Ballet, Jack Carter, Peter Darrell and Norman Morrice.

With *Blood Wedding* (Plate IX (a)), adapted from the Lorca play
for Sadler's Wells Theatre Ballet in 1953, Rodrigues gained his first
important success. The best choreography is to be found in the
ballet's *pas de deux*. Rodrigues' use of lifts was expressive of the
story and lovely to see. The ballet, too, combined the music of Denis
ApIvor and the designs of Isabel Lambert with dances which presented the drama strikingly and powerfully.

Darrell's *The Prisoners* (1957), Carter's *The Witch Boy* (1957) and
Morrice's *Two Brothers* (1958), *Hazaña* (1959) and *Conflicts* (1962)
show a comparable sense of theatre. At the same time each has
developed a particular field of work to which his style seems suited.
Darrell has given the Western Theatre Ballet most of its best new
works and has made a reputation as a television choreographer.
Morrice has become the latest significant product of the Rambert
Company. Carter, like Michael Charnley,[1] another choreographer
who has worked with Festival Ballet, has turned aside from the
crowded British stage to build a reputation abroad.

Carter is a choreographer of great experience with a marked
narrative ability. Ballets like *Past Recalled* (originally named *Ouverture*, to a theme by Proust) and *The Witch Boy* are strong in atmosphere and tell their story through well-created characters. It is hard,
though, to judge him properly against his contemporaries because
so much of his work is scattered through theatres in Europe and
South America. By such travels, he and others illustrate the growing
influence exercised by British choreography on the international
stage.

The choreographic picture in Britain since the war, therefore, is a
complex of narrative, mood and abstract creations in a rich variety
of styles. The complexity in part derives from a similar complexity
of contemporary music and in part has stimulated the catholicity of

---

[1] Creator of *Symphony for Fun*, one of the most successful of the original works
commissioned by Festival Ballet. It is regrettable that a choreographer of such
achievement should have been unable to find adequate recognition in Britain.

music which choreographers have used, from Bach and Mozart to the latest composers.

Not that *British* composers have adventured far in the cause of ballet. Generally speaking, British ballet music has held itself aloof from radical experiment, while its original sources have drawn small inspiration from the folk past. Vaughan Williams, an exception among our composers, shows the influence of folk tune in his music for *Job*. His score, for example, asks that the figures in the dancing of the opening pastoral should derive from the old tune *Jennie Pluck Pears* in Playford's *Dancing Master* on which the pastoral is based. But *Job* was Vaughan Williams' sole excursion into the ballet theatre. Other contemporary composers have sought more sophisticated inspiration for original works. At the same time British composers of the past have been summoned to inspire choreography through skilful arrangements of their works, like Lambert's use of Boyce for *The Prospect Before Us*.

In the thirty years of its life, British choreography has divided its musical attention evenly between existing scores and scores specially created. In pursuing this policy, it was lucky to have at Sadler's Wells a musical director of the quality of Constant Lambert. His taste and judgement, combined with wide knowledge, gave our choreography firm musical roots. Unfortunately, he was restricted for most of his time at Sadler's Wells by lack of money and always by the conservatism of the musical public and British musical thought.

This is not to say that British ballet music has not sometimes been distinguished. Lambert saw to that. It is to show, rather, that in the life of a nation its ballet requires the same collaboration between the worlds of music, painting, literature and choreography as a single ballet requires of single artists. This grander collaboration has yet to be achieved in Britain. It can only be achieved, musically, through stronger musical direction, better libretti and a more frequent association of our best composers with ballet.

Parallel with this has gone a development of stage design, although the work of British artists and lighting experts in this field matches neither the richness of British choreography nor the invention of stage designers in some foreign countries.

Partly this has been because the economic problems of new ballet companies everywhere have limited the designer to a more austere theatre than Diaghilev ever knew. There was less money for scenery and costumes. There was no money to deepen the shallow nineteenth-century commercial stages which ballet encountered once it stepped outside the opera houses where it had lived for two centuries and a half. Such stages restricted perspective and depth in design and choreography. Any design was questioned which occupied more than a minimum of valuable dancing space.

In Germany and America these pressures of money and space led to an emphasis on light at the expense of décor. In Britain, where a more careful balance was maintained between light and decoration, the decoration often acquired a simplicity which was almost functional.

Simplicity, so in keeping with the small resources and stages of the early Sadler's Wells and Rambert ballets, was the starting-point of the work of Sophie Fedorovitch, Hugh Stevenson and William Chappell. To some extent, too, it had to guide the work of later artists such as Rex Whistler, Leslie Hurry and John Piper. Out of these conditions came memorable occasions in the first decade of British ballet design. There were Whistler's *The Rake's Progress*, Chappell's *Les Rendezvous*, Fedorovitch's *Nocturne*, Beaton's *Apparitions*, Stevenson's *Jardin aux Lilas* and Hurry's *Hamlet*.

Today things are easier. The old distinctions between stage and studio hardly trouble artists. Easel painters are almost anxious to consider the theatre's use of their talent. Therefore, since the war, due to the growing numbers of painters commissioned to work in the theatre, British ballet has produced a wider range of important décors by artists such as Piper, Clavé (who exerted a significant influence on all early post-war ballet decoration), Rowell, Georgiadis, Koltai, Nolan and Isabel Lambert. Waiting, too, to be explored with choreographer and composer is the unmapped territory of back projection, the open stage and the new audience-artist relationship which could develop without a proscenium arch.

(ii) THE UNITED STATES

In America ballet was an occasional spectacle at least as far back as the American Revolution. At that time numerous ballets on patriotic themes were created by American choreographers. Later the romantic movement reached long fingers across the Atlantic. *La Sylphide* made its American debut on 15th April, 1835. An American production of *Giselle*, with an American dancer, Mary Ann Lee, in the title role, was seen for the first time in Boston on 1st January, 1846.

European dancers, too, came to America. The brother and sister-in-law of Marie Taglioni appeared in 1839. The same year the young Marius Petipa was seen in New York during a brief, mismanaged season at the Bowery Theatre. But the most brilliant appearance of all was the Austrian, Fanny Elssler. The success of her long tours from 1840–1842 remained unmatched for the rest of the nineteenth century. Only *The Black Crook*, an American extravaganza running from 1866 onwards, came near to rivalling it, helping too, to revive public interest in ballet.

Not until the first American visit of the Danish ballerina, Adeline Genée, in 1908, followed by the arrival of Anna Pavlova and Mikhail Mordkin in 1910 can it be said that classical choreography began to strike roots in American soil. The visits of these and other dancers, including the Diaghilev Ballet during the First World War, led to the establishment of ballet schools and ballet companies in some of the principal American cities. Public taste, encouraged by the appearance of the Russians and by the rising standard of public education, was able to sustain developments of a kind which could not have been sustained fifty years earlier.

By the time of Diaghilev's death in 1929 Russian choreographers and teachers like Kosloff, Fokine, Bolm and Mordkin had been working for more than a decade in America. They had founded important schools in New York, Chicago, San Francisco and Los Angeles. Thither came a stream of young Americans to study, inspired by the coast-to-coast appearances of Anna Pavlova and other great visiting dancers.

Pavlova had stirred the continent by her continual tours from 1911 onwards. During the years of the First World War America was her home. It was she who brought *The Sleeping Beauty* to New York for the first time in 1916, and she who began the battle for classicism as against other forms of theatrical dancing. It seemed natural, therefore, when many of the former Diaghilev dancers came together in the Ballet Russe de Monte Carlo in 1932, that America should be one of this Russian company's early calls. They made their New York debut on 21st December, 1933, forging links with the American public which remain unbroken today.

Meanwhile the expressionist[1] movement was launched in America

---

[1] The popular term in America for 'expressionist dance' is 'modern dance'. We have used the term 'expressionist dance' throughout this book to denote all those idioms and styles which have arisen on both sides of the Atlantic since the

by Isadora Duncan and Ruth St. Denis. Separately and differently each rebelled against the classical dance. They rejected its discipline and technique. They held that the classical dance had come to be used merely for spectacular purposes, devoid of content. Fokine, too, rejected the empty spectacle of most classical ballet at the end of the nineteenth century. But he was able to distinguish between this and the value of the technique behind it.

The expressionist dance flourished in America, bearing fruit in schools and companies. In time it enriched and modified the American *danse d'école* in a way which never happened in Britain, where its dance forms never took root. When expressionism influenced British classical choreography it did so at long range, from outside the national culture.

In America, on the other hand, the expressionist dance was nourished by Americans. St. Denis and Ted Shawn, for example, launched the Denishawn school and company in 1915. It became an educational and theatrical force, helping a whole generation of dancers to evolve American styles of movement. Among these dancers Martha Graham, Doris Humphrey and Charles Weidman developed personal vocabularies which gained a following far beyond the American theatre. They were reinforced from outside the Denishawn circle by Helen Tamiris and Hanya Holm who brought from Germany the potent influence of Mary Wigman's central European style. This influence gained powerful support in 1933 from the first appearance in America of Kurt Jooss and his company.

Such, then, was the climate of American dance theatre in the early thirties. The balance was swung decisively in favour of classicism by two events. First, the Ballet Russe de Monte Carlo under the impresario, Sol Hurok, began the decade of tours which educated, more than anything else, a ballet audience in America. Second, Lincoln Kirstein and Edward Warburg invited the Russian, George Balanchine, to establish a School of American Ballet. The school had begun already in a small way at Hartford, Connecticut. Balanchine transferred it to New York, opening its doors in January 1934, in Isadora Duncan's former studios. From it sprang an American style of classical dance and a succession of companies which have evolved into the New York City Ballet today.

Balanchine has been the most potent of all influences upon

end of the nineteenth century and are today also sometimes called 'modern', 'free' and 'central European'.

American choreography. He is a master of music—of musical construction, as well as rhythm and melody—and a master of the classical vocabulary which he inherited from Petipa through training at the Maryinsky School. From the beginning in New York these qualities began to be enshrined particularly in the plotless ballet. He made this ballet of 'pure' dancing so much his *genre* and the *genre* of the American companies he has guided, that it is recognised today internationally, as an American contribution to choreographic art.

Not that the abstract, or plotless, *genre* arrived unheralded. It has its origins in the *divertissement* which is as old as ballet itself. Perrot's *Pas de Quatre* and Fokine's *Les Sylphides* both stand on the unclear frontier between the mood and the abstract. During the twenties Nijinska in *Les Noces*, Massine in *Ode* and Balanchine himself in *Apollon-Musagète*, reconnoitred the frontier without crossing it. These ballets reached out to abstract territory but always retained for their dancers the garments of character or emotion. This was made clear on the programme. Not until the thirties was the frontier crossed and the adventure begun. The lands of narrative and mood were left behind. With Balanchine choreography entered the realm of 'pure' dancing.

By developing the classical ballet logically from the point to which Petipa brought it, Balanchine made America the home of neoclassicism. American choreography, as developed by him, is the direct descendant of Petipa rather than of Petipa, through Fokine, like British choreography. To Petipa theme always remained significant. But form, line and technique claimed his first attention. By making the theme subordinate to the dancing, he posed the possibility of doing without theme altogether.

Balanchine turned the possibility into reality. He has abstracted the Petipa vocabularly from mood and narrative, making movement the end of choreography. Sometimes he has kept a suggestion of an idea—as in *Ballet Imperial*—to give the whole thing a kind of motivation. Sometimes there is nothing but the structure of the music. *Concerto Barocco* is simply music made visible. The only sensible way to approach Balanchine's choreography is through its music.

Yet Balanchine responds no less vividly to physical material. He has developed classical brilliance, balance, harmony and proportion on American physiques and temperaments. It is these physiques and temperaments which give all American choreography the athletic quality and contemporary, almost rough, appeal found nowhere else. 'American style', Lincoln Kirstein prophesied in 1938, 'springs or should spring from our own training and environment which was not in an Imperial School or a Parisian imitation of it. Ours is a style bred also from basket-ball courts, track and swimming meets and junior proms. Our style springs from the personal atmosphere of recognisable American types. . . .'[1]

Balanchine's choreography reflects this environment quite as much as the choreography of de Mille, Robbins or Kidd. At the same time it has characteristics whose sum separates him from native American choreographers.

Generally, his dancers are anonymous. They are instruments of movement devoid of individual personality and so in a sense timeless. This approach has been emphasised by the choreographer's preference for lack of décor and for costuming his dancers in similar styles of tunic. Early on, the dancers were mostly feminine. The available male material was poor and Balanchine himself was more interested in creating for women. So there was little effective contrast between male and female movement. Male movement was hardly developed and there were few remarkable male roles before the end of the war. Today the balance is almost redressed by a supply of excellent male dancers. *Theme and Variations* in 1947, for example, contained a striking solo for Igor Youskevitch. Others have followed. But the emphasis continues to be upon the feminine element.

In form Balanchine's choreography was characterised early by long lines of dancers all doing the same movement. *Serenade* shows this, together with the choreographer's interest in the patterns achieved by changing lines. His orchestration underlines particular movements for particular music, whereas Ashton, Tudor and others orchestrate their *corps* to perform different movements.

Technically, Balanchine's classical steps are finely modelled with the *pointe* much used, often for movements taken from jazz sources. Frequently, he distorts the classical line of which he is such a master by introducing movements off balance or by sticking out hips, elbows and shoulders. This occurs in almost all his work from *Concerto Barocco* (Plate XV) to *Agon* (Plate XXXI (b)) and *Stars and Stripes*. But not in *Serenade*—*Serenade* is purely classical.

The School of American Ballet had to produce dancers who could be instruments for such choreography. It was the first classical

[1] L. Kirstein, *Blast at Ballet* (New York, 1938).

ballet school in America with a national, rather than a local, vision. With Balanchine in charge it gave American choreography an academic link with the tradition of European ballet and an academic vocabulary developed to suit national temperament.

Hence the School of American Ballet exerted its influence on American choreography through the classical style of dancing it transmitted to the ballet theatre as a whole (not just the Kirstein-Balanchine companies) and through the dancers it trained who have become the first generation of American choreographers.

Among these choreographers John Taras and William Dollar have developed most consistently the American classical style in terms of the plotless ballet initiated by Balanchine. Three other dancers from the school, Lew Christensen, Eugene Loring and Michael Kidd, have been among the principal creators of a style of choreography which mingles Balanchine's Russian classicism with home-grown dance influences. These were nourished particularly by Ballet Theatre after 1940.

The home-grown influences came largely from the pioneers of the thirties. Catherine Littlefield used American folk sources in *Barn Dance* (1936). Ruth Page's early dramatic ballets fused expressionist and classical styles. In particular, the expressionist dancing and teaching of Doris Humphrey, Charles Weidman and Martha Graham built on Denishawn's exploration of American folk themes during the 1920s.

Even so, the first widely successful all-American ballet did not come till 1938. This was *Billy the Kid*, presented by Ballet Caravan at the Chicago Opera House on 16th October. It had music by Aaron Copland, décor by Jared French and choreography by Eugene Loring, using a dance style no less American for being based on the *danse d'école*. The scenario by Lincoln Kirstein told the story of William Bonney, American outlaw.

Six months earlier in London Agnes de Mille created a suite of American dances, 'one of which was called *Rodeo*. This study contained every bit of gesture that was later used in the ballet *Rodeo*.'[1] Thus, in two works separately born on either side of the Atlantic, the aristocratic classical vocabulary was moulded to the American spirit. On this foundation was raised the repertoire of later ballets

[1] Agnes de Mille, *Dance to the Piper*, p. 226 (Bantam Books Edition, New York, 1954). See also, Peggy van Praagh, *How I became a Ballet Dancer*, p. 52 (Nelson, London, 1954).

by de Mille, Robbins and others which mirrored America more directly than the academic classicism of Balanchine. Yet Balanchine showed as early as 1936, in *Slaughter on Tenth Avenue* for the revue *On Your Toes*, that new America and traditional classicism could strike a workable compromise.

At that time, the compromise was neither clear enough nor complete enough to satisfy those who sought to translate America as *Billy the Kid* had done. Therefore many important choreographic developments of the early forties took place outside the framework of the School of American Ballet which lost, in any case, Lincoln Kirstein's decisive presence for the duration of the war.

The seedbed of these developments was Ballet Theatre. The strongest influence was Antony Tudor, who arrived in America after the outbreak of war in Europe in 1939.

Ballet Theatre was formed early in 1940 around the nucleus of the Mordkin Ballet which had been formed in turn in 1937 around the Mordkin School in New York. Here again was a direct link with Imperial Russia. But the link was with the Bolshoi in Moscow, whence Mordkin came, rather than with Balanchine's Maryinsky in St. Petersburg. Whereas Balanchine continued the Maryinsky tradition of dance and spectacle, Mordkin had trained his company in the Bolshoi's tradition of dramatic character ballets. This was helpful to Ballet Theatre in the task it set itself to become the representative American company.

At first, though, neither the Russian nor the few American works in its huge repertoire carried most weight with dancers and public. It was the English ballets of Antony Tudor which attracted attention. Tudor's extension of the mood ballet into psychological drama, his particular development of expressive dance gesture and preference for contemporary stories and types of people became part of the tradition of American choreography. In the same *genres* as his revivals of earlier ballets he added *Pillar of Fire* (1942) (Plate XXV (b)), *Romeo and Juliet* (1942) and *Undertow* (1945), powerful ballets built for American dancers.

The treatment of almost all these ballets had the inevitability of Greek drama. Within the psychology of their characters lay a destiny from which they could not escape. But also within these ballets lay a destiny from which, it seemed, their choreographer could not escape. Tudor's approach to his characters was somewhat detached. He watched them, played with them as a cat plays with a mouse, before destroying them. The detachment grew and widened until it came between the choreographer and his public so that his appeal faded. Nevertheless, he left an imprint upon American choreography which can never be erased. His ballets have become classics in America, if not American classics. They gave artistic stability to the erratic, proudly American, self-consciously national venture which was Ballet Theatre in its early days.

The war roused national interest and scattered ballet ventures across the country, as it did in Britain. Under this stimulus young American choreographers wove the influence from abroad and the influences from home into new styles which caught the imagination of the public. The most successful among them were Agnes de Mille, Jerome Robbins and Michael Kidd.

De Mille combines the classical vocabulary with expressionist ideas, like so many American choreographers. She was the first to bring an American idiom of choreography to international notice. The idiom is intensely realistic and often humorous without losing the poetic qualities of dancing. One can see it in *Rodeo* (1942) (Plate IX (b)), *Fall River Legend* (1948), *The Harvest According* (1952) and in her ballets for *Oklahoma* and the many musicals which followed.

This idiom, like her themes, has been shaped by her interest in American folk-lore and history, as well as what she has absorbed from Martha Graham. In *Rodeo*, for example, a series of attitude turns *renversé* with the arms sweeping to the ground represented a cowboy's trick while riding his horse. The cowboy's natural movement was cleverly assimilated into classical movement. Often, de Mille uses diagonal lines and great sweeping *jetés*. Like the expressionists, but unlike Balanchine, she has used the floor a great deal, and used turned-in movements, impulses, natural humour and acting. In grief or humour she can project strong emotion till it hurts the spectator. There are few scenes in American musicals sadder than the funeral in *Brigadoon*. The jokes in *Rodeo* have pathos as well as wit. She feels her characters deeply and draws them as sharply as the edge of Lizzie Borden's axe. Agnes de Mille 'knew exactly what she wanted', said Nora Kaye of *Fall River Legend*. 'It was she who determined that Lizzie must be conceived as a tragic heroine. . . . In the choreography she mingled freely invented movements and dramatic gesture with traditional ballet steps and movements.'[1] With such an approach it seems small wonder that de Mille should

[1] To Walter Terry, *Sunday Times*, London, 15th March, 1959.

become the first American choreographer to reach and hold a mass public.

Jerome Robbins has developed Americanism in other directions. Very few other choreographers in this century have had so wide an artistic training. It recalls the catholicity of a Blasis or Viganò. He was trained in dancing by Antony Tudor and Eugene Loring, and trained in acting by Elia Kazan. He is a student of the piano and the violin, and of oriental, Spanish and modern dancing. As a choreographer he is the first American to unite in his own style the classicism of Balanchine, whom he resembles in musicality, with the contemporary influences of young America, which Kirstein defined.

Robbins's ballets range as widely as his talents. The plotless *Fanfare* (1953) can be countered with the extrovert humour of *Fancy Free* (1944) (Plate XXXI (a)) and *Interplay* (1945). The intensely serious *Age of Anxiety* (1950) and the psychological study of lonely people in *Facsimile* (1946) find their opposite in the almost classical exploitation of jazz by young America in *N.Y. Export Op. Jazz* (1958). The tender understanding of youth displayed here and earlier in *The Afternoon of a Faun* (1953), where a new scenario by Robbins was set to Debussy's score, is developed further in *West Side Story* (1957). In this Robbins achieves a remarkable synthesis of the performing arts with dance as the unifying element.

A master of the theatre and of choreographic construction, Robbins has dedicated himself to the advancement of American dancers and American choreography. In doing so he has shown a continuing sympathy for ordinary people in tragic or humorous circumstances. Such observation and contact with daily things is his to an unusual degree, reproduced with a simplicity which is the overriding characteristic of his work.

Robbins's feeling for ordinary things is not unique among American choreographers. In different ways (in the contrasting styles of Todd Bolender and Herbert Ross, for example) most of them express it. The growing regional ballet movement, which is such an encouraging feature of the American ballet scene, is producing promising choreographers who stress themes from their own localities.

Cinema and television encourage the same trend. Michael Kidd, for instance, was classically trained by former members of Diaghilev's company and in Balanchine's School of American Ballet. Then he showed in *On Stage* (1945), produced for Ballet Theatre when he

was only twenty-six, an exceptional talent for adapting the aristocratic *danse d'école* to the theatre of an egalitarian society. Like
Robbins, his choreography reflects a mixture of folk and expressionist
influences. He has the same sincerity, the same sense of humour and
gift of observation, and the same belief in dancing and dancers.
Unlike Robbins he has developed his talent more in musical comedy
and the cinema than in the ballet theatre. His choreography for the
film *Seven Brides for Seven Brothers* (1955) remained the best union
between choreography and the camera until *West Side Story* was
filmed in 1960.

Of all choreographers Robbins has been most successful in mingling Balanchine's Russian-American classicism with the character
and demi-character styles illustrated in the work of de Mille. It is
important to emphasise that these two strands exist in America side
by side. Both are necessary to American ballet and will depend for
some time to come upon each other. But in the work of Robbins
and younger choreographers they are united in a style which one can
recognise already as beginning an *American* School of Choreography.

CHAPTER IX

OTHER CONTEMPORARY CHOREOGRAPHY

(i) FRANCE

IN France, during the thirties and early forties, choreography was dominated by the single figure of Serge Lifar. As a dancer, organiser and publicist Lifar revived the fallen reputation of the Opéra and of French ballet. For this ballet in France stands permanently in his debt.

As a choreographer Lifar's style has been based on a vocabulary learned from Cecchetti and influenced in its early days by Balanchine. But his use of this vocabulary has been to stress the bizarre and the grotesque, posture rather than movement, in works which have been almost always over-ornamented, ill-constructed and ill-balanced.

'He settles his ballets very quickly,' wrote Irène Lidova, one of the most acute of French ballet *animateurs*, 'but takes long over the details of a *pas de deux* and fusses over the *variations* of the soloists. The plastic details hold his interest more than the evolutions in space, which generally lack variety. Most of his ballets are very unequal, containing some passages which are moving and strong but then suddenly declining into the conventional. His ballets which contain big *ensembles* are few. The most successful certainly is *Suite en Blanc* to the music of Lalo (revived for the Ballet de Monte Carlo under the name of *Noir et Blanc*). Here Lifar uses the rich vocabulary of classical dance in *pas de deux*, *pas de trois*, *pas de quatre*, *variations* and entrances of *ensembles*. The ballet is fresh and dynamic, particularly in its very first version, for which its interpreters were perfectly chosen. In *Les Mirages*, where the groups are fairly important, they still have only a decorative role.'[1]

Lifar became a creative force in French ballet soon after Diaghilev's death by virtue of his enormous output and energy, his dominance of the hierarchy of the Paris Opéra, his reforms and his theories. These theories were outlined in *Le Manifeste du chorégraphe* and executed to some extent in the ballet *Icare*, both produced in 1935.

[1] Irène Lidova, 'Serge Lifar, the choreographer' (*Foyer*, London, Autumn, 1951—trans. Edmée Wood).

Icare has a certain significance for choreography. In it the choreo-grapher sought to free himself from musical control by imposing his own rhythms on the musicians in accordance with the movements and steps he had composed. The significance, however, has been overrated. It did not emancipate ballet from music, as has been claimed. The idea of using only the sounds of percussion and similar instruments in the 'score' was so far from being new that it was a return to the earliest forms of musical accompaniment to dancing.

As a choreographer Lifar has little importance. His lasting influence lies in his introduction of the Russian school of classical ballet at the Paris Opéra and his extension of the French public for ballet. He raised the dignity of the dancer's calling in France. He was an authority and point of reference for many young French dancers and choreographers who grew up during and after the war. The most important of these was Roland Petit.

Guided not only by Lifar, but by Jean Cocteau and Boris Kochno (Plate XI (b)), artistic heirs of Diaghilev's last days, Petit has de-veloped a French style of choreography with qualities of taste and originality not found in Lifar's work.

Erratic, deficient in discipline, but exceptionally versatile, he is a master of narrative-drama and of the mood ballet. *Carmen* (1949), *Le Loup* (1953), *Cyrano de Bergerac* (1959), show the development of his narrative style from one-act to three-act works. *Les Forains* (1945) and *Le Jeune Homme et la Mort* (1946) show the dramatic overtones usually given to his ballets of mood.

With a poet's feeling for atmosphere in large and small things these ballets reflected post-war France in the fate of their characters. Not that the reflection was praiseworthy or flattering to France. All of them, except *Cyrano* and *Les Forains*, have an air of decadence. The bedroom scene in *Carmen* is pornographic, with a naturalism which is incompatible with art. *Le Loup* is pathological, unhealthy and revolting in its subject. *Le Jeune Homme et la Mort* is macabre, a poem to death. *Les Forains*, by contrast, sparkles, full of life and sympathy.

Possibly due to economic circumstances Petit has usually worked with small companies. This may be why his use of a *corps de ballet* has rarely been successful. *Cyrano* fails in this respect and in the mixture of styles through which the story is presented. It comes to life best in its *pas de deux* and *soli*. As in other Petit ballets these often include phrases of great invention with exciting acrobatic lifts.

Petit's work was first seen in London with Les Ballets des Champs-Élysées in 1946 and 1947, the company which had developed out of Irène Lidova's organisation of young talents in 1944. It made an enormous impression. Through these and subsequent visits of the Ballets de Paris, Petit influenced young English choreographers, notably Cranko and MacMillan. His influence flowed from the public approval of works such as *Les Forains*, *Le Jeune Homme et la Mort* and *Carmen* (Plate XXX (a)). The originality and economy of their décors, their strong sense of theatre and the remarkable stylisation of passions in their *pas de deux* illustrated Petit's gifts. They illustrated, too, the ability of his scenarists who were often Cocteau and Kochno themselves. France at least understands the nature of the ballet libretto and the poet's role in ballet.

Meanwhile other choreographers in France have explored some of the directions suggested by Lifar and Petit. Janine Charrat, neo-classical in style, is endowed with a vivid imagination and has a sure grasp of choreographic language. She showed strong dramatic ability in *Les Algues* (1953) and lyrical talent in *Concerto de Grieg* (1953), but she overloads her ballets emotionally so that they often become indigestible.

Jean Babilée, in many ways the most brilliant, sensitive and talented of French post-war male dancers, brings the same qualities of intellect and feeling to choreography which he brings to dancing. He is always interesting and promising, but never, like Peter Pan, quite grows up.

France is a land of promise for such young men. Since she is unique in the opportunities she offers young choreographers she is rich in the variety of styles they offer her. Whether they come from France or abroad, the great French tradition of artistic experiment provides someone somewhere somehow to dance their new choreography in public. There is no other country where this has happened so much. Thus the Russian-American George Skibine, the Yugoslavs Milko Sparemblek and Vassili Sulich, the Dane Harald Lander (now a French citizen) and the Frenchman Maurice Béjart have been encouraged to enrich the French scene.

George Skibine has translated the elegance of his own style of dancing into ballets for the Grand Ballet du Marquis de Cuevas, the Opéra, the Opéra-Comique and other companies. Less inclined than any of his French contemporaries to twist and distort the classical line, he has used the classical vocabulary, nevertheless, to express a wide range of feeling. He is a poet rather than a dramatist, using his poetic gifts to create small works of touching beauty like *Idylle* (1954) and Edgar Allan Poe's *Annabel Lee* (1951), or larger ballets inspired by famous poems like Pushkin's *Le Prisonnier du Caucase* (1951).

Outside the circle of the Opéra, Milko Sparemblek and Maurice Béjart, two choreographers of the newest generation, present, as it were, the choice before French choreography.

Milko Sparemblek is a Yugoslav dancer, resident in France, who has shown in *Quatuor* (1956) a fine imagery, a talent for flowing, plastic composition and a gift of mingling the classical vocabulary with other influences without destroying this vocabulary in the process. His themes are topical and intellectual, his technique firmly based on the traditional *danse d'école*.

Equally topical and intellectual, Maurice Béjart, the most dynamic of the latest generation of French choreographers, has taken the movement initiated by Nijinsky to its logical conclusion. Where Nijinsky, Nijinska and those who have followed them have bent, battered and twisted the classic line into new shapes and angles, Béjart has broken it. In his hands the classic line lies fractured, all but unrecognisable. Just as the *musique concrète* he uses dismembers sound and dissolves the laws of musical composition, so his movements destroy the classical harmony of the human body and presents, it seems, distorted limbs in the service of themes which reflect the confused philosophies of post-war Europe. In sum these themes elevate pessimism to an ideal. Death and psychological complexes become almost a natural state.

It appears that Béjart is trying to build a new choreographic language and a new relationship between sound and movement. The instrument of this language, the human body, is required to wear a minimum of decoration so that it is expressive by itself alone. It is required to learn a new discipline of movement, laid upon the classical foundation, but broken and rearranged in a way which no other French choreographer has attempted.

The relationship between sound and image is developed with the help of *musique concrète*. The image Béjart creates in choreography is never a realistic image nor are the sounds of *musique concrète* exactly realistic sounds. Both are approximations of reality. By setting the two in juxtaposition, like a piece of film montage, a new sound-image is created distinct from either the sound or the image. A new quality is realised in both, when put together, which raises a new emotional response in the audience. If, to express this idea in its simplest form, there is a sound of breaking glass and a dancer clutches her heart the resulting sound-image of the two together is a strongly poetical impression of anguish.

Béjart is a choreographer with a wider vision than most of his young contemporaries. His version of Stravinsky's *Le Sacre du Printemps*, has enormous theatrical power and shows a remarkable gift for orchestrating movement. In *Orphée*, ideas of *musique concrète* and *chorégraphie concrète* have full play. These works suggest that the new language for which he is searching will be neither the classical language nor any of the expressionist idioms so far evolved. The French scene, indeed, poses the question whether classical choreography is to retain its world harmony and unity, or whether it is to split into a babel of forms bereft of a common language.

This fever for experiment is not new, nor peculiar to the choreography of post-war France. It was a feature of the last years of the Diaghilev Ballet in design and music almost more than in dance. Between the wars the theatrical experiments of painters like Picasso, Dérain, Miro, Roualt and Tchelitchev continued to enrich the theatre and distinguished ballet production. Since the war the original work of designers such as Clavé, Wakhevitch and Daydé has influenced ballet decoration far outside Paris.

Throughout the century the experimental approach of French composers has extended musical technique in many directions, even if the journey has led sometimes to the desert.

Satie and Les Six with their 'ideals of simplicity, sobriety and linear workmanship';[1] Guy Bernard mingling music and sound effects to recreate the mad world of *Les Algues*; Pierre Schaeffer and Pierre Henry collaborating with Béjart to reflect *musique concrète* in *chorégraphie concrète*—such men have used to the full new technical methods to enlarge the scope of ballet music. The pity is that, for all this experiment, the range of French choreographic idiom, themes and achievement has not in this century matched the achievement of French music and, especially, French stage design.

(ii) Scandinavia and Central Europe

Harald Lander stands pre-eminent among Danish choreographers. One of his country's foremost artists, he, and the great teacher Vera

[1] Martin Cooper, *French Music*, p. 185 (Oxford University Press, 1951).

Volkova, have carried the Danish School into the twentieth century from the ways in which it lived since the death of Bournonville. It is Denmark's loss that Lander should have become a French citizen and work outside Denmark.

He was appointed Royal Ballet Master in Copenhagen in 1932. This post carries the triple responsibility of teacher, choreographer and principal dancer. From that year until 1951, when circumstances forced his resignation, Lander built the Royal Danish Ballet into the company it is today. Firmly founding his work on the traditions and repertoire of Bournonville he added to this the reforming ideas of Fokine, under whom he studied during the twenties. He realised, too, the need to introduce Russian methods of teaching so that the dancers could undertake not only the works of Fokine, Balanchine and the Petipa classics, but the demanding choreography which he himself devised in about thirty original ballets during these years.

In style and theme his choreography is linked with Bournonville, while its technical level reflects the advances made under Fokine and other Russians. His first ballets used folk themes from different sources. Then, as the technique of his dancers improved, he turned to larger works, using internationally known composers. Finally, under the stress of the German occupation he returned to national themes and music, producing, as the war ended, the shining splendour of *Étude* (1945) which showed that Danish choreography had caught up with its classical brothers in Western Europe and America.

Étude[1] (Plate XXIX (a)), on the one hand, and *Qarrtsiluni* (1942) (Plate XXIX (b)), on the other, presented the two faces of Danish choreography. Both used richly orchestrated scores by the Danish composer Knudåge Riisager.

Étude shows the full development of the Danish style in a plotless ballet of classical dancing based on classroom exercises. Two qualities stand out. The whole ballet, from the opening scenes at the barre to the virtuoso finale, has remarkable musicality. This is one of Lander's most valuable assets as a choreographer. The other quality is his exploitation of technical virtuosity. If we compare *Étude* with *Konservatoriet* we see how alien a quality this is in the Bournonville School. *Étude* exploits female virtuosity in the passages for the leading ballerina and sets it in competition with male virtuosity. It makes virtuosity the climax and principal quality of the ballet. This is done with sensitivity and great good taste. Nevertheless it marks a depar-

[1] Titled *Études* outside Denmark.

ture from the Bournonville tradition, which is necessary if the Danish School is to face the challenge of twentieth-century choreography.

Qarrtsiluni is a character ballet with the epic qualities of Nijinsky's *Le Sacre du Printemps*. Set in Greenland, its theme is the sun's return to the Eskimo after winter darkness. It translates musical rhythm into dance rhythm through the counterpoint of a single soloist against the massed *corps de ballet*. Fokine, Nijinsky and Massine might all claim to find themselves reflected in *Qarrtsiluni* just as Balanchine might claim a reflection in *Étude*. Chiefly, however, the two ballets stand as the high points of twentieth-century Danish choreography. When Lander left Copenhagen and was appointed to the staff of the Paris Opéra he brought these and other examples of his work into the French repertoire. The School of Vestris returned to Paris in a Danish form.

No other choreographer of international reputation has yet emerged from the Danish School. Indeed, few other names in Scandinavia and central Europe can claim international reputations in classical ballet, except Aurel Milloss in Italy and Germany, and Birgit Cullberg and Ivo Kramer in Sweden.

All three combine central European styles of dance with the classical *danse d'école*. Milloss has been the principal choreographer of Italy for several decades with work almost equally well known in Germany. His idiom emphasises the psychological and emotional elements in his themes through flowing plastic movements. These are full of gentle poses and sudden twists and turns for women but fail sometimes to exploit all the technical resources of a classically trained ballerina. Male dancers benefit from his effective understanding of male line which appears in many choreographic patterns. Milloss often lets this line flow strong and unbroken from the fingers of a raised arm, down the side of the body, and out into space through the raised thigh and foot.

Outside Germany and Italy his choreography has been seen in *Le Portrait de Don Quichotte* for Les Ballets des Champs-Élysées (1947) and in *Coup de Feu* for the Grand Ballet du Marquis de Cuevas (1952). *Le Portrait de Don Quichotte*, in particular, has been revived several times since, most recently in Cologne. It formed part of the repertoire also in São Paulo, Brazil, where Milloss was *maître de ballet* from 1953-1954.

The strongest inspiration in Ivo Kramer's idiom comes from Kurt Jooss. Kramer is less classically influenced than Milloss or Cullberg and makes great use of mime, being himself outstanding as a mimetic performer. But unlike Jooss, Kramer's work has been created on companies whose first allegiance is to the *danse d'école*, principally the Royal Swedish Ballet and the Norwegian Ballet. *The Prodigal Son*, which he produced in 1957, is one of the first truly Swedish ballets likely to live in the repertoire. In music, décor, theme and choreography its style is completely Swedish, completely expressive of Swedish national temperament.

The best known creator of Swedish ballets, however, is Birgit Cullberg. Her *Miss Julie*, even more than *The Prodigal Son*, may become a Scandinavian classic. It is now in the repertoire of American Ballet Theatre and the Royal Danish Ballet as well as the Royal Swedish Ballet. *The Moon Reindeer*, too, is a ballet of Scandinavian significance. Drawing its theme from Lapp legend, it was created in Copenhagen before being reproduced in Stockholm and America.

Today, Cullberg is the only Scandinavian choreographer besides Lander whose work has been seen in America. She has created new choreography there and introduced several of her Swedish ballets, including her dramatic and striking *Medea*. Yet these ballets still achieve their greatest effect when performed by Scandinavians. Equally, the Scandinavian dancers Elsa-Marianne von Rosen, Mariane Orlando, Erik Bruhn and Caj Selling have had some of their principal successes in her choreography. Cullberg places a particular emphasis on dramatic themes, taking great trouble to evolve the plot before creating choreography. Where Milloss is a philosopher, and Kramer a poet, she is a dramatist with special talent for exploiting dramatic conflicts through strong characterisation. Although she lacks a wide vocabulary in the *danse d'école*, Cullberg admires this school and has turned more and more towards it in her recent choreography. Like Kramer, the basis of her idiom remains her original Jooss vocabulary, but she has expressed this vocabulary always through classically trained dancers. The first success from this combination came with Elsa-Marianne von Rosen, the creator of Miss Julie.

Undoubtedly, Kurt Jooss personifies Germany's contribution to choreography in the present century. He is an expressionist choreographer whose masterpiece is *The Green Table*, who has never worked with a classical ballet company, but who exerted a strong influence over many choreographers of the classical *danse d'école* through his Ballets Jooss in Germany and England during the thirties and early forties.

After the First World War this *danse d'école* virtually disappeared from the German theatre. It was replaced by the expressionist choreography of Jooss, Mary Wigman, Harald Kreutzberg and others. Since the Second World War a reverse trend has been apparent. Opera house after opera house has turned to the *danse d'école*. Germany, East and West, is now a land of opportunity for classical choreographers. It is too early for many new names to have arisen, although Stuttgart has given John Cranko opportunities he could not find in Britain.

(iii) The Soviet Union

The arrival of the Bolshoi Ballet in London in October, 1956, opened a new chapter in the relations between Soviet ballet and the ballet of the West. Henceforth Western choreographers are likely to feel more and more the influence of Soviet choreographic thought in a process which is two-way. Choreography in the Soviet Union, no less than in America and Western Europe, will be enriched by the exchange of ideas.

What is this Soviet ballet which has grown up with such vigour in the last thirty years? It is much more than the Bolshoi in Moscow and the Kirov in Leningrad. It embraces a vast number of teachers, choreographers and dancers in ballet companies spread over all the nationalities of the Soviet Union. It speaks with Georgian accents in the Caucasus and the accents of many other peoples in the far north and east.

The Bolshoi and the Kirov are the centres of this world. But the Soviet dance world, already great, is constantly growing. Therefore the demand for teachers and choreographers is growing. We have to understand this problem of size before we can understand properly the Soviet choreographic scene.

Choreographers spring naturally from the great companies at the Bolshoi and Kirov Theatres. There is also the choreographic faculty of the State Institute of Theatrical Art (G.I.T.I.S.) in Moscow. The Dean is Anatole Shatin, a pupil of Gorsky. Other leading professors on the faculty are Leonid Lavrovsky and Rostislav Zakharov. Its training is theoretical and practical, including a general study of aesthetics, and the history and theory of the fine arts, music, theatre and ballet.

The war seriously disrupted plans already laid for the development of this training. After the war, when more than thirty new ballet companies and schools were formed to serve new theatres in the Soviet republics, the need for some higher college to train choreographers and ballet-masters became even more urgent. The choreographic faculty of G.I.T.I.S. was opened in 1946 to satisfy this need.

The first task was to train artistic directors for the new theatres, people who could provide artistic and administrative leadership without necessarily being expert choreographers or teachers. At the same time the faculty began the longer term task of developing a course for choreographers and teachers. Nowadays, candidates for its five-year course must have graduated from full ballet school and have had three years' practical experience in a ballet theatre or folk dance company. The course itself is described fully at Appendix VIII A.

In Leningrad choreographic advice is given principally by Feodor Lopukhov, brother of the Diaghilev ballerina, Lydia Lopukhova. He is an honoured figure in Soviet choreography, the creator of some fifty ballets, and one of the most powerful influences upon the latest generation of choreographers and dancers. Born in October, 1886, Lopukhov graduated at Leningrad in 1905, dancing Acis in Fokine's *Acis and Galatea* at his graduation performance. Between 1909 and 1911 he undertook many private engagements in France and America with his sister, Lydia, and with Alexander Volinin, but he never danced for Diaghilev.

Now officially retired, his opinions are much sought by young choreographers whose inspiration he remains. There is no doubt that he, in particular, is responsible for much of what the West regards as acrobatic in Soviet choreography. From the early 1920s he worked intensively on difficult lifts and gymnastic movements evolving also very advanced ideas on training. He was a close collaborator with Vaganova, creating ever more difficult choreography to challenge the dancers she produced. His modernist experiments and those of his contemporary, 'Kasyan Goleizovsky, the outstanding, daring ballet master',[1] were an important influence on the young Balanchine before he left the Soviet Union to join Diaghilev.

None of Lopukhov's nor Goleisovsky's ballets, and very few other Soviet ballets, have been presented in the West. Lavrovsky's *Romeo and Juliet* (Plate XXVIII (a)), Zakharov's *The Fountain of Bakchisharai*,

[1] Yuri Faier, 'Notes of a Ballet Conductor', *Sovetskaya Muzyka*, No. 10, 1960. Reproduced *Anglo-Soviet Journal*, London, Summer, 1961, p. 14.

Grigorovitch's *The Stone Flower* (Plate XXVIII (b)), Belsky's *Shosta-kovitch Seventh Symphony*, Bourmeister's *Swan Lake* and *The Snow Maiden* and a few films are the extent of our knowledge of full-length ballets. Apart from these there have been miniatures like Jacobson's *Gossiping Women* and *The Snow Maiden*, and a few extracts from ballets like Vainonen's *The Nutcracker* and Fenster's *Taras Bulba*.

The early work which Lopukhov and Goleizovsky produced in the 1920s inclined towards abstraction with little literary or political content. Hence it was often frowned upon, and very few of their ballets from this period survived. There seems now to be a reawakening of interest in what they were trying to do. A programme of miniatures by Goleizovsky, for instance, roused enormous enthusiasm when presented one evening in Moscow in 1962. None of them told any kind of story and nearly all of them included a great deal of *pas de deux* in which the dancers crawled round each other in strange, unclassical positions. The choreography gave little actual dancing to the men who mostly provided support, often performing marvellous lifts.

Following the experiments of the 1920s came a period of dance drama with an emphasis upon ballets of political or literary content in which the influence of Stanislavsky was strong. Many of the ballets of this period are as forgotten as the ballets of the earlier period but it was at this time that the first generation of Soviet choreographers became established. The principal names are Lavrovsky, Zakharov, Bourmeister, Vainonen, Fenster and Jacobson.

Most of these never graduated from the ballet schools of Moscow nor Leningrad but came from the world of folk dance or from theatre institutions. They were producers first and dancers second, a bias which encouraged the trend towards dance-drama. Both Zakharov and Bourmeister, for instance, acquired their dance training after maturity. Even Lavrovsky, who passed through the Leningrad school, was never a good performer. Among the second generation of choreographers now coming forward Grigorovitch and Belsky have shown important talent and Changa and Dodishkilvani have done interesting work. The first two are products of Leningrad, the second two graduates from G.I.T.I.S.

From what we have seen, or learnt from Soviet sources, four developments seem to us outstanding in Soviet choreography. First, the fusion of the Leningrad and Moscow traditions of classical ballet;

second, the development of the choreographer's human material as a result of Vaganova's teaching and Lopukhov's choreography; third, the emphasis on content; fourth, the evolution of the *genre* of dance-drama, strongly influenced by the dramatic teachings of Stanislavsky.

In the past the St. Petersburg and Moscow Schools had distinct styles. The St. Petersburg-Leningrad style was the more aristocratic of the two. More emphasis was laid on classical purity, less on qualities of acting and character. Moscow placed the emphasis on demi-character and character ballet, with vivid characterisation and usually a greater realism in acting. Under the Empire, St. Petersburg was generally held to be the most influential company. Since Moscow became the Soviet capital this tendency has been reversed. Many of Leningrad's leading dancers, including Ulanova, Semyonova and Yermolaiev, and choreographers like Lavrovsky and Zakharov, have gone to Moscow. Yet the school of choreographic thought in Leningrad still exerts a considerable influence. It remains a kind of choreographic laboratory where experiments can be made before being passed on to Moscow and other stages. Differences in style can be discerned still in dancers from the two schools but a fusion of the best from each is certainly one reason for the enormous success of the Bolshoi Company wherever it has been seen abroad.

One of the main architects of this Soviet School was Agrippina Vaganova. Trained in St. Petersburg, she graduated into the company in 1897, became a ballerina in 1915 and retired in 1917. From 1919, when she began to teach at Leningrad, her methods made her one of the greatest teachers of this century. She was also a vital link between the Imperial Ballet which trained her and the new Soviet ballet whose finest artists were her pupils.

A notable choreographer as well as a remarkable teacher, Vaganova combined both qualities in her theory 'dancing out of the body'. This profoundly influenced the development of classical technique in the Soviet Union, emphasising, in particular, the dance rather than technical qualities of a step or movement. The methods she used in her training of female dancers (often methods present in great teaching of the past) became the basis of training in the Soviet School and also influenced the training of men.

The effect of these methods has been to develop the plasticity of the upper body and to release the personality of dancers. To understand the importance of this we must recall Fokine's demand for expressiveness in the whole body. This required a new emphasis in training, a freeing of the *danse d'école*. It is this which Vaganova seems to have developed, while retaining the discipline of the *danse d'école*. We noticed it particularly in the looseness of the upper back and the arm movements of the Bolshoi dancers when they first appeared in London.

In choreography their greater plasticity, and the freeing of the dancer's personality which accompanies it, appears in several ways. There is the long and perfect line of the dancers' extension, particularly in *arabesque*, and the development of academic steps combined with *élan* which sometimes gives an exceptional excitement to their performance (in all kinds of *jetés*, for example). We have already spoken, too, of the lifts and feats in *pas de deux* which Lopukhov developed to complement Vaganova's teaching. All this adds to the resources a choreographer can command to express his themes. It makes it easier for the *danse d'école* to absorb the influences of national dance on which Soviet choreographers place such emphasis.

The way Soviet choreography has used this virtuosity in large-scale three-act dance-dramas has helped to translate the tradition of the full-length ballet from nineteenth-century forms into twentieth-century forms within the context of Soviet life. In so doing, Soviet choreography as a whole attaches great importance to the content of a work. This contrasts strongly with the general attitude in the West. Here, the emphasis is placed more often than not on the invention of elaborate movement rather than the communication of ideas. Soviet choreography has begun to admit only recently the validity of a plotless ballet of mood like Igor Belsky's *Shostakovitch Seventh Symphony*. For such ballets Soviet theory holds that the choreographer should follow the programme of the music, where this exists. Where the music has no programme the choreographer is free to attempt his own choreographic interpretation.

Following the traditions of Russian art, Soviet ballet themes are conceived often on an epic scale. Jacobson's *Spartacus* recalls the historical sweep of a Tolstoy novel as well as the spectacular qualities of a Viganò work, while his ballet, inspired by Mayakovsky's *The Bug*, ranges the entire history of the Soviet Union, from 1917 to the present day. This, incidentally, takes a fresh, enormously interesting form. Jacobson has called it a choreographic poster! It has little virtuoso dancing and resembles in some ways the living newspapers, or theatrical posters, presented dramatically in many countries during the late twenties and thirties.

One can see that Soviet choreography indulges particularly in the Broad Statement. This leads sometimes to a lack of subtlety in choreographic characterisation. Choreographic images are tied too much to traditional classical form. Until recently romantic *pas de deux* tended *always* to have classical steps; character dances to have national dance steps. It is rare for a whole ballet to be stylised, as *Dark Elegies* was, *pas de deux* and all.

Yet choreographers try hard to express contemporary life in themes and characters. Workers from factories and fields, soldiers, sailors, ordinary men and women, appear in their ballets as well as the allegorical figures of myth and fairy-tale. How rarely in the West do characters from contemporary life appear on the ballet stage.

The problem of adapting classical forms to contemporary life faces Soviet choreographers in a particularly acute form. This is not because of any demands made on them by Marxist theoreticians. It is because of life itself. Life in the Soviet Union has been changed so quickly and in such a degree that the solution of the problem is bound to be difficult and slow. No-one would suggest that even the most successful choreographer has done more than reach out to the opportunities before him. Yet if his problem is more intense it is still the same as that faced by choreographers everywhere. And the Scylla and Charybdis of his art are the same. He must avoid naturalism on the one hand and aesthetic formalism on the other.

In seeking his solution the Soviet choreographer draws on the same four sources of movement as the Western choreographer. The *danse d'école*, national dance forms, painting and sculpture and movements from real life ; these compose his vocabulary. The dominant element appears to be the basic form of the *danse d'école* in its present Soviet development. The most important influence after this flows from the movements and patterns of the Soviet Union's rich store of national dancing. To this gold-mine Soviet choreographers turn to enlarge the range and artistic expression of their classical vocabulary. They have done so with good effect. The national dancing of the Moiseyev and other ensembles, or the gypsy dances in *The Stone Flower*, are more brilliant than anything Fokine or Massine were able to achieve with the material at their disposal. By contrast, we in the West have mingled the classical vocabulary with jazz and modern dance elements in order to match the development of our music.

In the long run, of course, a choreographer's opportunities to develop his vocabulary are conditioned by the skill and training of his human material, almost as much as by his own invention. Hence the emergence of Soviet dancers of exceptional technical strength, such as the young Vasiliev, Michel Lavrovsky (son of the choreographer), Besmertnova and Sorokina, all recent graduates, is likely to encourage choreographers to place greater emphasis on dance as opposed to dance-drama so as to use their great gifts.

Music has exercised an even greater influence over Soviet choreography than it has exercised over choreography in the West. Soviet ballet gives to music an importance which, regrettably, is not always accorded it by Western dancers. Whereas in the West many dancers only dance *to* the music, in Soviet ballet one *dances* the music, and is expected always to do so. Not that musical development has been easier than choreographic development. Prokofiev and, later, Shostakovitch have been the pioneers. Prokofiev's score for *Romeo and Juliet* in 1940 broke completely with the long-lived formulae of musical set pieces for dances in ballets and shocked, in so doing, a large part of the Moscow dance world.

'The day came', wrote Yuri Faier, 'when Prokofiev brought the score of *Romeo and Juliet* to the Bolshoi. Nearly every member of the ballet company gathered in the dark-red Beethoven hall. Prokofiev was pale but outwardly calm. Few could observe his emotion. As he played, the number of his listeners dwindled. Most of them did not understand Prokofiev's music. They said it was unthinkable to dance to such music, that nothing like it had ever been known in ballet previously, and could never be. The theatre turned down *Romeo and Juliet*.'[1]

Subsequently it was the Kirov, Leningrad, not the Bolshoi, which created *Romeo and Juliet* on 11th January, 1940. In fact, the ideas in the score were not entirely new. The composer's *Cinderella* had already pointed the way. *Cinderella*, however, was not produced as a ballet until 1945. *The Stone Flower* continued the process although this is not so impressive a score.

Prokofiev's long development of musical passages, particularly in *Romeo and Juliet*, demanded a similar long development of choreographic passages. Old habits of set piece *divertissements* had to be rejected, although one finds them still in Khachaturian's *Spartacus*.

[1] Yuri Faier, 'Notes of a Ballet Conductor', *Sovetskaya Muzyka*, No. 10, 1960. Reproduced *Anglo-Soviet Journal*, London, Summer, 1961, p. 13.

Therefore the issues posed by Prokofiev were fundamental to the nature of Soviet choreography. He challenged not only choreographic form but the established relationship of music and dance. Is music merely a rhythmic accompaniment to dance, as choreographers too often seemed to regard it, or is it an integral part of dance, the foundation of choreography? Prokofiev's *Romeo and Juliet* showed that it was inseparable from the development of the action on stage. Music and dance are indivisible.

So deep is the dramatic content in *Romeo and Juliet*, so finely woven and counterpointed are the four main themes of the principal characters, that dancers and choreographer found themselves facing new dramatic problems.

The dancers were able to solve these problems because the schooling of their talent embraced far more than a development of technique. Musically, the Soviet dancer is much better trained than his Western counterpart. Because he has to learn to play and read music during his school days he has a better ear and understanding.

Similarly, he has more training as an actor and interpretative artist, largely because of the influence of Stanislavsky's ideas on all theatre training in the Soviet Union and because of the emphasis which Soviet choreography places on the content of a work. But in any case, the Soviet dancer is not as divorced from Fokine's reforms as many Western authorities believe. Fokine produced fifteen ballets in Russia, including all but two of his Diaghilev successes. The two missing ballets are *L'Oiseau de Feu* and *Coq d'Or*. Following Fokine, and long before *Romeo and Juliet*, the Soviet dancer began to develop acting through dancing and characterisation in depth. For example, *The Fountain of Bakhchisarai*, created in 1934, is an infinitely more demanding choreographic drama than *Schéhérazade*, with which it is often compared.

The Soviet actor-dancer, in fact, is a product of the 1930s. At that time the emphasis upon literary and political themes combined with the influence of Stanislavsky's methods to produce both the artists and the works of art through which they could express themselves. *Romeo and Juliet* is the highest expression of the choreography of this period just as Ulanova is its greatest exponent. Difficult though the problems were with which Lavrovsky and Prokofiev faced their dancers the dancers were well prepared for the encounter.

Lavrovsky's conception of dance-drama in *Romeo and Juliet* is more complete than anything seen up to that time in the West. Such a conception, of course, develops the ideas of Noverre, Viganò and Fokine in contemporary form. His published notes on *Romeo and Juliet* (1940) even seem to echo Fokine: 'The depths of passion and ideas, the intensity of feeling conveyed by the protagonists of Shakespeare's tragedy, demand the fusion of Dance with Mime. In Ballet, words are absent and the effect of every phrase of mime must correspond with the spoken language of the stage characters.

'Mime should never descend to trivial, commonplace, imitative gestures, but become a genuine theatrical performance in which characters, emotions, and passions are expressed by the movements of the body, instead of by the varied intonations of the voice. Ballet is a choreographic play in which the dancing must arise naturally from the mimed action, or the mimed action be the logical sequence of the dancing.'[1] As far as we can see most of the younger Soviet choreographers now adopt this view as their starting-point.

The effectiveness of such choreographic ideas, when they have been realised on stage, suggests that the ideas of dance-drama will occupy the ballet world more and more in future. Dance-drama, of course, has no fixed rules. It has room for many creative styles, forms and individualities, depending on talent and craftsmanship while recognising that art without romance and dreams is grey and drab. It must be balanced, too, with the *divertissements*, spectacles and lighter works which have always played their part in ballet repertoires.

But as a choreographic form the dance-drama, or ballet-play, seems able to reach popular post-war audiences more powerfully than other forms. This, therefore, may be the *genre* appropriate to our age, as the romantic ballet was to Paris in the 1840s and the classical ballet was to St. Petersburg in the 1880s. The full development of this *genre* will need new kinds of choreography, lighting, design, music, even theatres, with a new relationship between the dancer-actor and his audience.

It will need, for certain, bolder, better constructed themes. Works of art, after all, mean very little if they do not 'have a central unifying dilemma which springs from the heart, from being alive'.[2] In choreography, as in all art, the theme is fundamental.

[1] L. Lavrovsky, quoted by Cyril Beaumont in *Supplement to the Complete Book of Ballets*, pp. 190-191 (Beaumont, London, 1942).
[2] John Cranko interviewed in *Monitor* by Huw Wheldon, B.B.C. Television, 24th April, 1960.

PART III

THE CHOREOGRAPHER'S THEMES

CHAPTER X

THE AUTHOR–CHOREOGRAPHER AND OTHERS

THE author is the person who conceives the idea of the ballet. He may be the choreographer. He may be someone else. Whoever he is he should be associated with every phase of choreographic creation. Principally, though, he is concerned with the earliest phases: first, the conception of the idea and its composition into a written scenario; second, the working out of a choreographic plan, or libretto, with the choreographer and the other collaborators.

In this chapter we talk about the author. In the next chapter we discuss the phases of creation with which he is most concerned. Both chapters indicate points of craft but are not intended to lay down rules or fix methods of creation. Such a thing would be impossible, even if it were desirable.

There are, for example, no rules to define the pedigree of a ballet author, but there are three groups of people among whom he may be found. He may be a choreographer. He may be one of those who collaborate with choreographers—a composer, designer, or even a dancer. He may be a writer, or a poet, like the earliest authors.

History has many examples of the work of each of these groups. In recent years Gavin Gordon wrote the scenario and composed the music for *The Rake's Progress* (1935) before Ninette de Valois ever became the ballet's choreographer. Hugh Stevenson wrote the scenario and created the designs for *The Planets* (1934) before Madame Rambert commissioned Antony Tudor to do the choreography. This became Tudor's first lasting success with her company. Milko Sparemblek, a principal dancer, was the author of *L'Échelle* (1958), which Dick Sanders choreographed for Milorad Miskovitch's Ballets des Étoiles de Paris.

Each group has advantages and disadvantages. Scenarios by musicians often emphasise the musical element of a ballet at the expense of the other collaborating arts so that the impact of design and dancing suffers. Nevertheless, composers from Lully till today have made important contributions to balletic authorship. Stravinsky played a major role in this department during the first decade of the

Diaghilev ballet. British ballet, especially the early work of Frederick Ashton, owes an incalculable debt to the authorship of Constant Lambert, composer, writer and first musical director of the Sadler's Wells Ballet.

Designers naturally produce visual ideas which have choreographic possibilities. Noverre acknowledged this quality by emphasising the link between ballet and painting. To him ballet was essentially a series of *tableaux vivants*, 'a series of pictures connected one with the other by the plot which provides the theme of the ballet'.[1]

Of course, a designer's ideas may be too static, too much a series of pictures. But, Bakst and Benois in Diaghilev's time, Hugh Stevenson and Sophie Fedorovitch in our own time, have created movement, not only through the shapes of their designs, but through scenarios of their devising. British ballet, indeed, is deeply in the debt of British painting, past as well as present. 'The narrative element that is so often to be found here', said Dame Ninette de Valois, acknowledging the debt, 'has resulted in our school of painting acting as a strong national inspiration for our ballets.'[2] (Plate X.)

Choreographers are most likely to produce ideas suitable for interpretation through movement. These ideas may be their own invention, like Fokine's scenario for *Le Carnaval*. Or they may be adapted from another medium, from literature, say, or painting, in the way that Ninette de Valois drew her inspiration for *The Gods go A-Begging* from Watteau's pictures.

Choreographers think naturally in terms of movement. Hence they began to assume a principal part in balletic authorship as soon as the *ballet d'action* was born out of the separation of ballet and opera. Weaver and Noverre, for example, seem to have prepared most of their own scenarios (Appendix I). Today, so general has this practice become in Britain and America that choreographers almost always bear the double burden of scenario and choreography.

The value of this is questionable. The practice rejects, in effect, the full assistance of trained writers, especially poets, in ballet. Yet literature underlies ballet and is really its fourth estate. Choreographic talent confers no automatic talent in scenario composition, even if some successful ballet authors have been choreographers with an

[1] Noverre, *op. cit.* p. 9.
[2] Speech to the Royal Society of Arts, 29th May, 1957, reproduced in *The Ballet in Britain* (O.U.P., 1962).

ability to translate poetic ideas into well-constructed scenarios. Such choreographers are rare. Too often, the majority are inclined to emphasise their own choreographic contribution at the expense of others, or to regard scenario and content as secondary to choreographic movement. A few go further still. Instead of considering ballet from the point of view of life they consider life from the point of view of ballet. Dancers and audiences have suffered often from such an attitude. On each occasion a part of the audience on which ballet depends for survival has been lost. Art and economics are alike defeated.

Choreographers, then, *may* be good ballet authors. We show some examples of their work at Appendices I–III. So, too, may professional writers and poets, given the chance. Already, such writers hold an honourable place in the history of ballet. Petipa was not too proud to use the scenario of Begitchev and Geltser for *Swan Lake*, nor to acknowledge his indebtedness to Vernoy de Saint-Georges, the French scenarist. Of the five major nineteenth-century ballets which have survived in the repertoires of Western Europe, three—*Giselle*, *Coppélia* and *Swan Lake*—are by literary authors working alone or in collaboration with the choreographers. The remaining two—*The Sleeping Beauty* and *The Nutcracker*—have scenarios whose precise authorship is uncertain. They are less well constructed than the scenarios of the other three ballets by professional writers.

Diaghilev gave equal place to the writer among his collaborating artists. The scenario of *Le Spectre de la Rose* was by the poet, Vaudoyer, after a poem by Théophile Gautier. Nijinska's *Le Train Bleu* was by Cocteau. Massine's *Le Tricorne*, his most famous ballet, was by Martínez Sierra, after Alarcón. Other early Massine ballets were by Cocteau and Boris Kochno, a name which arises also as the author of many early Balanchine ballets.

Today, it is a recognised practice in France and the Soviet Union to employ professional scenarists, although choreographers in the Soviet Union complain that not enough writers come forward for this work. Writers in France, on the other hand, have originated almost all the most memorable ballets created there since the war. Among the ballets of Roland Petit *Les Forains* is by Boris Kochno, *Le Rendez-Vous* by Jacques Prévert, *Le Jeune Homme et la Mort* by Jean Cocteau, *Les Demoiselles de la Nuit* by Jean Anouilh, and *Le Loup* by Anouilh and Georges Neveux. *Carmen*, the only exception, closely follows the original operatic scenario by Meilhac and Halévy. During the same period John Taras' *Piège de Lumière* is by Philippe Heriat; Janine Charrat's *Les Algues* is by Louis-Bertrand Castelli; and Georges Skibine's *Idylle* is by Alwyn Camble, a writer and designer. *Prométhée*, which first firmly placed Maurice Béjart upon the choreographic map, was conceived by the poet, Pierre Rhallys, in a scenario reproduced at Appendix III B.

Writers, therefore, have a strong claim for consideration as likely ballet authors. Certainly there is no justification (other than unconvincing economic reasons) for them to be ignored in Britain and America.

Ballet needs the skill in plot and denouement which writers bring to their work. It needs the link with contemporary literature of which it has been starved since it took its first steps in the Anglo-Saxon countries. Above all, it needs to unite, as Noverre dreamed, 'the poet's genius and the painter's genius; the one to conceive the other to execute', for 'ballet is brother to poetry'.[1]

Because poetry is brother to ballet, poets have qualities which can be of special value in creating ballet scenarios. Given a knowledge of ballet and an understanding of subjects suitable for ballet, poets have the attributes of ideal scenarists. They speak in rhythms like musicians, choreographers and dancers; they speak in images and create metaphors in the manner of choreography; they are particularly concerned, as ballet is, with the world of imagination. In the imagery and way of thought which are the poet's special gift they have the means to realise this world even, sometimes, without a knowledge of choreographic needs. Their talent can create the themes which others can translate into scenarios and libretti. 'While the contribution of a theme cannot be classified as a composition, the implanting of the first seed of an idea is at times the foundation for success of the entire structure of a ballet.'[2] He is a wise choreographer who numbers writers and poets among his friends.

But writers and poets will not become scenarists without encouragement and guidance from the world of ballet. They must be trained to ballet like composers, designers and choreographers. They must have flair for the work, a technique which depends on visual images, not literary explanation, and a detailed knowledge of all the choreographic problems outlined in the next chapter. Choreographers,

[1] Noverre, *op. cit.* p. 53.
[2] Fokine and Chujoy, *Fokine, Memoirs of a Ballet Master*, p. 180 (Little, Brown & Company, Boston, 1961).

composers and designers, of course, may have as much, or more, flair in selecting subjects. They may have more detailed choreographic knowledge. But writers, having mastered the technique of the matter, add to these qualities their special ability in handling themes and embodying them in well-constructed scenarios. 'Yet I think the Author of the Piece not improper to be consulted,' said Weaver of the writers of his day, 'and excellent Hints may be taken from him, that may be of singular service.'[1]

Whoever he is a good ballet author is so rare, requiring so fine a talent, that he deserves a constant search, and careful training when found. More than this, he deserves a proper place in the world of ballet so that he ranks, in fact and on the programme, equal with the other collaborating artists. Being found, he should set to work always to realise the great principle of Belinsky, that in art, 'there is no beautiful form without beautiful content'.[2]

[1] John Weaver, *Essay towards an History of Dancing*, p. 166 (London, 1712).
[2] V. G. Belinsky, *Selected Philosophical Works* (Foreign Languages Publishing House, Moscow, 1956). Belinsky, 1811–1848, Russian realist critic, philosopher and historian.

CHAPTER XI

THE AUTHOR AT WORK

(i) CHOICE OF THEMES

'THIS art,' said Noverre, 'born of good taste, can become beautiful and varied to an infinite degree.'[1] No theme is inappropriate to ballet if it can be expressed visually through movement. But the theme of a ballet which hopes to live as a work of art must reflect a true and noble aspect of mankind.

The choice of theme is the most important single act in the art of choreography. Good themes have no rules to define them, except Belinsky's principle. Even apparently sordid themes can achieve 'beautiful content' through correct treatment. An example is Kenneth MacMillan's *The Burrow*. It examines the reactions of people in hiding. Its basic theme of fear is not in the least noble. Yet MacMillan treats it in such a way that the situation reveals nobility in the human character. Treatment is all important.

The author arranges the theme into a scenario. This will be realised in dance images on stage, through a libretto, or choreographic plan, prepared principally by the choreographer. The scenario, therefore, is the seed from which the ballet will grow if, as Blasis once decreed, it 'be chosen with taste and constructed with art'.[2]

Faults of scenario construction, or libretti which do not draw the collaborators closely enough together, often lead to the failure on stage of ballets with excellent themes. Ballets with superficial or ignoble themes sometimes succeed through being well constructed. There is even a school of thought which holds that weak themes and loose scenarios are in themselves no proof that a ballet will fail. The choreographer, this school argues, may make something of any material if he is sufficiently gifted. In fact, the number of times a skilful choreographer can turn an unpromising scenario into a good ballet is far fewer than the failures which flow from loose thinking and woolly construction at this first stage of choreography.

Themes may be dictated by historical circumstance. Ballet is often

[1] Noverre, *op. cit.* p. 11.   [2] Blasis, *op. cit.* p. 236.

summoned to celebrate great occasions because it is the theatre's highest form of poetry. A nation's principal choreographer becomes a kind of theatrical poet laureate.

Thus the betrothal of the Duc de Joyeuse to Marguerite de Lorraine in 1581 inspired the *Ballet Comique de la Reine*. Similarly, the coronation of Elizabeth II of England in 1953 imposed upon Frederick Ashton the theme which became *Homage to the Queen*. Between these two ceremonies lie countless other balletic *pièces d'occasion*.

Whether dictated by history, drawn from literature, or inspired by legend the theme of a ballet should reflect the observation of life. It will, in any case, be the product of outside experience however much it may seem to have arisen unconsciously within the author. A special experience, a conversation with a friend, or a piece of music will nourish some nascent idea until it flowers into what we call inspiration. Inspiration realises the theme by suggesting the form in which the theme can be expressed. *Petrouchka* was conceived roughly in this way, as we show at Appendix IV.

But the observation of life can be interpreted in choreography in many ways. To Frederick Ashton, choreography must express 'the choreographer's vision of experience as truthfully and beautifully as possible. In so far as it does this, it will express his most profound sense of values and thus be likely to concern itself with matters of more permanent significance than topical issues. He should deal with that which is spiritual and eternal rather than that which is material and temporary.'[1]

Other authors may find their deepest satisfaction in themes of material and topical significance, so long as these can be expressed in the ways of choreography. Unlike the cinema, television and some drama, choreography should *never* be naturalistic because of the stylised nature of its movements. It always remains 'brother to poetry', always a language of symbols.

Each age, in general, draws these symbols from a particular source. The eighteenth century used the characters of classical gods and goddesses in the mythological ballet; the nineteenth century turned to the mystical wilis and sylphs of romantic poetry. The twentieth century prefers folk tales or characters in real life situations and has added the mood and the abstract ballet to the traditional form of the narrative ballet. But when it takes real life situations, as it does in

[1] Sir Frederick Ashton, 'The Subject Matter of Ballet', *Ballet Annual*, *13*, p. 39 (Black, London, 1959).

The Rake's Progress, Miracle in the Gorbals and *Billy the Kid*, the twentieth century uses them in a symbolic manner. And when it steps beyond real life into fantasy it moves into a world in which ballet is supreme in the theatre, a world of poetry combined with symbolism in *Petrouchka* and *Job*, of almost pure poetry in *Les Sylphides* or of absolute symbolism in *Checkmate*.

This need of choreography to speak in symbols governs the choice and treatment of theme. If a theme cannot be expressed in movement it is useless to a choreographer. Every author, therefore, must have more than good ideas. He must understand perfectly the limitations of choreography. Since the medium is movement, he should be wary of static situations. As a general rule nothing should be attempted in ballet which can be achieved better in another art-form.

Why, then, was Robert Helpmann able to translate *Hamlet* into a successful ballet? Other choreographers had failed before. *Hamlet's* situations do not lend themselves to balletic treatment. The strength of the play, as in all Shakespeare's writing, lies in the beauty and rhythm of the words, particularly Hamlet's soliloquies. The plot has too many minor characters, is too complicated in detail and too particular to be used for ballet as Shakespeare used it for drama. Helpmann handled it successfully by developing a single idea in Hamlet's soliloquy, 'to be or not to be'—

> For in that sleep of death what dreams may come
> When we have shuffled off this mortal coil,
> Must give us pause . . .

The ballet begins as the dead Hamlet is carried off stage. Helpmann then shows some of the play's main incidents following quickly one on another, as they might have flashed through Hamlet's mind just before he died. At its end the ballet returns to the opening death scene. This is a rare example of the successful use of 'flash-back' in ballet.

So Helpmann succeeds in giving an impression of Hamlet, the Prince, although he cannot show choreographically all the Prince's nuances of character. At the same time he contrives a fast-moving plot, full of incident. Shakespeare's narrative becomes fantasy. Its incidents become symbols.

The author should not only conceive his theme in terms of movement according to the limitations of ballet, as Helpmann did. He must make sure that all the significant action can be realised in movements large enough to reach the back row of the gallery seats. It is no use hanging an important incident upon a wink or movements of the fingers. Ballets for cinema or television can do this because the camera can pick out details. Not so a ballet on stage.

The author should remember that even the smallest trait of character has to be represented by gesture or movement. So, because the audience can learn only from movements and gestures what kind of person a character is, the character must not be too complex nor too difficult to describe visually. And he must be established in the first few minutes after his entrance.

For this reason authors need to draw their characters boldly. Often, they will have to draw types of people. Colas in *La Fille Mal Gardée* is a typical ballet hero of the early nineteenth century, extrovert, young and handsome. His successors this century are the sailors in *Fancy Free*. Hagar, the neurotic sister in Antony Tudor's *Pillar of Fire*, is another twentieth-century type. By showing her jealousy of her successful younger sister and her scorn of the life of her older spinster sister Tudor conveys to the audience the reason for her neurosis. But Tudor could not have told the audience, even if it had been true and necessary to the plot, that Hagar was neurotic because at the age of three she saw her father hit her mother.

This introduces the problem of time, a rock upon which many scenarists and choreographers founder. Through costume and décor, time, period and place can often be established pictorially, but it is not possible to show, during a ballet, the lapse of many years—or even days—forward or backwards, except with great ingenuity or through an elaborate change of scenery as in *The Sleeping Beauty*. Generally a ballet must start at a particular point in time and work forward.

Many scenarists solve this problem by wrapping up their themes in fantasy or symbols and placing their ballets in the land of nowhere at any time at all. Thus Coralli's *Giselle* (see Appendix II A), Perrot's *La Esméralda* and Petipa's and Ivanov's *Swan Lake* (see Appendix II B) each presents the struggle of good and evil in its own way. But only *La Esméralda* is precisely placed in a definite historical period. It was a 'perfect model of ballet building', wrote *The Times* in 1844, after its première at Her Majesty's Theatre, London, with Carlotta Grisi in the name role. 'Never did we see those parts of a long story that might be dramatically effective selected and arranged with such skill as in this ballet. The catastrophe of the novel is altered. The incidents selected are greatly modified, but the tact with which five *tableaux* have been taken out of the romance, and combined into a neat pantomime of action, without a gap, deserves unqualified praise.'

The secret of *La Esméralda's* success, like the secret of Helpmann's *Hamlet*, was the simplicity of its scenario, based on a thorough understanding of all the limitations of the art. 'Situations', said Frederick Ashton, 'must be direct and fundamental and understood through plastic statement, which must be clear and portray the situations with clarity, truth and dramatic understanding.'[1]

(ii) CONSTRUCTION OF THEMES

There is no one way to translate a theme into choreography. That way is best which produces the best results in the circumstances of the moment. The outline which follows therefore provides only general guidance to the student author.

Scenarios should suggest how the ballet can be developed in choreographic, musical and visual terms. They should indicate which of the three contemporary forms of choreography will best express the theme, and in what period, if any, it is to be set. The author may use a *narrative* form, as Nuitter did with Saint-Léon in *Coppélia*, a *mood* form, as Tudor did in *Jardin aux Lilas*, or he may wish to *abstract* certain qualities of choreography so that these can be presented alone upon the stage. Fokine did this in *Les Sylphides*, which 'contains no plot whatsoever. It was the first abstract ballet.'[2]

One or other of these three forms should always dominate the ballet. Even if elements of other forms appear in certain scenes it should be made clear in the scenario whether the ballet is conceived primarily as a narrative, mood, or abstract work. Otherwise the collaborators will lack a clear understanding of the author's intention, and this lack of clarity will be communicated, ultimately, to the audience. In ballet there is no room for the make-what-you-can-of-it school of art. The ballet author who adopts this kind of obscurity will soon find each collaborator taking him at his word and going his own way, so that the ballet will fall apart.

What, then, are the characteristics of the three forms through which the author can express himself? The narrative ballet will tell

[1] Sir Frederick Ashton, 'The Subject Matter of Ballet', *Ballet Annual, 13*, p. 38 (Black, London, 1959).
[2] Fokine and Chujoy, *Fokine, Memoirs of a Ballet Master*, p. 131 (Boston, 1961).

its story best through characters distinctly drawn, and often named individually on the programme, like 'Dr. Coppelius' or 'Swanilda'. These characters should be vivid personalities, sharply focussed and presented in a story which brings the characters naturally into dramatic conflict one with another. The scenario should demand from its characters acting ability as well as dancing ability. It should be conceived, in other words, as dance-drama whether its inspiration is real life or a fairy-tale.

The mood ballet presents a particular mood and emotion rather than a story. It ranges from the gentleness of Le Spectre de la Rose to the psychological storms and neuroses popular today in much European and American art. Its problems of construction are more easily solved by poets than by novelists.

The scenarist who purposes a mood ballet proposes something which will come to life on stage, not through the interaction of character and incident as in a narrative, but through the representation of one part only of a human being, the emotions. It is as if the outer shell of personality had been removed to reveal what takes place within the heart and mind. Hence the characters of a mood ballet are less individual people than symbols of emotions. For this reason creators of mood ballets usually describe their characters in rather general terms, as types rather than individuals. Fokine's Le Spectre de la Rose has 'The Young Girl' and 'The Spirit of the Rose'. Tudor describes the characters of Jardin aux Lilas as 'Her Lover', 'The Man she must marry' and so on, Cranko's characters in The Shadow are called 'A Youth', 'His Romantic Love' and 'A Young Girl'. So, too, 'The Faded Beauty', 'The Rich Man', 'The Poor People' and others who represent the moods of MacMillan's Noctambules. (Appendix III c (ii).)

This is the particular approach and the peculiar distinction the scenarist must bear in mind when he works in the mood genre. This and the caution that the mood genre, by its nature, cannot be extended into three acts. Mood and abstract ballets are one-act forms only, even though their special qualities may be combined at certain times in a full-length narrative work. So the mood ballet and the abstract ballet can never be more than secondary forms in the mainstream of choreographic development. The three-act narrative ballet, like the three-act play, must bear the main burden of development from period to period.

Apart from this the rules of scenario construction apply to the

creation of mood as fully as they do to narrative. A suitable choreographic theme, clearly drawn characters within the *genre*, proper
climaxes and a good finale—all these are part of a task which is
singularly difficult and designed especially for poets.

The abstract ballet goes one step further. It peels away the emotions, as well as character, leaving only bodies with a technique of
dancing. Usually, the dancers have no description on the programme.
The principal roles in these ballets are used to reflect, like prisms,
heightened qualities of the ensemble, or individual technical qualities
of the dancer.

What does abstract ballet abstract? Mostly, one element of
choreography—the technique of dancing—from the narrative and
emotional context in which it has lived until now. Dancing becomes
a thing in itself; its movements stem only from the music as if all the
symbols on the musical stave had come to life on stage. Instead of
being a means of portraying character or evoking a mood, it
becomes the end product. No longer the servant of dancers, it is their
master.

There can be no scenario or libretto for such a *genre* in the formal
sense. Instead, the scenario itself is often an abstraction representing,
perhaps, a single idea unrelated to anything else, like the idea of
'meetings' in Frederick Ashton's *Les Rendezvous*. Or there may be
some emotional feeling which is undefined but inspires the dancing
and often derives from the music. 'I think', wrote Frederick Ashton,
'that ballets without librettos, popularly known as abstract ballets,
though appearing to convey nothing but the exercise of pure dancing,
should have a basic idea which is not necessarily apparent to the
public, or a personal fount of emotion from which the choreography
springs. Otherwise, in my opinion, a cold complexity emerges
which ceases to move an audience.'[1]

Not every choreographer who uses the abstract *genre* would limit
himself as Ashton does. Some choreographers, like Jerome Robbins
and Maurice Béjart, have abstracted dancing even from music so that
movement literally exists on its own. Their choreographic shapes
and patterns, created by dancers' bodies in silent ballets, are un-
embellished by scenery or music.

Yet it needs to be emphasised that an abstract ballet is abstract,
not because of the nature of its choreography, but because of the

[1] Sir Frederick Ashton, 'The Subject Matter of Ballet', *Ballet Annual*, *13*, p. 38
(Black, London, 1959).

conception behind it, and the manner in which this conception is realised. Often the realisation will show how narrow is the frontier between mood and abstraction. After all, a mood ballet is already half way to being abstract. This is particularly true of Balanchine's work. In *The Four Temperaments* the contrast of rhythm and type of movement produces a shadow of a story which is, in fact, an abstraction of four moods. Fokine's *Les Sylphides* also has elements of both forms. Hence some people attempt no distinction beyond grouping the two kinds together as 'plotless ballets'.

Whatever its form, then, the author's scenario should be clearly constructed with a strong central idea to hold it together and give everything motivation.

This idea should be developed through an introduction, development and finale. The introduction should state the theme, present the characters and place them in a situation which they have to resolve. The middle section should develop the theme and situation, exploring and deepening the conflicts between the characters, which the situation has created. The finale should provide the climax which resolves the situation and makes clear the author's intention.

All themes should be developed in this way. The scenario should provide for minor climaxes at the end of each scene, or act, to intensify the situation, as well as a major climax at the end of the ballet to resolve the conflicts. Situation and incidents, of course, must be able to be expressed visually, through the physical movements of dancers before an audience within an allotted span of time and within the three-dimensional framework of the proscenium, stage and backcloth.

The choreographic form of the conflict will be suggested by the theme itself. In abstract works, where dancers are disposed as bodies in space, the conflict may be no more than the contrast of strong and soft movements, *corps* and soloists in *Ballet Imperial*, or male and female in *Birthday Offering*.

In mood ballets, such as Andrée Howard's *La Fête Étrange*, the conflict will be emotional, represented in movements symbolising emotions, rather than through the actual creation of character. The people of mood ballets are themselves symbols of emotion. Thus in *La Fête Étrange*, bride, bridegroom and country boy are linked in clear conflict which is never directly expressed by any of them, but which ends in solitary grief for all three, having been visible as a whole only to the audience. Narrative ballets, on the other hand, require the open, physical conflict of living characters in opposition to one another on stage. These characters may represent the clash of good and evil in *Swan Lake* or the more complicated physical and emotional struggles of Lavrovsky's *Romeo and Juliet*.

Once the scenario is evolved it will be discussed with the artistic director, choreographer, composer and designer. Phase two begins. On the basis of this discussion the choreographer will draw up a choreographic plan, or libretto. This must be a very detailed plan because it will guide all the collaborators when they set about their separate tasks. It will show the course of the dramatic action in even more detail. It will be broken down into sections for the composer, showing the length, speed and character of each dance in minutes and seconds, and will show, for the designer, the major requirements of costumes, scenery, properties, colours and lighting.

We show at Appendix IV how Stravinsky's slender musical idea of Petrouchka's cry became a scenario, then a choreographic plan, through discussion, first with Diaghilev, then with Benois. Let us see now how the collaborators discussed John Cranko's early ideas for his three-act work, *The Prince of the Pagodas*, until this ballet evolved its final shape.

Cranko combined the roles of author and choreographer, weaving certain choreographic ideas into his scenario from the start. 'I was asked by the Sadler's Wells Organisation', he said, 'to submit a scenario for a three act ballet. How was one to provide a vehicle for creative choreography, rather than "classical" pastiche, which would still have the immediate box-office appeal required? I decided that the mythological fairy-tale would supply the framework needed. . . .

'My idea was to make a series of images from traditional fairy stories, linked by a thread of plot which was as important or un-important as the audience chose to make it. These images would provide the various divertissements I wished to make.

'My choreography was to take Petipa as a starting-point, but there were to be differences. Firstly, no "deaf and dumb" mime passages. Relationships of dancers to each other or to objects, or the quality of their movement, were to convey all the meaning. The classical dance was to be quite freely interspersed with acrobatics or popular dance steps as long as these were used poetically, and not merely as stunts to steal a cheap gasp from the audience: the moon would be like a white trapezist swinging in a crescent through the air, the fishes would tumble and somersault through the waves. The result of these deliberations was a first rough scenario of *The Prince of the Pagodas*.'

The rough scenario had to be turned into a detailed choreographic plan. This was done by discussion with the other artists.

'When I explained these ideas to John Piper', said Cranko, 'he understood and was excited about them. We decided in favour of relating "The Pagodas" to the strange edifices of Steinberg and Paul Klee, and against making a pastiche of eighteenth century chinoiserie. By using sharply defined shapes in contrasting colours which advanced or receded, we would make our feeling of space and the Palaces and Places would be in the imagination, rather than realistically represented.

'The scenery was to move, too, and become part of the dance. That is, its movements would have a beauty of their own and not be merely illustrative, such as realistic storms at sea, volcanoes erupting and so on; in short, nothing was to be conveyed by scenic effect which would not be conveyed in the dance.

'One evening I asked Britten if he had any ideas about composers, little dreaming that he would become excited enough with "Pagodas" to undertake it himself.

'The whole ballet was rediscussed and Britten suggested various themes on which he would make variations short enough to provide the episodic dances, but which would give the work as a whole a sense of continuity.

'Together we worked out a sort of "shooting script" of the whole ballet, almost as if we were planning a silent film. For example:

Belle Rose enters sadly and looks off-stage to see if she is alone (*short introductory bars*).

She dances her loneliness. (*One minute.*)

She sees a vision of a prince dressed in green. (*Slow music, to allow for smoke to spread, then quickening when she sees prince, whole time not more than four minutes.*)

The prince vanishes. (*Some sort of crash, but very rapid.*)

'Then Britten started to compose. As the music grew the ballet sprang to life, and, carefully as Britten had followed my script, his imagery was so strong that the entire choreography had to be revisualised. This is often the case with specially composed ballets. There are stages of metamorphosis like a butterfly. Firstly the scenario; then the emotional and rhythmic framework provided by the music; and last of all the movements; thus a choreographer may find his original idea grown and developed differently from his first conception by the time he actually goes into rehearsal.'[1]

In *The Prince of the Pagodas*, the 'shooting script', or libretto, for choreography and design appears to some extent to have been separated from the libretto for choreography and music, though both were linked through the author-choreographer. This separation of the ballet's component parts remained one of its qualities even on stage, and was noted by several critics as a fault of construction.

A more serious fault of construction was the lack of real motivation in the ballet. It has no strong narrative thread. The first act is well enough drawn. The characters of the king, the good and bad dwarfs, the old counsellors and Belle Epine are clearly stated. But the Prince has no reason whatever for his appearance. He is not even Belle Rose's dream of her ideal lover. So why should she journey off, trustingly, on his invitation? And when she does journey, into the elemental world of Act II, she is given no choreographic link with the elements. In any case the dances of the elements are much too long, like the *divertissements* in the third act which celebrate Belle Rose's marriage to the Prince.

Lacking motivation and narrative thread *The Prince of the Pagodas* loosely assembles all three types of ballet into one work. Act I and the first scene of Act III are narrative. Act II is mood. The *divertissements* in Act III are abstract. They are held together by the music and by the interest of Cranko's endless choreographic invention. But this is not enough to involve our feelings.

Cranko, nevertheless, brought to the preparation of his 'shooting script' a knowledge of choreographic construction which ought to be part of the equipment of every ballet author, even if he is not a choreographer. From the start, the author must be able to envisage a general choreographic shape for the ballet within which different sections of dancing can be related to one another and the whole built to an effective climax.

Certain details of choreographic construction, generally speaking, are common to the shape of all ballets. They are required by the nature of the art. If the author understands these he can provide for them in his scenario so that the collaborators can build the full libretto more easily.

The author should know, for example, that it can be convenient to open a ballet with some kind of ensemble dance like the hens in

[1] John Cranko, 'Making a Ballet', *Sunday Times*, 20th January, 1957.

Ashton's *La Fille Mal Gardée* and the *corps* in Tudor's *Gala Performance*. This prepares the way for the principal characters by establishing place, period and atmosphere. Usually, the principal characters should be introduced early on, although their solo dances will often come later in the ballet when demanded by the dramatic action or when it is necessary to lift the dance pattern by some kind of choreographic highlight.

The dramatic action and/or the dance pattern (if the ballet is a plotless *divertissement*) usually build up to the *pas de deux* which will be placed probably where the biggest climax is required. This *pas de deux* generally holds pride of place in the ballet, or act, because it contains not only the best dancing by the best dancers, but is the emotional centre of the piece.

From the point of view of shape the *pas de deux* presents author and choreographer with a problem. How to avoid an anti-climax to the act or ballet after the *pas de deux*? How, in other words, to devise a suitable finale? We discuss this problem in Chapter XXII in choreographic terms. The author, however, has to offer a solution in his scenario by providing a proper emotional ending or twist to his story, developed naturally out of the *pas de deux*. Cranko does this very well with a *coup de théâtre* at the end of *The Shadow*.

As often as not it is the ensemble which comes to the rescue in the finale, just as it is the ensemble which holds the stage when the principal characters are absent. The author must understand that the *corps* is a choreographic link between the highlights of action and dancing, as well as a crowd of characters who are part of the narrative in their own right. Very often the principals have to leave the stage to rest or change costumes. The author must give these necessary exits a proper motivation and provide the ensemble, too, with a proper reason for holding the stage.

No wonder, then, that the author must devise a scenario with a developed thread of thought linking everything together. If there is no consistent motivation in the scenario the choreographic construction will seem contrived, however well it is done. The motivation may be strong, as it is in *Blood Wedding*, or slender, as it is in *Les Rendezvous*, but motivation there must be arising from a properly conceived situation.

These generalities make it clear, too, why the author must know something of the mechanical problems to be solved in realising his scenario, although he may not actually solve them himself and may not prepare the choreographic plan. The best kind of scenario, of course, will suggest solutions for each of the main problems facing the collaborators. But this is rare. Boris Kochno, Diaghilev's secretary and a moving spirit of French ballet, not only wrote the stories of ballets but suggested the style of music, the nature of scenery and costumes and the character of important passages of choreography. This guide for each collaborator is the ideal scenario and the best preparation for an effective libretto.

Once the libretto is complete the ballet can go forward through its remaining stages of production. It may change many details as its parts are created, but it will never lose the shape and direction worked out originally in scenario and libretto.

PART IV

THE
CHOREOGRAPHER'S COLLABORATORS

CHAPTER XII

THE ARTISTIC DIRECTOR

THE problem of harmony between choreography and its associate arts has been an issue over which artists and critics have always argued. The problem has been resolved best whenever someone has appeared strong enough to maintain a balance between the arts in the interests of the whole. History shows that this someone may be either a choreographer or a person who is of the arts but not necessarily a specialist. It is the task of this person to achieve harmony and to stand above the collaborators, even when he is one of them.

In the eighteenth and nineteenth centuries the effective artistic director of a ballet, or a season of ballets, was usually the choreographer, at that time called the ballet-master. Occasionally an exceptional theatre director or impresario with a strong enough personality might have claimed the title, had he wished. In those days, the tendency towards specialism in the arts and sciences, which the industrial age brought with it, had not created the need for a fifth person to hold the balance between the collaborators.

Noverre was one of the first ballet-masters whose taste and knowledge raised him above his fellows to be also an artistic leader. One might call such a person a master-choreographer. In the same century one could give the title, perhaps, to Hilferding van Wewen of Austria and the Italian Gasparo Angiolini.

The following century produced from France the master-choreographers, Charles Didelot, Jules Perrot and Marius Petipa. Each best realised his talents in England or Russia. Denmark produced August Bournonville, who gave to his country what Petipa gave to Russia. Italy's contribution to the list was Salvatore Viganò.

While ballet evolved its master-choreographers the world of the theatre evolved another kind of ballet leader. Often he combined the role of *animateur* and impresario, whose taste and knowledge helped to make his theatre or his period especially brilliant.

A prototype of this man, perhaps, was David Garrick, the actor-manager, who presented Noverre's ballets in London and deeply influenced the doctrine of the *ballet d'action*. But Garrick was the greatest actor of his day, an artist with London at his feet. The ballet-theatre directors of the nineteenth century were of a different stamp. Those who most influenced the art were Benjamin Lumley in London, Ivan Vsevolojsky and Prince Volkonsky in Russia, directors of the Imperial Theatre at St. Petersburg from 1881–1902, and, possibly, the Frenchman, Louis Véron.

Véron was more of a good business man than an *artistic* director. He knew how to give people what they wanted. Nevertheless, he assisted at the birth of the Romantic Ballet as director of the Paris Opéra and played an important part in the creation of *La Sylphide*. The glory of Taglioni and the volubility of Gautier have overshadowed the contribution of a man who presented some of the Romantic Ballet's greatest dancers.

Benjamin Lumley, too, overshadows Véron in the history of the Romantic Ballet. During the 1840s Lumley, one of the great impresarios of the English theatre, 'succeeded in outshining by the brilliance of his ballet even the fountain-head of the classical dance, the Paris Opéra'.[1] And this in a decade which saw the first performance of *Giselle*.

Under Lumley's management Her Majesty's Theatre, London, became a capital of the dance. When this management ended in 1858 a hundred years were to pass before London achieved an equal ascendancy in the world of choreography. 'His vivid imagination enabled him to plan on a bold scale. For his taste and enterprise he was rivalled by no other opera house manager of his day. It was on his suggestion that Perrot set to work to create a ballet out of Hugo's *Notre-Dame de Paris*; it was his drive that surmounted the obstacles standing in the way of the fabulous *Pas de Quatre*.'[2]

He even established a ballet school to support his company which, for a time, looked like becoming a permanent centre of ballet in England. Lumley, more than any other theatrical manager of the nineteenth century, displayed qualities which Diaghilev was later to show belonged especially to the artistic director.

In Russia the Director of the Imperial Theatres was a court official. As such, Vsevolojsky and Prince Volkonsky were patrons and supporters of Petipa during the time he created the works which have come down to us. Vsevolojsky, a painter in his own right, created designs for *The Sleeping Beauty*, *The Nutcracker*, *Raymonda*, and other

[1] Ivor Guest, *The Romantic Ballet in England*, pp. 83 ff. (Phoenix House, London, 1954).   [2] Ivor Guest, *op. cit.*, p. 84.

ballets. For some of these he also wrote the scenario. Petipa complained bitterly at the 'irreparable loss in the departure of this never-to-be-forgotten Director', who placed ballet enormously in his debt by introducing the music of Tchaikovsky and Glazunov.

'The creation and staging of a big ballet', Petipa wrote in his memoirs, 'presents enormous difficulties; in outlining the scenario or programme, one must think of all the individual roles; having completed the story and pantomimic part of the ballet, one must invent and create the appropriate dances, pas, and variations, and make them conform to the music. This work becomes pleasant when one finds in the director such a well-informed and gifted adviser as M. Vsevolojsky, or when one works with a composer of genius, such as Tchaikovsky.

'All the décors, costumes and accessories, which conformed to the style, period and character of the subject, were devised by M. Vsevolojsky. He himself made the sketches, which naturally lightened the problems of everyone connected with the production. The Director knew how to use for the ballet the power and genius of the great Russian composer Tchaikovsky, who wrote three such works as *The Sleeping Beauty*, *Swan Lake* and *The Nutcracker*. Under the same Director the talented composer Glazounov also wrote for the ballet. He gave us *Raymonda*, *Ruses d'Amour* and *The Four Seasons*.'[1]

Later, Petipa credits Vsevolojsky with giving him and Ivanov the opportunity to rechoreograph and represent *Swan Lake* after the failure of its first production by Reisinger in Moscow. 'To whom were we indebted for this opportunity, if not to M. Vsevolojsky?'

When Volkonsky succeeded Vsevolojsky in 1899 it seemed that the Imperial Theatres had been lucky again in their director. 'Loving art in general, and the theatre in particular,' wrote Petipa, 'the new Director devoted himself enthusiastically to his new duties.' But Volkonsky lasted less than three years to be replaced by Teliakovsky, for whom Petipa had less respect.

Even so Volkonsky's short reign saw the strengthening of the new movement in Russian ballet. Fokine made his first choreographic essays; Cecchetti was appointed as teacher; Benois and *The World of Art* painters were brought into the theatre; Diaghilev was entrusted with a new production of *Sylvia*, but displeased the administration

---

[1] *Russian Ballet Master*, edited by Lillian Moore, p. 60 (Black, London, 1958). Pepita refers presumably to *Les Saisons*.

and was dismissed. From this period, nevertheless, dates Diaghilev's life-work for ballet.

Diaghilev developed and fashioned the figure of the twentieth century artistic director as a dynamic force. First, in collaboration with Benois, then alone, he replaced the state administration to meet the special needs of the itinerant Russian Ballet in Western Europe.

Diaghilev's position was justified for other reasons, too. The circumstances of the Ballets Russes compelled a division of the ballet-master's traditional responsibilities. Choreographers no longer had time to be teachers, choreographers and directors all at once as Petipa had been. It was enough to be a choreographer. The duties of ballet-master and teacher in the company were given to other talents, leaving the duties of selection and guidance to the man who became the first artistic director, as such, in the history of ballet. Here was someone who was neither dancer, painter nor composer but 'who was listened to by all three; who was not an impresario, but a cultural dilettante who kept a travelling ballet company alive for twenty years; a Maecenas with the money of others. There is no name to describe his function; he has left no successor.'[1] This man was Serge Diaghilev.

One cannot name Diaghilev's functions because history imposed upon him tasks beyond the duties of artistic directors as we know them today. (Plate XI (a).) History has not repeated itself and so he has no direct successor. But he proved the value of independent artistic direction in ballet and pioneered the role itself. Because of him Ninette de Valois and Marie Rambert in Britain, George Balanchine, Lincoln Kirstein and Lucia Chase in America, are principal figures in their national ballets as *artistic directors*, quite apart from any leadership they may exercise in other ways.

In Paris, the traditional organisation of the Opéra was not much changed with the appointment of Serge Lifar in 1932. Nevertheless, the dominant position and influence of Lifar as ballet-master-choreographer after 1932 represented a significant shift in the seat of power which might never have happened but for Diaghilev's example. Denmark and the U.S.S.R., on the other hand, had no lasting contact with the ideas represented in the Diaghilev ballet. They retained their traditional organisation. The ballet-master is often the chief choreographer, teacher and inspiration of their state companies.

[1] Arnold Haskell, *A Picture History of Ballet*, p. 19 (Hulton Press, London, 1954).

Yet there seems to be a need for someone to fulfil the duties of artistic director in these state theatres. 'Under the regulations of the Committee for Art Affairs', argued the ballerina Ulanova, in Moscow in 1953, 'the artistic director of the ballet must also be the chief theatrical choreographer. This means, however, that he is constantly engaged in current productions. Yet the artistic director is also the leader of the whole ballet team. I feel that his role is primarily that of creative organiser, whose job it is to pursue the new, to be always thinking of prospects for the development of ballet as a whole, and to study its artistic improvement.

'It is the task of such a director to draw in the composers and the script writers to the theatre and to integrate their efforts with those of the producers and performers, so that there is no crying dissociation between them, as there is now.'[1]

The role of artistic director in today's ballet theatre could hardly be better expressed—'leader of the whole ballet team . . . creative organiser, whose job it is to pursue the new, to be always thinking of prospects for the development of ballet as a whole. . . .'.

Such a person requires above all, aesthetic and personal discernment, a sense of theatre, powers of leadership to promote his ideas, and a working knowledge of ballet to carry them out.

By discernment is meant not only personal taste but the ability to relate personal taste to public taste. On occasion, it may even be necessary to impose personal taste so that the public is led rather than leads.

The taste of an artistic director will be reflected in the nature and balance of his company's repertoire, his choice of collaborators to create new ballets, and the quality of his dancers. He must want the best in everything. He must have talent and be able to discern it early on.

Having spotted talent he must be able to mould it, educate it. In forming choreographers in the early thirties, for example, Dame Marie Rambert had to turn Ashton's eyes inwards on his ballets to improve them because he paid too much attention to his audience. Antony Tudor needed opposite guidance. Tudor was too self-absorbed. His eyes were fastened too much on his ballets and not enough on his audience.

By a sense of theatre is meant the fulfilment of all those conditions

[1] Galina Ulanova, 'The Demand on the Artist', *Sovetskaya Muzyka,* April, 1953, reproduced in *Ulanova on Soviet Ballet,* (S.C.R. London, 1954).

which can render ideas theatrically effective. There must be a sound artistic policy in a company. Probably, the repertoire will be based upon the narrative ballet, balanced by mood and abstract works, tragedy, comedy and so on. This balance will guide the artistic director in his choice of new ballets and of collaborators. He must be able to recognise which ideas and themes submitted to him are especially suitable for ballets. He must be able to fashion these ideas to a proper size for his theatre and his company. Finally, through his collaborators and a wise choice of cast, he must bring the ideas to the stage so balanced in all their elements that they make the greatest theatrical impact.

To achieve this the artistic director must be as able as Diaghilev to reject even the work of famous artists if this fails to satisfy him or satisfy the collaboration. 'Picasso's original *Pulcinella*', recorded Stravinsky, 'was very different from the pure *commedia dell' arte* Diaghilev wanted. His first designs were for Offenbach period costumes with side-whiskered faces instead of masks. When he showed them, Diaghilev was very brusque: "Oh, this isn't it at all", and proceeded to tell Picasso how to do it. The evening concluded with Diaghilev actually throwing the drawings on the floor, stamping on them, and slamming the door as he left. The next day all of Diaghilev's charm was needed to reconcile the deeply insulted Picasso, but Diaghilev did succeed in getting him to do a *commedia dell' arte Pulcinella*.'[1]

If Diaghilev sometimes went too far, many producers and artistic directors today fail to exercise a strong enough control over their team. This control should come in the first place from the respect commanded by artistic erudition and fine taste. It is inhibited sometimes by an excessive and mistaken regard on the part of directors for 'artistic freedom' or the self-expression demanded by individual collaborators. Freedom of this kind has no justification in a collective artistic organisation, particularly if it detracts from the quality of the final work. Freedom must be relative to the interests of the production as a whole. In this interest it is the duty of the artistic director to blend and edit, where necessary, the work of the collaborators. The ultimate work should represent the taste of one person, the director, rather than four separate tastes. Likewise the repertoire should reflect the taste of this one person. Where a ballet company

[1] Stravinsky and Craft, *Conversations with Igor Stravinsky*, p. 105 (Faber and Faber, London, 1959).

is based on an opera house, this again will require a blending between the interests of the ballet and of the opera house.

The director's powers of leadership, therefore, will be shown in his ability to choose and stimulate collaborators as a team rather than as individuals. Everything in ballet ultimately depends on the choice of collaborators, the right artists for the right themes. False judgement in assembling the team almost always leads to disharmony in the production, visible only when it is too late to put things right.

Three paths lie open to the artistic director in exercising his leadership and choosing the collaborators. He can initiate a theme himself, then find the right artists to achieve it; he can bring together artists whose meetings will produce a theme; or he can accept, reject or reshape ideas brought to him by collaborators who have already come together and made their choice.

Whichever path is appropriate to the moment, the principles of collaboration always require an equal balance between the theme and the manner of its interpretation. There should be an equal balance between the talents of each artist, and an equal balance between the interpretations of the theme which each artist contributes. The rhythms and colours of the design, for example, must not be in conflict with the rhythms and colours of the music.

Collaborators must *want* to collaborate, as people as well as artists. Diaghilev knew this and joined Benois to Stravinsky for *Petrouchka* accordingly (Appendix IV). Ballet history is full of such partnerships, the most fruitful of which, perhaps, was between Petipa and Tchaikovsky. Our time links Stravinsky with Balanchine, Ashton with Sophie Fedorovitch, Tudor with Hugh Stevenson, MacMillan with Nicholas Georgiadis, Jerome Robbins and Leonard Bernstein with Oliver Smith.

Collaboration, of course, goes deeper and further than the work of the four creators. It includes the relations of the artistic director with his musical director, examined at greater length in the next chapter, and extends to the back-stage staff and the dancers. But if the initial collaboration of scenarist, composer, designer and choreographer fails, everything fails. Even in an outwardly excellent team there is danger. 'Two's company, three's a crowd.' The choreographer and the composer may be particularly close, leaving the designer outside. The artistic director must overcome this by the way he guides their joint work from his independent position. In doing precisely this so often for so long lay Diaghilev's greatest achievement.

The achievement, of course, rested on a thorough working knowledge of ballet and attention to detail. Every artistic director must have these qualities if he is to command the respect of his artists. Working knowledge needs to be exercised at every stage of production. It has to include a sound theoretical, if not practical knowledge, of dance technique, music and painting.

The period between a ballet's commission and its first rehearsal, for example, may last weeks or months. During this time the artistic director must see all the collaborators, approve their contributions and see that each maintains the time schedule. (Plate XI (b).) Otherwise one will hold up another. Before the first rehearsal takes place he must approve the piano score. Then he must agree the cast with the choreographer.

When rehearsals begin he must keep in touch with the progress of the ballet in every department. This includes such details as the preparation of orchestral parts and costume fittings for the dancers. It is too late to wait to see how everything has been realised at the dress rehearsal.

The artistic director then must have confidence in himself and be able to inspire the confidence of others. He must stamp his personality and his taste on the ballet of his time as Dame Ninette de Valois has done by raising English ballet to preeminence in a brief thirty years. He must be on both sides of the footlights, producer and critic, seeking in the harmony of separate arts the success of them all. His mind must know that the 'art of the theatre is neither acting nor the play it is not the scene nor the dance, but it consists of all the elements of which these things are composed'.[1] His heart should feel that the theatre is 'a place in which the entire beauty of life can be unfolded, and not only the external beauty of the world, but the inner beauty and meaning of life'.[1]

[1] Edward Gordon Craig, On the Art of the Theatre (Heinemann, London, 1911).

CHAPTER XIII

THE COMPOSER

(i) THE COMPOSER AT WORK

As the designer provides a framework of space within which the choreographer moves his dancers, so the composer provides a framework of time.

The two arts, music and dancing, form a partnership which demands the utmost of each. The choreographer must explore in his *visual* art all the suggestions in the music. The composer must explore in his *aural* art every musical device which can enrich and realise fully the libretto.

Ultimately, of course, the realisation of the partnership depends on the performance. Many dancers hear only one quality in music, its measure or rhythm. If this were the only musical quality they needed a tom-tom would be sufficient, or, at most, the pipe and drum repetitions of the Catalan *Sardanas*. Such an attitude destroys what composer and choreographer labour to create.

The modern composer has a multiplicity of rhythms with which to illustrate a story and make a dancer's work more difficult. But besides rhythms to which dancers can dance a composer has to create musical characters for the principal members of the cast and the *corps de ballet*. His music has to supply these characters with emotions and a soul in the way that Stravinsky gave life to Petrouchka. He has to create atmosphere and lyrical feeling as Delibes did for Swanilda's dance with the ear of corn in *Coppélia*. More than this, he has to provide the ballet with proper punctuation—the commas, semi-colons, full stops, sentences and paragraphs which help words, or steps, to tell their story. This is why (to return to the scenarist for a moment) a good libretto must be based on full discussion between the collaborators.

Composer and choreographer, therefore, should devise their ballet together. 'Perfect analogous concord should subsist between what we see and what we hear. The ideas of the composer should accord with those of the author; and the labours of both should be ever most closely and agreeably united.'[1] This is the ideal of which *The Sleeping Beauty*, *Petrouchka* and Ashton's *Ondine* are different, but fine, examples. Dramatic and narrative ballets, in particular, require specially composed scores.

The choreographer should prepare for the composer a detailed plan for composition, based on the libretto. This should show not only the course and timing of the dramatic action, but each section of the ballet, each role in it, the length, speed, rhythm, character and purpose of each dance, the proper pauses, the highlights of *pas de deux*, and the climaxes. 'I gave him', said Frederick Ashton, of his instructions to Henze, the composer of *Ondine*, 'strict minutage, like Petipa used to give Tchaikovsky, detailing the length of each dance and section. . . .'[2] (See Appendix III (iv).) 'I much prefer to be in constant touch with the composer while he is writing it,' said Balanchine of a commissioned score, 'I must be able to convey to him exactly what I require, so that the music accords with my action and harmonises with my movements.'[3] Choreographers should remember, none the less, that music has its own inner life which must be satisfied. The composer must be allowed the same freedom the choreographer claims for himself.

What sort of composer does a ballet need? He must, of course, be a good composer, not just a competent one. He should be experienced in other fields of composition. He must be in sympathy with the choreographer, and his musical style must accord with the theme of the ballet. He may be chosen in consultation with the musical director. The choice is vital to the success of the ballet. His music will require a feeling of theatre, strong sense of rhythm and clear delineation of episode and character. Especially, he must 'combine the gifts of dramatist and musician, otherwise he will be unable to express the idea of the whole work and reveal human thoughts, feelings, experiences and conflicting passions in his music. If the music lacks dramatic excitement, and the characters lack clear, musical imagery in their delineation, then the music will be no more than an illustration, a rhythmical accompaniment to the scenes and dances.'[4]

Nowadays, this dramatic composer will not be the rather second-

---

[1] C. Blasis, *The Code of Terpsichore*, p. 189 (London, 1830).
[2] *Sunday Times*, London, 26th October, 1958.
[3] *Dance Journal*, London, August-October, 1931.
[4] R. Zakharov, 'The Urgent Needs of Soviet Ballet', *Sovetskaya Kultura*, 12.10.54 (trans. S.C.R., London).

rate specialist he often was a century ago. 'A composer', said the composer of *Blood Wedding*, speaking of British conditions, 'should "know" ballet in a general way, be familiar with the repertoire, and have some technical knowledge of what can or cannot be done by particular types of dancers, and of what is required for special types of dance, e.g. the *pas de deux* in its various forms; the *pas seul* for the male soloist, with its heavy demand on physical energy; the sort of vigorous rhythms required for the men's ensemble, and so on.'[1]

Both sides need to remember that they approach ballet from different starting points. This is one of the problems of collaboration. Musical themes, for example, usually are capable of longer development than choreographic themes. The composer must be aware of this difference. But there are times when a musical phrase must develop along its own lines. The choreographer must match his ideas to it rather than dismember the music.

Maybe the musical conception can be matched by an abstract choreographic conception which explores the music in its own way. Balanchine is a creator of this kind of abstract or symphonic choreography. Basing himself wholly on the music as a source of inspiration he seeks to translate auditory impressions into visual impressions.

On the other hand, an equally musical choreographer might interpret music in a way quite opposite from the obvious. At the greatest musical climax in Tudor's *Jardin aux Lilas*, for example, the whole cast stands still on stage. Again, a choreographer may use concert music which has no evident programme, for programme purposes, say, to make a narrative ballet.

Frank Martin's *Concerto for Wind, Tympani and Percussion* is a case in point. The music suggested to Kenneth MacMillan the series of dramatic incidents which became *The Burrow*. In this interpretation MacMillan was helped by the natural reaction of some audiences to absolute music, which is to attempt to give the music a programme. *The Burrow* demonstrates how one kind of music (and a particularly difficult one at that) might be used for quite a different choreographic purpose. It also demonstrates very well an aspect of adapting existing music which is discussed further in the next section.

Rhythm is another problem. It is the most powerful ingredient of music and dancing. It derives from the heart-beat and is basic to our natures. Breathing, walking, habit are all expressions of it. It is our constant battle with gravity, with mother earth. Dancers

[1] Denis ApIvor, *Dancing Times*, London, April, 1959, p. 346.

heighten and glorify this struggle to the limit of physical possibility. Musicians, freed of physical restraint, reach beyond this limit to explore rhythmic forms of great complexity, which it takes dancers time to learn and even more time to dance.

To musicians and dancers rhythm 'covers the ensemble of everything pertaining to what may be called the *time* side of music (as distinct from the *pitch* side) i.e. it takes in beats, accents, measures or bars, grouping of notes into beats, grouping of beats into measures, grouping of measures into phrases and so forth'.[1] The choreographic equivalent of this is the amount of time it takes a dancer to perform one step, then a combinations of steps and, finally, whole passages or movements.

In ballet, therefore, it is for the composer to remember the dancers' limitations. No matter what varieties of rhythm and speeds attract him there must be a fundamental pulse running through his music. Romantic music from Adam to Delibes and Tchaikovsky was always strong in pulse. So is Prokofiev's *Romeo and Juliet*. Pulse to a dancer is not only being in time with the music, nor only syncopated beat. It is the source of energy and character because it represents the natural human reaction to the rhythmic qualities in music. Audiences react to it as instinctively as dancers. Hence pulse is an expression of the primitive link between the community, music and dance. In this way, ballet, however sophisticated, remains a communal activity.

Cadence, too, is inseparable from the rhythmic structure and must be matched choreographically. A musical cadence, Mary Skeaping remarked to us on one occasion, is a tonal progression which gives a sense of partial, or complete, finality at the point where it occurs. It is analogous to punctuation in language. Rhythmic patterns in dance are punctuated by the completed movement and/or point of rest.

Often today choreographers have to use music of great complexity. Occasionally, complex time changes can be emphasised effectively by being ignored in choreography, as sometimes happens in *Petrouchka*, but usually musical complexity inspires a like complexity in choreographic movement and rhythm. Frequently, it becomes impossible for dancers to do more than remember the steps which go with the music because each is equally intricate. Inner feeling and character have become lost, so we need a new simplicity in ballet music because ballet needs and always will need a clear

[1] Scholes, *The Oxford Companion to Music*, p. 795, Seventh Edition (O.U.P.).

melodic line. Somehow composers must give this to dancers, even while they enrich their scores with the innovations of Stravinsky and his successors.

Choreographer and composer need to appreciate similar problems in smaller matters, like the exact interpretation of descriptions in the libretto. Since the choreographer probably knows more about musical language than the composer does about choreography the choreographer should use musical terms in his plan.

If the collaboration goes well the result should be a score stamped with the composer's creative style, written in self-contained shortish sections representing episodes or changes of mood suitable for dancing, all clearly stated musically. The score 'should describe the characters and passions belonging to it; striving to strengthen and complete the picture.'[1] Architecturally, it should be complete in form and yet imply a visual treatment to realise it fully.

During the composition of the score the composer will be in close touch with the choreographer. (Plate XII (a).) Once the music is created he should play it to the choreographer, the artistic and musical directors, the designer and the company, or at least to the principal dancers. This is so that they understand the composer's intended *tempi*, the emotional colouring of his score, its shape and so on.

Ideally, a piano score should be complete before the choreographer starts work. Better still, an orchestral recording or tape should be made for rehearsals because a modern orchestration often sounds different from the piano score. The score's colour and texture, for example, depend on the orchestration.

Once absorbed, the choreographer begins to divide the music into counts, or phrases, for rehearsal purposes. If the composer has fulfilled his side of the bargain, choreographer and dancers must fulfil theirs. There must be no tampering with *tempi*, no arbitrary *accelerando* or *ritardando* because a dancer prefers it that way.

More than this. Many ballet scores, like Britten's *The Prince of the Pagodas* and Vaughan Williams' *Job*, give careful descriptions of the composer's intention. In spite of previous discussion, this may not always agree with the choreographer's interpretation. Depending on their training and musical feeling dancers can find in the score and music a guidance which is fuller than the most careful choreographer can put into words. The music sets the scene, creates atmosphere and

1 Blasis, *op. cit.* p. 189.

offers a constant commentary on the characters, events and emotions in the ballet. So it demands thought by each member of the cast, not just by the choreographer. For this reason we give, as illustration, a study of the music of *Job* at Appendix V, considering the way the choreographer has used the score, compared with Vaughan Williams' instructions.

(ii) THE COMPOSER ADAPTED

The ideal music for a contemporary ballet is a score specially commissioned. Often lack of money and/or time prevents this, so that a search has to be made for suitable music to fit the theme. Sometimes, an existing work provides a choreographer with an idea, as Chopin's music inspired Fokine's *Les Sylphides*. Or a ballet's theme may require the use of period music rather than music in a contemporary style. Both Balanchine and de Valois used Handel's music, arranged as a suite by Sir Thomas Beecham, for their versions of Kochno's *The Gods Go A-Begging*.[1] Here, the choreography was in a classical idiom with no attempt to reproduce exact period steps. Quite different was Mary Skeaping's choreography for Handel's *Alcina* at the Swedish Opera and her *Cupid out of his Humour* to Purcell's music at Drottningholm. Here the period music was matched by period choreography.

Between the ideal of period music for historical themes and contemporary music for contemporary themes lies the wide use of existing music for all kinds of choreography.

The problems of using such music, however well arranged, are very different from the use of commissioned scores. To begin with there are special aesthetic problems.

The fitness of using music never intended for dancing at all (i.e. music designed to stand by itself as music) was a principal debate of the thirties around Massine's symphonic ballets. But there remains the deeper problem of translating music, primarily intended to be heard, into visual images which do not have the motivation of narrative or mood. 'Balanchine is a master of this difficult transition', wrote Birgit Cullberg. 'He allows the dance patterns to dissolve and come together again like rings on water in a wide, never-ending flow. He has the gift of revealing the symphonic character of the

[1] Kochno's scenario was the basis of both ballets, the first in 1928, the second in 1936.

music in choreography. . . . But he is no slave of music. He builds his ballets in accord with the aesthetic laws of choreography.'[1]

When music has to be found to fit an idea the fit is nearly always approximate, rarely exact. The musical punctuation may not be altogether suitable, the ending or the minor climaxes or certain sections of the score may not be appropriate to the mood or the plot. In *Gala Performance*, for example, Tudor had to add most of the first movement of Prokofiev's Third Piano Concerto to the composer's Classical Symphony to make the music fit his story. This was exceptional for Tudor who is generally meticulous about using music as a composer wrote it. Even when possible changes have been made there may still remain areas of music which will tax the ingenuity of librettist and choreographer.

When, on the contrary, the music has suggested the idea, the choreographer/librettist must place himself entirely at the receiving end, allowing dance images to be born in his mind out of the music. In this case, said Balanchine, 'I familiarise myself with the music and try to fathom what the composer had in mind when writing it, or endeavour to conceive a theme which will harmonise with the mood of the music.'[2] Balanchine is an example of the type of choreographer whose usual starting point is the music. Such choreographers are influenced all along more by the music than by anything else. 'The composition of my stories,' Norman Morrice told us, 'is a process of listening to music ten thousand times.'

But once the idea and the images are born, choreographic craft has to be applied as forcefully as it would be to a ballet conceived in another way. The choreography must have its own integrity and unity, must stand on its own feet.

Petrouchka shows this very well. The ballet was inspired by Stravinsky's short piece, *Petrouchka's Cry*, which is now the music for the scene in Petrouchka's cell. Yet 'today', wrote Benois, 'when I listen to the music of this second act of *Petrouchka* and watch what the artist is expressing, more or less successfully, in his gestures and mime—*demonstrating* the absolute coordination of action and music —it is difficult even for me to believe that the music was not written to a set programme, instead of the programme being subsequently fitted to the music.'[3]

---

[1] Birgit Cullberg, Programme Note of the Royal Swedish Ballet.
[2] *Dance Journal*, London, August-October, 1931.
[3] Benois, *Reminiscences of the Russian Ballet* (Putnam, London, 1941).

In practice, existing music can be used by a choreographer in one of two ways. It may be used as the composer wrote it, in the way Walter Gore interpreted Britten's *Simple Symphony* for the ballet of the same name. Or it may be selected and arranged by a contemporary composer in the way Constant Lambert adapted Meyerbeer's music from *Le Prophète* and *L'Étoile du Nord* for Ashton's *Les Patineurs* in 1937. The emphasis must be on selection because what counts above all things is the actual suitability of the chosen music. No amount of arrangement can make good a bad choice. When the choice is a good one, as in Mackerras' use of Verdi for *The Lady and the Fool* and Sullivan for *Pineapple Poll*, clever arrangement can make it even better.

Liszt's *D'après une lecture de Dante—fantaisie quasi sonate* was similarly well chosen for *Dante Sonata*. Lambert later described in a broadcast the way in which he and Ashton worked together on the creation of this ballet:[1] 'The general lay-out, by which I mean not the dancing as such but the association of various characters with various themes and the general dramatic sequence, was then established mutually by Ashton and myself. I played the piano at almost all the rehearsals while the choreography was being created, so that when it came finally to orchestrating the ballet, I had the whole stage picture in my mind. I am certain that, apart from whether people like *Dante Sonata* or not, it has a visual-cum-musical unity which could only have been achieved by this form of collaboration.'

Lambert here was playing the role of professional arranger and rehearsal pianist as well as musical director. The success of the result points the wisdom of using professional arrangers to make musical arrangements rather than the hacks of an earlier period. Lambert understood this. He set a creative standard of selection and arrangement which has been matched by Charles Mackerras' *Pineapple Poll* and *The Lady and the Fool*, and John Lanchbery's *House of Birds* and *La Fille Mal Gardée*.

(iii) COMPOSER AND MUSICAL DIRECTOR

Balanchine's abstract ballets are a sort of apotheosis of the ballet composer. From being subordinate to the choreographer, a despised hack (except for Delibes and Tchaikovsky) through most of the nineteenth century, the composer achieved the equality of a true collaborator through Diaghilev and Stravinsky. Now, through

[1] Mary Clarke, *The Sadler's Wells Ballet*, p. 141 (Black, London, 1955).

Balanchine, he dominates the stage. It is the composer's hand which dictates the movements of Balanchine's choreography. This does not minimise Balanchine's achievements as a gifted choreographer-musician. Except that one wonders sometimes where lies the soul in these beautiful, dry steps and patterns.

This kind of changing balance is perpetual in life. Perhaps a perfect equality of the arts in ballet is difficult to maintain for long. But the ideal balance of music and dancing ought to be expressed, in the artistic direction of a modern ballet company, through the relations between the artistic director and the musical director. Their collaboration should be the visible sign of the partnership of music and dance in the company's policy, just as the collaboration of composer and choreographer fulfils this policy in every ballet.

A good musical director, like Constant Lambert, will be counsellor and friend to choreographers, composers and dancers. A choreographer, of course, should seek his musical director's advice in the choice of music. In this case a wise director will not confine his advice to naming a single composer. If the music is to be existing music the musical director can name a group of composers appropriate to the period with remarks about each one, leaving the choreographer to make a selection. If the music is to be composed and the choreographer has no particular composer in mind the musical director may name one or two composers whose style is likely to suit the theme and appeal to the choreographer.

In any case, the final decision about a composer cannot be made by the choreographer alone. It must be made in agreement with the musical and artistic directors of the company, because every ballet company should have a musical policy which will affect, and be affected by, the composers who work for it. This policy will insist on the use of the best composer appropriate to the ballet, compatible with the choreographer and available within the budget.

Lambert's budget as musical director at Sadler's Wells was never large. During the war economies were particularly necessary. So his use of Liszt for *Dante Sonata* exactly fulfilled the musical policy of the company at that time. The music was of good quality, cheap because free of copyright, and appropriate to its theme. In execution, moreover, it fulfilled an artistic ideal through its unity with the choreography, founded on the close collaboration of musician and choreographer from the beginning. It showed, as *Symphonic Variations* was to do six years later, how proper collaboration and the skilful choice of music can help a choreographer to realise visually the music's line, phrasing and emotional colour.

The musical director should be a familiar figure in rehearsal rooms, sometimes playing the piano for choreographer and dancers, learning the peculiarities of each in their reactions to music. Much can go wrong with the music of a ballet in rehearsal rooms, or rather with the collaboration between music and choreography. The musical director's presence can minimise misunderstandings and help the performance on stage.

For one thing he must see that rehearsal pianists give an orchestral interpretation of the score. Their playing for the dancers should expound the score creatively with an orchestral texture, always at the *tempi* at which it will be performed. For another thing, the musical director must keep his choreographer constantly aware of the orchestration of the score. In this way what has been rehearsed and planned will not be upset, as it was at the dress rehearsal of *Petrouchka* in Paris in 1911, because the orchestration seems strange when first heard.

'The conductor', wrote Yuri Faier, musical director of the Bolshoi, 'is, above everything, an excellent musician, knowing how to reveal the content of the music and its dance features deeply and sensitively. He knows not only the music score, but also the choreographic score, so difficult to fix in one's mind. He must study all the richness and variety of the language of the classic dance, all the infinite possibilities of combining various steps in consequential, logically developing musical action and dance. It is very good when the conductor begins work on the ballet at the stage when the libretto is being written. Ideally, he is not only a more or less talented performer, but also one of the creators of the ballet, able to make many suggestions to both the composer and the ballet-master.

'The ballet conductor must have a clear idea of each performer's part. As much as the performer (ideally even better) he must remember the whole "dance text" of the role—movement after movement. He should know the possibilities of each dancer, male and female, and be able to suggest to them the type of performance which would bring out the strong side of their talent and hide the weak. Most important of all is his love for the art of ballet; the desire and *ability* to give his time, his soul and his life to ballet.'[1]

[1] Yuri Faier, 'Notes of a Ballet Conductor', *Sovetskaya Muzyka*, No. 10, 1960 (*Anglo-Soviet Journal*, London, Summer, 1961).

Thus the ballet conductor is the dancer's best friend on stage. It was Lambert's special quality, for example, to be able to unite the movement of stage and pit in a way which drew the best from each. Yuri Faier has the same rare skill. Since Lambert's day at Covent Garden, Robert Irving and, most noticeably, John Lanchbery have displayed it among British conductors.

The ballet conductor, also, should add to theatricality, which is all important, something of the dramatist, the painter and the dancer as well as the musician. He must understand the physical problems of dancing and be able to balance these against the claims of correct musical *tempi* so as to produce musical coherence within the wider coherence of music and dance. This implies an ability to view changes of *tempo*, as it were, under a microscope, an extreme sensibility to the minute changes which will help the dancing.

As an executant his musicianship must be such that he can command from his orchestra in performance the same high standard it would give in the concert hall, even while his eyes watch the stage to anticipate the dancers' movements.

By being all these things, the director will become established as the musical guardian of dancers, composers and choreographers. He will make his company a creative force in musical life for which composers will compete to create. Above all he will effect that union of choreography with good music without which choreography cannot succeed.

CHAPTER XIV

THE DESIGNER

(i) THE DESIGNER AT WORK—SCENERY

To the Greeks the theatre was 'a place for seeing'. By and large it has remained so to modern audiences. The designer's job is to help the audience to see in a way which adds understanding to pleasure. He does this through illusion, by making magic for the choreographer. He casts the spell the moment the curtain goes up, establishing through décor and costumes a ballet's period, atmosphere and locale.

The designer's other principal task is to create space for dancing. In this he is quite unlike the designer of stage plays who can afford designs which fill the stage. Dramatists, too, do not compete with their designers for the eye of an audience in the way the choreographer does. This creates a special problem in their collaboration.

A designer's work is three dimensional and *static* in its scenery. Though the scenery should imply movement the designer must say what he has to say through the colour and arrangement of two-dimensional designs on wings and backcloth, and, perhaps, through a limited amount of architectural construction. The choreographer's work is three dimensional and *mobile*. He must say his piece through movement, the flow of steps and patterns and the juxtaposition of dancers, individually or in groups.

The two arts meet on two levels. First, in the similarity of their creative approach. Second, on stage through their costumes. The costumes are the link between scenery and choreographic movement.

In their creative approach both arts are subjective. Both synthesise elements of visual experience stored in the artist's mind. Both depend for this synthesis on the quality of imagination and sensibility which the artist brings to the selection. Both are arts of space. They 'have the same object in view, whether it be for the achieving of likeness, the admixture of colours, the play of light and shade, or the grouping and draping of figures, posing them in graceful attitudes and giving them character, life and expression'.[1]

[1] Noverre, *op. cit.* p. 35.

But choreography is an art also of time, so it is this art which unites on stage music and design. Music, the art of time, and painting, the art of space, are related in the qualities of rhythm and movement. Rhythm and movement are also fundamental qualities of dancing.

Musical rhythm is a succession of beats, bars and phrases. It is the feeling of progression obtained by infinitesimal alterations of the exact note lengths. Pictorial rhythm is the repetition of certain forms and colours over a canvas or stage design so that they are coherent to the eye and stimulate it. These repetitions may be slow or quick, as musical rhythms may be slow or quick. The pleasure they give is not the same as the pleasure communicated by a design's descriptive meaning. Rhythmic pleasure has to do with man's most primitive instincts.

Musical movement is the primary self-contained division of a large composition, each of which is usually given a separate indication of speed. Pictorial movement is the movement of compositional lines in a painting or stage design, directing the eye of the audience and giving unity to the work.

So rhythm, movement and other qualities in music, painting and dancing are fundamentally similar, as they are in all the arts. By understanding these qualities we understand more exactly how to achieve an ideal balance between the choreographer and his collaborators. Not only should each be the equal of the others in taste and accomplishment; each of the qualities of their work should be in harmony with like qualities in the other. Such an absolute harmony reigns in the English *Symphonic Variations* and in the Soviet *Romeo and Juliet*.

On stage the choreographer makes a series of visual statements to his audience through the movements of his dancers. He develops his argument through a succession of dance pictures set to music. The music presents similar aural arguments. The designer's settings and costumes must parallel these arguments, pointing the underlying dramatic unity of the choreographer's pictures and heightening their meaning. Hence his colours and designs are inseparable from choreography and music. They are never only an embellishment.

Whatever the designer's preference, whether he uses a great deal of scenery, or symbolic bits of wood and canvas, or only lighting against drapes, his job is to relate the ballet visually to its audience within the conception of the author. This requires more than an eye-catching picture or a set establishing locality and period. The design should establish these things but, principally, it should state the ballet's theme, its inner meaning.

Decorating a ballet, therefore, is a matter of interpreting a choreographic idea in pictorial terms. Somehow the designer's work should rouse the audience emotionally to convince it of the reality of what it sees, however fantastic the stage world may be. If the design fails to do this no amount of beauty nor taste can make good the deficiency.

Hence the collaborators must agree collectively at an early stage on the meaning and interpretation of the libretto, which each will underline in his own work. This agreement is as important for productions of the classics as it is for new ballets.

The moment when the designer will be able to enter the discussion depends on the way he is chosen to design the ballet. He may be consulted from the beginning, if he conceived the idea, or if he is a resident designer such as one still finds in a number of opera houses. He may be, and usually is, approached as soon as the artistic director has approved the scenario and begins to build the creative team. But if the music to be used already exists, the approach may be delayed until choreographer and artistic director have heard the score and decided which designer can best match it.

Thereafter, the designer may sketch a few ideas, but he cannot advance far without hearing the music himself and studying the choreographer's style at rehearsal. The choreographic line is fundamental to the style of the design. At the same time the choreographer should bear in mind the particular qualities of the designer he has chosen. He should adapt his line to these qualities where necessary. Frederick Ashton and Nico Ghika effected such an exchange with great success in *Persephone* (Plate XXXII) at Covent Garden. Music, too, can suggest colour to a designer, because colours have emotional associations. Through colour, Repin once wrote to his friend Kramsky, 'painting, for me . . . must affect the mood of the spectator like a chord of music'.

It is rare that the designer can attend many rehearsals. Usually, he cannot afford the time. Happy, then, the designer who inspires a choreographer and is inspired by him. English ballet is the richer for the personal and artistic friendship of Ashton and Fedorovitch, Tudor and Stevenson, Cranko and Piper, MacMillan and Georgiadis. (Plate XIV.)

Having absorbed the idea, the music and the choreographic line, preliminary sketches of sets and costumes can be made. Often these preliminary sketches are created in two phases. In the first phase the designer searches for original ideas and a style. He jots down shapes and drawings without particular regard for technical limitations. When he has found what he wants he modifies and builds his ideas into a practical form. These early sketches can be discussed with the artistic director, the choreographer, the production manager, the scene painter and the wardrobe staff.

Already in these sketches it will be clear whether the theme has inspired the designer. The most beautiful music and the most perfect choreography cannot replace this inspiration. This is why the power of the original theme to move each collaborator is fundamental to the success of all. Beauty of form, as every designer learns, cannot be created out of nothing nor imposed on nothing. It must arise from the strength of the content to inspire and absorb him in his work.

The quality of the designer's drawings may indicate, too, the quality of the designs to come. They may be sketchy because they assume his presence during realisation. But also they may lack theatrical quality or be impractical because the designer has insufficient training in theatre craft. They may be too literary or too flat, like book illustrations or a picture on a wall. They may, especially if the designer has come to the theatre from architecture, employ too many structures and take too long to mount. Or they may overcrowd the stage through not visualising the dancers in the set. Paradoxically, bad drawings may contain excellent ideas which can be translated in the workroom into theatrically effective décor. Sophie Fedorovitch, for example, was never very good at drawing, although the final effect was always evocative. (Plate XIV (b).) An artistic director must be able to see weaknesses of this kind in early sketches so as to correct them. He must assure himself that there is a proper organic connection growing up between the style of the designs and the style of the production.

In all his work the designer will be guided by three unalterable factors; the shape of the stage, the shape of the human body, and the fact that his costumes and scenery are to be used for dancing.

The scenery is the pictorial framework for the choreographic picture. It may be naturalistic like all nineteenth-century designs or realistic like the designs of Rex Whistler for *The Rake's Progress*. (Plate X (b).) It may be fantastic and allegorical like Piper's set for *The Prince of the Pagodas*. It may be abstract like Fedorovitch's set for *Symphonic Variations* (Plate VIII (a)), although the distinction between mood and abstraction is as hard to make in design as it is in choreography.

The designer must plan his scenery according to the proportions of the stage and make it reasonably able to fit other theatres of different proportions on tour. He must be sure that, on any stage, all the audience can see all the design. Behind the set there must be adequate working space for the stage staff and for dancers' entrances and exits. In front of it nothing must impede the dancers' movements. The designers must always keep in mind the scale of the human figure against his scenery and the demands of stage illusion. Nijinsky's famous leap through the window in Le Spectre de la Rose is tribute to the power of this illusion. The window sill 'was made slightly over a foot in height'.[1] Yet the leap became legendary for its height and daring.

Once the rough sketches of the scenery have been agreed by the artistic director, designer and choreographer, a ground plan, scale design, and scale model should be made. The ground plan is a map of the scenery usually drawn to the scale of half an inch to a foot. This shows at once the actual amount of space occupied by the scenery on the floor of the stage. Exits and entrances are marked clearly, indicating, too, the dimensions of stairways and other properties. It is a necessary guide for the scene builders, the scene painters, the stage director and the choreographer.

Painting usually takes place in a special paintshop where the great canvases can be hung in a paint frame on the wall, or laid out on the floor. The designer, of course, supervises the execution of the design, but rarely does his own painting.[2]

At the same time the properties are put in hand. Every property used on stage, however small, must be designed by the designer and constructed under his guidance in materials of his choice.

Meanwhile the choreographer knows from the ground plan how much space will be available for dancing during the performance. The essentials of this plan can be drawn with chalk on the rehearsal room floor, or, better still, on a stage cloth which can be moved from one rehearsal place to another. More than one scene should be shown by different colours. Thus inexperienced dancers, in par-

---

[1] Fokine and Chujoy, Fokine, Memoirs of a Ballet Master, p. 181 (Little, Brown & Company, Boston, 1961).

[2] For a more detailed explanation of scene painting, costume design, and so on, see William Chappell, 'Problems of Ballet Design' in The Ballet in Britain (Oxford University Press, 1962).

ticular, can become accustomed to the dimensions and gain confidence for dancing in the full set.

The scale design and scale model, within which scale models of dancers can be placed, will show the cast the picture of the set and help to eliminate many practical problems of fitting the set on to the stage. With a scale model proper masking and borders can be planned in advance to hide the 'off-stage' part of the stage from the audience. Much of the lighting plot also can be prepared in practical detail from a scale model, although the creative purpose of the lighting should have been in the mind of designer and choreographer from the beginning.

A lighting plot can require a hundred or more sources of light, ranging from 250 watts to 1500 watts each. Sometimes a ballet has no scenery in the traditional sense and lights have to do all the work of creating locality, mood and so on, aided only by dancers. Balanchine, like Jooss, has used lighting in this way, partly for economic reasons, but partly to emphasise the element of choreography in ballet. Thus he solves the inherent conflict in the competition of choreography and design for the audience's eye by discarding tangible scenery in favour of a scenery of lights and the patterns of his *corps de ballet*. (Plate XV.)

(ii) THE DESIGNER AT WORK—COSTUMES

Costume has exerted a primary influence over dance technique throughout ballet history. There is an organic connection between the two. The dancer's impulse towards freedom of movement struggles always against the restriction of moral fashion.

On stage, costumes are the link between a ballet's static and mobile pictures, that is, the scenery and the choreography. They fall into two groups. Either they adapt period or contemporary clothing, or they are fantasy creations, more or less elaborate. Whichever group they belong to they must be easy to dance in. They must not distort the line of the body in movement. And they themselves should embellish movement in the way their material falls. They should reveal the psychology and character of the role to the back row of the gallery. They ought to describe the role visually, helping to create or interpret mood, period and place. The most striking costume is valueless unless it can do these things.

Costumes, then, achieve their effect by emphasis and exaggeration, although they should never be so exaggerated that they draw attention from the wearers to themselves. Their starting point should be the physical characteristics of the role and its interpreter. These characteristics will guide the colour, materials and cut so that, when finished, every character will stand out clear against the background décor and the important characters will be distinguished from the less important. Bakst's costumes for Fokine's *Carnaval* fulfilled all these needs.

It follows that costume designers for ballet need many other qualities besides a strong sense of theatre. They should add an understanding of psychology, dance movement and line to the knowledge of period, materials, colours and lighting effects which should be theirs already.

The great rule is simplicity of colour, texture and design. Costumes should be comfortable, light, easy to move in, provide ample breathing space and use a minimum number of fastenings. They should catch and emphasise the beauty of the body's movement, never distorting the natural line except for dramatic purposes. Although the contours built into a costume must be suitable to the period and character of a role and the style of the dancing they should also be complimentary to the physique of the dancer who will wear it. John Craxton showed how to do this in the costumes for Ashton's *Daphnis and Chloe*.

With all this in mind choreographers should watch carefully that the costume designs agree with their choreographic plan. If, as sometimes happens, the costumes are conceived without regard to the choreography, they will hide the important lines of the dancing so that the choreography will be meaningless.

After the designs have been agreed the choreographer should be consulted about the texture and weight of the materials to be used. The designer, of course, will know the theatrical effect of material he uses. But often the way material hangs, lights and moves can be used to achieve important choreographic effects. In Andrée Howard's *Veneziana* the principal gondolier enters suddenly and catches La Favorita's cloak as it is being carried past him off stage. He stops and the cloak falls behind, continuing the line of his arm. The movement shows how punctuation and accent in choreography can be aided by the skill of the designer (in this case Sophie Fedorovitch) in choosing material which carries and falls in precisely the right way.

If the material has to be dyed the designer may supervise this or even do it himself. Then the materials are cut. The designer should attend every fitting, instructing the costumier exactly how the costumes should be made. The choreographer, too, should be present on occasion so that no disparity arises between costume and movement.

There is no margin for error. Everything must fit perfectly like a second skin so that there is no hindrance when the dancer is in action and no strain in pirouettes or complicated lifts. The material and its making must be strong enough to survive *grands jetés* and a hundred other stresses. This is the task of the wardrobe. A great wardrobe mistress becomes every designer's strong right hand.

As soon as parts of the costume are made the designer should let the dancers use them a little to see how they will look, move and light in practice. He may change details, adding or taking away. The dancer, too, can help at this point with suggestions from his knowledge of the role's difficult movements.

As with properties for the set, so with properties for the costumes. There must be separate designs for every headdress, wig and piece of jewellery. *Appliqué* work on the costumes is usually carried out by the designer himself who must be careful to use nothing which will cut or injure a partner. The dancer wears the costume while the designer decorates, paints and moulds it like a sculptor at work. Picasso painted the design of the acrobats' costumes in *Parade* on to the dancers' bodies in this way.

Finally, the designer should advise the dancers about the hair styles and make-up of each character because this completes the costume. Make-up, except for *commedia dell' arte* characters and elaborate maskings, only became an important skill with the introduction of gas light. Before that the light of candles made strong make-up unnecessary. During the thirties of this century ballet make-up was greatly exaggerated. Today dancers have learned to use only so much as is necessary.

Simplicity must be the designer's rule. It is the mark of taste and the way to truth in the theatre. He who designs simply, sees clearly. He need not fear the moment when the movements of the dancers and the brightness of the lights bring his work to life.

PART V

THE CHOREOGRAPHER'S MATERIAL

CHAPTER XV

THE DANCER

THE dancer is the choreographer's human instrument. This instrument ranges from the experienced artist to the child fresh from school, and from the brilliant technician of small interpretative ability to great dancer-mimes.[1] The possibilities are limitless.

The dancer is part formed when he enters ballet school at the age of eight or ten years. The child possesses physical, emotional and intellectual characteristics which determine the type of dancer he or she will become—classical, character or *demi-caractère*. These are the types of dancer with which this chapter deals and which are recognised today in classical ballet. School and choreographer can mould and develop the characteristics of each type, but never change them completely.

Physique should be the first consideration of a would-be dancer. (Plate XVI (a).) It is not the only criterion of future success, but it is the earliest guide. It must be visually and mechanically suitable for dancing. Given this, the ballet school will train it so that it becomes a supple instrument of great endurance, aesthetically pleasing to the eye. (Plate XVI (b).)

'There are certain physical characteristics peculiar and constant to dancers', wrote Agnes de Mille of the ideal finished product. 'Dancers are nearly all smaller and more tautly knit than other people. . . . Their chief and most appealing characteristics are their slenderness and their posture, a soldierly spine and a sense of supple readiness that no other people acquire, not even great athletes.'[2]

Today, popular interest in ballet, coupled with a new regard for physical excellence, has roused public esteem for the perfections of the dancer's physique. The dancer is elevated as a social being higher than ever before. He has acquired a social significance over and above his significance as an artist.

To understand the reasons for this in public psychology is to

---

[1] Mime: used in Greek sense as the actor whose means of expression are gestures, features and line of body.

[2] de Mille, *And Promenade Home*, p. 59 (Hamish Hamilton, London, 1959).

understand more profoundly how choreography, which is a sculpting of the human body, can play upon the imagination.

Partly, the dancer's greater prestige derives from the improved methods of training which have made his physique more perfect and so more worthy of public admiration. Partly, the prestige arises because the dancer today offers one of the few representations of an ideal human form to be found in contemporary art.

Gone from contemporary art is the kind of physical ideal once created by Greek, Renaissance, neo-classical and even Romantic art, an ideal which was real enough to seem attainable by ordinary people.

Today, in British, French, American and other modern art, the ideal human form appears less and less often. Art instead expresses emotional and psychological states through a representation of the body which seems unbalanced and even distorted.

The general public, however, continues to demand an ideal physique. This should be aesthetically satisfying, not just athletically heroic as a great runner is, or a great footballer. The ballet dancer has come to fulfil this need, especially among women. The emancipated modern woman is athletic, well-groomed and chic with good proportions and fewer curves than in earlier periods. Markova, Jeanmaire, Fonteyn and Maria Tallchief are ideals quoted in fashion magazines.

The male dancer, too, has established a claim to respect and even envy for his athletic prowess. In physique, he restates at best the Apollonian ideal, a male perfection of form which has hardly been achieved so well since classical Greece.

Since sculpture and painting no longer try to represent the kind of physical perfection which moves the onlooker in Michaelangelo's David, this creative task has devolved upon the dancer. History has added it to his other tasks as an artist of the theatre. True, the shapes which choreographers make from limbs and bodies sometimes resemble the shapes of Braque or Moore or the elongations of Buffet. But in the end choreographers return to the beautiful, trained physique which nature and the classical ballet gives dancers for their starting point. This physique closely corresponds today to the physical proportions which were ideal in fourth- and fifth-century Greece.

Not only aesthetic considerations lie behind the dancer's need for a perfectly balanced body. The *danseur* and *danseuse noble*, who perform the leading roles in the big classical ballets, *need* beautifully proportioned bodies. Their technique and artistry are developed to exploit this beauty. But a well-proportioned body is necessary in every dancer as a protection against the physical strains of a dancer's profession. A well-balanced body is less likely to weaken under these strains. More dancers fail to complete their training through physical weakness than for any other reason.

Today's ideal dancing physique should show a balance between the upper and lower halves of the body. (Illustration 2 (a).) 'A good guide for the best proportions may be taken from ancient Greece in which the length from the crown of the head to the pubic arch or fork is equal to that from the fork to the ground. Following the same pattern, the length from the fork to the lower border of the knee cap should be equal to that from the lower border of the knee cap to the ground.

'According to the classical tradition, the shoulders of the man are broader than the hips, in the woman they are somewhat narrower. Here we diverge somewhat for it has been found by experience that the ideal ballet figure is the better for some slight extra width across the shoulders, whether male or female.'[1] This extra width in feminine shoulders is accepted today by women of all professions. It is a divergence of the twentieth-century ideal from the Greek ideal.

(a)

2. THE DANCER

(a) The ideal physique—dancer *de face*

Arms and hands must be similarly, though less strictly, proportioned. The head, neither too large nor too small, must be well poised upon a neck which is not too square nor too short. The body must be borne with an easy, upright carriage upon legs which are straight and well formed, and upon feet which are flexible and strong with a good instep and firm, straight toes of medium length.

Perfect proportions, however, are rare. Most dancers, as Noverre observed, are permanently *arqué* (bow-legged) or *jarreté* (slightly knock-kneed). The *arqué* dancer usually has speed, elevation and facility for *batterie*, while the *jarreté* dancer is better at flowing,

[1] Celia Sparger, former consulting physiotherapist to the Royal Ballet School, *Ballet Physique*, p. 11 ff. (A. & C. Black, London, 1958).

lyrical movements. Muscles are important and equally fixed. The *arqué* dancer usually has long muscles which have short tendons, while the *jarreté* dancer with short muscles and long tendons will find that this greatly helps his line. Hence his superiority in classical roles.

The other limbs, and the body itself, can be distinguished in their types. The body with a short back and correspondingly long legs is more likely to make a dancer of great classical roles than a long back and short legs, which are better suited to character dancing. Similarly, different types of foot formation include one with a high arch which is aesthetically pleasing in a *pointe* shoe, but not always very serviceable. On the other hand a strong foot which is good for jumping is often not so attractive to see. It is a question of balancing one need against another.

The face is especially significant. For women, the almond-shaped, delicately-boned face is the face traditional to a classical ballerina, while a mobile, strongly expressive face is necessary for a character dancer. All dancers use their eyes a great deal to give themselves the eloquence they lose by being unable to speak. Therefore large eyes set far apart, like Pavlova, Karsavina and Fonteyn, are specially to be prized. It is a good thing, too, to have the eyes which Gautier admired, 'jet in a sea of crystal'—large irises surrounded by clear white. Thus the eyes will seem more vivid and be more easily seen.

In colouring it is traditional that a classical ballerina should have dark hair contrasted with a pale face. This particular contrast is not essential. What matters is contrast of some kind, whatever the colour, so that the dancer will be more interesting visually. Dark hair makes the best frame for the face to hold the eye of the audience. Here, the hairdresser can reinforce nature.

The male classical dancer should have strong classical features for the noble roles. The face should be clean cut and sensitive. The nose should be straight, the cheek-bones well defined, the jaw line firm, the lips neither too full nor too thin, the eyes clear and set well apart. The effect, in sum, should be poetic, eloquent and commanding.

Weighing all these considerations, dancers and teachers work to develop what nature has given, not to add what nature has omitted. Between them they produce for the choreographer three kinds of instrument.

The *classical* dancer (Illustration 2 (*b*)) will perform the great roles of the classical repertoire and create new roles in the classical or romantic tradition. The *character* dancer will perform national dances and acting roles of a serious or comic nature which range from old Coppelius to the stable-boys in *Petrouchka*. Between them stands the *demi-caractère* dancer (Illustration 2 (*c*)), the man of many parts. He will have a classical technique brilliant enough for the Blue Bird, a lyrical quality equal to Elihu in *Job* and the strength and knowledge

                    (*b*)   (*c*)

2. THE DANCER

(*b*) The classical physique—line in arabesque
(*c*) The *demi-caractère* physique—elevation

to assume the character of any national dance. Really talented *demi-caractère* dancers are able to fill roles in either of the other categories. They are the backbone of every ballet company.

Often temperament, a dancer's emotional character, redresses the balance of physique. Emotional character is twin to the physical and should be equally considered in the training of a dancer. Children come to ballet school, and pass from ballet school to ballet company, with temperaments as definite as the shapes of their bodies. The problem of the teacher is not to define these temperaments, still less

C.A.—12

to restrict them, but to judge how they can be developed under proper guidance.

For choreographic purposes temperaments fall chiefly into two groups, the extrovert and the introvert. The reserved, withdrawn temperament has difficulty in expressing emotion. The others do not. There are degrees and divisions, of course. Generally, withdrawn personalities have the restraint so valuable to the classical dancer. The extroverts, who have no difficulty in projecting their personalities, make good character and dramatic dancers. Between them, the *demi-caractère* dancer holds a balance, inclining to one side or the other.

Sensibility to music is a primary element in emotional make-up. The best material for a choreographer, temperamentally speaking, is a dancer of whatever type who has the gift of response to music and a natural feeling for musical phrase. This is the gift one remarks among really good musical soloists because it makes the difference between mere performance and interpretation. A sense of rhythm may be taught in school, but the best teacher can never replace a natural sense of time and the gift of musicality.

The other important element in emotional make-up is an intellect acute and strong enough to control movement, never to be its slave. Contrary to general belief a dancer needs special intellectual qualities, a quick 'study', wit, intelligence, artistic humility, aesthetic judge-ment.[1] The kind of intelligence a dancer needs is not the highly cerebral kind. The dancer inclined to analysis and academic thought rarely makes a great dancer, though he may make a choreographer. The intelligence needed implies, rather, a wonderfully sensitive awareness of emotional expression in physical movement. And this movement, remember, has to conform to the technical vocabulary.

Above all, a dancer needs self-discipline. Without self-discipline he can never dedicate himself entirely to his art, never submit, as he should, to teacher and choreographer, while retaining personal con-trol over the use of the physical, intellectual and emotional gifts he has brought with him to the dance. In this way, if it does not rest with him to choose which kind of instrument he will become, if he must accept the decision of nature, he can still be master of himself. Intellect, 'real artistry and the gift of movement will always weigh heavily in the balance against physical imperfections'.[2] They always have. Were it otherwise ballet would have lost most of its finest artists.

---

[1] I.e. ability to learn quickly.   [2] Sparger, *op. cit.* p. 8.

CHAPTER XVI

THE DANCER'S SCHOOLING

THE teacher, himself a product of his school and the work of former choreographers, passes to the young dancer the knowledge which can develop his talents.

The foundation of this knowledge is a technique which can be taught only gradually and continuously, 'ever reverting to the basic movements, while dissecting and adding new accomplishments'.[1] This technique is similar throughout the world, but varies from country to country according to history and social background.

It takes about five years, with one lesson a day, to develop a basic technique in a dancer who starts between the ages of eight and ten years. After this, technical training needs to be intensified, mingled with knowledge of theatre craft and emotional development so that the dancer understands how to project himself to the audience. It is best if the whole training is linked with the theatre from the beginning.

Ideally, a dancer's classical training should continue until he has gained control over his body and he has learned to project his personality into his movements. At this point, when technique ceases to be a dictator and becomes a helpmate, perfection begins to be born. Only at this point is a dancer valuable to a choreographer.

The time taken to reach this point varies with every dancer and every school. Usually it is about ten years. But too often a dancer is taken out of school before time for reasons of economy or company expedience. And too often a dancer is given important roles before he has had time to grow as an artist on stage. This growing period usually takes a number of years with a company, dancing *corps de ballet* and small solo roles.

The translation from school to company before a dancer is fully formed emotionally often leaves the dancer unable to give more than a technical performance on stage. This is a fault which many teachers condone, or never notice. Technique needs to be considered as a

[1] Dame Margot Fonteyn, Speech to Canadian members of the Royal Academy of Dancing, December, 1955.

means, never as an end. Yet many teachers and dancers seem to think of it as an end in itself.

Technique, craft, emotional development, all these things must be combined in the service of the dancer to allow him to interpret roles, to be an artist. A dancer who thinks no further than multiple *tours en l'air* or strings of *pirouettes* is an acrobat, not an artist. He has no place in ballet.

The emphasis a school gives to the physical and emotional elements in choreography may quickly be discovered by studying the style the school transmits to a dancer, the dancer's 'schooling'. From the first *plié* of his school days, and forever after, a dancer absorbs this schooling from his teachers. The schooling will have evolved over many years and will be the result of social, geographical, historical and other influences combined with the basic technique of ballet derived originally from France and Italy. It is what each country develops from this technique to suit its national circumstances. It is the material of dance architecture. Classical ballet, like houses, fulfils the same functions everywhere, but is built in different national styles.

The builders are the teachers. Thus the French school is built on the teaching of Beauchamps, Noverre and Vestris, though much of their tradition was lost in France in the late nineteenth century. It was maintained outside France, however, in Denmark and Russia.

The Danish School is the school of Vestris-Bournonville, the French School (Vestris) being developed by a Dane (Bournonville) on Danish temperaments and Danish physiques. The Italian School is the school of Viganò and Blasis (both trained in the school of Vestris) and of Cecchetti who was trained mostly in Italy by Lepri, a pupil of Blasis. Viganò, Blasis and their successors adapted the French School to suit Italian temperament and physique.

The Russian School is the school of France, Italy and Denmark, as we have shown in Chapter V. 'Thus', observed Nicolas Legat, one of the Russian School's best-known exponents, 'the "Russian" school of dancing is an eclectic school—the French, the Scandinavian and the Italian—all welded into an artistic whole by the genius of the Russian people.'[1] Only the young English School has a comparable pedigree.

Ninette de Valois, the founder of the English School, was taught by Édouard Espinosa of the French School and Cecchetti of the

[1] Nicolas Legat, *The Story of the Russian School*, trans. by Sir Paul Dukes, p. 24 (British Continental Press, London, 1932).

Italian School. She worked with the choreographers of the Russian School who were her colleagues in the Diaghilev company. Through her the English School has moulded the French, Italian and Russian schools to the needs of the English physique and temperament. The result, de Valois herself observed, is a dancer who 'has immense dignity, a great capacity for objectivity, a reserve upon which too much emphasis is often placed, and an excessive humility'.[1]

Thus the dancers of every school of ballet speak the same language of movement, but with different accents, which indicate special traits. For this reason, national ballet companies do not like to have their dancers trained outside their school. Apart from the economics of training this would make the company's dance style heterogeneous, greatly complicating choreographic creation.

The permanent choreographers of a national company play an important part in developing their country's school and its dancers. Choreographers tend to use again and again types of movement and steps which appeal to them. In time, when the dancers in their ballets become teachers, these steps and movements are absorbed into the school which develops corresponding strengths and weaknesses.

Today, the English school reflects Frederick Ashton's preference for lyrical, flowing movement compared with the quicker, more brittle, brilliance which is a legacy of Balanchine's choreography to the dancers of America. The English school reflects also the influence of de Valois' narrative style and Tudor's treatment of emotion in ballet, or perhaps one should say rather, of Rambert's insistence on interpretative qualities. The American school has been influenced similarly by Tudor, the narrative style of de Mille and the persistently American idiom of Jerome Robbins.

Dancers of today rarely work under a single choreographer as they did in Petipa's time in Russia. They face, too, technical problems never encountered by their predecessors. Not only has the general level of technique developed far beyond the level Diaghilev showed Paris, but the range of repertoire demands a more extensive understanding of styles than was needed at the turn of the century. 'The ballets of Petipa and those of Fokine', Dame Margot Fonteyn pointed out, 'cannot be danced in the same way. The dancer of today needs such a pure and honest technique that changes of style present no problems.'[2]

[1] Speech to Cecchetti Society, *Times Educational Supplement*, 5th August, 1955
[2] Speech to Canadian members of the Royal Academy of Dancing, December, 1955.

The same is true of the emotional element in dancing. Always the most significant element it has ever been the most neglected. Noverre complained of this neglect, Fokine sought to correct it, and long before Noverre, John Weaver in London was asking his dancers to give less attention to the brilliance of feet and steps and more to emotional expression through the arms, body and head.

'The Feet and Steps,' he wrote, 'which seem to claim the greatest Share towards the Perfection of this Art, will not, as I shall show, appear so material a Qualification towards the Masterly Perform-ance of it, as the *Address* of the body, and just and regular Movements of the Arms; neither is it so difficult to obtain an Excellency in the former, as in the latter; for whereas the Feet require only Agility, and constant Practice, to arrive at the utmost Perfection; the *Motions* of the Body and Arms require a Judgement, and knowledge in several Arts, to qualify them for a just Performance; for it is by the *Motion* of the Body and Arms, that he must express the *Design*, and form the *Imitation*. . . .'[1] From then until now the arms and the body remain the secret of expressing the emotions as the emotions remain the first means whereby the dancer can move his audience.

The environment of home, school and company will be decisive in a dancer's emotional and intellectual development. The dancer is nothing without a company. It is his setting. Its environment makes him what he is and what he will become. Yet few professional dancers outside Russia today are left time by their companies to study more than the technical problems of their roles, still less to consider deeply the arts related to dancing. Their intellectual interests are restricted by company economics and the need to earn their living at too early an age.

Most dancers, as Ulanova has observed, reach their highest tech-nical proficiency before they are thirty, whereas artistic maturity comes only after the experience of many years. This is the tragedy of a dancer's profession. Schools and choreographers could mitigate it if they would, the one by providing a more thorough artistic education alongside technical education, the other by a more con-sidered use of talent as it develops to maturity.

Nowadays, at most ballet schools, the education of the mind—aesthetic, mimetic and histrionic—is allowed to take second place to the education of the body. In the theatre producers sometimes allow the substance of a role to take second place to its technical

[1] John Weaver, *Essay towards an History of Dancing* (London, 1712).

performance. The effect of this is to create puppets rather than people.

Even choreographers are guilty sometimes of stressing technical brilliance above emotional expression. There is nothing creative about such choreography or its performance. When, however, expression and technique are perfectly balanced in choreography and dancing the choreographer has put to creative use the instrument the school has given him. Dancer and choreographer then become one in the 'soul's soaring flight' for which Pushkin immortalised Istomina in *Eugene Onegin*.

CHAPTER XVII

THE DANCING

A CHOREOGRAPHER'S dance vocabulary is the sum of the movements he uses. This vocabulary is drawn from four sources: the traditional academic steps of classical ballet; other traditional dance sources such as folk dance and social dance; modern expressionist dancing; and original movements created by the choreographer himself. Cementing these movements, as mortar cements bricks, are mime and acting.

(i) DANSE D'ÉCOLE

The foundation of all choreography in classical ballet is the academic vocabulary of the *danse d'école*. The origin of this vocabulary was discussed in Chapter III. Its terminology is French, which has become the language of ballet as English is of sport.

The steps which compose the vocabulary are always developing and changing. (Illustration 3.) A *pas de bourrée* in Louis XIV's time was not the movement we know by this name today. The ballerinas of 1841 danced the steps of *Giselle* differently from the way we dance them. Thus the vocabulary of ballet reacts to outside influences like a vocabulary of words. And it gathers a variety of accents from country to country, like the accents gathered by the English language in America and the Commonwealth.

There are three main branches of the *danse d'école*—French, Italian and Russian. To these we are beginning to add a fourth school, the English School. It does not matter which of these a choreographer studies at first. The vocabulary is the same even if the style and terminology are different.

The three main schools are represented in most West European countries and in America. Often the best of each has been absorbed by dancers during their training. Many dancers study more than one school. Many teachers teach more than one school, seeking the best from each. Indeed, the schools today are so intermingled that it is hard sometimes to identify individual techniques. Dancers with

184

choreographic ambitions should make it their business to study the origins of each school as far as possible. One can trace, for example, an unbroken evolution of the French, Italian and Russian Schools

(*a*) Late seventeenth century   (*b*) Mid eighteenth century

(*c*) Mid twentieth century

3. DEVELOPMENT OF 'PORT DE BRAS'

from the period of Vestris. Today, each of these schools manifests individual characteristics which yet owe a great deal to each other.

The contemporary French School is notable for the excellence of its leg work, its high extensions (e.g. Jeanmaire) and brilliance in *batterie* and elevation (e.g. Babilée). It does not appear to stress what is understood today by 'classical line'—or *épaulement* and the subtler movements of the upper body, except in rare cases, such as the ballerinas, Chauviré and Vyroubova.

In Denmark where the modern Danish School has developed from the teachings of Bournonville (see Appendix VI A) the French influence is still strongly noticeable. To this has been added influences from Fokine and, more recently, the Vaganova trained teacher, Vera Volkova.

In Britain the French School provided the first technical basis of the Royal Academy of Dancing. Édouard Espinosa, son of a famous French dancer and teacher, became one of the Academy's founders; Dame Adeline Genée, the Danish ballerina, became its first president. This influence was later absorbed, and largely submerged, by stronger Russian-Italian influences.

The Italian School was the style of Vestris developed by Carlo Blasis through the Italian physique and temperament. From this evolved the School of Milan. In the nineteenth century this school developed such virtuosity as to make its products everywhere in demand. An example of its teaching towards the end of the century can be found at Appendix VI B in the notes of the ballerina, Pierina Legnani, already described in Chapter V. These show us something of the technical equipment which Italian dancers took to Russia. They help to complete our knowledge of the development of the School of Milan from Blasis through his pupil, Lepri, to Lepri's pupil, Cecchetti.

The visits to Russia of Italian ballerinas such as Zucchi and Legnani, and the long residence there of Cecchetti as dancer and teacher initiated a fruitful exchange. The Russians absorbed Italian methods and the Italian School in the person of Cecchetti acquired Russian influences. Later, this Italo-Russian method was developed and modified further to suit Russian physiques and temperaments when Cecchetti became the teacher of the Diaghilev company. Today, the method which Cecchetti evolved in concert with his many pupils is known as the Cecchetti system and is taught in all parts of the world, where these pupils have settled. It was codified under Cecchetti's guidance by Cyril Beaumont and Stanislas Idzikowski in *A Manual of the Theory and Practice of Classical Theatrical Dancing* published in 1922. Many times reprinted, this manual perpetuates Cecchetti's principles and exercises.

The great teacher laid considerable stress on posture. The carriage of the upper body had to be lifted well off the hips, to give a firm gripped waistline and squareness in the placing of the body. Considerable attention was given, also, to *port de bras*. Arms and head must be placed exactly to give perfect coordination and to make the best use of *épaulement*. The strong *pirouettes* and slow turns in many positions, which are a feature of the system, reflect the traditional attack and control of the Italian School. It was this which brought fame to many of its exponents eighty years ago.

Cecchetti's principle of drawing the soles of the feet together in the air, before landing in the fifth position from a high jump, has largely gone out of fashion. It is argued that it destroys the line of the leg. With it, to some extent, has gone the quality of high elevation. Certainly female dancers today find it hard to complete the slow Cecchetti *allegro enchaînements*. These make for great strength, but, in the opinion of some experts, are inclined to develop too much the thigh and calf muscles, and to restrict plasticity.

Such criticisms were levelled against the virtuoso Italian ballerinas of the last century. They are levelled still today by those who feel that the exceptionally strong technique produced by the Cecchetti method is more suited in women to *demi-caractère* or soubrette ballerinas than to the purely classical dancer. Nevertheless, the method has yet to be surpassed for strength, placing and *port de bras*.

When talking now of the Russian School one must remember that this, properly speaking, is found today only in the Soviet Union. We mean the entire training from the class of beginners to the class of perfection taken in complete sequence as taught at the Bolshoi or Kirov Schools. The 'Russian' methods still taught by émigré Russians all over the world communicate Russian influence and principles, but not the contemporary Russian School to their pupils. It was these methods in their early days, of course, which produced well-known dancers such as Baronova, Toumanova and Riabouchinska, thus earning an honourable place in the history of classical technique.

Historically, the Russian School includes elements of the French and Italian Schools as we have shown. Over the years it has extended the line of the French School, modified Italian 'roundness' and added, above all, plasticity and expressiveness.

Technically, it has evolved a back energetically concave and gripped in the waist giving particular beauty to all *arabesques*. It commands great breadth of movement, high elevation, high extensions and a free, generous line. These qualities were especially evident at the beginning of this century in the dancing of Trefilova, Pavlova and Karsavina. During the Soviet era, the great teacher Vaganova developed many of the School's qualities further, most of them illustrated at their best in the dancing of Ulanova.

The technical characteristics of the English School have been summarised by Dame Ninette de Valois as 'neatness, speed and precision'. She couples with this a stress on analysis which results from the School's efforts to build itself on a sound academic basis, examining everything from first principles. 'We are on the way', said Dame Ninette, 'towards the modification, harnessing and compromising of both the Russian and the Blasis-Cecchetti Schools, coupled with an exceedingly sound academic theory set up by the Royal Academy of Dancing.'[1] More cannot be said at the moment.

Each of these four schools group steps and movements in different ways for teaching purposes, according to the emphasis of the school. This is a matter of conviction. It does not alter the international character of the ballet vocabulary.

Vaganova divided the vocabulary of the Russian-Soviet School into *battements*, jumps, beats and so on, ten groups in all.[2] Cecchetti and the teachers of his method grouped the movements into six sets of exercises laid down in the manual of the Cecchetti method, one set for each day of the week.[3] Cecchetti's method directly corresponds with the first codification of the classical technique by Carlo Blasis, but develops it further.

Every choreographer of ballet absorbs this vocabulary during his years at school and while he is dancing with a company. Throughout his life it remains the basis of his work, comprising, nowadays, about one hundred and fifty steps, poses and movements affecting every limb of the body. These are capable of infinite variety.

A choreographer can use this vocabulary in three ways. He may create or reproduce a ballet which requires the performance of classical steps in an earlier style. (Plate XVII (a).) He may use the steps in a contemporary way, for virtuoso purposes, as Ashton does in *La Fille Mal Gardée* (Plate XVII (b)) and Balanchine does in *Ballet Imperial*. He may modify classical steps not for virtuoso purposes, but to show qualities of character or emotion as Tudor does in

---

[1] Ninette de Valois, *op. cit.* p. 231.

[2] Vaganova, *Basic Principles of Classical Ballet* (A. & C. Black, London, 1948).

[3] Beaumont and Idzikowski, *A Manual of the Theory and Practice of Classical Theatrical Dancing* (Beaumont, London, 1955).

Dark Elegies and MacMillan in *The Burrow*. Here the steps are still the steps of the *danse d'école* but they are moulded in new ways and combined with new movements created by the choreographer for emotional effect.

(ii) OTHER TRADITIONAL DANCE SOURCES

The social dances and folk dances of the past and present are source material to choreographers no less important than the *danse d'école*. From the folk dance sprang the social dances of the French court and the first vocabulary of ballet in the seventeenth century. Since that time the folk dance has continually enriched the classical vocabulary. Whenever the connection between folk dance and the *danse d'école* has been forgotten or worn thin the classical ballet has become arid and ossified.

Within the term 'folk dance' we include the dances created by modern working youth in industrial towns. If dancing is an expression of human emotion, individual and collective, choreographers cannot separate themselves from its modern expression in the *palais de danse*. These social dances, so vibrant with life, are, in a sense, the folk dances of our industrial society. Choreographers handling contemporary themes can do worse than draw inspiration from them. And if the dances are not always very beautiful, Belinsky's principle that in art 'there is no beautiful form without beautiful content', may help to guide their selection.

Richer veins of inspiration lie in older folk dances. Folk dances and country dances are descended from a nation's agricultural past, often looking back, as we have shown, to early magical ceremonies. In many areas these dances continue to be the social dances of the countryside. They range in form from the circle of many dancers to the smallest unit of two people.

The skips, hops, stamps and pivots of these dances all over Europe, their leaps and jumps and carriage of the body, are the movements from which the vocabulary of the *danse d'école* was born. 'There can be traced', Dame Ninette de Valois told the Royal Society of Arts,[1] 'from the Basque country to the highlands of Scotland, not only the steps but the very style of the classical dance. I know of no pastime that gives me more delight than to witness the annual display of folk dancing at the Albert Hall. I am able to recognise and name,

[1] Speech to the Royal Society of Arts, London, 29th May, 1957.

according to the academic terminology of the classical ballet, every step that I can see executed. Here I see these steps unadorned, yet neatly executed in their original simple form.'

Bournonville's *La Sylphide* in Denmark, now the earliest ballet in the British repertoire,[1] uses these Scottish dances in its first act. Many other romantic ballets reflect folk influences, the clearest late romantic examples being the mazurka and czardas in the first act of *Coppélia*.

Petipa stylised folk dances according to the canons of the traditional classical ballet. A three-year stay in Spain when he was a young man must have contributed to the Spanish dances in his ballets. They show Spanish characteristics in costume and movements for *épaulements* and *port de bras* imposed upon a costume and movements for the legs which remain formally classical. Compare this approach with Massine's Spanish dances in *Le Tricorne* and the dances presented by Antonio's Spanish Ballet today.

Not until the appearance of Fokine and Massine did the wealth of folk dances really begin to be exploited in ballet. Fokine set an example to his successors by using this wealth as a reference library, combining and adapting what he found there to the academic vocabulary. His studies even enabled him to create for *Prince Igor* the folk dances of a people about whose history and culture very little was known.

Massine studied and drew more widely on the folk dances of Europe. From this derives the truthful character and style-atmosphere of all his national ballets, from *Le Tricorne*, set in Spain, to *Donald of the Burthens*, set in Scotland. On each occasion Massine accomplished the difficult feat of transposing original folk steps into balletic terms. In *Le Tricorne*, especially in the *farucca* and the *jota*, the academic vocabulary remains the basis of the ballet. Nevertheless, the Andalusian character and dance-style imposed upon it so change the execution of the vocabulary that it seems something new.

Antonio, born and trained in Spain, founded his reputation directly upon the folk dances of his country. He arranged and adapted these for theatrical purposes but never had to transfer them, as Massine did, to dancers trained in another idiom. Latterly he has called in the discipline of classical ballet to strengthen and vary his choreography. So the wheel has gone full circle.

In America some classical choreographers of the forties and fifties,

[1] Produced by Elsa-Marianne von Rosen for the Ballet Rambert, 20th July, 1960.

such as Agnes de Mille, have drawn their deepest inspiration from folk dance and contemporary social dancing, especially jazz dancing. *Rodeo* is an example. In *Fancy Free* and *N.Y.Export:Op.Jazz* Jerome Robbins drew many of his movements from the social dances of American teenagers. Indeed his ballets often seem to be a direct reflection of the feelings and frustrations of young people in modern life. A similar inspiration is reflected in British ballet through the work of Cranko and MacMillan.

In the Soviet Union the link between folk-lore and the *danse d'école* has been carried furthest of all. An intense study of the history of folk dance and social dancing has helped choreographers to achieve the realism they seek. Lavrovsky built one of the most effective scenes of *Romeo and Juliet* upon a cushion dance of the Renaissance period. Two of the most outstanding contributions to the Bolshoi's first London season were Fenster's Ukrainian dance from *Taras Bulba* and Yagudin's dance of his own countrymen, the Bashkiri. From the opposite direction, Igor Moiseyev and other national dance companies have built their ensembles with classically trained dancers, although the choreography of their repertoire is drawn entirely from folk material. (Plate XVIII (a).)

Folk dances, of course, cannot be transferred wholesale to the ballet stage. Where classical ballet uses authentic folk material it does so in a way which refines and adapts the steps to its purpose and vocabulary. 'One must not', Moiseyev once remarked, 'turn the national dance in ballet into an ethnographic document. It is not slavish photographic reproduction of folk-lore that can stimulate the classical ballet. Artistic adaptation of folk-lore can stimulate it, however. . . . If the richness of folk choreography were infused into the classical ballet, its powers of expression would become immeasurably greater.'[1]

But in Britain the development of creative links between our classical dancing and our folk dancing still lies in the future. Although British folk dance is taught now in the Royal Ballet School, the wealth of folk steps danced naturally in the British countryside is mostly passed over by choreographers. Yet the Lancashire clog dance inspired one of the highlights in Ashton's *La Fille Mal Gardée* and there is rich inspiration to be found in the athletic Scottish and Irish dances and the virile English sword dances.

[1] I. Moiseyev, 'The Ballet and Reality' in *Ulanova on Soviet Ballet* (S.C.R., London, 1954).

'We have yet to solve the problem of our folk dance and its place in the theatre', said Dame Ninette de Valois acknowledging this weakness to the Royal Society of Arts. 'Certain folk dance and folk-lore ballets are necessary in every National Ballet Company; they should be fostered if only to develop the special characteristics of the native dancer; such works are a sure means of expressing a country's national form of musicality.

'The English dancer has shown himself to possess neatness, speed and precision in his technical feats. In his more expressive moments we are aware that he has a marked lyrical quality; in his dramatisation of a scene is shown a strong sense of detailed characterisation. I would say that, in performance, he unconsciously responds to his own folk dance and a closer contact with this source would help to develop and stabilise these qualities.

'We await a further generation of English dancers emerging from their own newly founded tradition. It is inevitable that this future generation of artists will bring forth some young choreographers bent on a more distinctly national form of self-expression.'[1]

(iii) MODERN EXPRESSIONIST DANCING

Unlike classical ballet, folk dance and social dance, modern expressionist dancing has no tradition outside the present century and no codified vocabulary which can boast international use. It looks back a mere seventy years to when the work of Isadora Duncan and Ruth St. Denis in America, Jaques Dalcroze in Switzerland and Rudolf von Laban in Germany was becoming known.

All the expressionist dancers and choreographers in Europe and America took as their starting-point the involuntary movements which express human emotions. Reflex actions provided their first vocabulary. They analysed these movements and other types of movement far removed from classical ballet. They looked back to the primitive beginnings of the dance. On these foundations they built their personal vocabularies. Sometimes they borrowed from folk dance, as St. Denis and Shawn did, or used movements derived from nervous, intellectual and emotional responses, as Laban and Jooss did, or combined these things with the discipline of classical

[1] Speech to the Royal Society of Arts, 29th May, 1957, reproduced as introduction to *The Ballet in Britain* (Oxford University Press, 1962).

ballet, as Graham did. All of them felt that their vocabularies of dancing expressed the contemporary world better than the strict technique of the *danse d'école*.

Often they were right, although the world of their dancing was serious, grim and sometimes absurd. Laughter was a rare visitor to their stages. Yet outside Russia, classical ballet everywhere, especially in America, was challenged by what they had to say. They forced the *danse d'école* to examine itself and bring itself up to date.

The first impact of these ideas on classical technique appeared in *Eunice*, one of Fokine's earliest ballets, created in 1907 as a direct tribute to Duncan. '*Eunice*', Karsavina recorded, 'was a compromise between our tradition and the Hellenic revival embodied by Isadora.'[1] Nevertheless, Duncan exerted no significant influence upon Fokine. The most startling demonstration of expressionist influence came later, in Nijinsky's two ballets, *L'Après-midi d'un Faune* and *Le Sacre du Printemps*. Probably the influence was unconscious. But the two ballets, building on the innovations of Fokine, gave something of a jolt to the *danse d'école*.

Looking back at this period of choreography it seemed as if classical ballet in Western Europe had climbed a long hill. Suddenly, it saw from the top a land of new expressive opportunities. Crossing this land during the twenties, thirties and forties of our century, it absorbed more and more from what it found there.

Classical choreographers found an attitude of mind which began always with the emotions. Previously, many of these choreographers would have started to create by conceiving dance patterns and steps. Then they would build emotion, even meaning, into these patterns. The difference can be seen in the way the classically trained Ashton handles a literary theme today compared with the Jooss trained Birgit Cullberg.

When creating *Romeo and Juliet* for the Royal Danish Ballet, Ashton first studied his dancers to discover the strong and weak points of his cast. Then he considered how best to use this material, even constructing his libretto to suit the dancers. But he never departed from Prokofiev's music nor Shakespeare's story. Cullberg, handling the same subject, was first concerned with story and content. She worked months on the details of her libretto before seeing her dancers. In the event she made several departures from Prokofiev's

[1] Karsavina, *Theatre Street*, p. 211 (Heinemann, London, 1931).

score and emphasised the psychological aspects of the story. To her, story and content dominate everything, including the music and the dancing.

This emphasis on content, especially emotional content, is reflected in expressionist technique. Every movement in expressionist vocabularies starts from the centre of the body and moves outwards to the limbs. Since the emotions are centred in the diaphragm, say the expressionists, the torso should first express itself in movement and so give movement to the limbs. Unlike the *danse d'école*, therefore, the limbs rarely move without being impelled by an expression of the torso. This general premise is not altered by the fact that a certain type of emotion produces peripheral movement only.

Such a doctrine implies a use of the torso and the limbs quite different from classical ballet. In ballet the legs must be turned out from the hips, and the upper part of the body, the arms and the head move only upon the relatively immobile lower torso. The immobility of the lower torso reflects the days when costume restrictions, especially corsets for men and women, made free movement impossible. Today the same immobility of the lower torso is needed to control the hips and to achieve virtuosity in *pointe* work, *batterie* and multiple *pirouettes*. All these require the straight back traditional to classical ballet.

Expressionist dancing requires no *pointe* work and often rejects shoes in favour of bare feet. The legs may or may not be turned out. It demands flexibility of the whole body, making great use of the middle and lower part of the back. Virtuosity for the sake of virtuosity is foreign to it so that *batterie*, multiple *pirouettes* and other demonstrations of physical skill have no place in its vocabularies.

These vocabularies explore space differently from classical ballet. The floor is a plane to be used in the dance, not just a base to support the dancing, as it is in ballet. 'Instead of the classic ballet's striving upwards to a floating (*svävande*) lightness,' wrote Birgit Cullberg, 'Martha Graham accepts the floor as a platform for sculptural lines. Her dancers often lie like statues, knocked over in horizontal positions, supporting themselves on one knee, a shoulder or an elbow as often as on their feet.'[1]

Under the same reasoning expressionist *port de bras* and the bends and inclinations of the body are conceived in terms of directions in space. The movements forward and backward, high and low

[1] Programme of the Royal Swedish Ballet, June, 1958.

diagonals, circles and figures of eight, all have an emotional origin, or at least an emotional explanation.

The emotional roots of expressionist dancing dictate also the execution of movements and the terms which describe them. Classical ballet may perform its movements at different speeds and rhythms but does not consider particularly the degree of tension in these movements. Expressionist dancing emphasises different tensions in execution and explores these tensions in its teaching to produce dynamic effects. One can see the influence in Jerome Robbins' choreography. It is what distinguishes his work from, say, Ashton or Balanchine. With him the deep romantic *fondu* has become a deep bend whence the dancer is released like a spring. Robbins' choreography does not burn like fire, as Russian choreography does, but like electricity. The bodies, the angular movements, are feverish with action, suddenly exploding in bursts of energy.

The descriptive terms of expressionist steps reflect emotional roots, as well as an occasional debt to the *danse d'école* for an exercise or a discipline. In the classroom one may hear of *impulses, bumps, contractions, rises* and *bends* alongside the balletic *plié* or *battement*.

The high point of expressionist dancing on the European stage came with Jooss's *The Green Table* and *The Big City* in 1932. Throughout the twenties and thirties Germany was the home of expressionist dancing, with a direct influence reaching as far as Holland, Sweden and Poland. Then the rise of classical ballet in Western Europe and America during the Second World War renewed the influence of the *danse d'école* in these parts of Europe.

In America expressionist ideas dominated serious dance theatre until the thirties. Classical ballet then began to gain an ascendancy, fostered by the presence of Balanchine, Massine and the Ballets Russes, Dolin, Markova, and later, Tudor. During the forties, as we have shown, a generation of American choreographers came forward, who acknowledged the *danse d'école*, expressionist dancing and folk dance equally as their teachers. In the work of Agnes de Mille, Jerome Robbins and Michael Kidd these three dance forms have been combined to produce choreographic styles which are new, specifically American.

In Britain ballet was never challenged by any home-grown expressionist movement. The Greek Dance of Ruby Ginner, the Margaret Morris Movement and the Natural Movement of Madge Atkinson were Britain's equivalent of Duncan's ideas. They never took root in the theatre but have been of value in the educational field.

Even so, British choreographers could not ignore what was happening on the Continent and in America. Most clearly influenced were de Valois and Tudor, although the theories and explorations of expressionist choreography affected all British choreographic thinking.

Since the war expressionist influences have fused more solidly with classical ballet. The work of younger choreographers in France, Britain and America shows the ideas of the expressionists absorbed into the *danse d'école* and reproduced as part of the post-war idiom. (Plate XVIII (b).) We can see more clearly how expressionism has changed classical choreography. In *content*, expressionist dances are usually about things felt rather than representations of things seen. Therefore the movement has helped significantly to develop the *genres* of mood and abstract ballet. In these *genres* particularly, the expressionist movement has helped choreographers to adapt the classical vocabulary to contemporary thinking. Since, for instance, classical ballet in its purest form reflects the confidence of privilege, it is unsuitable to express insecurity and unstable emotions. Through the expressionist movement these barriers have been removed. In *technique*, the expressionists have upset the universal application of the classical canon to 'let your body be, in general, erect and perpendicular on your legs'.[1] The essential difference between expressionist dancing and classical ballet is the displacement of the centre of gravity away from the vertical. In introducing this displacement lies the greatest single influence of expressionism over classical technique.

In Scandinavia we have shown how the work of Birgit Cullberg and Ivo Cramer reflects a reverse process. Latterly these expressionist choreographers have used much of the classical style and vocabulary, often with striking effect. Their success suggests that the expressionists can benefit from a study of the *danse d'école*, no less than classical choreographers can learn from the expressionists.

(iv) Original Movement

So far we have spoken of existing vocabularies which a choreographer can use. Any competent dance arranger who has learned from the *danse d'école*, folk dance and modern dance can build dances

[1] Blasis, *Code of Terpsichore*, p. 65 (London, 1830).

from these vocabularies. He takes what he needs from each source. He is the choreographic journalist of whom we spoke in Chapter XIII.

A choreographer does this too. But he gives something extra to the dance. Choreography, in fact, 'begins when the teacher or choreographer substitutes an unconventional movement for the conventional one'.[1] The choreographer handles established steps so that they appear in new forms. He has talent for creating original movements and patterns.

When he creates movement a choreographer's starting-point is the dancer. The dancer is his plastic material. The dancer places at the choreographer's disposal every variant of movement his trained body can produce.

These almost limitless possibilities are limited in practice by the dancer's training, the choreographer's training and the needs of design, gravity and rhythm.

From many vocabularies of dancing a choreographer will select the types of movement which seem to suit him best; he will evolve a personal idiom. This is why every choreographer should study widely as a dancer. His choreographic idiom will be enriched then by experience. Fokine, Massine, Balanchine and Ashton all show how this experience can influence his art.

Given the choreographic gift, invention takes two forms: the discovery of new movement and the arrangement of old movements in original ways. Choreographers lean to one form or the other. The real difficulty is to build the invention into a statement which has meaning for the onlooker, avoiding the repetition of personal devices which recur in every choreographer's idiom. 'I have an affinity for diagonal movements on the stage,' wrote Agnes de Mille, 'with figures entering at one corner and leaving at the opposite, and unless I watch myself, this pattern recurs tiresomely.'[2]

Choreographers learn to guard against themselves, learn to select wisely from their own inventions. The same wisdom has to guide their selection from the past. The wealth of sources available to a choreographer must be used sparingly, only taking that which applies to the moment. 'The best form', said Fokine, 'is that which

[1] Dame Ninette de Valois quoted by Joan Lawson, *Classical Ballet* (Black, London, 1960).
[2] Agnes de Mille, *And Promenade Home*, p. 177 (Hamish Hamilton, London, 1959).

most fully expresses the meaning desired, and the most natural one, that which most closely corresponds with the idea to be conveyed.'[1]

Whence come these forms and the originality for which every choreographer seeks? They lie in the choreographer's personal style. Hence the aspiring choreographer's first task is to search inside himself for this style.

(v) MIME AND ACTING

The choreographer has behind him a tradition of mime and acting. Their quality and emphasis vary from country to country.

Mime, descending from the *commedia dell' arte*, is one of the parents of choreography and deserves special study from this point of view. In choreographic history there have been two opposite approaches to mime. Those like Perrot and Fokine favour the story told entirely in expressive dance. Those like Petipa introduce a stylised mime to tell the story between passages of dancing.

Weaver and Noverre were two of the earliest advocates of expressive dance forms in ballet as against empty brilliance. By the Romantic period many of their ideas had taken root even if Romantic aesthetics distorted them. Some of the story was danced; most of it was told in a conventional mime-gesture directly descended from the *commedia dell' arte* through the French theatre of the Rococo. About two hundred of these gestures are known to us today, although only about fifty are in general use in the romantic and classical ballets we perform. Perfectly understood by the audience of nineteenth-century balletomanes, they were used for the mime passages in ballet which told the story, the dancing generally being quite separate. Danish and Russian dancers today excel in this mime-gesture.

At the end of the nineteenth century Petipa, interested more in dancing than story-telling, relied entirely on such gestures to carry forward his slender stories and provide excuses for the dance. (Plate XIX (a).) Not that the gestures were boring, formal or inexpressive in themselves any more than they need be so today in contemporary versions of Petipa's works. 'The most fascinating movements of all were those when Petipa composed his mimic scenes', wrote Nicholas Legat about Petipa's methods of choreography. 'Showing each

[1] Fokine, in the Russian periodical *Argus*, No. 1, 1916, quoted by Beaumont, *Michel Fokine and His Ballets*, p. 135 (Beaumont, London, 1935).

participant in turn he would get quite carried away by the parts, and the whole hall would sit with bated breath, following the extra-ordinary expressive mimicry of this artistic giant. When the scene was set there would be a terrific outburst of applause, but Petipa paid little attention. He would return quietly to his seat, smiling and licking his lips in a characteristic gesture, lighting a cigarette, and sitting silent for a time. Then the whole scene would be repeated while Petipa put finishing touches to the actions of the individual artists.'[1]

The difficulty about such *récitatif* scenes is that they disturb the choreographic unity of the work, its overall form, however well they are composed. Better that the dancing itself should express through the dancer's body what the mime takes time off to say. Ivanov, Gorsky and Fokine at the end of the nineteenth century redeveloped the principle of earlier ballet-masters that narrative and dancing should be integrated in a single whole.

Fokine rejected utterly the conventional mime we see preserved today in *The Sleeping Beauty*. He evolved dance forms which used the whole body to express ideas. 'Man can be and should be ex-pressive from head to foot,'[2] he wrote in his famous letter to *The Times*.

Massine applied these principles further in character dancing. In his ballets, especially in their principal roles, we see emerging the actor-dancer. The actor-dancer goes one better than the dancer who uses only an expressive body to reflect or create mood and emotion. The actor-dancer acts realistically with his face, his hands, everything he has. (Plate XIX (b) and (c).) He fulfils Weaver's dream that 'as a *Performer*, his Perfection is to become what he performs'.[3] To be able to act in this way, as well as have an expressive body, should be the aim of every dancer. 'It is as actor-dancers,' empha-sised Zakharov, the Soviet choreographer, 'that celebrities like Ulanova, Semeyonova, Vecheslova, Lepeshinskaya, Dudinskaya, Shelest . . . and others have become famous.'[4]

In Britain during the thirties and forties ballets were developed which fused acting and dancing in many of their roles. *The Rake's Progress* and *Miracle in the Gorbals* perfectly show this in character

[1] N. Legat, *Story of the Russian School*, p. 37 (British Continental Press, London, 1932).   [2] Fokine, letter to *The Times*, 6th July, 1914.
[3] John Weaver, *Essay towards an history of Dancing*, p. 166 (London, 1712).
[4] Rostislav Zakharov, *The Art of the Ballet Master* (Moscow, 1954).

ballet (Plate XIX (c)); *La Fête Étrange* shows it in a *demi-caractère* idiom.

But the straight classical ballet continued to demand little of the actor. Balanchine in America abandoned acting altogether. His choreography does not ask even for facial expression, only expression through the body in dance movements which are often pure abstraction.

Today, in spite of the advances of the thirties, the union of mime and acting remains unconsummated in the minds of most choreographers. They agree only that the conventional mime of Petipa should be rejected.

Yet 'the dancer is as much concerned with Stanislavsky as Cecchetti. The ballet is only interesting as a branch of the theatre; only the complete theatrical personality is interesting as a dancer.'[1] Soviet choreographers applying to ballet the principles of Stanislavsky, require the projection of the artist into the psyche of a role so that the role is realised *from the inside*. To achieve such a projection the artist must study the character he is to portray very thoroughly, if possible in real life. This experience helps him to assume the inner personality of the character. Once he has mastered the inner personality its physical manifestation in gestures, mannerisms and so on, will follow naturally, as in life.

A few choreographers outside the Soviet Union have adopted the same principles. They maintain that if a dancer who is naturally slow moving has to portray an impulsive person he must learn to move quickly and impulsively, probably with small sharp gestures. He will not maintain these movements convincingly over a long period unless he has learnt how to assume the mental outlook of an impulsive person. If all dancers could be trained successfully to assume the whole personalities of their roles and maintain them throughout their ballets, they would be less likely to make wrong gestures. The gestures would feel out of key at once, even to themselves.

Zakharov pleads for the wide application of the Stanislavsky method in Soviet ballet and the creation from it of living 'dance images'. But 'our ballet schools have not yet introduced this form of dancing into the training of our future dancers. It is still only the technique of the dance that is studied there, and there is no scientifically evolved method of training for the image-evoking *pas d'action*. This shows more clearly than anything else how backward our ballet

[1] Arnold Haskell, *The National Ballet*, p. 35 (Black, London, 1943).

schools are in relation to stage practice.'[1] The same might be said, of course, of all ballet schools throughout the world.

Desirable though it is that choreographers should give dancers the opportunity to act, this should not be at the expense of dancing. 'Nobody would think of belittling the significance of clever miming in ballet,' wrote Moiseyev a few years ago. 'But the most expressive, most emotional, most poetic language of ballet is the dance. . . . Unfortunately, even in a production of such great stature as *Romeo and Juliet* . . . the choreographer, L. Lavrovsky, gives undue weight to the element of mime, as if mistrustful of the language of the dance. . . .'[2]

Outside the Soviet Union the choreographer who has applied Stanislavsky's principles most consistently in his ballets is Antony Tudor. Because of his residence in America since 1939 the important contribution he might have made to the development of British actor-dancers has been lost. Sadder still, the younger generation of British choreographers have missed an influence which could have balanced their tendency today to concentrate on movement at the expense of acting and expression.

In America choreographers on stage and screen have developed a specifically American kind of realistic gesture. American actor-dancers can feel very much at home with the mime element of *Fall River Legend*, or *Fancy Free*. 'They dance down the street with typical sailor movements', says Jerome Robbins' scenario for *Fancy Free*, illustrating the common roots of dance and mimetic style in everyday American events.

In France some of the best choreography since the war has shown a preference for strong dramatic ballets based on tragic stories. The choreographers, often performing the principal roles themselves, have created memorable characters. But their inability to create effective minor roles has sometimes weakened the total effect of their work. Presently, this might be corrected under the spreading influence of the post-war French mime schools. Here, even if dancing plays no part in training, the performance is often accompanied by music, with the whole body used for expression.

Generally speaking, British choreographers make surprisingly few demands on the acting ability of their dancers, in spite of the strong

[1] R. Zakharov, *op. cit.*
[2] I. Moiseyev, 'The Ballet and Reality' from *Ulanova on Soviet Ballet* (S.C.R., London, 1954).

dramatic tradition in British drama and literature. Because of this and because almost every British dancer leaves ballet school histrionically untrained, the acting of our dancers usually is poor. Robert Helpmann was an outstanding exception in the thirties and forties. Since the war Julia Farron and Gillian Martlew, Alexander Grant, Ray Powell and Stanley Holden are a few who have strengthened the tradition of acting in ballet. But the lack of the use of acting remains a great weakness of British choreography.

The problem in Britain is intensified by the absence of a firm link between British drama and British ballet. Danish and Soviet ballet has such a link because the state drama, opera and ballet schools exist under one roof or work closely together. Students of one art often take the stage in performances of the other theatre arts. They are brought up in an atmosphere of total theatre so that they often become good actor-dancers even if, in Zakharov's opinion, they could still study Stanislavsky more thoroughly.

The chance of developing similar links in Britain was lost when the opening of the Sadler's Wells Theatre in 1931 led to the separation of drama, opera and ballet in the Vic-Wells Organisation. Drama stayed at the Old Vic; opera and ballet settled at Sadler's Wells. Circumstances, not people, were to blame for this. But it would have been possible then, and is still possible now, to emphasise in drama and ballet schools that these arts are interdependent, not independent.

Strong characters and clear dance images are inseparable from good choreography just as acting is an essential part of a dancer's art. This has always been so for Noverre's good reason that 'it is impossible to create interest by . . . merely executing some beautiful steps; the soul, features, gestures and attitudes must all speak at once and always with energy and truth'.[1]

[1] Noverre, *op. cit.* p. 107.

PART VI

THE CHOREOGRAPHER AT WORK

CHAPTER XVIII

CASTING AND PREPARATIONS FOR REHEARSAL

'In producing,' wrote Nicholas Legat of Petipa, 'the first thing he considered was his material.'[1] Casting is a vital part of choreography. A mistake at this point can change the character of a ballet or handicap it hopelessly. So it is important for a choreographer to study his dancers. He must know their technical ability and understand their personalities to judge what may be their contribution to the role he gives them. Usually a choreographer works with a company he knows. Often, therefore, a ballet's principle role will be conceived for a particular dancer, as *Giselle* was for Carlotta Grisi and *Le Spectre de la Rose* for Nijinsky. But there are always the minor roles to cast and the *corps* to be grouped.

If a choreographer does not know the company he is to work with he must attend its classes and performances, absorb its atmosphere and learn all he can of its dancers. Only then will he be able properly to prepare the casting of his ballet with the artistic director and the other collaborators.

In this work he must be guided by three considerations—the personality and artistic ability of his dancers, their technical ability and the size of cast required by his theme. 'Let the number of his performers be as his Subject requires. . . .'[2]

Sir Frederick Ashton, Antony Tudor and John Cranko use traits of personality and other individual characteristics in their dancers, as well as the dancers' technical abilities. This is a method of casting in which the choreographer exploits the available material. The material, in turn, makes a contribution to the choreography.

Kenneth MacMillan and Jerome Robbins apply this idea in different ways. In *The Burrow* MacMillan thought of exploring the reactions of a group of people in a situation where they were confined to a room under threat of discovery. When he started rehearsing the ballet he had the situation in mind, but no idea how he would develop it. The development came from the cast because he built the

[1] N. Legat, *Story of the Russian School*, p. 39 (British Continental Press, 1932).
[2] John Weaver, *Essay towards an history of Dancing*, p. 166 (London, 1712).

incidents around the personalities of the dancers available to him, imagining how traits of character might change under the stress of that claustrophobic burrow. Afterwards, the critics said his ballet was a version of *The Diary of Anne Frank*, a back-handed compliment since it showed the truth of his conception even if the critics were wrong.

Robbins goes further. In choosing dancers for his Ballets U.S.A. he looked principally for dancers who were different from each other, physically and temperamentally. This is the opposite of a classical ballet company where training produces at least a common physical pattern. Robbins' dancers are of many types, shapes, qualities of movement and expression. There is no company resemblance, except in their differences. His choreography then exploits and orchestrates these differences.

A quite different approach to casting is expressed by Dame Ninette de Valois in *Invitation to the Dance*. She maintains that dancers should be so much the instrument of choreography that the choreography should speak for itself and not rely on interpretative or emotional additions from individual dancers. In her view the important part of casting is the selection of dancers of the correct physical type who can fill roles and succeed each other when necessary. So a change of cast should never mean a change of interpretation or a lowering of standard due to the loss of a star personality.

In this argument Dame Ninette is very close to Balanchine. He thinks of his dancers impersonally as clay for the moulding, or like notes of music waiting to be assembled by the master.

'I do not discuss the ballet with my dancers', he once said. 'When I start to rehearse I do not even tell them the plot or anything about the ballet, but, as the work progresses, I may mention the name of a part to one and say, "you play the brother of so and so". My dancers do not know what they will have to do, or what characters they will be called upon to portray. . . .

'I expect them to do exactly what I show them and as I wish it to be done. I must make them see a movement as I see it, as if they saw it through my eyes. I do not tell them what they have to portray in their roles, because that would prejudice their conception of them. I make them drop naturally into their parts, so that they gradually come to live them. Nothing is left either to principals or *corps de ballet* to do for themselves; I show them every tiny movement and the least mimetic action; and I count their every step.'[1] (Plate XX (a).)

[1] *Dance Journal*, London, August-October, 1931.

Once the casting is done the choreographer needs to sink himself in study of his dancers, his libretto and his music. Perhaps the choreographer already knows the dancers well. Whether he does or not it is clear that choreographers like Balanchine, Massine, de Valois, and even Ashton, are not likely to use this period for any discussion of the libretto with their cast. They expect a dancer to appear at rehearsal without any preconceived ideas about the libretto. That way, they argue, the dancer is more pliable material. Many dancers would agree with them.

But most choreographers in the U.S.S.R., and American choreographers of the de Mille-Robbins school, discuss with their cast the way they intend to interpret the libretto and how they see the characters. 'When I began producing *The Fountain of Bakhchisarai* at the Leningrad Kirov Theatre in 1934,' said Zakharov, 'I invited all the performers of the main roles and their understudies to come to see me in turn, and had talks with them on the tenets of the Stanislavsky system, on the need to create Pushkin's characters . . . and also the characters introduced into the ballet . . . by means of expressive *pas d'action*. . . .'[1]

Other choreographers who believe in discussion with their cast do not necessarily follow the Stanislavsky system. Perhaps they should. But by discussion they achieve an understanding with their dancers which is their guide throughout rehearsals. The two English choreographers best known for this method are Tudor and Cranko.

In preparing a ballet many choreographers visit museums, read round their subject, and watch people or things to find out all they can about the characters they are to create. In this way they seek and receive inspiration, like Fokine did.

He studied all the Persian miniatures he could find, Cyril Beaumont told us, in his preparations for *Schéhérazade*. From these he took a number of poses which he arranged consecutively to form the beginning, middle and end of the ballet. Then he created movements in the same style to link these poses.

Such an approach presupposes the subtle aesthetic sense which choreographers ought to have. Sir Frederick Ashton displayed the sense in moulding the movements not of art, but of nature, to his ballet, *Ondine*. He drew most of his inspiration from water, because Ondine was a creature of water. 'I spent hours watching water

[1] R. Zakharov, *The Art of the Ballet Master* (Moscow, 1954).

move,' he said. 'All the choreography, especially that of the *corps*, moves in surges of movement like the swell of waves.'[1]

Such inspiration should be reinforced by study of the music, its atmosphere and structure. For this a pianist or tape-recorder will be essential.

'When the piano arrangement is ready the choreographer can begin work. First he must make a thorough study of the music, learn its melody, rhythm and dynamics in detail and its relation to the development of the plot. He must listen to it many times and follow the piano score, which is divided into numbered sections of a few bars each for reference during rehearsals. He must also study the full score to become familiar with the instrumentation. During this preliminary work, notes are taken and the ballet is sketched in outline, though the choreography is rarely definitely decided on at this stage.'[2]

Here the vital role of the composer is re-emphasised as we showed in Chapter XIII. It is the composer who first brings the libretto to life. The music embodies the libretto, all its characters, conflicts, and emotions. If the music is too long or lacks dramatic excitement, or if the musical image of the characters and their situations is unclear, the choreography will be handicapped.

Yet music and choreography, though fellow travellers in ballet, retain separate personalities. Neither can become merely an accompaniment for the other. Light and shade in the music does not necessarily require an exactly corresponding light and shade in the choreography. The music is the choreographer's guide, not his drill sergeant.

So if the score is good in itself in relation to the theme, and the choreography develops well, the choreographer will find he is building a dynamic, almost an explosive, relationship between the two arts. This is because each art has its own personal image of the ideas contained in the libretto. The images are not reflections of each other. Each visual and aural image, in fact, competes to some extent for the audience's attention. At the same time it rounds off the picture which the other is presenting.

The first stage in the building of this relationship is the blocking, or

---

[1] Frederick Ashton, interviewed by Peter Brinson, *Sunday Times*, London, 26.10.58.

[2] Niels Bjørn Larsen, *A Ballet is Created*. Programme of The Royal Danish Theatre, May, 1960.

phrasing, of the music to suit the needs of the choreography. With nineteenth-century music, nearly always written in phrases of eight or sixteen regular bars, phrasing was simple and fairly obvious. The beat and rhythm were clear.

With music of the last forty years such simplicity has disappeared. Musical structure and phrasing are more complex. This complexity makes it the more important for a choreographer to prepare his music in clear counts for his dancers. He must study it and break it down so that he can explain clearly his selection of the many cross-rhythms which present-day composers employ in a single piece. He will not necessarily divide the music musically, as a composer might. In preparing his ballet *A Place in the Desert* Norman Morrice used Surinac's *David and Bathsheba* for his score. He divided the score subjectively, 'per noise or note', according to convenience and its meaning for him. Then he numbered the divisions to correspond with the choreographic plan whose first page is shown in Appendix III c (v). When a choreographer works in this way it is best that he should do so in consultation with the person who will conduct the ballet.

Fokine always took the greatest care in the preparation of his music. It was the foundation of his choreography. 'He works for days', said Cyril Beaumont, 'until he has the sequence of music to his liking and has established a balance of mood which satisfies him. Then he studies the music in relation to movement, and the movement in relation to the mood and style-atmosphere required by the theme, which is finally considered in relation with the scenery and costumes. Gradually he conceives a mental picture of each stage in the development of the action, which becomes more and more detailed.

'On the day of the rehearsal he requires only dancers to bring into being the phantom pictures and movements that people his brain. He knows what phrase of movement is to be interpreted in such a movement, where there is to be a pose, and for how long. He composes like a painter, sketching a few movements here, arranging a few details of a pose there; it is one of the most entrancing experiences to see these apparently isolated elements gradually set in their proper order and combined to form a beautiful dance. The sensation received can only be compared to the witnessing of a film of a growing flower.'[1]

[1] Cyril Beaumont, *Complete Book of Ballets*, pp. 677-678 (Putnam, London, 1951).

Other choreographers, Dame Ninette de Valois among them, having absorbed and understood the music, prepare a ground plan on paper. This shows the general scheme of the action with probable groupings and directions of movement in relation to the music. The ground plan will be the last preparation before the choreographer meets his cast in the rehearsal room for the first time.

CHAPTER XIX

THE FIRST REHEARSAL

THE choreographer's work in the rehearsal room is the physical realisation of all the earlier creative processes, his own and those of his collaborators. His ideas, his long considerations in solitude at home or in the classroom, his idiom of movement, all this must find expression in movements created through his dancers' bodies.

'Whenever Petipa set about producing a ballet,' wrote Nicholas Legat, 'he waited till absolute silence reigned in the hall. Then, consulting the notes he had composed at home, he would methodically begin to work.

'He worked out many of his groupings at home, where he used little figures like chess pawns to represent dancers, arranging them all over the table. He would spend long hours studying these groupings and write down the successful ones in his note-book. Separate numbers, solos and *pas de deux* he composed at the rehearsals.

'First he had the music played through. Then he would sit for a time in deep thought. Then he would usually ask for the music to be played again, imagining the dance, making little gestures, and moving his eyebrows.

'In the middle he would jump up and cry: "Enough". He would then compose the dance eight bars at a time, call the dancer to him, and explain the movements at first in words rather than gestures. The whole dance having been explained, the dancer began again from the beginning, while Petipa frequently stopped, corrected or modified the movements.

'In the end he would say: "Now try nice", which meant the artist might try to execute the finished dance.'[1]

Many choreographers find the process of beginning, and the meeting with their cast at the first rehearsal, a fearful event. So it appeared to Agnes de Mille in the creation of *Rodeo*, her first big ballet for a major company.

[1] N. Legat, *Story of the Russian School*, p. 36 (British Continental Press, London, 1932).

'I asked for the men first,' she said. 'If I could break them, I would have the whole company in my hand. . . .

'I turned deliberately and faced them. There they were—nineteen of them. Male. Great muscled brutes leaning against the barre and staring with watchful smouldering eyes. Behind them were Paris, Covent Garden, Monte Carlo and, in three cases, the Maryinski. And behind me? A wall. It occurred to me at this precise moment that with the exception of five soloists I had never worked with men in my life. Never more than one man at a time.

'I took a deep breath. "We are going to begin," I said in a scarcely audible treble, "with men riding horses in a rodeo. . . ." '[1] (See Appendix III D.)

Some choreographers at the first rehearsal start at the beginning and call only the few dancers who are to open the ballet. Thereafter they create the ballet straight through in the sequence it will be danced. This is the simplest way, especially for an inexperienced choreographer.

Sir Frederick Ashton varies the practice. 'In rehearsal', he said, 'I always start at the beginning of a ballet and go on until I find its style. Once this is established I jump about. For example, in *Ondine*, I completed Act I, then did all the show pieces in Act III, then Act II, which is mostly *pas d'action*. Act II was the most difficult because it takes place on board ship so that I wanted the movement to be fluid, like the rhythm of the sea, rather than set ballet steps. Also, I wanted it to rest the audience, as it were, between the two acts where the dancing is most intense.'[2]

Another method, used by Antony Tudor, is to choose one or two dancers from the cast with whom the choreographer is particularly in sympathy. With them he will experiment to find the type of movement most suitable for the work. Not only the solo roles, but even the ensemble steps will be worked out on these dancers.

Very often a choreographer will complete the solo roles before beginning the ensemble dance. In this way the solo roles are highlighted and the ensemble becomes a kind of chorus, support or contrast, with the soloists completing the picture.

Whatever method is used a choreographer should prepare something in his mind, if not on paper, before each rehearsal and will certainly have his music blocked into working sections of not more

---

[1] Agnes de Mille, *Dance to the Piper* (Little, Brown & Co., Boston, 1952).
[2] *Sunday Times*, London, 26th October, 1958.

than eight or ten bars as we showed in the last chapter. He may even write down steps to fit the musical phrases, clarifying the ground plan he has drawn on paper. Dame Ninette would certainly know exactly where each change of step takes place on the music and on which bar each character is to enter.

Balanchine, too, would have a clear picture of how he wants to use his music and group his dancers before each rehearsal, although he never makes detailed notes.

'I have no fixed method of procedure,' he said. 'Sometimes I arrange the end of the ballet first; sometimes I commence in the middle. I have the outline in my head—I never make notes—and then I work out every movement, showing each dancer what he or she must do to the slightest movement, and I expect everyone to copy me in the smallest detail. If I have plenty of time at my disposal I work with each dancer until he or she is perfect in his or her part; if I am pressed for time I expect the soloists to perfect themselves. This was the case with the ballet *The Prodigal Son*, which I had to produce in a fortnight. It was only an hour before the dress-rehearsal that I conceived and arranged the scene where the table is used as a boat. . . .'[1]

Choreographers of this type very often invent the steps by working them out on their own bodies instead of on another dancer. An extreme example of this approach is a choreographer, like Roland Petit, who improvises. It is not an intellectual process. Petit lets his body react physically and emotionally to the music. His dancers must be quick to follow and remember because the choreographer may not be able to repeat himself. When such a choreographer sees what his body has created he builds upon it without destroying the original spontaneity.

In a different method, the choreographer will come to rehearsal with a definite style of movement in mind, but not the actual steps. He will then experiment on his dancers by trial and error to find the steps he needs.

'The actual scenes and dances I do not work out before I commence my rehearsals,' said Massine, 'but I generally visualise them in my mind and form just a hazy outline of them, somewhat like the outline of houses seen through a London fog. I do not discuss the ballet with my dancers, unless it is of such an unusual character that I find it imperative for them to understand it, in order that they may grasp

[1] *Dance Journal*, London, August-October, 1931.

the situations. I regard the dancers as the elements for the realisation of my ideas, and as such I must be able to inspire them with the same feeling for my work that I have.

'When I begin to rehearse I may start with any scene or dance in the ballet; only gradually do I place the scenes and dances in their proper order. I work separately with my principal artists and the rest of the company, and it is only when the scenes take definite shape that I rehearse them altogether. During the rehearsals I create the dances and work out every detail for every member of my company; and I expect them to remember these details, as I may forget them when I get other ideas. . . .'[1] (Plate XX (b).)

Inevitably, this method is expensive in time because the choreographer has to experiment in many ways before deciding what is best. 'I think', said Jerome Robbins, 'about probably one-quarter of the work that I choreograph appears finally in the ballet. I think three-quarters of it gets thrown out in my attempt to find a better way of expressing it.'[2] Tentative searchings of this kind through ideas and movements are like the early drafts of a book or a painter's rough sketches. The choreographer is feeling his way towards the finished version.

Sir Frederick Ashton works a little like Massine, perhaps because Massine was Ashton's first important teacher. He, too, comes to rehearsal with only a general idea and the style of what he wants to do. This has to be ignited, as it were, by the dancers. Peggy van Praagh recalls a moment in the creation of *Valentine's Eve* in 1935. The music was Ravel's *Valses Nobles et Sentimentales*. As the music was being played, Ashton said, 'Dance some Cecchetti steps for me'. She danced some of the set *enchaînements* from the Cecchetti *allegro*. Out of these he evolved a complete dance to one of the waltzes. By changing the position of the body, the angle of the head and altering an arm here and there the original Cecchetti steps became unrecognisable. But initially it was these classroom pieces which inspired Ashton to create a lovely dance.

There are, therefore, as many ways of working as there are choreographers. The methods of work, which we have sketched, are neither set nor final. A choreographer is a creative being who adapts his method to his theme and even to the way he feels on the day he

[1] *Dance Journal*, London, February, 1932.
[2] Jerome Robbins interviewed by Peter Brinson on B.B.C. Television, *Monitor*, 13th September, 1959.

works. Sometimes at later rehearsals all the early work may be discarded for a fresh start. John Cranko scrapped his original version of
the first act of *The Prince of the Pagodas* and re-created it after he had
created Act II. It is at such moments with choreographers like
Cranko, who take their cast into their confidence, that the dancer
can be particularly helpful and make a major contribution to the
ballet.

But whoever the choreographer is, however he works and whatever his theme, he has three main, practical tasks when he steps into
a rehearsal room. He must develop the principal roles with highlights
of dancing, in *soli* and *pas de deux*. He must create his group dances
for the corps within the general pattern. Finally, he must create *pas
d'action* and dramatic climaxes, linking the whole together. In all of
this he must never lose sight of his story-line and the general shape of
his ballet.

CHAPTER XX

PRINCIPAL ROLES

(i) PRESENTATION AND DANCE STYLE

EVERY ballet, whether narrative, mood or abstract, unfolds itself through its principal roles. Therefore these roles must be presented properly to the audience so that each one commands attention and is instantly established. A perfect example is Odette in Act II of *Swan Lake*; she enters with a *pas de chat* into the centre of the stage, a great leap like a swan alighting on the ground, which almost always wins applause. All the great classical ballets have effective entrances of this kind for their ballerinas and other soloists.

At the same time as the choreographer presents his soloists he must establish their character and dance style. Success in this depends a great deal on the clarity with which the role has been conceived beforehand in the libretto and the music. There must have been complete understanding between librettist and composer about each role and its place in the libretto. If this understanding is present the *motif* of a role in a well-written score will help to define it emotionally, just as well-designed costume and make-up will define it visually. Through the music we can know something about the inner characteristics of a principal role, even before the dancer has appeared.

Given this help, choreographers indicate character and dance style through stance (how a character carries himself) and through steps and movements. Odette's character and dance style are established immediately after the *pas de chat* of her entrance in Act II through the swan-like movements with which she shakes the water from her head and neck.

In contemporary choreography Hagar's little mannerism in Tudor's *Pillar of Fire*, passing her hand up her face, shows her inner turmoil and agitation. Jasper's walk with turned-in feet in *Pineapple Poll* instantly shows him to be one of the pathetic little men who appear so often in Cranko's ballets.

Stance, therefore, springs from the conception of the character in the libretto and the score. The stance established, the choreographer must translate it into steps and movements, developing the character as he does so. This demands from the choreographer ability to represent the character's inner world of emotion in movement combined with the ability to create dance steps.

Here the dancer can contribute a great deal, principally through his talent as an actor. The better actor and dancer he is the more he will be able to bring to life the whole dance image. This is much more difficult than just being able to dance the steps correctly. Of course the dancer can help, too, in a practical way by showing that such and such a step does not *feel* right to the character, or by pointing out mechanical difficulties in what the choreographer wants. Usually the choreographer will be right to insist that what he wants must be achieved. But sometimes the dancer will be able to supply another, and perhaps a better, answer.

Margot Fonteyn has recorded how this happened in the creation of Frederick Ashton's *Ondine*. 'Take, for example, the little mime scene about Palemon's heart in the first act. Ondine comes out of the water. Palemon sees her and loves her. After this, in the original version, Ondine was attracted by Palemon's amulet and snatched it away. When he took it back she became petulant and angry.

'But when we did that scene it seemed false, especially musically. So now Ondine replaces the amulet round Palemon's neck. . . . At that moment he presses her hand to his heart. She is frightened by his heartbeat (Ondines don't have hearts, you know) and jumps back with surprise. Then, overcome by curiosity, she puts her hand over his heart to feel it beat again.

'Characters, incidents, dramatic details even, grow very much in this way, through discussion with the choreographer and other artists.'[1]

Many choreographers give their principal soloists a *motif* in movement corresponding to the role's *motif* in the music. This *motif* in movement will express the core of the character and will accord with the dance style. The choreography will return to it again and again throughout the ballet.

Take, for instance, the character of Giselle as it is defined in the dancing. Her early steps are joyous, free, trusting and spontaneous. When her trust is shattered the *same* steps are heavy and her limbs become uncoordinated because her brain has gone. When she is a wili the *same* steps recur with more maturity, fluidity and lyricism.

[1] *Sunday Times*, London, 8th March, 1959.

Albrecht's character is similarly portrayed, the choreography being repeated in different ways as he moves from the everyday world to contact with the supernatural.

Odette-Odile in *Swan Lake* is more complex than Giselle because Petipa and Ivanov had to create two characters who are at the same time the opposite of each other and yet, as in legend, two aspects of the same person.

Odette, the good aspect, is defined by fluid, lyrical movements. Odile has harsh, flashy, brilliant movements. It is the difference between pearls and diamonds. The pearl seems duller, but holds unseen qualities. The diamond flashes, but you see through it.

Some of the success with which this duality of character is represented in the choreography flows from the accident of two choreographers working on the role, Ivanov for Odette, Petipa for Odile. But there is more duality in the role than the twin aspects of character. Each aspect has a duality. The movements of the lyrical Odette have to reflect the swan in her from the waist up and the princess in her from the waist down. Odile similarly is half owl, half human although very few Odiles manage to express this in their movements.

Cinderella and Aurora in *The Sleeping Beauty* also require a great deal from their interpreters. 'The role of Aurora is typically feminine, demanding enormous charm, grace and spirit,' said Yvette Chauviré. 'The young princess is fresh, candid and very intelligent, but simple, too, and with a sense of humour. . . .

'In Act II the same qualities are apparent. This act, in which the Lilac Fairy shows the vision of Aurora to the prince, was created by Petipa in a manner softer than the sharp brilliance of Acts I and III. This does not mean that the choreographic architecture differs in this act from the first and last acts—only that the emotional content is different. It is the ballerina who must transmit this difference, and pay great attention to doing so because the vision scene is one of the most important in the ballet.

'What has Aurora become in this scene? She is not a spirit like Giselle, but she is immaterial, incorporeal. Moreover, she loves the young prince. So when he sees the vision of herself she tries to show him all the woman he will know. There must still be something about her of Act I, yet she must be light, gentle and unearthly. At the same time she must communicate the reason—not only by her gestures, but by her looks, expression, feeling and so on—why this man should become so desperately attracted to her. Unless she can do this all the rest of the ballet has no meaning.'[1]

Cinderella's duality of waif and princess is expressed in parallel fashion through Prokofiev's music and Ashton's choreography. Ashton has created movement *motifs* which correspond with the musical *motifs*. The waif dances in the kitchen with stilted, tentative, inelegant toes-turned-up steps. But sometimes in her dance with the broom, when she dreams of going to the ball, the movements become lyrical and noble. Thus the choreography of this scene heralds her different dance style with the prince in the ballroom.

In the ballroom the role is conceived along simple lines expressing the essence of Cinderella's unspoilt character. Her first entrance shows this particularly. It consists of *pas de bourrée couru* down the staircase into the centre of the stage. She does no other step whatever—the measure of her simplicity—but unlike Cinderella in the kitchen her stance, the carriage of her head and shoulders, has become the stance of a princess. The moment the clock strikes midnight the stance changes, the grand carriage vanishes and she becomes a frightened waif seeking to escape.

Among male character roles of the present day *Petrouchka* is pre-eminent for the brilliant way in which Fokine delineates the doll's tortured soul. Petrouchka, said Benois in his reminiscences, is the personification of the spiritual and suffering side of humanity. He is half man, half puppet. 'The great difficulty of Petrouchka's part is to express his pitiful oppression and his hopeless efforts to achieve personal dignity *without ceasing to be a puppet*. Both music and libretto are spasmodically interrupted by outbursts of illusive joy and frenzied despair. The artist is not given a single *pas* or a *fioritura* to enable him to be attractive to the public. . . .'[2]

In *Le Spectre de la Rose* Fokine created a similarly great male classical role, made greater by its dancer's exceptional technique. The basis of the choreography is a purely classical idiom for the legs. To this Fokine added movements in a contrasting romantic idiom for the shoulders, head and arms, establishing a dance style which suggested ethereality, the product of a young girl's romantic imagination. If he had done no more than this the role would have been attractive, but not remarkable.

[1] *Sunday Times*, London, 29th March, 1959.
[2] Alexandre Benois, *Reminiscences of The Russian Ballet*, p. 338 (Putnam, London, 1941).

Fokine made it a remarkable role of supreme virtuosity by contrasting Nijinsky's great elevation with his ethereal qualities. The famous leap through the window, one of the most effective entrances any dancer ever had, has been copied since, but never equalled. The leap into *entrechat huit* from a kneeling position beside the girl halfway through the ballet has hardly ever been attempted.

Nijinsky's brief period as choreographer gave a major role to male dancing in *L'Après-midi d'un Faune*. The character of the faun, indolently alone on the tree trunk, is established in his stance and dance style the moment the curtain rises. No matter that this dance style completely reversed the accepted classical positions and the classical line by eliminating turn-out, its image of the faun was absolutely clear, a physical picture, half man half beast with an inner character to match. The performance of the rhythmical movements and precise poses, always in profile, demanded such control that only a dancer of considerable experience could perform them well. At the same time the role made heavy demands upon the actor to show the faun's longing, curiosity and man-beast qualities.

Massine's contribution to the choreography of principal roles confirmed male equality, especially in character ballets. To him the world owes the Miller in *Le Tricorne*, the Peruvian in *Gaîté Parisienne* and other examples of the actor-dancer. The choreographic conception of the Miller, as a lively, vibrant contemporary human being, made extra demands upon the dancer as an actor. It enlarged the part of mime and acting in the dancer's art. In *Le Tricorne* Massine began as he continued, by placing the actor-dancer firmly in the centre of his choreography.

The example was not lost on the English School. Almost all the important male roles in English ballets of the thirties were character roles demanding high acting ability. De Valois's Satan in *Job* and the Rake in *The Rake's Progress* are outstanding examples. But in lesser roles like the Dago in Ashton's *Façade*, Massine's influence is apparent too.

The Rake is as testing a role, in many ways, as Petrouchka. Its choreography is precise, the libretto excellently conceived, the observation acute, especially in the mad scene; but much is left to be filled in by the dancer as an actor. And because so much depends upon the acting the impact of a performance can vary greatly.

In the early scenes, when the Rake is a young *nouveau riche*, the basis of the choreography is classical with the legs turned out. The *port de bras* is exaggerated to show his gaucheness, turning the palms of the hands down and lifting the elbows in an eighteenth-century manner. Character and dance style are thus established.

But the Rake's character changes. As it deteriorates through the ballet, from brothel to gambling room to prison and Bedlam, he loses bit by bit his classical style and stance. In the mad-house solo, there is no academic basis left at all. The turn-out of the legs disappears; the movements become wild, like those of an animal.

Two years after *The Rake's Progress*, Ashton's *Les Patineurs* gave English choreography a classical male role whose technical virtuosity, firmly based on the academic vocabulary, could contrast effectively with the great mime roles of Satan and the Rake. The Blue Boy in *Les Patineurs* was created like the Spectre, or any principal virtuoso role, to display the qualities of a particular dancer. In this case it was Harold Turner's mischievous, slightly cocky personality which gave the role its character. His clean, classical technique combined with skating movements to give it its dance style. Into this Ashton introduced the turns and *batterie* at which Turner excelled.

From all this we see that the effective presentation of principal roles, and the creation for them of suitable dance styles, provide the foundation upon which the choreographer builds his dances throughout the ballet. These dances will take the form of solo variations, *pas de deux*, ensemble dances and linking passages of *pas d'action*, which bind the whole together.

(ii) SOLO DANCES

Solo dances for principal roles are of three kinds. First are the virtuoso variations, romantic, classical or neo-romantic, which can stand alone usually, as dances complete in themselves. These are highlights of dancing in which the choreographer demonstrates the virtuosity of his dancers without advancing the story. Examples are Giselle's first-act solo and Aurora's variation after the Rose Adage. *Birthday Offering* is a modern development of this classical style. Frederick Ashton uses the classical idiom in seven different variations to show off seven different ballerinas, much as Petipa invented different variations for Aurora's fairy godmothers in the Prologue to *The Sleeping Beauty*.

Second are solos in contemporary ballets which combine elements of *pas d'action* with their virtuosity. Such solos grow out of the action and merge back into it. They cannot stand alone because their function is to advance the story or the mood, however slightly, as well as show off the dancer. Examples are Harlequin's solo in *Harlequin in April* and the solo passages for the two women in *Lilac Garden*.

Third are solos of *pas d'action* where movements are not designed to show virtuosity but to tell the story. Examples are Giselle's dance of madness, Petrouchka's dance in his cell, Juliet's taking of the potion in the ballets by Lavrovsky and Ashton, and the dances of the Betrayed Girl in *The Rake's Progress*.

The function of solo dances, except when used purely to display technical virtuosity, is to reveal *interior* conflicts, whereas *pas de deux* generally reveal *exterior* conflicts. Even a virtuoso solo, which has little to do with the story of the ballet, should have a thread of choreographic and musical argument running through it, deriving from the libretto. This argument links the solo with the rest of the ballet, giving it an artistic unity within itself and within the ballet. Nowadays, indeed, every solo in a narrative or mood ballet should have an element of *pas d'action*, advancing the audience's understanding of the story, the mood or the character.

In the craft of orchestrating movement for ballet the choreographer should see his solo dances, in Massine's phrase, 'as melodies written for a single instrument'. These dance melodies must have proper shape with a beginning, middle and end like the whole ballet. They usually last from half a minute to two and a half minutes, being shorter for a man than a woman because the male dance is more athletic. Always they seem longer than they are to everyone concerned, including the audience. Three minutes is already taxing; four minutes becomes an endurance test. The seven minutes of the Chosen Virgin's solo in Massine's *Le Sacre du Printemps* were an agony which only someone like Sokolova, who danced the role, could properly convey.[1]

Again, like the ballet, the solo dance is governed by its music. Length, quality, mood or action to be conveyed, will have been agreed beforehand by choreographer and composer. Once the music is written the choreographer must search for steps and dance phrases which equally fit the music's rhythm and melodic line and convey the mood of the dance. Odette's solo variation in *Swan Lake*, Act II, has no more than three musical phrases. Giselle's first-act solo has only four. In both solos there are choreographic phrases corresponding to the music. Both begin with a quiet movement in which the

---

[1] See Richard Buckle, *Dancing for Diaghilev*, pp. 159-168 (John Murray, London, 1960).

choreographic stress is on balance. The second phrase in *Swan Lake* is one of elevation, using jumping steps. The second in *Giselle* is one of turns, using a slow turning step. The third in *Giselle* is a travelling step of hops on *pointe* diagonally across the stage. Each phrase in each solo is more exciting than its predecessor, creating tension. The last phrase in both dances is a crescendo of *pirouettes*, an ending we meet often in the classical dance form.

But the choreographer should not follow the musical rhythms too precisely. His task is to find variations of the rhythm and to present a variety of rhythmic and dynamic patterns within the music. The structure of the dance and the structure of the music thus run parallel to each other without being equivalent. Each has its own pattern in time.

The dance also has to have a pattern in space, a ground pattern. To create this is one of the most difficult tasks of choreography. The choreographer with his one dancer must draw upon his invention and his knowledge of dance vocabulary (Chapter XVII) to find steps which communicate his meaning to the audience. At the same time these movements must be combined so that the directions and ground pattern of the dance are interesting and arise naturally out of the character, helping to express it.

It would be boring if the dancer did everything in perfect symmetry and travelled only in straight lines from side to side or back to front of the stage. Sometimes, in keeping with the character, the choreographer must use asymmetrical movements and must devise a variety of travelling movements in curves, circles and diagonal lines for his dancer.

The choreographer must give extra variety to the dance through the ways in which he presents the dancer's body to the audience. This is best illustrated in Cecchetti's principle of the square. (Illustration 4.) Here a dancer's body can face in any of eight directions, each one presenting him differently to the audience. In these directions the audience sees the dancer *de face* (Illustration 2 (*a*)), *croisé*, *écarté* or *effacé* to front or back. By adding *épaulement* (changes of the shoulder line) to these directions still more variety of body position can be achieved. (Illustration 5 (*a*).) By adding again to this variety the infinite combinations of leg, arm and head positions (*Effacé*, Illustration 5 (*b*)) the choreographer will complete his picture like a painter adding colours to a painting from his palette.

Such are the possibilities of the static pose. But the dancer moves.

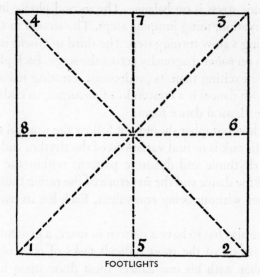

FOOTLIGHTS

4. THE EIGHT DIRECTIONS OF MOVEMENT

(a)   (b)

5. THE CREATION OF MOVEMENT

(a) *épaulement* with working foot *dégagé*

(b) *effacé en l'air*

So wherever he moves on stage our square moves with him, translating the static pose into movement.

The choreographer's task is still unfinished. Beside horizontal
patterns and the patterns of the static pose he must create a vertical
pattern. His dancer may be shown lying down, kneeling, standing
on the whole of his foot, on half point, full point or in the air, jumping. (Illustration 5 (c).) Such vertical patterns are contrasted particularly well by John Cranko in solos for the four kings in the first

(c)

5. THE CREATION OF MOVEMENT

(c) elevation—a Soviet *jeté*

act of *The Prince of the Pagodas*. Between them the kings explore
every plane, the King of the South, for example, performing movements in which his body is flat on the ground for much of the dance.

This combination of possibilities becomes an unconscious process
on the part of the choreographer. It is the way he speaks, his dance
language. But these things are, in fact, what make a dance interesting.
Variety of rhythmic patterns (patterns in time), of directions of
movement, levels of movement and directions of the body (patterns
in space) combined with variety of step, and proper motivation,
these are the stuff of creation. Doris Humphrey has summarised them
all as 'the four elements of dance movement . . . design, dynamics,
rhythm and motivation'.[1]

[1] Doris Humphrey, *The Art of Making Dances*, p. 46 (Rinehart, New York,
1959).

C.A.—15

Variety does not mean promiscuity, nor dancing for dancing's sake, nor the choreography of every note of music. Stillness, pauses, are as important as action. Stillness can underline meaning and make a brilliant passage or step seem more brilliant.

Simplicity should be the choreographer's watchword. The great classical ballets and their well-known solo variations use limited palettes. The basic steps and movements of *Swan Lake* and *Giselle* are extraordinarily few, about twenty-one for *Giselle* and thirty for *Swan Lake*,[1] but their combinations are masterly. Fokine's *Le Cygne* (*The Dying Swan*), to quote a famous solo, is largely built on a single step, the *pas de bourrée couru*.

In composing his dances, therefore, but especially in composing the solos, the choreographer should aim at using a few steps well. True variety implies a right selection of steps to convey what is meant with the greatest economy, neither mixing styles, nor over-crowding the canvas.

(iii) PAS DE DEUX

A *pas de deux* can be any dance for two people. The clowns in *The Lady and the Fool*, the Popular Song for two men in *Façade*, and the red girls in the original version of *Les Patineurs* are *pas de deux* of their kind. But usually the *pas de deux* expresses some relationship between a man and a woman. In the development of a narrative or mood ballet it illustrates a climax in this relationship, tragic, romantic or comic. In choreographic terms it is similar to a duet in opera, a climax of contrast in performance of the same instrument—the male and female voice, the male and female body.

Thematically and technically the *pas de deux* usually marks a climatic point. Hence it is the most important dance a choreographer has to create. For this reason, and because it is one of the pleasantest forms of dance on which to work, many choreographers create it first, before soli or ensemble dances.

The modern choreographer has many models and periods from which to learn. Examples on the international ballet stage today range from Galeotti's late eighteenth-century character *pas de deux* in *The Whims of Cupid and the Ballet Master* at Copenhagen to the most recent creations of Ashton, Balanchine and Lavrovsky.

---

[1] Cf. Cyril Beaumont's analysis of *Swan Lake* and *Giselle* in *The Ballet Called Swan Lake* and *The Ballet Called Giselle* (Beaumont, London, 1952 and 1944 respectively).

The romantic style, loose in construction, can be seen in the *pas de deux* passages of *La Sylphide* and *Giselle*. These mirror the social conventions of the nineteenth century. It was then immodest to make love in public, so the Sylphide barely touches James, and Giselle and Albrecht dance mostly apart. Today, the lovers in Petit's *Carmen* hardly rise from their bed. (Plate XXX (a).)

Technically, there is little formal arrangement of the *pas de deux* between Giselle and Albrecht or James and the Sylphide. Their duets are of the simplest kind, but the man has not yet been eclipsed as a dancer. Albrecht dances almost as much as Giselle. So does the peasant boy with his girl in the first act of the ballet. This peasant *pas de deux* was created to display the virtuosity of the principal *demi-caractère* dancers at the Opéra. It is more formal in architecture than the *pas de deux* for the principals. Here we see already the elements of the structure which Petipa and Tchaikovsky later fashioned into the *grand pas de deux classique*, much as the Palladian architects transformed their Gothic inheritance into the clean lines of English Georgian and Regency styles.

The *grand pas de deux classique* was the glory of Petipa's creative work. Of all his choreography this part exerts the strongest influence today over ballet music and choreography wherever the classical vocabulary is danced. It consists usually of an *entrée* and *adage* for the two partners, followed by a solo variation for the man, a solo variation for the woman and a closing coda for the two together.

The Black Swan *pas de deux* in the third act of *Swan Lake* is an example of this elegant classical structure, so different from the looser romantic form of Perrot half a century earlier. The *pas de deux* between Aurora and Prince Florimund in the third act of *The Sleeping Beauty* would be an even better example did not Western Europe continue Diaghilev's unfortunate precedent of using the music of the coda for the dance of the three Ivans. The Aurora *pas de deux*, as danced by the Royal Ballet, therefore has no coda.

The *grand pas de deux classique* was created to be the climax of every full-length ballet in the classical style. Two other kinds of classical *pas de deux*, the *demi-caractère* and the character, were evolved also out of romantic precedent to suit classical needs. The dance of the Bluebird with the Enchanted Princess and of Puss-in-Boots with the White Cat are examples of these in *The Sleeping Beauty*.

The chief technical difference between the *grand pas de deux* and its *demi-caractère* brother lies in the role of the man. The *grand pas de deux classique*, following late romantic fashion, made the man a *porteur*. So strong is the influence of this conception that he is still a *porteur* in innumerable dances by contemporary choreographers, copying the classical style.

In such dances the man's function is to display the ballerina. He must support her, lift her, balance her. The choreographer invents his movements and poses around these tasks of the man, placing the technical emphasis upon whatever the ballerina can do best. Because of Legnani's virtuosity in turns, for example, Petipa made thirty-two *fouettés* the climax of the coda of Odile's dance with the Prince and so, in effect, the climax of *Swan Lake*'s third act. Similarly the leaps and lifts, in which Nadia Nerina and David Blair excel, are the fabric of the dance for Colas and Lise in the first act of Frederick Ashton's *La Fille Mal Gardée*.

In classical *demi-caractère* and character *pas de deux*, by contrast, the architecture of the dance is often the same as in the *grand pas de deux* (*entrée, adage, solo, solo, coda*), but the man is not a *porteur*. He dances with the women, displaying all the virtuosity of which he is capable.

Many *demi-caractère* dances are still created in this classical form. Like the *grand pas de deux*, their vocabulary is dictated by the technique of the artists for whom they are conceived. But the choreographer, instead of using the man to show off the ballerina, now has to orchestrate two dancers equally so that each complements the other and each shows off the other, yet together they are an ensemble.

Demi-caractère pas de deux of this kind, like the dance of the Bluebird, helped to keep alive the tradition of male dancing in Russia while men were eclipsed from the ballet stages of Western Europe at the end of the nineteenth century. These dances are still great tests of male virtuosity.

When Fokine's ideas infused new style and purpose into the *pas de deux*, the male again became the dominant partner. Dancing heroes returned to ballet. Side by side with the classical *pas de deux* of formal architecture, arose once more the *pas de deux* whose *primary* purpose was to advance the mood or story of a ballet, not display the virtuosity of the dancers. This type of dance for two, like the one in *Les Sylphides*, abandoned formal architecture. It was built according to the needs of the ballet in which it appeared. Or it even stood alone, a little ballet by itself, as it did in *Le Spectre de la Rose* (Plate XXIII (a)) and has done many times since, in Petit's *Le Jeune Homme et la Mort*, for example, and Robbins's *Afternoon of a Faun*.

With Fokine, classical conventions were set aside. The *pas de deux* began to grow into the wide variety of forms it enjoys today. Sir Frederick Ashton in particular has emphasised and extended the emotional qualities of the *pas de deux*, sometimes using a classical structure, sometimes a freer style. Always this dance is the most sublime moment of his ballets as it is the loftiest expression of his art. He has introduced to it a new plasticity, developing its form as a poet would develop his imagery. (Plate XXI (a).) In all British choreography there are few more lovely moments than the *pas de deux* passages in *Symphonic Variations* and *Ondine*.

Balanchine has directed the *pas de deux* differently in America, building on the example of Petipa, as we saw in Chapter VIII. Movement is his keynote, as emotion is Ashton's, and sensuality Petit's. So he has developed the *pas de deux* technically and in complexity, adding an enormous number of new *pas* and emphasising the element of display inherited from Petipa. Brilliance of choreographic construction and technical execution mark every Balanchine *pas de deux*. This approach has limitations to which we have drawn attention. A master-creator of movements which seem to bring musical notes to life, Balanchine rarely shows interest in content.

Soviet choreography, also building on Petipa's model, has developed its virtuosity beyond the point at which Petipa left it. We have shown how this development has been a perfection of Petipa's classical technique, not a fusion of its technique with other schools or dance forms as has happened in America, even in Balanchine's choreography. Elements in Soviet *pas de deux* which appear acrobatic are only admissible, said Vaganova, if based on classical exercise.[1] We find, therefore, stronger, more exciting lifts and aerial supports than Petipa could have used, more graceful flight, more plasticity and defiance of gravity.

Just because the *pas de deux* is so flexible a dance form and plays so significant a part in choreography, its placing and construction in a ballet have to be considered with special care. If the ballet's author and composer have done their work well the choreographer will know the purpose of his *pas de deux*, its place in the scheme of things and its style long before he enters the rehearsal room.

The style will follow the style of the ballet. Usually this has been

[1] V. Kamenev on Vaganova, *Anglo-Soviet Journal*, Summer, 1959. Other issues of the Journal since 1955 contain valuable assessments of Soviet choreography by Kamenev.

established before the *pas de deux* begins, so that the *pas de deux* will continue it. Giselle, shown to be intangible when she rises from the grave in Act II, must remain intangible throughout her dances with Albrecht.

In Tudor's *Dark Elegies* the *pas de deux* is the second dance of a ballet whose style of grief and tranquillity was established in the first dance. Dictated by the theme, the music, and the influence of Jooss upon Tudor at that time, the *pas de deux* developed the theme and embroidered the style and dance vocabulary. Among post-war ballets, John Cranko's *pas de deux* in *Harlequin in April*, *Pineapple Poll* and *Bonne-Bouche* notably fulfil the same dual task. So does the dramatic *pas de deux* which comprises the second scene of Jack Carter's *The Witch Boy*.

The *pas de deux* is regarded rightly as the most interesting of dances, because its combinations are infinite in theme and execution. Usually, too, it marks the emotional climax of a ballet. Invariably, the *pas de trois* is less satisfying, unless devised for a particular purpose in the narrative like Sir Frederick Ashton's *pas de trois* for Lise, Colas and Alain in *La Fille Mal Gardée*. With the help of the *corps de ballet* Alain is constantly deceived in a *pas de deux* for three which is one of the ballet's most delightful dances.

Of course, the *pas de trois* can be used solely for virtuoso display, as it is in the first act of *Swan Lake*, but it appears best when it is an extension of plot or mood in the manner of *La Fille Mal Gardée*. Chiarina and the two white ladies in Fokine's *Le Carnaval*, for instance, provide a moment of calm and contrast in a ballet mainly composed of *pas de deux*. Andrée Howard's two *pas de trois* to the songs in *La Fête Étrange* are so evocative that they enhance the mood of the whole ballet. Captain Belaye's justly famous conquest of his fiancée and her aunt in *Pineapple Poll* provides the comic highlight of the work.

Pas de quatre and larger dances for soloists are less of a problem. They have wider possibilities which range from the spectacle of the cygnets in *Swan Lake* to the emotional conflicts of *Lilac Garden*, where the climax of the ballet comes in a dance for the four principal characters. Sometimes, today, these larger dances even become virtuoso one-act ballets in the classical form. The structure of *Birthday Offering* to Glazunov's music follows this form exactly. It consists of a Grand Entrée for seven ballerinas and their partners, followed by a solo for each ballerina, and a *pas de sept* for the men. The climax comes with a grand *pas de deux* for one couple only, the prima ballerina assoluta and her partner, followed by a final Grand Coda for the ensemble.

The choreographer's problem in all these dances, is to devise lifts, turns, poses and *pas* in an already established style. Problems of pattern in space and time, discussed in the last section, apply equally. But the designs can be more varied because the two or more dancers can move through all the directions of the chess-board square and all the levels of vertical pattern in unison with each other or in opposition.

In all such compositions the creative process demands first an understanding of the purpose of the dance. This should be clear in the libretto. Is it to express love, hate, anger, what? Where is the dance placed in the ballet as a whole and why is it there? When he has answered these questions to himself the choreographer can begin to experiment in the rehearsal room. He and his dancers will try out different movements—lifts, jumps, turns and other highlights— which seem to be suggested by the mood and style of the ballet. To this process the dancers may contribute a great deal. (Plate XXI (b).)

The process can develop in one of two ways. It may be that the choreographer and his dancers will begin their experiments without music. Having devised their lift or turn—whatever it may be—they work out how long the movement will take, how to get into it and out of it and how it will be related to the music.

Or they may hear the music first and decide how its climaxes will determine the climaxes of the dance. Then they will work out the kind of lift, turn or other highlight which will best interpret the music's mood and feeling. Whichever approach is adopted a dance must be devised whose movements clearly express the emotional relationship between the characters. The relationship is then developed in movement to a climax and resolution, the beginning-middle-and-end framework of every dance in every ballet, however long or short.

Once the framework is established and the steps and highlights set (with the strongest highlight as the dance's climax) the choreographer must polish and polish, investing the movements with extra touches to express better the purpose of the dance, tilting a head, changing an arm movement, adjusting an *épaulement*. (Plate XXI (a).)

Simple variety again must be his watchword. Whatever faults he may have as a choreographer will be discovered most quickly in *pas de deux*. But in this dance, too, his virtues can be most richly displayed.

CHAPTER XXI

ENSEMBLE DANCES

A HUNDRED AND FIFTY years ago the chief function of the *corps de ballet* was one of visual decoration and atmosphere, a kind of moving backcloth. But it had a collective life of its own as well, to which Viganò principally contributed. In *Gli Strelizzi* and other Viganò ballets the *corps* represented real characters, animated by human feelings which guided their collective movements in the way Noverre envisaged. This has remained the ideal of *corps de ballet* composition.

By the time of the Romantic Ballet the corps had developed to provide a silent comment on the narrative, taking part in it, helping to underline and emphasise particular passages. In *Giselle* it contrasts the real world of demi-character dancing with the spirit world of classical technique. The ensemble of peasants and courtiers should underline the tragedy of Giselle's madness through their acting as precisely as the ensemble of Wilis reflect the cruelty of their Queen in fulfilling her commands.

Of course, old conceptions of the *corps de ballet* persisted then as they do today. But leading choreographers since Viganò's time have stressed the special importance of the *corps* dramatically (Perrot— Ivanov—Fokine) and technically (Petipa—Balanchine). Hence the modern *corps* must be as good at acting as it is at dancing.

Petipa gave the *corps* a special place in classical architecture. It is the *corps* in *The Sleeping Beauty* which emphasises the drama and provides some of the continuity. Its terror reveals the power of Carabosse; its grief measures the tragedy which overtakes Aurora.

But the *corps'* principal function at St. Petersburg was a decorative, dancing function, best illustrated today in the Petipa ballets at the Bolshoi and Kirov Theatres. There, remarked Balanchine to us, the Garland Dance in *The Sleeping Beauty* is a spectacle of a kind never seen elsewhere. At the Kirov Theatre in Leningrad about one hundred and fifty dancers appear in it—fifty girls, fifty boys and fifty children. Elsewhere[1] the Petipa choreography for this famous

---

[1] The Royal Ballet does not use the Petipa choreography for this dance, which has been re-created by Sir Frederick Ashton.

ensemble is used with fewer dancers. His choreography retains its magnificence, even if the impact is less strong.

By using his *corps* to provide such spectacle Petipa re-emphasised dancing's spectacular function, which the romantic ballet had reduced, but not eliminated, in the interests of dramatic expression. The *corps* was the instrument of this new kind of spectacle. Ground patterns became straighter and bolder. Technique developed, especially in speed of footwork and general precision. But the style of Petipa's ensemble dances varied little from ballet to ballet. Every dancer performed the same step and wore the same costume as her neighbour. Such formalism was only dispelled when Gorsky and Fokine demanded a new range of style and expression.

During the twentieth century the dramatic and choreographic functions of the *corps* have changed radically. The multiple use of the ensemble for character, national and classical dancing within the compass of a single full-length work went out of fashion. Instead, Fokine's short ballets concentrated on one type of dancing only, classical in *Les Sylphides*, character in *Prince Igor* and so on. The dancers, too, began to be used individually, like an orchestra of separate personalities.

Practical reasons of finance and transport made the ensembles of touring companies smaller than was considered proper in state theatres like the Maryinsky. After the First World War in Europe and America the *corps* sometimes vanished completely, leaving only individual dancers who might be all ensemble or all soloists.

Technically and dramatically the clear distinction between ensemble and solo dances, on which Petipa had insisted, becomes blurred from Fokine onwards, although no ballet in the classical tradition can lose the distinction completely. The use of the *corps*, too, becomes less formal, even individual. No longer does it move about only in circles and straight lines. Pattern and shape become submerged in groups and masses. After Fokine the *corps* begins to turn in its feet and turn up its toes. Instead of dancing in a simpler idiom of its own, as in Petipa's day, its movements begin to reflect those of the principals.

We noted, in Part II, how this choreographic revolution broke with the classical tradition of two hundred years. In ballets like *L'Après-midi d'un Faune* and *Le Train Bleu*, not a single movement could be recognised as stemming from the classical tradition. 'It is danced by the real Russian Ballet,' said Diaghilev of *Le Train Bleu*, 'but it has nothing to do with Russian Ballet. It was invented for Anton Dolin, a classical dancer who does nothing classical.'[1] Yet these were ballets in the repertoire of the most famous classical ballet company of the day.

The ensemble, along with every other element of classical choreography, felt the force of the revolution. At one moment, in Nijinska's *Les Biches*, it could be reduced to a group of individuals. At another, in the same choreographer's *Les Noces*, it could be moved across the stage boldly, plastically, in a nameless mass. But when all the excitement of these years had subsided the strongest memory was Massine's conception of mass movement in his symphonic ballets of the thirties. The strength and importance of such ballets lay in the way their ensemble was used to represent the questions of life and death with which the scenarios dealt.

The principal living choreographers today are still those influenced by Diaghilev and his collaborators—de Valois, Ashton, Balanchine, Tudor, Robbins and so on. Yet Petipa remains a point of reference. This is so, not only for Balanchine, the choreographer, or de Valois, the artistic director. Petipa is a point of reference even to choreographers like Ashton and Cranko, because the full-length ballet has begun to return to the European stage. Petipa is the only available model to choreographers of a State Company using large ensembles dramatically and spectacularly for the first time. Therefore, in Ashton's *Cinderella*, *Sylvia*, *Ondine* and *La Fille Mal Gardée*, and in Cranko's *The Prince of the Pagodas* Petipa and Diaghilev's successors join forces.

In choreographic practice today, the ensemble generally fulfils one or more of four dramatic functions. It can be used at the beginning of a ballet or an act to prepare the entrance of the principals, as in the first act of *The Sleeping Beauty*. It can support the dancing of the principals by decorating the stage (third act of *Swan Lake* and *Homage to the Queen*), or by commenting on the action (Giselle's mad scene and the fight scenes in Lavrovsky's *Romeo and Juliet*). It can provide spectacle and contrast through the dancing of the whole ensemble. It can be used to provide a finale, such as Massine creates in *Mam'zelle Angot*.

These uses show again how important it is for the creators of a ballet, especially the librettist, composer and choreographer, to plan a proper balance between *corps* and soloists from the beginning.

[1] Beaumont, *Complete Book of Ballets*, p. 810 (Putnam, London, 1951).

The *corps* must not hold up the action which centres on the soloists. Rather its dances, usually in *divertissement* form, must be part of the action as well as a means of setting the scene, creating atmosphere and providing contrast, colour or comment. 'The thoughts, emotions and behaviour of the characters are revealed through *pas d'action*,' notes Zakharov. '*Divertissements* must reveal the character of their environment and the historical epoch. Here the choreographer must have a profound knowledge of national dancing, its history, the style of performance and so on.'[1]

This conception applies to ballets of mood as well as narrative. In Ashton's *Homage to the Queen* the *corps* are not mere background decoration; they are the environment, the elements themselves, through which move the Queens of Earth, Water, Fire and Air with their consorts. In *Job* and *The Rake's Progress* Ninette de Valois disposes a much smaller *corps* to achieve maximum effect in a different way. It enhances the majesty of God and the evil of Satan; it provides the central scene of group action before the Rake's downfall.

In each of these ballets, and even more in a three-act work like Ashton's *Ondine*, we see the *corps* used for contrast—obvious contrast between solo and ensemble dances, more subtle contrast when the *corps* supplies a rest, or break, in the rapid tempo of action involving the principals. We see, too, the librettist arranging for the logical presence of the *corps* on stage while the principals rest or change.

Choreographers, of course, vary in the way they create ensemble dances as much as they do in creating soli and *pas de deux*. For those like de Valois who come to rehearsal with patterns prepared, diagrams on paper and the mechanics of movement worked out, little remains but to teach the dancers. (Plate XXII.)

Others, like Tudor at the opposite extreme, work out a group dance on a single dancer who is particularly sympathetic to their style. Only when the style and type of movement are established on this dancer are such choreographers ready to face the *corps*. Between these extremes are many variations, none, perhaps, as odd as Perrot's method of creation. 'When the moment of inspiration seized him', recorded Charles de Boigne in his *Petits Mémoires de l'Opéra*, 'he squatted on the stage, his head between his hands. He might have been a china monkey. When the *corps de ballet* saw him seated on the ground like a tailor, they knew it would be for a long time, and so everyone made themselves comfortable accordingly; some

[1] Zakharov, *op. cit.*

embroidered, some lunched, some read, the solo dancers had re-
freshments brought to them. After a long interval a certain noise
was heard. It was Perrot snoring. He was awakened; the *ballabile*[1]
was finished; it had arrived with the snoring.'[2]

Many choreographers find the group dance the most difficult to
create, as if the problems were multiplied by the numbers they have to
handle. A choreographer who creates solo dances or *pas de deux* first
will have established the style of his ballet already and can transfer
this to the group. In this sequence, even if he wishes to contrast the
movements of corps and soloists, he will always have something from
which to start. If he begins creation with the ensemble he must
establish the style of the dancing on it before he does anything
else.

In practice a choreographer can handle his ensemble in one or more
of four ways, once he has decided on its dramatic functions. He can
give it separate, set-piece dances, such as Petipa might have done or
Ashton has developed in his three-act works. These set pieces can be
in any style—romantic, classical, national or character.

He can integrate all *corps* movement with that of the soloists. This
provides a framework within which the soloists dance. In the
Barcarole for the *corps* in Howard's *La Fête Étrange* the story is
unfolded while the chatelaine dances among her guests with the
country boy. Similarly, in Rodrigues' *Blood Wedding*, the wedding
scene is set within the framework of the *corps*—there are no set
dances for the *corps*, yet the *corps* dances all the time.

The choreographer can use the *corps* as a mass, not in formal
patterns, but boldly bunched in the manner of some expressionist
dances. Massine does this in his symphonic ballets, every dancer performing the same, essentially *anonymous* movement. Cranko achieves
great effect with a similar disposition of the *corps* in *Antigone*. (Plate
XVIII (b).) Ashton, in the second act of *Cinderella*, suddenly dissolves the formal, classical lines of his ensemble into just such a
nameless mass in order to emphasise the critical hour of midnight.
The mass sways from side to side, like the clock's pendulum and the
jester jumps high above it at each strike of twelve. Cinderella and the
Prince appear and disappear through this mass, the only characters
still recognisable as individuals.

Finally, the choreographer can use the *corps* as a crowd. Again

[1] A *ballabile* is a dance executed by a large number of persons, such as the *corps
de ballet*.   [2] Trans. C. W. Beaumont.

there is no formal pattern, but the members of the *corps* retain their individuality as against the anonymity of the mass, varying their movements according to the characters they are dancing. There may be different movements for every dancer. To achieve this the choreographer may determine the movements for everyone precisely, as MacMillan did in *The Burrow*, although the effect is one of improvisation. Or he may allow the dancers to improvise within the limits of character, situation and a general pattern of movement. Fokine attempted this second approach for the crowd in *Petrouchka*, and Helpmann did the same in *Miracle in the Gorbals*.

Within these variants some of the *corps* can be on stage for the whole ballet, as it is in Balanchine's *Ballet Imperial*, or it can make specific appearances to perform a dance. Such appearances may last anything from a few seconds to five minutes. The short entrées of the *pas de huit* throughout *Les Patineurs* never run more than a minute. The garland dance in *The Sleeping Beauty* usually lasts four minutes, five if played in full. The finale of Massine's *Mam'zelle Angot* for the whole ensemble lasts thirteen minutes.

The style and length of the dance having been established, its shape and structure are the next problem, as in solo dances. Here the golden rule is simplicity. The larger the *corps* the simpler must be the patterns and steps. The more complicated the pattern the simpler should be the steps. Complex steps appear best when a dance is not based on pattern.

In musical terms each ensemble dance will have an opening, a development, one, two or three climaxes, according to its place in the ballet, and a finale. This musical structure will have a corresponding choreographic structure in the steps and patterns. In contemporary ballets, where the music is particularly complex, the group dances tend to become kaleidoscopic, their patterns changing more quickly than in romantic and classical choreography because the musical phrases are so short.

Such movements and patterns can be achieved in various ways, remembering that 'the gradation of the heights of the dancers must be observed scrupulously whenever dances form part of the decorative scheme'.[1] Gradation of height is an element of pattern peculiar to the ensemble but it affects fundamentally each of the dispositions of an ensemble open to a choreographer. The dispositions are threefold. He may create static tableaux, as Fokine does for the Prelude in

[1] Noverre, *op. cit.* p. 45.

Les Sylphides. He may make bodies move, but not travel on stage, as de Valois does with the red pawns in *Checkmate*. Or he may make bodies travel and build an infinite variety of patterns as Ashton does time and again in *Ondine* and *Persephone*.

The translation of the *corps* from pattern to pattern is always a major problem in ensemble dances, whatever the period of the ballet or the use of the *corps*. Petipa was a master at it, as Karsavina observed, developing 'the intricate but always precise pattern of his grouping . . . with facility and logic'.[1] Such development implies the plastic ability of a film director, a 'continuity of vision'[2] vital to all choreography.

But the translation is also a mechanical matter. If, for example, the *corps'* dance involves a ground design which changes from a circle to a diagonal, one difficulty may be the mechanics of moving from the first pattern to the second within the limits of the music. Some dancers will have to travel further than others because of their position on stage. So a step must be invented of the right style, appropriate to the music and elastic enough to suit the dancers with far to go and those with only a short journey. Fokine handles such mechanics brilliantly in *Les Sylphides*. The *corps* in the *Grand Valse* changes constantly from diamond diagonals across the stage into circles, squares and other patterns.

In spite of such mechanical problems it is easier to devise patterns for an ensemble of many dancers than it is for a solo dance or even a *pas de deux*. The possibilities of orchestrating an ensemble are so large. It has such an infinite number of bodies, limbs and shapes, an infinite number of instruments. 'Group dances correspond to a piece orchestrated for a given number of instruments,' remarked Massine to *Dance Journal* in 1932. 'And, just as an orchestration should contain colour and contrast, so do I seek to invest my group and mass dances with similar qualities.'[3]

Colour and contrast are the essentials of ensemble choreography. They can be achieved by dividing the ensemble into groups of two, three or more dancers. Or by disposing it oddly, some into groups of two, some of three and so on. Or by moving it all in the same direction or in different directions, on the same level or on different levels. Thus all space can be explored, variety of vertical pattern

[1] Karsavina, *Theatre Street*, p. 156 (Heinemann, London, 1931).
[2] Audrey Williamson, *Contemporary Ballet*, p. 11 (Rockliff, London, 1947).
[3] Beaumont, *Complete Book of Ballets*, p. 841 (Putnam, London, 1951).

contrasting or complementing varieties of horizontal pattern on the ground.

This variety in space should be coloured by variety in movement. There can be uniformity of movement through use of the same step or a contrast of different steps. There can be contrast in the dynamics of movement and in movement between the sexes, the strong movements of the men countering the soft movements of the women.

Jerome Robbins achieves such variety in a most striking and personal manner. We have shown already how he searches for contrast in the casting of a company or ballet. The differences between his dancers are then exploited choreographically in every possible way.

Moves, for example, contrasts all kinds of male and female movement. The ballet is silent, without music, yet it is constructed musically, like a symphony in which bodies are instruments. First, there is an ensemble for all together. Next, all the men dance, then all the women. The ensemble returns, followed by a dance for six, two men and four girls, and so on.

In this and other ballets Robbins's dances contrast planes of movement, tensions, emotions, strengths and weaknesses in jumps, slides, jerks and swings. His bodies do not always sing, confident and glorious, like the Russians. Often they stutter and shake and hesitate, as people do in a harsh world. At his best, though, Robbins speaks with humanity and feeling. This appears most powerfully when he adds to other contrasts the rarest and most natural one of all between the negro boy and white girl in *Afternoon of a Faun*.

All patterns of space and movement will be developed as patterns in time through the rhythms of the music. Here, too, there must be variety. The dancers may follow the rhythm precisely, or groups may dance in counterpoint to them, to other groups or to the soloists. While exploring these rhythms they may even imitate the orchestral pattern, as Nijinsky did in *Le Sacre du Printemps*. 'When a theme was given to a certain instrument, certain dancers would detach themselves from the mass and dance apart, the main body being used as a static or quietly moving background for the new dance.'[1]

So the choreographer has another problem applicable in all dances, but especially in dances for the ensemble. The choreographic line of his dance, visual and aural, must correspond with the rhythmic line

[1] Beaumont, *The Diaghilev Ballet in London*, p. 74 (Black, London, 1951).

of the music. If the musical rhythm runs tum te, tum te, *tum*, regularly throughout one phrase, the choreographer can devise movements which match this rhythm exactly in time value, or he can cut across it. But whichever he does his movements must always be related to the music, confined within it, because they start and finish with it. Hence the shape, or line, of his choreography has the same boundaries as the music and can vary only within these limits.

But the variety is wide. 'Robbins', notes de Mille, 'is beset by rhythm, visual and bodily rhythms as well as auditory, and when he gets hold of a gesture he continues inventing out of the core of the matter until he has built an entire design and must wait for the composer to catch up. His rhythms will then work in counterpoint to the musical pattern. . . . Whereas Balanchine's rhythmic sense is spatial and linked to the music, Robbins's is independent. I, on the other hand, am totally derivative and lean and grow on melody. I cannot move without melody.'[1]

When rhythm has given life to the dance, when its style and length and shape and structure are established and all its movements invented and combined, the choreographer must devise a strong finish. The dreariest dance can be saved by an effective ending. The best can be ruined by a poor one.

[1] Agnes de Mille, *And Promenade Home*, pp. 179-180 (Hamish Hamilton, London, 1959).

CHAPTER XXII

LINKS AND ENDINGS

THE choreographer has two more tasks in the rehearsal room. He must knit everything together in an overall shape. He must devise an effective choreographic ending which fulfils the scenario's intention.

He will not leave such matters necessarily to his last rehearsals. He will have had the overall shape of his ballet in mind from the beginning. He and his collaborators will have discussed at the libretto stage the dramatic and mechanical problems involved in bringing on stage and taking off principals, soloists, ensembles and so on, according to the period and style of the ballet and the resources available. He may have devised an ending during the ballet's first rehearsals. Now is the time to put his work together.

The linking of dances into an overall shape, or form, calls for a detachment which many choreographers find difficult to achieve. 'Perhaps over-all form is the hardest part of choreography to grasp,' said Doris Humphrey of the making of dances, though it applies equally to whole ballets; 'there are so many pitfalls.' But 'the first thing about form is continuity. Anything, to be exciting, must build, and nothing should be allowed to damage this—not costume changes, casting considerations, or lighting and set ideas, no matter how brilliant. They are not worth it if everything stops cold for them.'[1]

Clearly then, the building of overall shape with effective links in all the action requires much more than adjustments to movement here and there. Often it requires the elimination of movements, even of whole passages, which impede or confuse the action. Almost every ballet and every dance starts out by being too long. The time when a dance must be shortened is the time when it takes its place in a ballet.

In some ballets the linking passages between dances are achieved mechanically by production effects. The mysterious noises from the house of Dr. Coppelius, for example, combine with the fickle behaviour of Franz and the burgomaster's tales to link together the dances in Act I of *Coppélia*. Or there might be a musical link, like the

[1] Doris Humphrey, *The Art of Making Dances*, p. 149 (Rinehart, New York, 1959).

drum roll in *Petrouchka*. When these do not involve the cast no rehearsal time will be needed.

In most ballets linking passages are effected by the mime scenes and ensemble *divertissements* of the kind found in Petipa's choreography. Or there are the *danses d'action* of post-Fokine choreography, which combine mime and acting into expressive dance movement. These involve the cast, so they must be worked out in the rehearsal room and be included in the time schedule.

The principal linking passages in romantic and classical choreography were mimetic, as we have shown, corresponding to the recitatif passages in opera of the same period. Petipa, especially, linked his major dances with mime which told the story through traditional gesture and often provided a reason for the dances which followed. The mime might be very formal, like that of the Princess Mother in the first act of *Swan Lake*. It might be character mime like the tutor's actions in the same ballet. Sometimes a single person, like Cantalbutte[1] in *The Sleeping Beauty*, would have to provide continuity for a succession of dances and events.

Busy, pompous, soft-hearted Cantalbutte, Master of Ceremonies to Florestan XXIV, fusses about the court, disposing visitors to Aurora's christening. He introduces the good fairies, their consorts and their gifts to the royal parents, and takes the blame, bravely enough, for not inviting the wicked fairy. He even tries, ineffectually, to protect the knitting women whose needles have been banned from the kingdom. He is the main link, or should be, between all the action of the ballet until the grown-up Aurora arrives more than an hour after the ballet has started. Later, of course, he returns to introduce the guests at Aurora's wedding ceremonies. Therefore, he is one of the principal examples in classical ballet of the use of a mimetic link. Leslie Edwards created this difficult role in the British production of *The Sleeping Beauty* at Covent Garden in 1946. He made Cantalbutte a living and, so far incomparable, figure on the British stage.

Romantics, like Perrot, used a more naturalistic mime than their classical successors, but its function was just as much to link dances and fill in the story. Not until Fokine's innovations were linking passages of mime abandoned altogether with the rest of the classical formula.

[1] Called Cattalabutte in the Royal Ballet's production. Cantalbutte was his name in the original production in St. Petersburg.

Today everything has to be expressed in movement which combines acting with dancing. At one end of the scale dances may be linked musically through the development of a score and choreographic style, but remain separate as in Ashton's *Façade* and most of Balanchine's abstract works. At the other end of the scale the dancing is made continuous through a number of *danses d'action*. The characters in the ballet are carried along on an endless belt of movement which arises from the conflict of one character with another. So Fokine brings together Ivan, Kostchei and the Firebird, and Tudor makes character play upon character in *Jardin au Lilas*. Or there may be linking passages of acting which are part of the movement, as in Lavrovsky's *Romeo and Juliet*. Or there may be danced scenes which are nothing but elaborate joints in a story, like the drop curtain scenes in de Valois' *The Rake's Progress* and the return from the siege in Petit's *Cyrano de Bergerac*.

Often it is impossible to separate *danses d'action* from other passages of dancing in contemporary ballets. The choreographer will have prepared them all together. So the separate bits of dancing created in the rehearsal room will resemble pieces of knitting which careful stitching can assemble into a garment.

The dancers can help with the stitches. By now they are beginning to work themselves into their roles. The motivation for their actions in the libretto and music will help them logically to stitch together what the choreographer has devised for them. The same motivation will guide the choreographer in creating extra linking passages, where these are needed.

Whatever devices he employs the choreographer's aim must be continuity. His ballet must develop logically, clearly and economically to its end.

'An ending', says Agnes de Mille, 'has to be a summing up, the logical total of all that precedes, the final statement; in other words, the point of view.'[1] Most choreographers create the ending early on, or at least three-quarters of the way through their rehearsal period. It should be planned from the beginning, never left to the last moment. The choreographer without an ending in mind is like a marksman without a target.

Fashions in endings have changed, like fashions in ballet. The original end of *Giselle* was a *tableau vivant* with Bathilde and the

[1] Agnes de Mille, *And Promenade Home*, p. 177 (Hamish Hamilton, London, 1959).

court returning to claim the lost Prince. (See Appendix II.) Today this has been modified in many different productions. Classical choreographers usually rounded off an act or a ballet with a grand *pas de deux*, followed by dramatic action which included production effects (*Swan Lake*, Act III), or a spectacular dance and tableaux for the whole cast, like the end of *The Sleeping Beauty*. 'An inevitable *divertissement* brought his ballets to an ever happy conclusion', wrote Karsavina of Petipa, 'while such of his heroes, for whom anything but a tragic end was an historical impossibility, found themselves crowned in a final apotheosis.'[1]

Romantic and neo-romantic choreographers were much less conventional. In *La Sylphide* and *Petrouchka* they even ring down the curtain on a solitary figure of good or evil triumphant. In other words, they end the ballet as the story dictates, without a formal grand finale unless this arises naturally.

There is, of course, no recognised way to end a ballet. But the end must be a logical climax, true, and inevitable or surprising. Originality alone is not enough. In *The Rake's Progress* Ninette de Valois leaves a dead man on stage. Massine, past-master of the finale, fills his canvas with dancing figures. Andrée Howard lets everyone depart to finish *La Fête Étrange* with an empty stage.

Frederick Ashton, the consummate craftsman, shows how wide a range of ending one choreographer may devise. He ends most of his classical ballets in the formal manner; creates the tableaux of a house façade to end *Façade*; and builds a finale of Massine dimensions in *Daphnis and Chloe*. In *Symphonic Variations*, he begins and ends with the same choreographic picture.

The younger generation of British choreographers have shown a fondness for endings which are strongly dramatic or *coups de théâtre*. Alfred Rodrigues in *Blood Wedding* lets a blooded moon sink on to a stage, empty but for the bodies of its two victims. Jack Carter makes the Conjur-man produce another witch boy to replace the lynched victim of *The Witch Boy*. MacMillan ends *The Burrow* after the conclusion of the music, with three knocks on the door, and a pause before the curtain falls. Most brilliant of all is Cranko's comic end to *Pineapple Poll*. Mrs. Dimple, the aunt, is presented suddenly as Britannia, complete with shield and trident. It is a master stroke of theatre exactly in keeping with the theatrical style of Sullivan's England.

[1] Tamara Karsavina, 'Souvenirs d'enfance' (*Musica*, December, 1912).

All these endings arise naturally from the libretto. They are truthful as well as original. They are the kind of full stop which Doris Humphrey and other choreographer-teachers always look for, 'an end, a statement, a resolution'.[1]

1 Doris Humphrey, *The Art of Making Dances*, p. 166 (Rinehart, New York, 1959).

CHAPTER XXIII

THE DANCER'S CONTRIBUTION

'WHATEVER the talents of all those dancers may have been,' wrote Pierre Rameau of the principal dancers of Louis XIV's time, 'they recognised the superiority of Pécourt and L'Étang. . . . L'Étang danced with nobility and precision, while Pécourt took all kinds of parts with a grace, precision and lightness. Moreover, they were both well versed in the manners of polite society, so that the greatest lords delighted in their company and admitted them to their receptions.'[1]

Two and a quarter centuries later the L'Étangs and Pécourts have become 'boys and girls with the true ballet look, the erect, brisk and quiet figures carrying their boxes and baskets of practice clothes'.[2] You may see them in Times Square, New York, and the shady Kongens Nytorv in Copenhagen. They walk to work through the vegetable boxes of Covent Garden, the traffic of the Place de l'Opéra, down wide Moscow streets and over the graceful bridges of Stockholm.

The dancer's position in society has changed and grown. But his contribution to ballet is essentially what it was in Rameau's day. He is still a being composed of technical and emotional qualities which inspire and stimulate the choreographer. These qualities, of course, embrace a wider range than anything Rameau knew. They contribute to choreographic creation in two ways—technical and interpretative —at two stages of creation, the pre-rehearsal period and during rehearsal.

In the pre-rehearsal period it is the qualities of the dancers available, and specifically of certain dancers, which inspire a choreographer. Often these influence him in his choice of theme and in his choreographic plan. Or a dancer might stimulate one of the other collaborators, as the young Dolin, practising in the rehearsal room at Monte Carlo, inspired Cocteau to write the libretto for Le Train Bleu in 1923. (Plate XXIII (b).)

This inspiration is a powerful one because the choreographer has

[1] P. Rameau, Le Maître à danser, Paris, 1725, p. xiii (trans. Beaumont, London, 1931).　　　　　　　　　　　　　　[2] Agnes de Mille, op. cit. p. 36.

to work with the instruments he finds. Throughout ballet history it has been customary for him to be attached to a particular company for long periods of his creative life. Therefore he works with the same group of dancers. Among these, he finds some dancers who are more responsive than others to his ideas. On this basis professional partnerships develop between dancers and choreographers, sometimes supplementing, sometimes cutting across, personal relationships.

A partnership of father and daughter, Filippo and Marie Taglioni, lay behind some of the principal romantic ballets. The collaboration of Fokine, Pavlova, Karsavina and Nijinsky was the foundation of Fokine's greatest choreographic period. (Plate XXIII (a).) In our own day Maria Tallchief, when Balanchine's wife, was responsible for many of the special characteristics of his ballets in the late forties, like *Bourrée Fantasque*, *Symphony in C* and his version of *The Firebird*. (Plate XXIV (a).) British ballet owes many of its finest works to the inspiration which Sir Frederick Ashton drew from the dancing of Fonteyn and Somes. (Plates XXI (a) and XXIV (b).)

As with Fokine and the great Russians, these two dancers have not been Ashton's whole inspiration. He would have found other instruments for other ballets had they not been there. Indeed, he has done so with Beriosova in *Persephone* and Fonteyn and Nureyev in *Marguerite and Armand*. But the presence of Fonteyn and Somes over so long a period turned his work in the particular direction of their special qualities.

Margot Fonteyn has a great fluidity of movement combined with exceptional control and discipline, producing remarkable clarity in all she does. To an unusual degree she combines the carriage of a classical ballerina with the plasticity demanded by contemporary choreography. Ashton uses this combination to great effect in many of his ballets.

Fonteyn's other special quality is her emotional restraint. We do not mean she does not give warmth, gaiety and wit to her audience. She has done this, for example, in *Daphnis and Chloe* and in the tango in *Façade*. But, like other English people, she always seems to hold something in reserve. Because of this, because one so often feels there is more to see, she can be seen again and again with enjoyment in the same role.

This quality has appealed so much to Ashton that he has used it constantly throughout his association with her from the poor girl in *Nocturne* to the translucent *Ondine*. It represents an emotional discipline corresponding to the discipline of her movement. So exactly does it reflect the English character that it makes her a personification of the English School, as well as its model.

In a similar way the staunchness of Somes's character, his security as a partner, his presence and nobility on stage have set a standard for other English male dancers. These qualities have been incorporated into Ashton's ballets as foils to the femininity of Fonteyn.

The collaboration of Fonteyn with Ashton has been the longest and the most fruitful in English choreography. It has affected the interpretation and technical composition of almost all Ashton's ballets since the mid-thirties. Often, since 1946, he has conceived his ballets directly for Fonteyn and Somes or made decisions in the light of their opinions. 'Before Frederick Ashton decided on *Ondine*,' said Fonteyn, 'we discussed several possible stories for a three-act ballet. I objected, a little selfishly, to *The Tempest* because I thought Miranda rather a dull character for me. Then *Macbeth* was considered. I was attracted to the idea in some ways, but for various reasons it was not pursued. Finally, Ashton hit upon *Ondine*. It was ideal from my point of view.'[1]

Obviously, the influence of a dancer's promise upon a choreographer before a ballet is created is different from the influence exerted during rehearsal. Once a ballet goes into rehearsal the specific talents of dancers are what limit and fire the choreographer. It is a two-way process since a choreographer can inspire and mould his dancers as much as they can influence his style.

During the creative period this interaction of dancer-choreographer-dancer continues. It may add to the choreography only the particular technical achievements of members of the cast; it may inspire the whole dance style of a ballet. In technique, for example, the use of the left leg as the basis of most of the Swan Queen's Dances in *Swan Lake* may be because the first Swan Queen danced best on this leg. The *fouettés*, in the third act, were certainly turned to the right, i.e. on the left leg. 'The Italians', remarked Nicholas Legat, 'permitted a great deal of one-sidedness for the sake of superficial effect.'[2] All dancers, however, turn better one way rather than another. It is up to the choreographer to exploit their ability.

Who can tell what difference the accident of illness made to the dance style of Ashton's *Cinderella*? The role was conceived originally for Fonteyn. She became ill and much of the role was built on Moira

[1] *Sunday Times*, London, 8th March, 1959.   [2] Legat, *op. cit.*

Shearer, who created it at the first performance in 1948. Since these ballerinas have very different qualities it is possible that the choreography would be different today had Fonteyn been able to complete the creation of the character with Ashton.

The moral and physical presence of dancers, then, can influence choreography in very practical ways. A dancer can be so helpful in devising the mechanics of movement that the collaboration is actually creative, or he can be unhelpful to the point of obstruction. A dancer's encouragement can provide the stimulus or suggest the missing step when a choreographer's creation temporarily flags. In particular, the attitude of dancers to their work and the atmosphere surrounding them will affect a choreographer. If a choreographer works for long with a company its atmosphere, composed of temperament, discipline and artistic integrity, becomes a formative influence upon everything he does.

Even after creation, choreography can be modified significantly by a change of cast or by transfer of the ballet to another company. Two illustrations will show, in practice, what it is that dancers and dancers' schooling can do to a ballet.

A change of cast in the Bolshoi's *Romeo and Juliet* was noted perceptively by the critic Vladimir Kamenev in London after Ulanova had shown the British public the remarkable qualities of her Juliet in Lavrovsky's choreography. (Plate XXV (a).) But Juliet, in the same choreography, seemed a different person when Raisa Struchkova danced the role. Struchkova's 'choreographic portrait of Juliet is equally full of tenderness and lyrical charm', wrote Kamenev, 'but she uses somewhat more vivacious colours. Her Juliet is less withdrawn and is more passionate. Her *élévation*, if less spectre-like, is more expansive in range. The difference in their individual styles is conditioned by their different physique.'[1]

Giselle has changed much in its revivals during the nineteenth and twentieth centuries. It has journeyed with many companies from France, to Russia and back to Western Europe. 'The fairly accurate revival of Coralli's masterpiece,' Karsavina once wrote, 'well done as it is, yet has lost much of its original style. It took me some time to puzzle out why the same choreography, the same set of steps, are not the same any more in their effect and in their emotional value. It is because the choreography of *Giselle* has been transposed into another key. Originally composed for a dancer of exceptional

[1] V. Kamenev, *Anglo-Soviet Journal*, London, Autumn, 1956, p. 25.

lightness, it was in my time reserved for ballerinas with more than average elevation. This seems to be no longer so.'[1]

When Karsavina analyses the reason for this 'transposition into another key', we see the interrelation of choreography and performance, choreography and teaching. 'The perfect technique of a classical dancer is becoming rare at present. The decline of it is manifest in ballets of Romantic style, such as *Giselle* and *Les Sylphides*. Though following the choreographic design fairly accurately, the steps are not what the choreographer intended them to be. They are transposed from an elevated sphere to the *terre-à-terre* execution. The *ballon* and the preservation of a pose when landing are seldom seen. The great and beautiful feature of Romantic style such as landing from a *fouetté en l'air* into a long-sustained *arabesque fondue* is practically a lost art. What is the cause of the decline from perfect seemingly effortless elevation? The answer is easy: the omission of exercises needed for *ballon*.'[2]

The Russians have retained these exercises in their school. As a result they, and a ballerina like Alicia Markova, Russian and Cecchetti trained, are able to reproduce the period qualities of *Giselle* more faithfully than younger schools. The stronger dramatic impact of the Bolshoi's *Giselle*, compared with any other version today, derives from this fact and from the dramatic training Soviet dancers receive throughout their career. Likewise Markova in her fiftieth year remained a greater English interpreter of the romantic style than many younger dancers.

In the contemporary British repertoire we find the qualities of particular dancers similarly preserved in the roles they created, but modified by succeeding generations. The special qualities of Anton Dolin, enshrined in the Satan of de Valois' *Job*, appear differently through the physique and temperament of a Grant or a Blair. The qualities of Maude Lloyd, Peggy van Praagh and Hugh Laing, which appear and reappear in Tudor's early ballets, have all but vanished from contemporary versions without, however, reducing the impact of the choreography on the audience. Similarly, the special qualities of Laing and Nora Kaye, which illuminated Tudor's ballets in America, are slowly disappearing. (Plate XXV (b).)

The extent of a dancer's contribution to choreography depends, of course, on how much the choreographer will accept from the

[1] T. Karsavina, *Ballet Technique*, p. 29 (Black, London, 1956).
[2] T. Karsavina, *op. cit.* p. 27.

dancer and whether the dancer's training has made him a passive instrument or an active contributor to choreographic creation. 'There are two kinds of choreographer,' observed the dancer, Milorad Miskovitch, to us on one occasion. 'One is very strong and imposes his style on you, making you do it. The other absorbs the dancer's style, then moulds it to his purpose as a sculptor moulds clay.'

Dame Ninette de Valois is of the first kind; Sir Frederick Ashton is of the second; while Antony Tudor seems to meet his dancers in both guises. De Valois is the most impersonal of the three. Her choreography shows none of that sympathy for particular dancers which is so marked a characteristic of Ashton's work and, in a different sense, of Tudor's too. She bends the dancers to her will. She does not mould them. Tudor, too, bends dancers to his will. Tudor will create almost in conflict with his dancers, where Ashton will make of creation a joint enterprise. Like Ashton, however, Tudor is inspired by qualities of movement in his dancers. Both choreographers feel deeply, in a physical sense, every movement they create.

Tudor draws on the personalities of his dancers more than Ashton. Personality is to him a most potent inspiration. Hence his best ballets are built on conflicts of character. His most fruitful collaboration since he left London has been with Nora Kaye, the great American actress-dancer.

Contributions from the dancer to the choreographer can be found at every level and period of choreography. The choreographer's art can reach the public only through the prism of the dancer, who executes choreography like the playing of a score. Sometimes, indeed, choreography becomes significant only because of the performance of a particular dancer. To many people L'Après-midi d'un Faune and Le Spectre de la Rose were significant only so long as Nijinsky danced the Faune and the Rose. Similarly, Le Cygne (The Dying Swan) is associated for ever with Pavlova.

PART VII

THE CHOREOGRAPHER
IN THE THEATRE

CHAPTER XXIV

THE COLLABORATORS AGAIN

THE ballet reaches the theatre. The collaborators begin their last phase of work together. Since they first assembled, a general idea has become a detailed libretto. A score has been created in careful discussion to realise this libretto in dance terms. Light, colour and design in sets and costumes have been devised to create atmosphere and point emotion and movement without encumbering either. Finally, a choreographic play, a 'mute eloquence',[1] has been fashioned to express the libretto, score and stage design through a succession of dance images. Now these elements must be transferred from the rehearsal room, the paint shop, the wardrobe, and the orchestral score to the theatre where they belong. Here they will be combined into the single work envisaged at the beginning.

The person who carries out this fusion is known as the producer. Usually the producer is the choreographer, sharing responsibility with the artistic director. Together they supervise the final rehearsals. But the producer does not have to be either of these people. Michael Benthall, a drama producer, directed the final rehearsals of *Hamlet* and *Miracle in the Gorbals*. Tyrone Guthrie lit *Sea Change*. Diaghilev supervised, lit and virtually produced every ballet for his company. Ballet could benefit from a more frequent use of such outside minds. For the moment, however, we assume that the producer is the choreographer in collaboration with the artistic director. The degree of this collaboration depends on the personalities concerned and their experience. If the choreographer is inexperienced the artistic director or another collaborator may assume complete production authority from the moment the ballet leaves the rehearsal room.

Whatever the form of the collaboration there are certain tasks to be fulfilled before a ballet enters the theatre, if the best use is to be made of valuable stage time. During the last weeks in the rehearsal room conferences about lighting take place between the choreographer, designer and stage director. Then a lighting plot is prepared. This can be done first on a model of the set or on paper with the

[1] de Lauze, *op. cit.*

designs, preparatory to a technical rehearsal later in the theatre with lights and sets but without the cast.

The process takes many hours, but they are hours well spent. 'I have learned by experience', wrote Noverre of stage lights, 'the heightening effect they give to figures, the sharpness of form they induce and the elegance they accord to groups.'[1] The possibilities of lighting are endless, but 'it is not the great number of lamps, distributed at chance or symmetrically arranged, which lights up the stage and sets off the scenery; the skill consists in knowing how to distribute the lights, or mass them in unequal groups, so as to afford plenty of light to those parts which require it, or bring darkness to bear on other portions which demand such treatment.'[2] The lighting plot is vital to a ballet's success. Many a poor ballet has been saved by imaginative lights; many a good one has been made better.

No-one understood this more than Diaghilev, who was a master of lighting such as Noverre himself might have acknowledged. 'Whoever saw his production of Petrouchka', recorded Lydia Sokolova in her memoirs, 'must remember the bitter cold light just before the snow fell, which was so realistic that it made one shiver. Nothing could be more beautiful than his lighting in L'Oiseau de Feu at the moment when the Princesses appeared on that enormously high rostrum in the moonlight, and then came slowly down the steps, to surround the magic tree whose golden apples shone with an unearthly glow. This was breath-taking. Diaghilev would start his lighting rehearsals with a full staff of electricians and a few scene shifters on the stage. Although every ballet had its lighting plot, each theatre was differently equipped, so in important towns he rehearsed each ballet afresh and refused to leave the theatre until the effects he desired had been attained. Sometimes he would sit calling out instructions all night long, and we would find him still there, tired and unshaven, when we arrived to rehearse at ten in the morning.'[3]

Like lighting, the properties must be checked and reviewed, although their scale and weight will have been decided at the first discussions with the designer. Now they must be all assembled. Wrong properties can kill a dance or stage effect almost as effectively as bad lighting.

The producer must ensure, too, that the management receives

[1] Noverre, op. cit. p. 42.　　　　　　　　　　　　[2] Ibid. p. 63.
[3] Memoirs of Lydia Sokolova: Dancing for Diaghilev. Ed. Richard Buckle, p. 129 (John Murray, London, 1960).

in good time a correct and final cast list with a good title for the ballet and programme notes, if any. Naming a ballet, and writing programme notes, are as much a part of the craft of choreography as casting. A title, like *Symphonic Variations*, should suggest the form of a ballet, or, like *Checkmate*, should convey an idea essential to its understanding. This information is supplemented by the list of characters on the programme, and, perhaps, a very short programme note which should be explicit and simple. Nothing irritates an audience more than incorrect or obscure programmes.

Probably the artistic director will have attended rehearsals to become familiar with the ballet and to criticise it. Criticism and self-criticism between the collaborators should have been continuous throughout creation, but now they are more important than ever. The balance will be held by the artistic director who will decide differences of opinion.

Choreographers, like all artists, need someone with whom they can discuss the progress of their work. This may be one of the collaborators, one of the cast or a personal friend. Ideally it should be the artistic director. The artistic director needs to be a psychologist in the matter. The choreographer should be able to lean on him, but not too much. It is a question of balance, of judgement.

In the immediate pre-stage period the collaborators must make sure that the agreed shape and balance of the ballet have been maintained throughout the choreography, and that the chosen style and period are suitable to the story and common to choreography, music and décor. (Plate XII (b).) They must check that the story, or idea, has been clearly presented in the choreography, with the characters well defined, not only to the dancers *but to the viewing public*. They must see that the cast is fulfilling the collaborators' intentions, technically and dramatically. If the choreographer finds a dancer has been miscast the dancer should be changed regardless of personal feelings. So too with other elements of the ballet. Finally, the collaborators must confirm that highlights and climaxes are properly placed, that the ending is effective and that the balance of each section and the whole work is correct. Cutting or lengthening may be necessary at this point. Continuity, pace and climax are the watchwords. Nothing irrelevant to the story or mood must be retained.

No wonder choreographers are a rarity! To remain creative within the limits of all these practical and artistic considerations

C.A.—17

implies enormous self-discipline. Complete mastery of theatre craft is essential, besides artistic knowledge.

The final stage rehearsals usually fall in the last week or fortnight before a première. In most state theatres the heavy demands of the general repertoire on stage time make longer periods than a week unlikely. Commercial companies must keep the time short for economic reasons.

Stage rehearsals are usually grouped so that each component part of a ballet can be examined alone before everything is pulled together. First the dancers are examined, dancing to a piano. Probably the set will not be erected, but its dimensions will be indicated on the boards. Since few rehearsal rooms have the dimensions of a stage, except in big opera houses, this may be the dancers' first opportunity to fit their steps to the proper dancing area. There may also be certain peculiarities of the stage, such as a rake or a difficult surface, to which they must adapt themselves, especially in virtuosity passages and lifts.

Probably, too, this will be the first time artistic director, choreographer and designer can view the work critically in perspective from the distance across the footlights. So, in consultation with the composer, more cutting and pruning often takes place to supplement what has been done in the rehearsal room. Be warned, though, that first rehearsals of this kind are often depressing affairs. Movement and acting somehow seem smaller, less important, than in the rehearsal room. The absence of costumes, scenery and lighting deprives the work of theatrical magic. Sir Frederick Ashton was in despair after the first stage rehearsal of La Fille Mal Gardée which, within a fortnight, became one of the greatest successes in the British repertoire.

Next, a technical and lighting rehearsal is called at which the stage director puts the set on to the stage without the dancers. Here carpenters, electricians, property men, scene shifters and other technicians are made familiar with the technical problems of the ballet and with their roles in the production.

At the same time the lighting plot is tested in practice. Lighting colours must be matched against sets and costumes. The distribution of the lights—spots, battens, perches, front of house lights and so on —must be determined. Cues for lighting changes must be agreed and marked on the stage director's score, commonly known as the prompt score, in a way similar to the practice shown in the cue sheet for *Ondine* in Plate XXVI. On the not infrequent occasions when choreographer and designer fail to agree about lighting the artistic director must intervene. Finally, changes of scenery must be rehearsed to ensure silence, especially when scenery is complicated or if some special effect is required.

The last of the ingredients for mixing in the theatre is the music. The orchestra assembles to meet the music for the first time. These rehearsals are taken by the conductor or by the composer. Often the composer of a commissioned score conducts the early performances, but in any case he should be present at orchestral rehearsals.

We recall sitting with Sir Frederick Ashton in the empty auditorium of the Royal Opera House, Covent Garden, during such an orchestral rehearsal of *Ondine*. Hans Werner Henze, the composer, was taking the orchestra through his score. On the seats around us were members of the cast sometimes making the movements of the choreography with their hands. A single white light from the domed roof drained the gold and plush auditorium of colour. The great place looked like the countryside in winter. Only a yellow glow from the orchestra pit suggested life. 'Too fast', murmured Ashton, and glanced sideways at his dancers.

Such early orchestral rehearsals concern the choreographer and dancers only in as much as they may be hearing the orchestration for the first time. Therefore, they will need to learn it and discuss tempi with the composer and the conductor. Adjustments in tempi should be small if composer and conductor have attended sufficient rehearsals. Often nowadays, as with *Ondine*, the cast will have learned the orchestration from a tape recording in rehearsals. In the event of disagreements on musical matters which cannot be settled amicably, the artistic director must give his ruling.

Once the dancing, costumes, sets, and music have been rehearsed separately they begin to be pieced together. First there is an *orchestral rehearsal* with dancers in practice costume for the conductor to begin uniting the stage and pit. Next, there is a *piano dress rehearsal* for the dancers in costumes and with sets. Accompanied by a piano, so as not to waste expensive orchestral time, the dancers get used to the feel of costumes and sets and learn special details of make-up. (Plate XXVII (a).)

The costumes, of course, have been made to fit the dancers, but this is the first time all the work of the designer has met all the work of the choreographer on stage. There are still many problems to be

C.A.—17 *a*

solved, and adjustments to be made. The set may have steps which dancers must use within the time limits of the music. A quick change may need to be timed. Some costumes may be difficult to dance in, or the material of a girl's bodice may slip in a man's hands when he tries to lift her. Dancers must learn where the lighting falls so that they dance in the proper place, and lights must be adjusted to avoid blinding dancers at difficult moments, particularly in pirouettes.

This rehearsal is often long and slow with many repeats of sections and many trials on tempers and patience. But usually a complete run through is achieved before it ends. The British Actors' Equity contract, however, limits rehearsals to three hours at any one time and even more stringent regulations prevail in the U.S.A. and elsewhere. So it is wise to follow Diaghilev's example by calling a dress parade on stage prior to the piano dress rehearsal whenever the cast is large or costumes are particularly complicated.

The piano dress rehearsal is the most important of all the stage rehearsals to a choreographer. It is his last real chance to adjust details with his dancers (Plate XXVII (b)) and solve the problems presented by stage and proscenium arch. If he is really creative he will solve these craft problems with inspiration.

All the parts of a ballet come together for the first time at the *orchestral dress rehearsal*, known in some countries as the general, or final, rehearsal. If the earlier rehearsals have been properly conducted no adjustments should be needed at this rehearsal. Everything should fit perfectly.

The main value of an orchestral dress rehearsal, therefore, is to accustom everyone to everyone else, to create a sense of unity. Also this may be the first time that the ballet has been performed straight through without a stop. And since a ballet does not come alive without an audience it is the custom of some theatres to invite an audience to watch this rehearsal. Two repetitions are enough on such an occasion. Too many will kill the spontaneity of the first night.

CHAPTER XXV

THE FIRST PERFORMANCE

No ballet is ever complete before it meets its audience. The first performance, therefore, sees the beginning of its final realisation, with hours and minutes of tremendous tension for all the creators. 'It is hard to explain', said Sir Frederick Ashton to us before the first performance of *Ondine*, 'the strain of creating a three-act ballet. It is not only the long labour with other people, but the weight of responsibility to the artists and the public. If it fails it is like a great house collapsing.'

At the first performance the collaborators usually know at once whether or not they have fulfilled their intention. But every ballet needs a number of performances to settle down. It is only after these performances that a ballet can be judged fairly by everyone, including the critics.

Two kinds of success can be achieved by a ballet; a popular, box-office success and a *succès d'estime*. The one does not always imply the other. Each kind of success implies a different kind of audience impact or appeal.

The appeal of a *succès d'estime* is to a relatively small number of people, but for these few it is profound. Many of the best ballets, like other works of art, have this appeal. Often, when first produced, they are in advance of the popular taste of their time. Nevertheless, their quality is such and their impact on their own public so powerful that they continue to live and grow in the repertoire. *Job* and *Dark Elegies* are examples in Britain.

The appeal of *Job* lies in its theme and the stylised interpretation of this theme 'as a masque for dancing' through music and choreography inspired by Blake. To some extent, too, it has acquired an emotional appeal for the regular ballet goer as the oldest British ballet still extant. It is nobly conceived, perfectly synthesising theme and music, dancing and design, perfectly English and perfectly individual in the work of its composer and choreographer.

In a popular success the appeal is wide and immediate. Two of the most outstanding popular successes in the British repertoire since the war have been *Pineapple Poll* and *La Fille Mal Gardée*. No ballet, in our experience, has been given the mark of public approval so completely, within ten minutes of the curtain rising on the first performance, as *La Fille Mal Gardée*. Yet Ashton told us he considers *Ondine*, his more lyrical work, to be the better ballet.

Why is *La Fille Mal Gardée* so successful? Why has it been acclaimed so universally? Each ingredient has a popular appeal, fulfils its task precisely and is properly located in the ballet. In a word, the ballet fulfils the conditions of ballet-making which we have outlined in this book.

The narrative is well constructed with sympathetic characters clearly drawn from life in contrast to each other. It contains romantic appeal, comic appeal and proper conflicts of character and situation. It has simple, danceable music, well arranged and orchestrated. The patterns and inventions of the choreography are original and well organised for ensemble and principals. The highlights and climaxes of plot and dancing are cleverly placed and brilliantly created, fully using the advantages offered by the technique and personalities of the dancers. Finally, the ballet itself is superbly executed by the cast.

These, then, are the ingredients of popular success. They help us also to discern the part played by the audience. The popular success asks the audience to receive what it has to say without demanding a special intellectual or emotional contribution. The *succès d'estime* demands from the audience a measure of active thought and feeling if it wants fully to appreciate the performance. In the theatre, as everywhere else, the number of people prepared to make this serious contribution is increasing, but it is still a minority of the total audience.

Either way, the audience's contribution at the first performance is a vital factor in the ballet's future. Once the impact has been established and the ballet has settled down on stage it is possible to see clearly where weaknesses lie. Adjustments can be made by the collaborators in choreography, music, lighting and design. Again, the artistic director can play a creative part in these discussions.

Most often adjustments take the form of cutting and rearrangement. Audience reactions frequently suggest how this should be done. The audience make it possible to feel where the argument is obscure or the action drags. The collaborators cannot see this themselves, because they are too close to the work and they are not, after all, the audience.

After the first performance, then, polishing takes place. Polishing is a process of adjustment by dancers as well as collaborators. The dancers grow into their roles, learn how to get the most from them dramatically, where to pause, where to speed up—in a word, how to punctuate their performances for the audience. It is only after this polishing has taken place that each component art is clarified finally and knit together.

As this goes on there is a qualitative, almost indefinable, change in the ballet. It begins to merge the talents and personalities of its creators, large and small, good and bad, with the characteristics of the national school which gave it birth. (Plates XXVIII–XXXII.) It acquires a personality, a life of its own, distinct from any of its creators, but distinctly national. It grows up. It is complete.

CHAPTER XXVI

THE PRESERVATION OF BALLETS

BALLETS have three kinds of life.

There are ballets which are produced once only, fall out of the repertoire and are never revived. Such ballets may be complete failures or limited successes. The failure will die after a few performances. The limited success remains for only one season. For some reason it fails to catch on. Its appeal is too special or too small. Often this is the fate of the *succès d'estime*.

Secondly, there are ballets which enter the repertoire and stay there. They may be popular successes like *Pineapple Poll* which are frequently performed, or established *succès d'estime* like *Job*, which are revived occasionally.

Thirdly, there are ballets which survive beyond the epoch in which they were created. These are the classics. *Giselle*, *Coppélia*, *Swan Lake* and *Les Sylphides* are obvious examples. *Job*, *The Rake's Progress*, *La Fille Mal Gardée*, *Jardin au Lilas*, *Rodeo* and *Symphony in C* are possible candidates for recognition among the classics of tomorrow.

No-one can say for certain what makes a ballet live, but there are a number of decisive factors, artistic and practical.

The most important artistic factor is the effectiveness of the collaboration. Is the ballet a complete unity? Next comes the quality of that unity and its parts. History shows that survival depends primarily on a good scenario and a good score. If these parts are poor good choreography and décor cannot save the work.

Beside these artistic merits, practical factors sometimes exert an influence beyond their apparent importance. There are six such factors.

First, usefulness to the company. Much depends on the needs of a company, or theatre, at a given moment. Every repertoire should be balanced for audience appeal. It may need a dramatic ballet, a comic ballet or a ballet which finishes the evening well. If even an indifferent ballet meets this need its chances of survival are much improved. On the other hand a good ballet would be in jeopardy if it was difficult to carry in the repertoire, whatever the reason.

Second, national taste. Petipa's classics, successful as they are in Britain, America and the Soviet Union, did not begin to enjoy a comparable success in France until the late fifties. Similarly, several popular French ballets have been poorly received in Britain. American ballets, too, have sometimes done badly in Britain and Australia in spite of success at home.

Third, period taste. A ballet might catch the mood of a moment of history, but die, like *Dante Sonata*, when that moment passes. Or it might reflect a phase of taste in art like the Diaghilev cocktail ballets, *Le Train Bleu*, *Le Bal* and *La Chatte*. *Giselle*, too, one could argue, reflects the taste of its period, but its theme is a fundamental theme applicable to any time, whereas the cocktail ballets had no fundamental theme and so only appealed to the taste of their day.

Fourth, press reactions. Newspapers do not always present accurate, or even reasonable, aesthetic judgements. Often their opinions are not those of trained critics but of journalists untrained in ballet who are unsuitable to judge the work as it should be judged; or the attitude of the writers is determined by private feelings which have nothing to do with the ballet—a bad meal, editorial whims or lack of space. It would be much better if critics did not have to write a hasty judgement within half an hour of the fall of the first-night curtain. It would be fairer if the press carried a news announcement of the première, leaving aesthetic judgement until trained critics had seen a number of performances. This is the case in the U.S.S.R. where critics only write a considered opinion after many viewings. Critics cannot kill a really good ballet at its first performance as they tried to kill *Dark Elegies*, but they can kill a borderline case.

Fifth, continuity of dancers. Ballets may die for lack of suitable dancers to play particular roles, or because the dancers who remember these roles have left the company and no other arrangements have been made to preserve the ballet.

Sixth, economic problems, especially on tour. If a ballet requires expensive staging (special effects, extra instrumentalists, singers and so on) it is difficult enough to provide this in the home theatre, but on tour it is often impossible.

Combinations of all these artistic and practical factors determine the length of life of a new ballet. But what makes a ballet live beyond its epoch? What makes a classic?

Clearly, a ballet which becomes a classic must have something more than the qualities which enable it to survive short-term tests. This 'something' is again a mixture of aesthetic and practical factors.

Aesthetically, classics become classics because what they say and how they say it have an exceptionally powerful appeal. The poetic spark which makes this appeal exceptional is governed by no rules and can have no definition.

In practical terms, classics fulfil all the requirements of a new ballet in the repertoire and include, besides, great roles which particularly challenge and display the dancers who appear in them. Hence each generation of dancers is as interested as the public in keeping the ballet alive.

But how is a ballet kept alive from generation to generation when there is no widely accepted system of notation? Unlike a play or a piece of music, ballets can only be preserved in something resembling their original shape by constant performance in a company. *The Whims of Cupid and the Ballet Master*, for example, has never left the repertoire of the Royal Danish Ballet since Galeotti created it in 1786. It may not be the best example of Galeotti's work, but circumstances were such that it alone has survived.

Libretti, music and designs can always be preserved on paper. We have ballets preserved in this form even from Weaver's time. But they are meaningless without the choreography which gave them life. Choreography can be preserved in four ways operating separately or in combination. The four ways are: the dancers' memory, critical comments, systems of notation and films.

The dancers' memory is the traditional method of preserving choreography. The memory may be that of the choreographer, the dancers, or a répétiteur, passing on the ballet from one generation to another.

Some choreographers can remember all their ballets and can reproduce every role as they created it, even after long periods without a performance. Other choreographers forget their choreography the moment they have created it. They clear their minds, as it were, for the next ballet. Between the two lies the choreographer who can remember the general shape and some, but not all the details, of his original work. This kind of choreographer will revive a work by creating new choreography to replace what he cannot remember or to improve what he can remember. Fokine was inclined to do this. So he has left us different, equally 'authentic' versions of *Les Sylphides*. Such changes are quite different from more purposeful changes, which bring an old ballet up to date in terms of audience appeal.

Diaghilev introduced several of these purposeful changes into Petipa's *The Sleeping Beauty*[1] at the Alhambra Theatre, London, in 1921. 'Diaghilev began by studying Tchaikovsky's score,' wrote Serge Grigoriev, the great man's régisseur. 'He deleted everything he considered dull, and replaced these excisions with material from other compositions of Tchaikovsky's. He also asked Stravinsky to re-orchestrate the Prelude and Aurora's variation in Act III. . . .

'Diaghilev took an active part in the *mise en scène*, directing much of it himself, and though what he aimed at primarily was a reconstruction of this ballet in its original form, he was prepared, where it seemed advisable, to introduce fresh matter. It was hence that Bronislava Nijinska came to take a hand in the choreography. . . . Diaghilev invited her without more ado to arrange some new numbers in *The Sleeping Princess*. She did this most successfully, the best known of these numbers being the afterwards celebrated *Dance of the Three Ivans*.'[2]

Another change in Act III affected what has become in Britain the *pas de trois* for Florestan and his sisters. Originally Petipa created a *pas de quatre* to this piece of music for the Fairies Diamond, Gold, Silver and Sapphire. Diaghilev retained it as a *pas de quatre* in 1921 but made the characters Pierrette, Pierrot, Harlequin and Columbine. Only in 1923, when he reproduced the third act as a one-act ballet, called *Aurora's Wedding*, did the dance become a *pas de trois*.

More fundamental changes, partly as a result of researches into the full Tchaikovsky score, partly to bring the ballet 'more into tune with Soviet life', have been made by Soviet producers in several versions of *Swan Lake*.

Departures of any kind from the original are always debateable. When made, however, they must continue the intention of the creator and pursue his choreographic idiom. Much, therefore, depends upon the accuracy with which the original roles and dance idiom are remembered.

Dancers who have danced a role for many years will remember that role and best be qualified to pass it on. This does not mean, unfortunately, that such dancers know all the other roles in the same ballet. Dancers able to remember many roles are exceptional and need

[1] Called by Diaghilev, *The Sleeping Princess*.
[2] S. L. Grigoriev, *The Diaghilev Ballet, 1909–1929* (Constable, London, 1953).

to be cherished. Leon Woizikovsky and Lydia Sokolova are examples from the later Diaghilev Ballet. Elizabeth Schooling is an example from the Ballet Rambert; Julia Farron from the Royal Ballet.

Woizikovsky demonstrated his dancer's memory in a remarkable way in Warsaw in 1958. The fortieth anniversary of his début on the stage in Warsaw was celebrated belatedly on 8th March that year at the city's Panstwowa Opera. He lived in Poland throughout the war and had had no contact with the Diaghilev repertoire for nearly twenty years, nevertheless, as we saw for ourselves, he reproduced the whole of *Schéhérazade*, *L'Après-midi d'un Faune* and *Petrouchka* with an accuracy that was uncanny, even in an art which has always fostered memory.

It is also a fact within the experience of dancers—attested by Tamara Karsavina and Lydia Sokolova in their memoirs—that a kind of muscle memory exists alongside conscious memory. It springs from the stimulus of music. Often, when dancers seem to have forgotten a role, the playing of the music will stimulate their limbs to respond with the appropriate steps.

Some dancers, blessed with special talent and good memories become ballet-masters or régisseurs. It is these dancers who are responsible principally for passing individual ballets, and even whole repertoires, on to a new generation. These are the really important memories. On them depends the quality of each new production of an old work.

Nicholas Sergueeff and Serge Grigoriev established high standards during the thirties as régisseurs respectively of the Maryinsky classics and the Diaghilev ballets. But for Sergueeff's work in England the Royal Ballet, and other companies outside the Soviet Union, would not enjoy the versions they know of *Swan Lake*, *Casse-Noisette*, *Coppélia*, *Giselle* and *The Sleeping Beauty*. But for Grigoriev the best of the Diaghilev repertoire would not be preserved, as it is today, in the companies of Europe and America.

Grigoriev recalled his first rehearsal for Diaghilev. It took place at the Drill Hall in Cheyne Street, London, in 1912. 'At the end of this, the first rehearsal that I directed, Diaghilev took me back to his hotel with him, and expatiated on the role of a ballet régisseur. It was similar, he suggested, to that of the conductor of an orchestra. Just as the latter conducts the performance of orchestral works by various composers, so the régisseur has to conduct ballets composed by various choreographers. Both must bring to this conducting all the talent and knowledge they can command. The only difference between them is that whereas the conductor of an orchestra remains with his musicians during performances, a ballet régisseur has in the end to leave his dancers to their own devices; and that whereas the conductor has a score before him, the régisseur must rely on his memory. The task of the régisseur is therefore harder than that of the conductor.'[1]

Nowadays a régisseur is sometimes called a répétiteur. His job, points out Zakharov, the Soviet choreographer, is to preserve the authors' version of a ballet as far as possible. If, in other words, the choreographer is living he must be consulted before any departure of substance is made from his original choreography, even when local conditions make such changes necessary. If the choreographer is not living, everything must be done to fulfil his intention and reproduce his work in the most vital and accurate form.

We need, remarks Zakharov, 'to train capable ballet répétiteurs who cannot only preserve the outer form of the production (exact adherence to the choreographic text, and smoothness and evenness in the ensemble dances) but can also set the dancers serious intellectual and artistic problems and help them to reveal the basic thought, the heart of the role. The répétiteur must have an excellent visual memory and an exceptional ear for music.'[2]

So important has the work of répétiteurs, or régisseurs, now become that particular attention is being paid to training these specialists in Britain and elsewhere, as well as the Soviet Union. This means that existing ballets by choreographers of the past, or ballets forgotten by their living creators, can be reproduced anywhere in the world with the help of a répétiteur familiar with the production.

But memory, however excellent, plays tricks. It is the least reliable method of preserving choreography. Each generation of memories takes us a little further from the original. To refresh their memories répétiteurs and others often use some form of notation and even turn occasionally to the writings of critics and ballet historians. Today the cinema can supplement these aids.

Critical records are useful because they often include an impression of a ballet's general shape and impact when it was first seen. Such impressions are of two kinds: evocative and highly personal, like the

[1] S. L. Grigoriev, *The Diaghilev Ballet*, 1909–1929 (Constable, London, 1953).
[2] R. Zakharov, *The Art of the Ballet Master* (Moscow, 1954. S.C.R. abridged translation).

writings of Gautier; or factual and descriptive, like the writings of Beaumont. Lucky the répétiteur who has both kinds of writing to help him. Notation and films cannot capture the quality of impact during a performance.

Since the seventeenth century, choreographers, teachers and ballet masters have evolved methods of notation to record steps and gestures. (Plate XXXIII.) Weaver in his day thought he discerned a universal notation evolving like music. In fact no simple universally accepted method has arisen which dancers can use as a matter of course to record movement with the accuracy of a composer writing down music. This deficiency must be made good if choreography is ever to achieve effective copyright protection, as well as accurate preservation. The case for a universal dance notation is as imperative today as the case for musical notation was in the fifteenth century.

Plates XXXIV and XXXV (a) give examples of three systems in use today. The Stepanoff notation, first published in St. Petersburg in 1891, uses a specially printed type of musical stave, with an adjoining floor pattern. It was taught to students in the ballet schools of St. Petersburg and Moscow and is still in use in the Soviet Union. Sergueeff recorded twenty-one Russian classical ballets in this system and used the records to mount the classics in Western Europe. These valuable records are now in the possession of the English ballerina, Mona Inglesby, founder of the International Ballet. Sergueeff became régisseur of the International Ballet from its inception in 1941 and remained in this position until his death, in Nice, in 1951.

Labanotation and Benesh notation have gained recognition in Western Europe and America, although it is regrettable that competing systems should ever have arisen. Labanotation originated in Germany in 1928 and is taught and used widely there and in America, less widely in Britain. It uses special symbols on three vertical lines read upwards from the bottom of the page. Already a number of ballets have been notated from current repertoires. The scores are available at the Movement Notation Bureau in New York whence they have been used to reproduce the works on other companies.

Benesh notation secured copyright in London in 1955 by Joan Benesh, then a dancer with the Sadler's Wells Ballet, and her husband, Rudolf Benesh. It uses a five-line musical stave, one for each dancer or group of dancers, running horizontally across the page.[1] It is taught

---

[1] *A Dictionary of Ballet*, by G. B. L. Wilson (Penguin Reference Books), carries an excellent short description of dance notations.

today to all students at the Royal Ballet School in London and is beginning to spread abroad.

The great problem of notation, of course, is to record moods and nuances as well as steps and movements. This problem has not yet been solved satisfactorily. Notation, too, records choreography alone, not the whole stage picture of choreography, décor, costumes and music assembled together. Such a record can be provided only by the cinema.

Ballet films can be of two kinds. They may be intended for public exhibition in cinema or on TV (see Appendix VII) or made for purely record purposes. Film records which are only for the archives and are not meant to be works of art should be shot from the angle which gives the best overall picture. They should record the actual stage production with the original cast in the complete theatrical setting, accompanied by the full orchestral score in perfect synchronisation.

Records of this kind have been made occasionally in the Soviet Union. Nothing so elaborate has been attempted in Western Europe and America, although Massine for years has recorded his ballets without music in a rehearsal room. (Plate XXXV (b).) The Royal Ballet in London now regularly records new works on film in a way whose value has been proved. The value would be greater but for difficulties of finance and trade union regulations, which prevent the music being recorded at the same time.

Films, however, cannot be the only record. They are expensive, move too quickly to make it easy for a répétiteur or dancers to learn particular steps, and rarely give a clear, unhindered view of each role, especially minor roles.

At this moment, therefore, the accurate preservation of choreography depends upon a proper collaboration of every method—memory, critical record, notation and the cinema. This could be helped enormously by the development of a central archive of the dance in each country charged with organising, maintaining and developing records. Ideally, every successful ballet should be notated, filmed and described. For the world of ballet in general and for national ballets in particular a proper system of archives has become essential. Too many works of choreographic art have been lost already or distorted beyond recognition to excuse more delay in providing this vital service.

CHAPTER XXVII

EPILOGUE: CURTAIN

WE have shown how choreography is the most universal of stage languages. It reaches its highest expression in ballet, which mingles the primary arts of music, painting, dancing and poetry as a painter mingles the primary colours. Out of this synthesis has been born an art of the emotions greater than any of its parts.

Looking North, South, East and West, from London, Moscow or New York, ballet and choreography can be seen growing, firm and strong today in countries which never knew them before. They exert an influence in world culture such as history has never seen and perhaps never expected. Dancers and choreographers have become ambassadors, speaking a language without frontiers.

This has come about following the successful international tours of Pavlova, Diaghilev and their companies. These journeys established the large international touring company as a permanent travelling show-case of choreographic art. Such a phenomenon became possible only through this century's technological advances, since the movement of a ballet company with its orchestra, tons of scenery and properties necessitates a major feat of transportation.

As a result the international audience for choreography has expanded many times. To meet the demand thus created even the great state companies of France, Denmark and Russia have moved abroad. They have left their ancient theatres for the first time in history.

Famous dancers and choreographers, of course, have travelled often before. The world of the dance has always travelled. But this is not the same thing as seeing whole companies from another country performing choreography in the true national idiom. This is why the representative national company makes such a strong impact when first seen in another country.

The impact is profound on the foreign public and no less profound upon its dancing profession. Hence the exchange of companies over the last half century has enriched choreographic art on a scale hitherto unknown. Such an exchange of ideas is vital to all arts. To choreography it is especially necessary because there is no true way of showing choreography, as yet, other than by the physical presence of dancers in their companies.

Yet choreographers remain the rarest of creative artists. Although the world of dancing has increased so much choreographers seem hardly more numerous proportionately today than when Weaver and Noverre first argued the cause of the *ballet d'action*. This is because a good choreographer is someone possessing very special gifts. Not only must he be born with many natural talents. He must have the opportunity to develop these talents and the chance to acquire training and skill in closely allied arts. Such provision is difficult. Even harder to come by are his dancers, his human material, the musicians to play for them, the theatre to present them and the money to pay them. Hardest of all is the creation of the right atmosphere, the *milieu* within which the choreographer can work.

Within the framework of national cultures, however, choreographers have won a new place of influence since the war. It may be hard for choreography to retain this place, let alone develop it. Nevertheless, the last few years in Europe and America have seen the creation of full-length works where none existed before, alongside lighter one-act works. For their themes many choreographers have begun to seek inspiration in contemporary thought and daily life, or if their themes are not contemporary they have adapted old stories to contemporary taste.

Somehow, choreography must hold the interest of its present public and reach an even wider audience. To do this it must come closer to the public in language and theme. It must involve people as well as entertain them.

This does not mean that a new language needs to be devised; only that the present one should be used in a more universal way. Nor should choreography express itself only through the extreme forms of pure dance or dance-drama. There needs to be a proper balance between these two, just as there should be a proper balance in every repertoire between the one-act work and the full-length ballet.

Choreography also requires urgently a universal system of dance notation. Imagine literature without a written script, or music without a score. Without some notation system choreography can have no individual existence. It must lean inevitably on music, can never be independent of other arts, never be a great art in its own right.

These are problems to be solved by the choreographers of the future. A start has been made, but there is still a long way to go. Society now needs to encourage what has been begun. Education is the key to this advance on both sides of the theatrical curtain.

A more widely based education is needed for dancers, those who will become performers and those who will teach. At present in Britain specialist dance education finishes at secondary school level. What is needed is some higher level, the equivalent of the university, which can provide a more advanced training in aesthetics, music, art and dramatic techniques alongside students of other arts. By these means the dancer will have the chance to acquire a broader outlook in an atmosphere where his talents and intellect can develop beyond what is possible in the more restricted curriculum of ballet school and company.

Something of this kind has been provided for a number of years at the Lunacharsky State Theatrical Institute, Moscow, and at the Leningrad State Conservatoire. Courses such as the Moscow course described in Appendix VIII A, will not necessarily suit conditions outside the U.S.S.R., but they provide a useful guide and starting point for discussion.

Such higher education will benefit choreographers, in particular, although it can never replace inborn talent and never replace initial work with a company. It can help them, saving as much as ten years of experiment, by teaching them the craft of choreography and passing on the knowledge of past masters. Therefore, a strong case exists for a similar higher institute of choreographic study in Britain where professional dancers and teachers, as well as choreographers, will be given time and guidance to enlarge their aesthetic experience. This institute, which might be an extension of a national school, would give training from which a dancer could not have benefited before reaching maturity.

The many financial and material difficulties still to be overcome, even at the level of secondary dance education in Britain, make it unlikely that any higher institute can be created for some years. The need is so great, however, that this should not prevent interim measures such as the short course outlined at Appendix VIII B through which potential choreographers and producers could be given facilities for choreographic study.

On the audience side of the curtain the education of the public can take place through the schools, universities, the press, books and television. Central and local government finance is the key to much of this. But financial help is only part of the need.[1]

British universities are far behind those in the United States in their contribution to the study of choreography. Yet choreography deserves now as much attention to its aesthetics and history as is given to music and other fine arts. Critics of choreography, too, need to be trained and properly qualified through the universities. Indeed, the development of a reservoir of trained critics, writers and lecturers is one of the most pressing needs in Britain today. For this reason we outline in Appendix IX certain courses which British universities might provide to meet the need internally and externally. The press and publishing houses, cinema, television and radio form contemporary public opinion. Without skilled representation in these fields the art of choreography will not receive the public appreciation every art requires, nor will it receive a share of help from the public authorities, commensurate with the standing it has won.

University extra-mural departments, local authorities and similar responsible bodies could encourage the study of this art by amateur performers through further education classes, at least to the extent that they encourage the study of other arts. Without roots in the educational system there can be no ballet and no choreography, because there will be no informed audience and no dancers. By the same token opportunity for dancing should form part of the general education afforded every child. 'Dancing, being that which gives graceful motions all the life, and, above all things, manliness and a becoming confidence to young children, I think cannot be learned too early.'[2] John Locke's words are as true today as when they inspired John Weaver two centuries ago.

In Great Britain and abroad specialised bodies like the Royal Academy of Dancing have done a great deal to introduce classical ballet to general education. As a result of the Academy's ballet-in-education syllabus about a quarter of a million children in Britain alone (more in the Commonwealth) study ballet each year as part of their physical education although very few ever intend to become professional dancers. Of these between thirty and forty thousand take the examinations of the syllabus itself. Professional ballet companies also do what they can with lecture demonstrations

[1] Problems of the relationship between dancing and the public are discussed further in *The Ballet in Britain* (O.U.P., 1962).
[2] Locke, *Essay Concerning Human Understanding* (London, 1690).

to schools, ballet and music clubs and other societies. Yet there is still a long way to go before dancing becomes a regular part of our national education system.

The same is true of the United States in spite of a much larger apparatus of dance education. There are now thirty thousand ballet schools in the States and many dance courses at university level for future teachers and critics. These provide in no sense a specialist dance training for performers; they should be seen rather as the basis of a more thorough general dance education for everyone. Parallel with this development has been the growth of the Regional Ballet Movement, stimulated by geographical conditions in the U.S.A. The movement's success in encouraging amateur and professional ballet centres all over the United States is one of America's principal dance achievements since the war.

Through movements of this kind, and expanding education everywhere, the influence of the art of choreography will spread and the choreographer himself will grow as an artist because what he has to say will fall less often on barren ground.

For the moment we have to remember that choreography developed with remarkable rapidity in Britain and America during the thirties and after the war. We live now in a period of reassessment when what has been achieved will be examined and absorbed or rejected. Out of this quiet period will come the choreographers of the next advance. Given an equal advance in educational and social conditions these young choreographers will undertake their difficult task better understood and supported on both sides of the theatrical curtain than any choreographers before them.

Yet when that curtain rises and the choreographer is judged it is talent, above all, which will count. No teacher can impart that priceless gift. All the choreographer's training and all his craft will pass for nothing unless he possesses the flair for inventing movement. This is the spark of creation which distinguishes the choreographer from his fellows. It is his alone, a private, magic fire which lights the art of choreography and gives it life.

THE CHOREOGRAPHIC PICTURE

Plate I. BEGINNINGS: THE ENGLISH MASQUE

(a) 1611. Inigo Jones' set for Oberon's Palace in *Oberon, the Faery Queen*, a masque by Ben Jonson. The palace was revealed after the opening of a pair of shutters painted to resemble rocks. Later the palace itself opened to reveal the land of the faeries.
Courtesy, the Devonshire Collection, Chatsworth

(b) 1931. An early production of *Job* by the Vic-Wells Ballet at the Sadler's Wells Theatre, showing Gwendolin Raverat's backcloth based on William Blake's designs for his *Book of Job*. *Job*, with scenario by Geoffrey Keynes, music by Vaughan Williams and choreography by Ninette de Valois, was created as a masque for dancing in eight scenes. Photo: Gordon Anthony

Plate II. BEGINNINGS: THE COURT BALLET

Ballet de la Jeunesse. Divertissement mêlé de comedie et de musique, first performed before Louis XIV at Versailles on January 28, 1686, with music by Michel-Richard de Lalande, décor and costumes by Jean Berain and choreography by Beauchamps. The entertainment consisted of *entrées de ballet* and sung *recitatives* between acts of a play by Dancourt. Nobles of the court and professional dancers took part. Photo: Satar

Plate III. BEGINNINGS: THE DEVELOPMENT OF COSTUME

(a) Mid-Eighteenth Century: Male

Costume for Jason in Noverre's *Médée et Jason*, showing the male tonnelet of the mid-eighteenth century

(b) Mid-Eighteenth Century: Female

Costume for Medea, showing the shortened skirt of the 1760's, and the heeled slipper

Both these designs, typical of costumes for dancers in the noble style, are by Louis Boquet, principal designer at the Paris Opera from 1760–1782 and the designer of many ballets for Noverre. Photographs from the Library of the University of Warsaw

(c) Early Nineteenth Century

A study of Salvatore Viganò and his wife, Marie Medina, showing the simple dress of semi-transparent material for women and the new line of the male costume in the neo-classical styles ushered in by the French Revolution. The shoes for both dancers are heelless allowing as much freedom to the feet as the costumes allow to the limbs

Plate IV. BEGINNINGS: DEVELOPMENT OF THE POINTE

(a) Acrobats. The Köbbler Family in 1812

The Dutch actor-designer, Jelgerhuis (1770–1836), made this, one of the earliest known drawings of the use of the *pointe*, 'at the theatre while the memory was still fresh in my mind'. Photo: Amsterdam Theatre Museum

(c) Marie Taglioni in *La Fille du Danube*, 1836, showing the costume, ethereal qualities and use of the *pointe* admired in the romantic ballet. Photo: Satar

(b) *La Sylphide*, Act I

Marie Taglioni in *La Sylphide*, 1832, from the painting by Lepaule. The spirit visits the sleeping James. The popularity of romantic themes of the kind introduced by *La Sylphide* encouraged the use of the *pointe* and was stimulated by its further development

Plate V. ROMANTIC AND CLASSICAL THEMES

(a) Romantic. *Giselle*, Act I
Giselle is elected Queen of the Wine Harvest
From the wood-engraving in Gautier's *Les Beautés de l'Opéra*, 1845

(b) Classical. *The Sleeping Beauty*, Prologue
La Belle au Bois Dormant at the Maryinsky Theatre, St. Petersburg, 1890. Prologue
and Act I were in the French Valois Period, later acts in the reign of Louis XIV. The
scene is a realistic presentation of a Renaissance Palace. Note the 'historical' costumes
of the mimes and supers, and the convention which permits dancers to wear out-of-
period ballet skirts. Photos: Courtesy, Cyril Beaumont

Plate VI. NEO-ROMANTIC THEMES

(a) Introduction of the one-act Narrative Ballet

Petrouchka. Opening scene of the Diaghilev production, showing Benois' décor.
Photo: Boris Kochno, *Le Ballet*, Paris

(b) Introduction of Mood and Abstract Ballet

Les Sylphides. A performance of the Diaghilev Ballet in Paris, 1909, showing
the original setting by Benois with Tamara Karsavina, *centre.*
Photo: Boris Kochno, *Le Ballet*, Paris

Plate VII. CONTEMPORARY THEMES

(a) Nijinsky's *Jeux* in 1913 was the first twentieth century ballet on a contemporary theme in contemporary costume. Photo: Boris Kochno, *Le Ballet*, Paris

(b) Massine's *Ode* with décor by Tchelitcheff, Paris, 1928. A kind of hymn to the Aurora Borealis, and one of the strangest of the Diaghilev Ballet's last productions. It was also a forerunner of the abstract *genre* which came in with the thirties. Photo: Lipnitzki and Boris Kochno, *Le Ballet*, Paris

Plate VIII. BALLET TODAY: MOOD AND ABSTRACT

(a) Abstract. The original cast of Ashton's *Symphonic Variations. Left to right* Danton, Shearer, Somes, Fonteyn, May, Shaw

The dancers are figures of movement, without emotional or narrative development. Photo: Baron

(b) Mood. The original cast of Tudor's *Jardin aux Lilas. Left to right* Laing, van Praagh, Tudor, Lloyd

The dancers are types, involved in an emotional situation with very little narrative development. Photo: Dunbar

Plate IX. BALLET TODAY: NARRATIVE

(a) Dramatic narrative. The original cast of Rodrigues' *Blood Wedding*, based on Lorca's play. *Left to right* Gill, Metliss, Fifield, Poole, Trecu. Photo: de Marney

(b) Comedy narrative. The principal characters in de Mille's *Rodeo*. de Mille herself is centre, rear. Photo: Fehl

Characters in both the above ballets are strongly drawn and involved in human situations

Plate X. THE AUTHOR AT WORK

The Rake's Progress
(a) Hogarth's cartoon. The Orgy. Photo: Sir John Soane's Museum

(b) Whistler's set and de Valois' choreography, the same scene

Hogarth's famous cartoons inspired Gavin Gordon, the composer, to write scenario and music for the ballet before de Valois became the choreographer. Rex Whistler's set and de Valois' choreography later took their inspiration from the same source.

Photo: Debenham

Plate XI. THE COLLABORATORS AT WORK

(a) Drawn by Picasso, Diaghilev watches Ballet Class with his manager, Salisburg

(b) Boris Kochno (*left*) discusses designs with Lepri, Berard and Serebriakoff.
Photo: Lipnitzki

Plate XII. THE COLLABORATORS AT WORK

(a) Fokine discusses the score of his one-act ballet *Cendrillon* with Baron d'Erlanger, the composer, in London, 1938. Photo: Anthony

(b) Kenneth MacMillan discusses with the designer, Kenneth Rowell, *centre*, a backcloth for his *Le Baiser de la Fée* in London, 1960. Photo: Dominic

Plate XIII. CHOREOGRAPHY AND DESIGN: DIAGHILEV

(a) Bakst and Fokine. *Schéhérazade* for the Ballets Russes.
Photo: Boris Kochno, *Le Ballet*, Paris

(b) Picasso and Massine. *Le Tricorne* for the Ballets Russes.
Photo: Boris Kochno, *Le Ballet*, Paris

Plate XIV. CHOREOGRAPHY AND DESIGN: BRITAIN

(a) Georgiadis and MacMillan. *Danses Concertantes* for the Sadler's Wells Theatre Ballet, 1955, with Maryon Lane, centre, and Donald Britton, front. Photo: Denis de Marney

(b) Fedorovitch and Howard. *La Fête Étrange* for the Sadler's Wells Theatre Ballet, 1954, with David Gill, Elaine Fifield and Pirmin Trecu, *centre*. Photo: de Marney

Plate XV. CHOREOGRAPHY AND DESIGN: AMERICA

Anti-décor. Balanchine's *Concerto Barocco* (1941)

Although the designer on the programme is Eugene Berman, the effective designer is Balanchine himself. The ballet is an example of anti-décor, danced usually in practice dress, the patterns of the dancers providing the stage decorations. Photo: Roger Wood

Plate XVI. THE CHOREOGRAPHER'S MATERIAL: THE DANCER

(a) Danish children being auditioned for entrance to the school of the Royal Danish Ballet, Copenhagen, in 1958. Ballet-master, doctor, teachers and other company officials are seated at the tables. Photo: von Haven Presse

(b) The junior class of the Bolshoi School performing exercises at the *barre*, Moscow, 1959

C.A.—19

Plate XVII. THE CHOREOGRAPHER'S MATERIAL: THE DANCING

(a) Traditional Classical Choreography

The *corps de ballet* of the Bolshoi Ballet in the second act of *Giselle* at Covent Garden, London, 1956. This remarkable action photograph also demonstrates very clearly some characteristics of the Russian School. Photo: Houston Rogers

(b) Contemporary Classical Choreography

David Blair, Nadia Nerina and the *corps de ballet* in the grand *pas de deux* from the first act of Sir Frederick Ashton's *La Fille Mal Gardée*. The poses also demonstrate characteristics of the English School. Photo: Dominic

Plate XVIII. THE CHOREOGRAPHER'S MATERIAL: THE DANCING

(a) Folk Dance

The Soviet Army Ensemble in *Friendship Dance* at the Empress Hall, London, in 1956.

Photo: Al Hunt

(b) Expressionist Influences

David Blair, Svetlana Beriosova, Michael Somes and *corps de ballet* in Cranko's *Antigone*, reflecting the impact of outside influences on the classical vocabulary.

Photo: Dominic

Plate XIX. THE CHOREOGRAPHER'S MATERIAL: MIME

(b) Contemporary Classical
Yvette Chauviré, as well known for her acting as her dancing, in the role of Marguerite in *La Dame aux Camélias*.
Photo: S. Enkelmann

(a) Traditional Classical
Anton Dolin and Alicia Markova in the Black Swan *pas de deux*, *Swan Lake*, Act III.
Photo: Anthony

(c) Contemporary Character
Robert Helpmann and Leslie Edwards as The Stranger and A Beggar in Helpmann's *Miracle in the Gorbals*. Photo: Dominic

Plate XX. THE CHOREOGRAPHER AT WORK

(a) Balanchine demonstrates music to his principal dancers (Svetlana Beriosova and David Blair) and the assistant director (Peggy van Praagh) in rehearsals for *Trumpet Concerto* at Sadler's Wells Theatre. Photo: Planet News Ltd.

(b) Massine demonstrates to dancers of the Ballet Russe de Monte Carlo during his creation of *Harold in Italy* at Boston, U.S.A., in 1954. Photo: Ballet Russe de Monte Carlo

Plate XXI. THE CHOREOGRAPHER AT WORK

(a) Sir Frederick Ashton, working like a sculptor, adjusting a lifted pose for a *pas de deux* in *Ondine* between Ondine (Margot Fonteyn) and Palemon (Michael Somes). Photo: Dominic

(b) John Cranko experiments with Judith Sinclair and David Boswell for a lift in *The Prince of the Pagodas*. Photo: Tony Armstrong Jones

Plate XXII. THE CHOREOGRAPHER AT WORK

Dame Ninette de Valois teaching hand movements to part of the ensemble in *Job*. Photo: Roger Wood

Plate XXIII. THE CHOREOGRAPHER'S INSPIRATION: DANCERS

(a) Fokine. *Le Spectre de la Rose*, Nijinsky and Karsavina

Le Spectre de la Rose so perfectly combined the talents of choreographer and dancers that it has never been matched since in performance by other dancers. Photo: Boris Kochno, *Le Ballet*, Paris

(b) Nijinska/Cocteau. *Le Train Bleu*, Dolin

Anton Dolin inspired first the scenarist, Cocteau, then the choreographer, Nijinska, in the creation of *Le Train Bleu* in 1923. Photo: *The Times*

Plate XXIV. THE CHOREOGRAPHER'S INSPIRATION: DANCERS

(a) Balanchine. *The Firebird*, Maria Tallchief

Maria Tallchief's brilliant technique and classical line became the perfect instrument for Balanchine's choreography and directly inspired some of his best work

(b) Ashton. *Horoscope*, the young Fonteyn

Frederick Ashton did much to mould the young Fonteyn, but she contributed greatly to Ashton's choreography.

Photo: Anthony

Plate XXV. THE DANCER'S CONTRIBUTION

(a) Lavrovsky. *Romeo and Juliet*, Ulanova

Ulanova, here partnered by Yuri Zhdanov, in creating her most famous role, has imbued Lavrovsky's choreography with her personality

(b) Tudor. *Pillar of Fire*, Nora Kaye and Hugh Laing

Nora Kaye's dramatic qualities made an important contribution to the nature, as well as the success, of Tudor's early American ballets.

Photo: Roger Wood

Plate XXVI. FINAL REHEARSALS. LIGHTING: STAGE DIRECTOR'S SCORE

Photostat of last page of score, marked with stage director's cues

Notes

This is the last page of the score for *Ondine* by Hans Werner Henze. The scene on stage is the final tableaux in the apotheosis. A gauze curtain has been dropped in front of the dancers to give a watery effect.

Each cue number and instruction, marked in *red* to be easier to see, requires the following orders by the stage director to the back-stage staff.

Cue 12, the gauze having been dropped.

Bring up in five seconds—
Batten 1 Green
Ripple effect lights
Spotlight to pick up Tirrenio, Ondine, Palemon and others till then invisible behind the gauze.

Cue 13. After Tirrenio's exit.

Bring up in 20 seconds—
Prompt and Opposite Prompt stage lamps
Prompt and Opposite Prompt fly spots
Pick up Ondine and Palemon through gauze
Special effects—stars on gauze
Front of House side lamps

Cue 14
Fade to Black Out
    except
Prompt and Opposite Prompt fly spots on Ondine and Palemon
Special Effects stars
Very Slow Curtain

Call Lights and lights for full company line-up and other curtain calls by the artists.

Plate XXVII. THE FINAL REHEARSALS

(a) Bronislava Nijinska adjusts the make-up of The Moor in *Petrouchka* watched by the late Marquis de Cuevas, artistic director of the Grand Ballet du Marquis de Cuevas. Photo: Serge Lido

(b) Leonid Lavrovsky, choreographer of *Romeo and Juliet*, discusses details with his principal dancers, Galina Ulanova (Juliet) and Alexander Lapauri (Paris) on stage at the Bolshoi Theatre

Plate XXVIII. THE FINISHED BALLET
The Soviet School

(a) *Romeo and Juliet*, by Leonid Lavrovsky

The Capulet Ball with Alexander Radunsky as Capulet and Elena Iliushenko as Lady
Capulet

(b) *The Stone Flower*, by Yuri Grigorovitch

Ekaterina Maximova (*right*) as Katerina and Nina Timofeyeva (*left*) as the Mistress
of the Copper Mountain

Plate XXIX. THE FINISHED BALLET
The Danish School

(a) *Étude*, by Harald Lander, with Toni Lander and Fredbjörn Björnsson.
Photo: H. J. Mydtskov

(b) *Qarrtsiluni*, by Harald Lander. Photo: H. J. Mydtskov

Plate XXX. THE FINISHED BALLET
The French School

(a) *Carmen*, by Roland Petit, with René Jeanmaire as Carmen and Roland Petit as Don José. Photo: Roger Wood

(b) *Les Noces Fantastiques*, by Serge Lifar, with Nina Vyroubova and Peter van Dijk. Photo: Lipnitzki

Plate XXXI. THE FINISHED BALLET
The American School

(a) *Fancy Free*, by Jerome Robbins. Photo: Ballet Theatre

(b) *Agon*, by George Balanchine. Photo: Fred Fehl

Plate XXXII. THE FINISHED BALLET
The English School

(a) *Ondine*, by Sir Frederick Ashton
Act II. The Shipwreck with Michael Somes and Julia Farron. Photo: Roger Wood

(b) *Persephone*, by Sir Frederick Ashton
Scene 3. Persephone's return from the Underworld. *Centre, left to right*, Svetlana
Beriosova, Alexander Grant, Derek Rencher. Photo: Dominic

Plate XXXIII. THE PRESERVATION OF BALLETS

Feuillet, Notation of a Minuet, 1700

PLATE XXXIV. THE PRESERVATION OF BALLETS

An extract from *The Shadow* (by kind permisson of John Cranko).

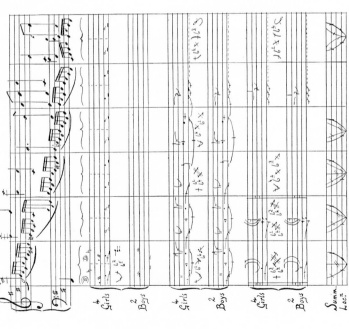

This extract is complete in every detail, including head, hands, and the precise movements of the various groups which are made up of twelve girls and six boys.

46

(a) Benesh notation, see page 270

Example reproduced from Rudolf and Joan Benesh's *An Intro-duction to Benesh Dance Notation.* (A. & C. Black, London, 1956)

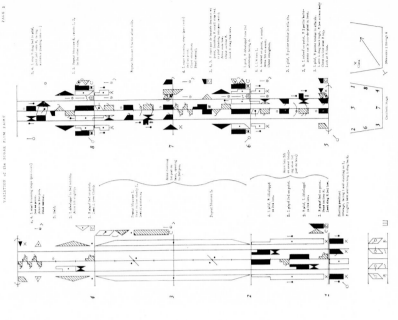

(b) Labanotation, see page 270

Example prepared by Dance Notation Bureau, New York

Plate XXXV. THE PRESERVATION OF BALLETS

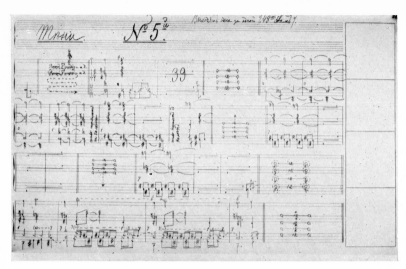

(a) Stepanoff Notation, see page 270
Example reproduced by courtesy Miss Mona Inglesby

(b) Massine showing film records of his choreography to dancers before
reproducing a ballet. Photo: G. B. L. Wilson

Plate XXXVI. THE BALLET LIBRETTO: *A MIRROR FOR WITCHES*

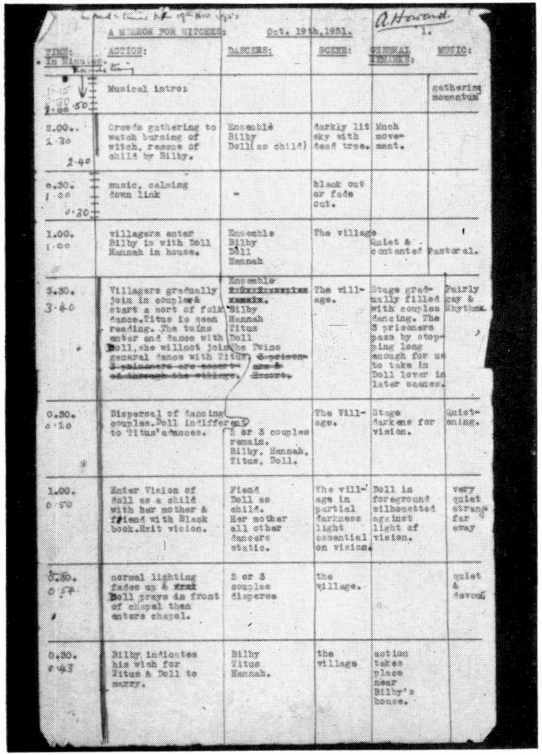

A MIRROR FOR WITCHES: Oct. 19th, 1951. 1.

A. Howard

TIME: In Minutes.	ACTION:	DANCERS:	SCENE:	GENERAL REMARKS:	MUSIC:
1.15 1.30 1.50	Musical intro:				gathering momentum
2.00. 2.30 2.40	Crowds gathering to watch burning of witch, rescue of child by Bilby.	Ensemble Bilby Doll(as child)	darkly lit sky with dead tree.	Much movement.	
0.30. 1.00 0.30	music, calming down link	-	black out or fade out.		
1.00. 1.00	villagers enter Bilby is with Doll Hannah in house.	Ensemble Bilby Doll Hannah	The village	Quiet & contented	Pastoral.
3.30. 3.40	Villagers gradually join in couples & start a sort of folk dance. Titus is seen reading. The twins enter and dance with Doll, she willnot join general dance with Titus. ~~3 prisoners are escorted through the village.~~	Ensemble ~~[illegible]~~ remain. Bilby Hannah Titus Doll The Twins ~~3 prisoners & Escort.~~	The village.	Stage gradually filled with couples dancing. The 3 prisoners pass by stopping long enough for us to take in Doll lover in later scenes.	Fairly gay & Rhythmic.
0.30. 0.10	Dispersal of dancing couples. Doll indifferent to Titus' advances.	2 or 3 couples remain. Bilby, Hannah, Titus, Doll.	The Village.	Stage darkens for vision.	Quietening.
1.00. 0.50	Enter Vision of Doll as a child with her mother & friend with Black book. Exit vision.	Fiend Doll as child. Her mother all other dancers static.	The village in partial darkness light essential on vision.	Doll in foreground silhouetted against light of vision.	very quiet strange far away
0.30. 0.57	normal lighting fades up & ~~exit~~ Doll prays in front of chapel then enters chapel.	2 or 3 couples disperse	the village.		quiet & devout
0.30. 0.43	Bilby indicates his wish for Titus & Doll to marry.	Bilby Titus Hannah.	the village	action takes place near Bilby's house.	

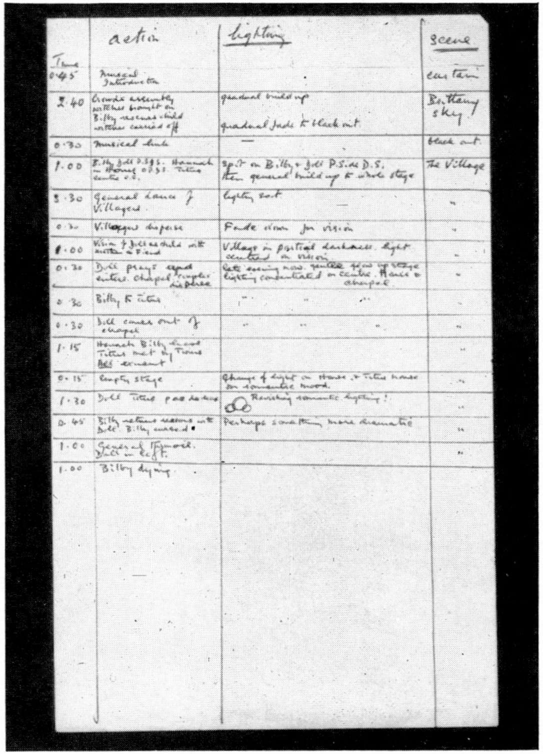

Time	action	lighting	scene
0.45	Musical Introduction		curtain
2.40	Crowds assembly witches brought on Bilby rescues child witches carried off	gradual build up gradual fade to black out	[illegible] sky
0.30	Musical link	—	black out.
1.00	Bilby Doll [illegible] Hannah [illegible] Titus centre [illegible]	Spot on Bilby + Doll P.S. [illegible] D.S. then general build up to whole stage	The Village
3.30	General dance of Villagers	lighting [illegible]	"
0.30	Villagers disperse	Fade down for vision	"
1.00	Vision of Doll as child with mother & Fiend	Village in partial darkness. light centred on vision	"
0.30	Doll prays and enters chapel couples disperse	[illegible] evening now. [illegible] up stage lighting concentrated on centre. House & chapel	"
0.30	Bilby & Titus	" " "	"
0.30	Doll comes out of chapel	" " "	"
1.15	Hannah Bilby [illegible] Titus [illegible]		"
0.15	Empty stage	Change of light on House & Titus house [illegible] romantic mood.	"
1.30	Doll Titus pas de deux	Ravishing romantic lighting!	"
0.45	Bilby [illegible] with Doll. Bilby [illegible]	Perhaps something more dramatic	"
1.00	General [illegible]. Doll [illegible]		"
1.00	Bilby dying		

Opening Scene

(a) Libretto for Composer/Designer

(b) Choreographer's lighting draft

For explanation see Appendix III c (iii), pages 309-310

Plate XXXVII. THE BALLET LIBRETTO: *ONDINE*

Act III

Prelude & Vision
under water.   5 min +
Pas-de-Supplication
Bent. & Hul interrupted
y'arrée & promenade of guests   2 min
Grand Pas Classique   1 min.
                                                                    6½ mins.
  Adagio boys & girls   2
    Var girls   1½   } =
    "   Boys   1½   }
    Coda general fast   1½   ]
Entree of Kublebar
Followed by rush of Neapolitans   ¼
Divertissement consists of 12 boys & 12 girls   ½
+ 3 principal boys & 3 principal girls.
ie. All boys & all girls   1 min]
   into which enter Soloists   ]
   pas-de-six   1   ]
   pasde-Trois }   ]
   2 boys 1 girl }   1   ]
   pas-de-Trois }   ]
   2 girls one boy }   1   ]
   12 girls & 12 boys   1   ] 11 mins.
   Var 3 girls   1   ]
   Var 1 boy   1   ]
   Var 2 girls   1   ]
   All six to finish   1   ]
   All 12 boys & 12 girls &   ]
   all pas-de-six.   2   ]

Solemn dance interrupted by Ondines
in frenzy – fright of Bertalda all
exit = Pas-de-action   2 mins.
Pas-de-deux. O & U.   3 mins.
Apotheosis   1 min ?
                                                    ─────────────
                                                          32¼ mins
                                  or better   30 mins.

Sir Frederick Ashton's notes to the composer of *Ondine*

Plate XXXVIII. THE BALLET LIBRETTO: A PLACE IN THE DESERT

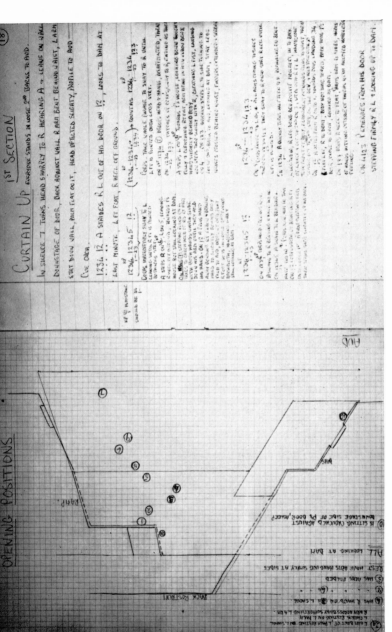

Opening scene

(a) Position of the dancers   (b) Their movements

The Choreographer's personal notes *before* rehearsal. See Appendix III c (v), page 310

Plate XXXIX. THE BALLET LIBRETTO: *RODEO*

Rodeo — 8 counts —

girl alone until skip 4 sixes — (> 6, 3, 1, 5, 12)
skip + galop 3 tens + 5 12 eights + 7.
men join — 7 counts — 6 and
1 - 3 - 5. 7.8.9. 10. 11 — 12 slow.
3 jumps + ... pause in air — 14 and
galop. pause. 15 - 16 - 9 10
1. 3 - 5. 7 - 8 - 9 10
4 bucks + pause in air
galop — 11 - 14.
corner passage — to 10 9
crossing step — 5 4 5
stationary step with turns — shoot. 4
leg. 3
pulse. 8
Horse necks — 16 — turn 4
balance necks 6
balance 6 + each
turn — 1 and 2.
Side jumps — 8.

Balance — 8. attack back group on 6.
tacit 5

Finish — 14

2nd group —

galop 13.
crossing step 5.
galop in circle 7.
2 slow développé turns — 8.
galop — 10 -

Opening Scene
The Choreographer's personal notes *after* some rehearsal.
For explanation see Appendix III, page 311

APPENDICES

APPENDICES I, II, III

THE DEVELOPMENT OF THE BALLET SCENARIO

COMPARATIVELY few written scenarios have survived the three centuries of classical ballet history. Today the scenario casualty rate remains as high as ever. The following scenarios, therefore, are among the best available to us, but not necessarily those we would have chosen had history been kinder. All of them, particularly the later examples where we can compare performances, illustrate the differences which frequently arise between a ballet's appearance on stage and its original conception in the scenario. Where possible we have indicated such points of difference with italics in the scenario.

APPENDIX I

The Ballet Scenario: Eighteenth Century

A. England

The Loves of Mars and Venus, by John Weaver, with choreography by John Weaver. First produced at Drury Lane, London, on 2nd March 1717.

Several copies have been preserved of this scenario, probably Europe's first *ballet d'action*. One of them was in the possession of the late Mr. P. J. S. Richardson, O.B.E., who allowed us to study it and later to reproduce the following transcription, which he published in *The Dancing Times* of September 1949.

Cast

Mars—Danc'd by Mr. Dupré, Senior.
Vulcan—Danc'd by Mr. Weaver.
Venus—Danc'd by Mrs. Santlow.
Aglaia, Thalia, Euphrosyne (Three Graces, Attendants on Venus), Mrs. Bicknall, Mrs. Younger, Mrs. Willis.
The four Followers of Mars—Danc'd by Mr. Prince, Mr. Bovall, Mr. Wade, Mr. Birkhead.
Four Cyclops—Workmen to Vulcan.
Three more Cyclops.
Gallus—Attendant on Mars.
One of the Hours attending on Venus.
Cupid.
Jupiter, Juno, Apollo, Diana, Neptune, Thetis—Gods and Goddesses.

SCENE I—A CAMP

The Entertainment opens with a Martial Overture; at the Conclusion of which, four Followers, or Attendants of Mars, arm'd with Sword,

279

and Target, enter and Dance a Pyrrhic to a March; then follows a Warlike Prelude which introduces Mars attended by Gallus carrying his Sword and Buckler; he performs his Entry, and then joyns in Pyrrhic Mood with his Followers; wherein he appears engaged sometimes with two at a time, and sometimes with all four: At last he clears the Stage; which finishes the Entry, and first Scene.

Note by Weaver

The manner of the Performance of the Pyrrhic Dance seems to have consisted chiefly in the nimble turning of the Body, the shifting, and avoiding the Stroke of the Enemy; and therefore, this was one of the Exercises in which young Soldiers were train'd; and was in such Esteem in Thessaly that they stil'd their Princes, and Generals, Leaders of the Dance. The Nature then of this Dance being warlike; and as we have shewn, made use of by the Ancients for the Discipline and Marshalling their Soldiers, I thought it the most proper for the introducing the Character of Mars.

SCENE II

After a Simphony of Flutes, etc., the Scene opens and discovers Venus in her Dressing-Room at her Toilet, attended by the Graces, who are employ'd in dressing her. Cupid lies at her Feet, and one of the Hours waits by. Venus rises, and dances a Passacaile: The Graces joyn her in the same Movement, as does also the Hour. The Dance being ended, the Tune changes to a wild rough Air. Venus, Graces, etc., seem in Surprize; and at the Approach of Vulcan, the Graces, and Cupid run off.

Enter to Venus, Vulcan: They perform a Dance together; in which Vulcan expresses his Admiration; Jealousie; Anger; and Despite; And Venus shows Neglect; Coquetry; Contempt; and Disdain.

Note by Weaver

This last Dance being altogether of the Pantomimic kind; it is necessary that the Spectator should know some of the most particular Gestures made use of therein; and what Passions, or Affections, they discover; represent; or express.

Admiration. Admiration is discover'd by the raising up of the right Hand, the Palm turn'd upwards, the Fingers clos'd; and in one Motion the Wrist turn'd round and Fingers spread; the Body reclining, and Eyes fix'd on the Object; but when it rises to

Astonishment. Both hands are thrown up towards the Skies; the Eyes also lifted up, and the Body cast backwards.

Jealousy. Jealousy will appear by the Arms suspended, or a particular pointing the middle Finger to the Eye; by an irresolute movement throughout the Scene, and a Thoughtfulness of Countenance.

Upbraiding. The Arms thrown forwards; the Palm of the Hands

turn'd outward; the Fingers open, and the Elbows turn'd inward to the Breast; shew Upbraiding and Despite.

Anger. The left Hand struck suddenly with the right; and sometimes against the Breast; denotes Anger.

Threats. Threatening is express'd by raising the Hand, and shaking the bended Fist; knitting the Brow; biting the Nails, and catching back the Breath.

Power. The Arm, with impetuous Agitation, directed forwards to the Person, with an awful Look, implies Authority.

Impatience. Impatience is seen by the smiting of the Thigh, or Breast with the Hand.

Indignation. When it rises to Anguish, and Indignation, it is express'd by applying the Hand passionately to the Forehead; or by steping back the right foot, leaning the Body quite backward, the Arms extended, Palms clos'd, and Hands thrown quite back; the Head cast back, and Eyes fix'd upwards.

These are some of the Actions made use of by Vulcan; those by Venus are as follows:—

Coquetry. Coquetry will be seen in the affected Airs, given her self throughout the whole Dance.

Neglect. Neglect will appear in the scornful turning the Neck; the flirting outward the back of the right hand, with a Turn of the Wrist.

Contempt. Contempt is express'd by scornful Smiles; forbidding Looks; tossing of the Head; filliping of the Fingers; and avoiding the Object.

Distaste. The left Hand thrust forth with the Palm turn'd backward; the left Shoulder rais'd, and the Head bearing towards the Right, denotes an Abhorrence, and Distaste.

Detestation. When both the turn'd-out Palms are so bent to the left Side, and the Head still more projected from the Object; it becomes a more passionate Form of Detestation, as being a redoubled Action.

SCENE III

With this last Action Venus quits the Stage in order to meet Mars; Vulcan remains, and moving up the Stage strikes at the Scene which opens to Vulcan's Shop, where the Cyclops are discover'd at Work; some at the Forge; some at the Anvil; some Hammering; and some Fileing; while Cupid is pointing his Arrows at the Grindlestone. Jupiter's Thunder; Mars's Armour; Neptune's Trident; Pallas's Spear, etc., are all laid on the Floor. A rough Comfort of Musick is heard while they are at Work, adapted to the particular Sounds of the Shop; after which four of the Cyclops advance, and perform their Entry; with whom Vulcan joyns; and in the Dance, delivers Wire to the Cyclops to form a Net; and turns them in, to their Work, and the Scene shuts.

Note by Weaver

To exalt, or lift up the stretch'd-out Hand, expresses some notable Exploit in Hand.

Scene IV—A Garden

A Prelude of Trumpets, Hautbois, Violins and Flutes alternate; to which
Mars with his Followers enter on one Side; and Venus, with Graces,
etc., on the other. Mars and Venus meet and embrace; Gallantry,
Respect; Ardent Love; and Adoration; appear in the Actions of
Mars: An affected Bashfulness; reciprocal Love; and wishing Looks,
in Venus; they sit on a Couch, while the four Followers of Mars begin
the Entry; to whom the Graces joyn; and Afterwards Mars and
Venus: At which time Cupid steals away the Arms of Mars and his
Followers.

Note by Weaver

This Performance is alternate, as representing Love and War: It
is somewhat in Imitation of a Dancing among the Ancients, in
which; the Lacedemonian Youth delighted much, as being equally
inclin'd to Love, and Arms; one singular Beauty in this sort of Dance,
is; that Strength, and Softness, reciprocally, and alternately are seen
in their full Power: when in the same Representation; and at the same
time; the Fire; Robustness; and Strength of the Warrior is seen, mixt
with the Softness, and Delicacy of Love; Boldness, and Vigour, in
one, and a coy, and complying Reluctance, in the other.

As to the Gestures made use of in this Scene; they are so obvious,
relating only to Gallantry, and Love; that they need no Explanation.

The Dance concludes, with every Man carrying off his Woman.

Scene V

Vulcan is discover'd leaning in a thoughtful Posture on his Anvil; the
Cyclops appear working the Net; they joyn it together; Vulcan
dances. The Cyclops having finish'd, bring it forward, and shew it
Vulcan, he approves of it, and they carry it off, etc.

Note by Weaver

Pleas'd at some Contrivance. To rub the Palms of the Hands
together, after the manner as those who take Pains to heat their Hands;
is an Expression of being pleas'd at some Thought of Deceit.

Scene VI

A soft Symphony of Flutes, to which the Scene draws and discovers Mars
and Venus sitting on a Couch; Gallus sleeping; and Cupid playing;
etc. Mars and Venus express by their Gesticulations, equal Love, and
Satisfaction; and a pleas'd Tenderness which supposes past Embraces.
Vulcan and Cyclops enter; the Net, falls over Mars, and Venus, who
seem slumbering, and being catch'd, appear in the utmost Confusion.
An insulting Performance by Vulcan and the Cyclops. After which
enter Jupiter, Apollo, Neptune, Juno, Diana and Thetis. Vulcan shows
them his Prisoners. Shame; Confusion; Grief; and Submission, are
discover'd in the Actions of Venus; Audacity, Vexation; Restlessness;

and a kind of unwilling Resignation; in those of Mars. The Actions of Vulcan are of Rejoicing; Insulting; and Derision. Neptune intercedes with Vulcan for them. Vulcan at length condescends; and forgives them; and they are releas'd. Mars, with the rest of the Gods, and Goddesses, dance a Grand Dance, which concludes the Entertainment.

Note by Weaver

Triumphing. To shake the Hand open, rais'd above our Head, is an exulting Expression of Triumph, Etc.

Entreaty. The stretching out the Hands downward toward the Knees, is an Action of Entreaty, and suing for Mercy.

Grief. Grief is express'd by hanging down the Head; wringing the Hands; and striking the Breast.

Resignation. To hold out both the Hands joyn'd together, is a natural Expression of Submission and Resignation.

Forgiveness. To extend and offer out the Right Hand, is a Gesture of Pitty, and Intention of Forgiveness.

Shame. The covering the Face with the Hand, is a Sign of Shame.

Reconciliation. To shake the given Hand, or embrace the Body, is an Expression of Friendship, Reconciliation, and the like.

FINIS

B. France

Médée et Jason, a tragi-ballet by Jean-Georges Noverre, with choreography by Noverre. First produced at Stuttgart on 11th February, 1763.

This was one of Noverre's greatest *ballets d'action*. Several versions of the scenario are in existence from illustrated accounts of his ballets which Noverre sent to the courts of Europe. Two of the most lavish of these accounts, written with great labour in long-hand, went to King Gustav III of Sweden and King Stanisław Poniatowski of Poland. They lie now respectively in the Royal Library at Stockholm and in the Archives of the University of Warsaw, with whose help we have reproduced the costumes of Medea and Jason in Plate III.

The 'Polish' scenario of *Médée et Jason*, with many photographs of costumes for Noverre's ballets, was reproduced recently in Irena Turska's Polish edition of Noverre's *Theory and Practice of Dancing*, published in Wrocław in 1959, an important event in European dance literature. This 'Polish' scenario follows of course, the same story-line as the 'Swedish' scenario but is more concise, appearing to summarise parts of the elaborate action described in the 'Swedish' account. Since both are equally authentic reasons of space decided us to translate the Polish scenario here.

Cast

Medea	Princess of Colchis, wife of Jason.
Jason	Prince of Thessaly, husband of Medea and lover of Creusa.
Creusa	Princess of Corinth, lover of Jason.

Creon   King of Corinth, father of Creusa.
Governess of Medea's children and Medea's confidante.
Medea's two children.
Princesses and Princes of Corinth.

Fire	Jealousy
Iron	Hatred
Poison	Vengeance

The scene is Corinth.

SCENE I

The theatre represents the Peristyle of the Palace of Creon, superbly decorated for a festive occasion. Through the peristyle the magnificent gardens of this prince are discovered, ornamented with fountains and various waterworks.

Creon, who fears the just pretentions of Medea to the throne of Corinth and wants to assure this throne for ever to his family, feels he cannot do better than unite Jason with his daughter Creusa, so separating the hero from Medea. To achieve this, he arranges for Jason the most brilliant entertainments so that his daughter shall have more opportunity to seduce Jason by her charms. To these charms Jason is already only too sensible, while Creusa on her side is equally disturbed. But their passion, in spite of its strength, has not yet been declared.

Love carries them away for the first time at the most recent of Creon's entertainments. Jason's attentions to Creusa, his eagerness to please her, the ceaseless favours he grants her and which Creusa demands of him, all these rouse in Medea the most dreadful suspicions. These suspicions become certainties and, convinced of Jason's unfaithfulness, Medea departs hiding a troubled heart while forcing herself to disguise her anger and despair. Creusa, whom passion has betrayed, hastens to reveal to her conqueror some part of her subterfuge.

SCENE II

Creon uses this moment to offer Jason his throne and Creusa, on condition that Jason repudiates Medea. Jason hesitates; gratitude to Medea struggles with the demands of love. He is still in this uncertainty when Medea appears with her children.

SCENE III

Medea makes a final effort which is for Jason particularly painful. She flings herself at the feet of her husband, recalls their first vows, begs him to give her his love once more, shows him her children, the precious tokens of the faithfulness she pledged him. She offers him a dagger and her breast, urging him to pierce her to the heart if he does not wish to be hers. Jason, deeply moved, repents and flings himself into the arms of Medea, embraces her tightly, bathes her in tears—he is going to be faithful to her, he will refuse the crown, refuse Creusa . . . when Creusa appears, and triumphs.

Scene IV

Jason leaves the arms of his wife to hurry to those of his lover. Passion makes him forget how much he owes to Medea. He goes so far as to order her imperiously to leave his presence and depart for ever the lands of Creon.

Scene V

Medea, her eyes fixed on the ground, stands motionless; the suddenness of her disgrace absorbs, so to speak, every faculty; she is crushed completely when, suddenly, she gives herself over to fury. She repudiates her children; she calls upon the elements, hell and heaven. She transforms the peristyle into a dreadful cavern. Infernal spirits fly through the air, monsters and serpents range themselves round her. Jealousy, Hatred and Vengeance come running at her voice. She commands them to serve her anger and these three daughters of Hell present to her Fire, Iron and Poison.

She orders Fire to lock inside a casket, destined for Creon, the most devouring flames and inflammable objects. She commands Poison to spread deadly venoms and infected vapours upon a diadem, which her cruelty reserves for Creusa. Of Iron she demands an instrument which can truly satisfy her anger and takes from his breast a bloodied dagger. This Jealousy, Hatred and Vengeance disguise and give Medea. Then the enchantress, congratulating herself on the crimes she is about to commit, orders the infernal troupe to vanish.

Scene VI

Drunk with fury Medea summons her children. They will be her first victims, but her arm refuses to obey her; the weapon falls from her hand and nature seems to reproach her with the awfulness of her crime. She gives her children the poisoned gifts and goes with them to ensure the means whereby she has resolved to satisfy her vengeance.

Scene VII

The scene represents a great salon of white marble veined with gold; the architectural style is Corinthian, in gold. In the body of the salon stands a magnificent throne.

Creon is seated on the throne. He descends from it and leads Jason to it in his place. To Jason he surrenders his sceptre and his crown before all his people. He orders his subjects to take the oath of loyalty to the new king, a ceremony which is carried out by the heads of three Estates of the Realm. Cries of allegiance sound on all sides; the noise of cymbals and trumpets rends the air. The people rejoice with dances led by Creon himself.

Jason and Creusa mingle their own joy with that of their subjects and express their mutual happiness. At the height of these happy scenes Creon presents the lovers with the nuptial cup. Jason takes it eagerly and has already raised it to his lips, when—Medea appears, her demeanour totally changed.

Scene VIII

Jason is filled with shame and anger; Creusa, seized with terror, dares raise her eyes no more; Creon shows his fury while the frightened people, trembling, await the outcome of this meeting.

Medea is hardly able to conceal her emotion at the sight of the cup which Jason holds so joyfully. Fearful of betraying herself, and hiding her rage beneath a veil of hypocrisy and dissimulation, she faces her enemies with signs of complete resignation. She smiles upon them agreeably that they might feel reassured and understand she is far from wanting to upset their happiness. She has come only to give them what she can. She shows them the presents in the hands of her children. Creusa and Jason feel easier; Creon's face softens. One of the children humbly offers him the casket on his mother's behalf. Medea herself takes the diadem and appears pleased to adorn her rival, whom she gathers into her arms with every sign of the most sincere good will. She takes a tender farewell of Jason, feigning to ask the blessing of Heaven on so perfect a union. Jason, touched at the sight of this, embraces Medea and his children. Creusa follows the example of her lover and the cunning Medea withdraws, secretly showing her joy that she has fulfilled already part of her scheme.

Scene IX and last

The departure of Medea brings peace again to every heart, but not for long. Suddenly Creusa feels the deadly effect of Medea's gift. A devouring poison courses through her veins and fixes her face in the image of dreadful death. At this moment Creon opens the casket whence leprous flames rise to suffocate him. He staggers back, reels and falls dead on the steps of the throne. Jason in despair tries vainly to aid the victims of Medea's fury. The enchantress appears triumphantly in her chariot drawn by monsters breathing awful flames. Hatred, Jealousy and Vengeance are grouped about her. One of her children dies at her feet, her arm is raised to strike the other.

Jason flings himself upon his knees and begs her to spare at least this final victim, but the implacable Medea laughs at his prayers and, heaping crime upon crime, plunges the dagger into the breast of her youngest son, who himself begs mercy. She hurls the dagger at Jason who seizes it, strikes himself and dies in the arms of Creusa who mingles her last breath with his.

The heavens darken; the earth trembles; the palace bursts into flame and collapses. All flee while the villainous Medea, rising into the air, flies off, congratulating herself on her black deeds.

The Ballet Scenario: Nineteenth Century

A. The Romantic Ballet

Giselle, by Vernoy de Saint-Georges, Théophile Gautier and Coralli, with choreography by Coralli and Perrot. First produced at the Paris Opera on 28th June, 1841.

The following translation was made by Mr. Cyril Beaumont for his *The Ballet Called Giselle* from the original published scenario of the ballet. This was titled '*Giselle ou Les Wilis*', *ballet-fantastique en deux actes par MM de Saint-Georges, Théophile Gautier et Coraly*, pp. 19. Paris 1841. Reproduced here by permission of Mr. Beaumont, it shows a number of differences between the authors' original conception and the ballet today. It also illustrates the author's contribution to a ballet as against that of the librettist. The libretto for the first production of *Giselle* showed a number of departures from the scenario because some of the original ideas were impractical—the idea of having the wilis in several different costumes, for example, and the presentation of Moyna and Zulma as odalisque and bayadere. Nevertheless, the original scenario and libretto both possessed a continuity of story and strength of motivation from which most productions today could benefit. Sections of this scenario which are not performed today or were changed at the first production have been placed in italics as far as possible, together with our own comments and the scenic description for each act.

Cast

Albrecht, Duke of Silesia	Bathilde, the Duke's fiancée
The Prince of Courland	Berthe, Giselle's mother
Wilfrid, the Duke's squire	Giselle, a peasant girl
Hilarion, a gamekeeper	Myrtha, Queen of the Wilis
An Old Peasant	Peasants, courtiers, wilis, etc.

ACT ONE

The scene represents a pleasant valley in Germany. In the distance are vine-clad hills, across which runs a steep path leading into the valley.

SCENE I

This represents the vintage on the Thuringian Hills. Day is just breaking. The vine-dressers withdraw to fetch more grapes.

SCENE II

Hilarion enters and looks about him as if seeking someone; then he lovingly points to Giselle's cottage and angrily indicates that of Loys, which is his rival's home. If Hilarion ever has the opportunity to revenge himself upon him he will gladly seize it. The door of Loys's cottage opens mysteriously. *Hilarion conceals himself to observe what is about to happen.*

SCENE III

The young Duke Albrecht of Silesia, disguised in humble clothes and having assumed the name of Loys, comes out of his dwelling, accompanied by his squire Wilfrid. The latter seems to persuade him to abandon some secret project, but Loys is obstinate. He points to Giselle's cottage, that lowly roof that shelters the object of his love. He commands Wilfrid to leave him. Wilfrid still hesitates, but, at a peremptory gesture from his master, he salutes him with respect and withdraws.

Hilarion is stupefied to see a fine lord like Wilfrid display such regard for a simple peasant like his rival. He appears to conceive suspicions which he will clear up later.

SCENE IV

Loys, or rather Albrecht, goes towards Giselle's cottage and knocks softly at the door. *Hilarion remains concealed.* Soon, Giselle comes out and runs into her lover's arms. Mutual transport and delight of the two young people. Giselle relates her dream to Loys. *She was jealous of a beautiful lady whom Loys loved in preference to herself. Loys, troubled, reassures her; he loves Giselle, and will never love anyone else. 'If you deceived me,' the young girl tells him, 'I should die; I feel it.' She presses her hand to her heart as if to show him how often it aches. Loys calms her with loving caresses.*

She gathers daisies, from which she picks the petals to be convinced of Loys's love. *The test succeeds* and she falls into her lover's arms. Hilarion, no longer able to contain himself, runs towards Giselle and reproaches her with her conduct. He was there and saw everything.

'Well, what does it matter?' gaily replies Giselle. 'I'm not ashamed of it. I love him and shall never love anyone else.' Then she abruptly turns her back on Hilarion, laughing at his expense, while Loys pushes him away and threatens him with his anger if he does not cease making love to Giselle.' Very well,' says Hilarion, with a threatening gesture, 'we shall see what happens later.'

SCENE V

A band of peasant girls come to fetch Giselle for the vintage. Day has dawned and it is time to depart, but Giselle, passionately fond of dancing and pleasure, delays her companions. After Loys, she loves dancing more than anything else in the world. She proposes to the young girls that they shall amuse themselves instead of going to work. At first she dances alone to convince them. Her gaiety, her joyous ardour, her lively and seductive steps, in which she expresses her affection for Loys, are soon imitated by the other girls. Baskets, bundles, and tools are cast away, and, thanks to Giselle, the dance soon becomes a mad revel. Then Berthe, Giselle's mother, emerges from the cottage.

Scene VI

'You will always dance then,' she says to Giselle, 'night and day . . . it's an absolute passion . . . and this, instead of working in the vineyards or doing the housework.'

'She dances so well,' says Loys to Berthe.

'It's my one enjoyment,' replies Giselle, 'just as he,' she adds, pointing to Loys, 'is my only happiness!'

'Bah!' says Berthe, 'I'm sure that if this little madcap were to die she would become a Wili and dance after her death, *like all girls who are too fond of dancing.*'

'What do you mean?' cry the frightened girls as they press close to one another.

Then Berthe, to lugubrious music, seems to depict an apparition of dead people returning to the world and dancing together. The terror of the villagers is at its height. *Giselle alone laughs and gaily replies to her mother that she is incorrigible and that, dead or alive, she will dance always.*

'Nevertheless,' adds Berthe, 'it's not good for you . . . it will affect your health, perhaps even your life!'

'She's very delicate,' she tells Loys, 'if she were to become over-tired or too excited, it might be the death of her; the doctor told her that dancing may do her harm.'

Loys, troubled by this confidence, reassures the good woman, and Giselle, taking Loys's hand, presses it to her heart and seems to say that with him she has nothing to fear.

A hunting call is heard in the distance. *Loys, uneasy at the sound, quickly gives the signal for departure to the vineyards, and drives the girls away;* while Giselle, forced to return to the cottage with her mother, blows a farewell kiss to Loys, who goes away followed by everybody.

Scene VII

No sooner does Hilarion find himself alone than he explains his project. He wishes at all costs to discover his rival's secret, to find out who he is. Making sure that he is unobserved, he furtively enters Loys's cottage. At this moment the calls sound nearer and huntsmen and whippers-in appear on the hillside.

Scene VIII

Soon the Prince of Courland and his daughter Bathilde appear *riding on horseback*, accompanied by a numerous following of lords and ladies, and falconers with falcons on their wrists. *The heat of the day is overpowering* and they seek a favourable place for repose. A huntsman points out Berthe's cottage to the Prince. He knocks at the door and Giselle appears on the threshold, followed by her mother. The Prince gaily requests the vine-dresser's hospitality. She begs him to enter her cottage, although it is a poor place in which to receive so fine a lord. During this time Bathilde goes to Giselle and, glancing at her, finds her charming. Giselle exerts herself to the utmost to do the honours of her modest dwelling; she begs Bathilde to be seated, and offers her fruit and milk. Bathilde, charmed with

C.A.— 22

Giselle's grace, takes a gold chain from her neck and clasps it round that of the young girl, who is both proud and shy at this gift. (N.B.—*No mention of Giselle feeling Bathilde's costume.*)

Bathilde questions Giselle on her work and pleasures.

She is happy and has no sorrows or cares; in the morning she works, in the evening she dances. 'Yes,' says Berthe to Bathilde, 'dancing above all, that is her passion.'

Bathilde smiles and asks Giselle if her heart has spoken, if she is in love with anyone. 'Oh, yes,' cried the young girl, indicating Loys's cottage. 'He who lives there is my lover, my betrothed. I should die if he did not love me any more.' Bathilde seems to take great interest in the young girl—their case is similar, for she, too, is going to be married to a young and handsome lord. *She will give a dowry to Giselle, who seems to please her more and more. Bathilde wishes to see Giselle's fiancé,* and re-enters the cottage, followed by her father and Berthe, *while Giselle goes to fetch Loys.*

The Prince *signs to his followers to continue the hunt;* he is tired and wishes to rest a little while. He will sound his horn when he desires to recall them.

Hilarion, who appears at the door of Loys's cottage, sees the Prince and overhears the commands which he gives. The Prince and his daughter go into Berthe's cottage.

Scene IX

While Giselle looks up the road to see if she can perceive her lover, Hilarion comes out of Loys's cottage bearing a sword and a nobleman's mantle. At last he knows his rival; he is a great lord. Now he is sure he is a seducer in disguise. He can now take his revenge, and wishes to confront Loys in the presence of Giselle and all the villagers. He conceals the sword in a bush, waiting until all the wine-dressers are gathered for the feast.

Scene X

Loys appears in the distance. He looks uneasily about him to make certain that the hunt is far away. Giselle perceives him and flies to his arms. At this moment joyful music is heard. (N.B.—*This scene omitted in some productions, included in others.*)

Scene XI

A march begins. The vintage is over. Slowly there comes into view a wagon decorated with palms and flowers, followed by all the girls and youths of the valley, with their baskets filled with grapes. A little figure of Bacchus sitting astride a cask is borne in triumph, according to an ancient local custom. (N.B.—*Bacchus very rarely included today.*)

Giselle is surrounded. She is declared Queen of the Vintage and crowned with flowers and palms. Loys is more than ever in love with the pretty wine-dresser. The villagers soon give themselves up to the most extravagant expressions of joy.

The vintage festival must be celebrated. Giselle can now indulge her favourite pastime; she leads Loys away from the midst of a group of vine-dressers and dances with him, surrounded by all the villagers, who soon join in with the young couple, whose dance ends with a kiss which

Loys bestows on Giselle. On seeing this, the envious Hilarion's pent-up jealousy can no longer be controlled. He leaps into the midst of the crowd and tells Giselle that Loys is a deceiver, a seducer, a nobleman in disguise! Giselle, at first alarmed, tells Hilarion that he does not know what he is saying; that he has been dreaming. 'Oh, I've been dreaming, have I?' continues the gamekeeper. 'Well, then, see for yourself,' he cries, displaying to the villagers' gaze the sword and mantle of Loys. 'These are what I found in his hut—proof enough, I should think.' Albrecht, enraged, dashes at Hilarion, who takes shelter behind the villagers.

Giselle, overcome with surprise and sadness at this revelation, seems to receive a terrible blow and *leans against a tree, breathless and on the verge of collapse.* The villagers remain dumb-founded. *Loys, or rather Albrecht, runs to Giselle, and, still convinced that he can deny his rank, tries to restore her confidence and calm her with tender avowals.* 'It is all a mistake,' he says; 'he is only Loys, a humble peasant, her lover, her betrothed.'

The poor girl asks nothing better than to believe him. Already hope seems to be reborn in her heart. She allows herself to go, happy and confident, to the arms of the perfidious Albrecht; while Hilarion, following up his vengeance and remembering the Prince's order to his suite, to return at the sound of his hunting-horn, *seizes one belonging to a nobleman,* which is attached to a tree, and blows it with all his might. At this signal the hunting-party come running up and the Prince emerges from Berthe's cottage. Hilarion points out to the Prince's suite Albrecht on his knees before Giselle, and each, on recognising the young Duke, *overwhelms him with marks of respect.* Giselle, perceiving this, can no longer doubt Albrecht's exalted station and her own misfortune.

Scene XII

The Prince goes forward in his turn, recognises Albrecht, and, discovering him so, asks the meaning of his strange conduct and the purpose of the costume he is wearing.

Albrecht rises, stupefied and distracted by this encounter.

Giselle has seen all. She is now convinced of this new betrayal on the part of the one she loves, her grief is boundless; she seems to make an effort to control herself and avoids Albrecht with a sense of aversion and horror. Then, as though overwhelmed by this new blow, she runs towards her cottage and falls into the arms of her mother, who at this moment comes out, *accompanied by Bathilde.*

Scene XIII

Bathilde goes quickly towards Giselle and questions her with touching interest regarding her manifest distress. Her sole reply is to point out Albrecht, oppressed and confounded.

'What do I see?' says Bathilde, 'the Duke in such a guise! But it is he I am to marry. He is my fiancé,' she adds, showing the engagement ring on her finger.

Albrecht goes to Bathilde and vainly attempts to prevent her uttering this terrible avowal; but Giselle has heard everything, understood all. The deepest horror is depicted on the unfortunate girl's features; her brain begins to reel, a horrible and sombre delirium seizes her as she sees herself jilted, lost, dishonoured. Her mind wanders, she bursts into tears, then she gives a nervous laugh. She takes Albrecht's hand, places it on her heart, and soon pushes it away in fear. She seizes Albrecht's sword still lying on the ground, and at first plays mechanically with the weapon, then she falls on its sharp point *just as her mother leaps upon her and drags it away*. The poor child recalls her love of dancing; she imagines she hears the melody of her dance with Albrecht; she darts forward and begins to dance forcefully and passionately. But so many sudden griefs, so many cruel shocks, added to this final effort, have at last exhausted her failing strength. Life is about to forsake her, her mother takes her in her arms, a last sigh escapes from poor Giselle's heart; she throws a sad, despairing glance at Albrecht; then her eyes close for ever.

Bathilde, kind and generous, sheds tears. Albrecht, forgetting everything, tries to revive Giselle with burning caresses. He places his hand on the young girl's heart and finds to his horror that it has ceased to beat. *He raises his sword to kill himself, but the Prince stops Albrecht and disarms him.* Berthe supports her unfortunate daughter's body, while Albrecht is *led away*, crazed with despair and love.

The villagers, *noblemen, and all the members of the hunting party* close round and complete this sad picture.

ACT TWO

The setting depicts a forest on the banks of a pool. A damp and chilly spot with intermingled rushes, reeds, clumps of wild flowers, and water plants. Birch trees, aspens, and weeping willows droop their pale foliage. To the left, beneath a cypress, stands a white marble cross, carved with the name—Giselle. The tomb is almost hidden beneath dense masses of grass and wild flowers. The bluish gleam of a very bright moon gives a cold and misty appearance to the scene.

Scene I

Some gamekeepers arrive by different paths in the forest. They appear to be seeking a suitable observation post and are about to decide on the bank of the pool when Hilarion runs up.

Scene II

Hilarion evinces the liveliest fear on learning of his companions' plan. 'It is an evil spot,' he tells them, 'where the Wilis dance their nightly round.' He shows them the tomb of Giselle, Giselle who was always dancing. He points out the crown of vine-leaves which she wore on her brow during the festival, and which is attached to the marble cross. At this moment, midnight is heard striking in the distance: it is the gloomy hour at which, according to local legend, the Wilis foregather in their ballroom.

Hilarion and his companions are terror-stricken on hearing the clock strike. Trembling, they look about them as though expecting the apparition of the airy phantoms. 'Let us flee,' says Hilarion, 'the Wilis are pitiless; they seize upon wayfarers and force them to dance until their victims die of weariness or are engulfed in the lake you see here.'

Fantastic music is heard. The gamekeepers grow pale, falter and flee in all directions with every sign of fear, pursued by will-o'-the-wisps, who appear from all sides.

A sheaf of bullrushes slowly opens and from the depths of the humid vegetation darts a pale, transparent shade, the airy Myrtha, Queen of the Wilis. She sheds a mystic radiance which suddenly illumines the forest, piercing the shades of night. This light is ever present when the Wilis appear. On Myrtha's white shoulders tremble and flutter the diaphanous wings with which the Wili can envelop herself as though in a gauzy veil.

This intangible apparition cannot remain stationary, and darting now on a clump of flowers, now on a branch of willow, she bounds here and there, traversing and seeming to explore her tiny empire, of which she nightly resumes possession. She *bathes in the waters of the lake*, then suspends herself from the willow-branches and swings on them.

After a solo dance she plucks a branch of rosemary, with which she touches in turn every plant, every bush, and every clump of foliage.

Scene IV

Hardly has the flower sceptre of the Queen of the Wilis rested on an object than the plant, flower, or bush opens to set free another Wili, who in her turn joins the graceful group which surrounds Myrtha, like bees about their queen. The last-named, on hearing the azure wings of her subjects, signs to them to dance. Several Wilis successively appear before their sovereign.

First Moyna, the odalisque, executing an oriental dance; next, Zulma, the bayadère, displaying her Indian poses; then two Frenchwomen, dancing a kind of fantastic menuet; and afterwards some German women, waltzing among themselves. Finally, they are joined by the whole band of Wilis, all of whom *perished from having loved dancing too well, or passed away too early in life to gratify sufficiently that foolish passion*, to which they appear to surrender themselves with fury in their graceful metamorphosis.

Presently, at a sign from the Queen, the fantastic ball ceases. She informs her subjects of the arrival of a new sister. All range themselves about the Queen.

Scene V

A bright and vivid ray of moonlight outlines Giselle's tomb, and the flowers which cover it *rise erect on their tall stems* as if to make way for the pale being they cover.

Giselle appears swathed in her thin shroud. She goes towards Myrtha, who touches her with her branch of rosemary; the shroud falls off and Giselle is changed into a Wili. *Her wings grow and unfold*. Her feet skim the ground. She dances, or rather darts, into the air like her graceful sisters, joyfully recalling and sketching the steps which she danced in the first act, before her death. A distant clamour is heard. The Wilis disperse and hide in the rushes.

Some village youths, returning from a festival at a neighbouring hamlet and led by an old peasant, gaily cross the scene. They are about to depart when strange music is heard, the dance melody of the Wilis. The villagers, in spite of themselves, are seized with a strange passion for dancing. The Wilis soon surround them, twine about them, and fascinate them with their sensuous poses.

Each of the Wilis attempts to detain the villagers, trying to please with steps appropriate to her nationality. The affected wayfarers are about to succumb to their wiles, to dance and die, when the old peasant, horror-stricken, dashes into their midst, tells them of the danger they run, and rescues them all, pursued by the Wilis, furious at the sight of their prey escaping them.

SCENE VII

Albrecht appears, followed by Wilfrid, his faithful squire. The Duke is sad and pale, *his dress in disorder;* he has almost lost his reason as a result of Giselle's death. He goes slowly towards the cross as if seeking a memory in order to collect his confused thoughts.

Wilfrid entreats Albrecht to accompany him and not to linger near the fatal tomb, which recalls so many sorrows. Albrecht bids him depart. Wilfrid renews his entreaty, but Albrecht orders him so forcefully to leave that the squire is compelled to obey. He goes out determined to make one last effort to induce his master to leave this fatal spot.

SCENE VIII

No sooner is he alone than Albrecht gives vent to his grief. His heart is filled with anguish; he sheds tears. Suddenly he grows pale, his gaze fixed on a strange being who takes shape before his eyes. He remains stricken with surprise, almost terror, on recognising Giselle, who looks endearingly at him.

SCENE IX

A prey to the most violent delirium, to the most lively anxiety, he still doubts and dare not credit what he sees, for it is not the pretty Giselle whom he adored, but Giselle the Wili, in her new and strange metamorphosis, who remains motionless before him. The Wili seems to invite him with a look. Albrecht, believing himself to be dominated by a charming illusion, goes towards her with slow and cautious steps, like a child desiring to capture a butterfly poised on a flower. But, no sooner does he extend his hand towards Giselle than, quicker than lightning, she darts far away from him, to take flight and soar through the air like a frightened dove, to alight in another quarter, where she throws him loving glances.

This dance, or rather flight, is repeated a second time, to the great despair of Albrecht, who attempts in vain to join the Wili, now and again fleeing before him like a faint wisp of mist. Sometimes, however, she makes him a loving gesture, throws him a flower which she ravishes from its stem, or wafts him a kiss, but, intangible as a cloud, she vanishes just as he believes her within his grasp.

At last he gives up, kneels beside the cross, and places his hands together in an attitude of entreaty. The Wili, as though attracted by this mute sorrow, so charged with love, bounds lightly beside her lover. He touches the Wili, and, swooning with love and happiness, is about to seize her, when, gliding softly between his arms, she vanishes among the roses, while Albrecht brings his arms together to clasp only the cross on the tomb.

Evincing the deepest despair, he rises and is about to leave this abode of sorrow, when he encounters a spectacle so unusual and so fascinating that *he is somehow stayed, held fast, and forced to witness the strange scene unfolded to his gaze.*

Scene X

Hidden behind a weeping willow, Albrecht perceives the unfortunate Hilarion, hunted by a whole band of Wilis.

Pale, trembling, and almost dead from fright, the gamekeeper collapses at the foot of a tree and seems to beseech the mercy of his playful enemies. But the Queen of the Wilis, with a touch from her sceptre, forces him to rise and imitate the dance movement which she herself begins to dance about him. Hilarion, impelled by a magic force, dances in spite of himself with the lovely Wili until she surrenders him to one of her companions who, in turn hands him to another, and so on to the last of all.

Just when the hapless wretch believes his torment ended with his wearied partner, another replaces her with new strength, and, compelled to put forth unimaginable efforts to the ever-quickening rhythm of the music, he ends by staggering and feeling overwhelmed with lassitude and grief.

At last, resolved on a desperate course, he tries to flee; but the Wilis surround him in a great circle which gradually contracts, closes upon him, and becomes changed into a rapid waltz movement, in which a supernatural power forces him to take part. Seized with giddiness, the gamekeeper escapes from the arms of one waltzer only to fall into the power of another.

The victim, ever enmeshed in this graceful and deadly web, soon feels his knees give way under him. His eyes close, he can no longer see, yet he continues to dance with a burning frenzy. Then the Queen of the Wilis seizes Hilarion and makes him turn and waltz with her for the last time, until the poor devil, *the end link in a chain of waltzers, arrived at the edge of the lake, opens his arms, thinking to clasp a fresh waltzer,* and goes tumbling into the abyss. The Wilis, led by their triumphant Queen, begin a joyous bacchanale, *when one of their number discovers Albrecht and conducts him,* still astounded by what he had just seen, into their magic circle.

Scene XI

The Wilis seem to congratulate themselves on finding another victim, their cruel band already begins to hover about this new quarry; but, just as Myrtha is about to touch Albrecht with her enchanted wand, Giselle darts forward and restrains the Queen's upraised arm.

Scene XII

'Flee!' cries Giselle to her beloved, 'flee, or thou art a dead man, as dead as Hilarion!' she adds, pointing to the lake.

Albrecht is momentarily horror-struck at the thought of sharing the gamekeeper's awful fate. Giselle takes advantage of this instant of indecision to seize Albrecht's hand; impelled by a magic force, together they glide towards the marble cross; she indicates this sacred symbol as his shield, his only salvation!

The Queen and all the Wilis pursue him to the tomb, but Albrecht, ever protected by Giselle, reaches the cross, which he embraces, and, just as Myrtha is about to touch him with her wand, the enchanted branch breaks in the hand of the Queen, who stands immovable, as do all the Wilis, overcome with surprise and dismay.

Furious at being baulked of their cruel hopes, *the Wilis circle about Albrecht, and frequently dart towards him, ever repelled by a power superior to their own.* Then the Queen, determined to be revenged upon the one who carried off her victim, stretches out her hand towards Giselle, whose wings immediately open and who begins to dance with the utmost grace and ardour, as if carried away by an involuntary madness.

Albrecht, motionless, watches her, overwhelmed, astounded, at this curious scene, but the Wili's graces and ravishing poses soon attract him against his will, which is what the Queen intended; he forsakes the holy cross which protects him from death and goes towards Giselle, who pauses from fear and implores him to regain his sacred talisman. But the Queen, touching Giselle anew, forces her to continue her captivating dance. This episode is repeated several times until, giving way at last to the passion which consumes him, Albrecht forsakes the cross and darts towards Giselle. He seizes the enchanted branch, for he would rather die and rejoin the Wili than be parted from her.

Albrecht seems to have wings, he skims the ground and leaps about the Wili, who from time to time endeavours to restrain him. But, carried away by her new nature, Giselle is soon forced to join her lover. They begin a quick, airy, and frenzied dance. They seem to vie with each other in grace and agility. Now and again they pause, to fall into each other's arms; then the fantastic music lends them new strength and fresh ardour. The whole band of Wilis accompany the two lovers, surrounding them with sensuous poses.

Albrecht is seized with a deadly weariness. He still struggles, but it is clear that his strength is beginning to be exhausted. Giselle goes to him and pauses for an instant, her eyes filled with tears; but a sign from the Queen forces her to take flight anew. A few more seconds and Albrecht is about to perish from weariness and exhaustion, when dawn begins to break. The first rays of sunlight illumine the silvered ripples of the lake.

The fantastic and tumultuous round of the Wilis slows down as the night fades away. Giselle seems to be filled with fresh hope on seeing the disappearance of the terrible enchantment which was leading Albrecht to his doom. Subjected to the bright rays of the sun, *the whole band of Wilis gradually droop and wilt, and in turn are seen to stagger, expire, and collapse in a clump of flowers, or on the stem which saw them born, like night flowers dying at the approach of day.*

During this charming spectacle, Giselle, subject, like her ethereal sisters, to the influence of daylight, slowly frees herself from Albrecht's enfeebled arms. She goes towards her tomb as though impelled by fate. Albrecht, conscious of the doom threatening her, bears Giselle away from the tomb and places her on the mound, amid a tuft of flowers. Then he kneels beside her and kisses Giselle as if to infuse her with his spirit and restore her to life. But Giselle, pointing to the sun, now shining in all its strength, seems to tell him that she must submit to her fate and leave him for evermore.

At this moment loud fanfares echo in the heart of the forest. Albrecht hears them with apprehension and Giselle with a sweet joyfulness.

Scene XIII

Wilfrid runs in. The faithful squire is ahead of the *Prince and* Bathilde, *accompanied by a numerous suite.* He leads them to Albrecht, hoping that their efforts to induce him to leave this vale of sorrow will be more successful than his own.

Everyone stops on seeing him. Albrecht leaps towards his squire to hold him back. Meanwhile, the Wili nears her last moments; the surrounding flowers and grasses have begun to rise and cover her with their slender stems; already the graceful phantom is partly concealed.

Albrecht retraces his steps and remains spellbound with surprise and grief on seeing Giselle sink slowly and gradually into this verdant tomb. Then, with one arm she still keeps free, she shows Albrecht the trembling Bathilde, kneeling some paces from him and stretching out her hand to him with a gesture of entreaty.

Giselle seems to tell her lover to bestow his love and fidelity on the sweet young girl; that is her sole wish, her last prayer, from one who can love no more in this world. Then, making him a poignant and eternal gesture of farewell, she vanishes amid the flowering grass which now completely engulfs her.

Albrecht rises heartbroken, but to him the Wili's command seems sacred. He plucks some of the flowers which cover Giselle and lovingly presses them to his heart, next, to his lips, then, weak and staggering, he stretches out his hand to Bathilde and falls into the arms of those surrounding him.

B. The Classical Ballet

Swan Lake, by V. P. Begichev and V. G. Geltzer. First produced at the Bolshoi Theatre, Moscow, on 4th March, 1877. The choreography for the first three productions of the ballet—in 1877 by Reisinger and in 1880 and 1882 by Hansen—was a failure. It only became a success when produced with choreography by Petipa and Ivanov at the Maryinsky Theatre, St. Petersburg, on 27th January, 1895, more than a year after Tchaikovsky's death.

For the following text we are indebted again to Mr. Cyril Beaumont who obtained a copy of the original scenario from the Bakhrushin State Theatrical Museum, Moscow, for inclusion in his book *The Ballet Called Swan Lake.* Presenting fundamentally the same action which we know in the ballet, it is reproduced here by his permission in a translation by Dr. V. France. Occasional departures from the scenario in contemporary versions are again indicated where possible in italics, together with our own comments and the scenic descriptions for each act.

Cast

Odette, a Good Fairy
A wealthy Princess
Prince Siegfried, her son
Wolfgang, his tutor
Benno von Sommerstein, the Prince's friend
Von Rothbart, an evil geni
Odile, his daughter, who exactly resembles Odette
Baron von Stein
Baroness von Stein, his wife
Freiherr von Schwarzfels
His Wife
1st Courtier ⎫
2nd Courtier ⎬ *Friends of the Prince*
3rd Courtier ⎭
Herald
Messenger
1st Peasant Girl
2nd Peasant Girl
3rd Peasant Girl
4th Peasant Girl
Ladies and Gentlemen of the Court, Guests, Pages, Village
    Girls and Youths, Servants, Swans, and Cygnets

ACT ONE

The action takes place in Germany.
Scene. A beautiful park. In the far distance a castle watered by a stream,
which can be crossed by a pretty little bridge.

At the rise of the curtain, the wealthy Prince Siegfried is seen celebrating
his coming-of-age. Seated at small tables are his friends quaffing wine.
Village youths and maidens, who have been previously coached by Wolfgang, come to offer their congratulations to the Prince, while his aged
tutor, who already seems to be slightly intoxicated, begins to dance. The
Prince invites the peasant youths to partake of the wine, during which old
Wolfgang dallies with the peasant girls and bestows upon them presents
of posies and ribbon favours. The dancing becomes livelier.

Suddenly a messenger enters. He announces the imminent arrival of the
Prince's mother, the Princess, who desires speech with her son. This news
cuts short the merry-making. Dancing ceases and the peasants withdraw
to some distance away. Servants hasten to remove the tables, conceal the
flagons, and so on. The respected tutor, conscious of affording a bad
example to his pupil, endeavours to assume the mien of a sober and
scholarly man.

At last the Princess herself appears, accompanied by her suite. All the
guests and peasants bow in homage to her. The young Prince, followed by
the slightly tipsy and staggering Wolfgang, goes forward to welcome the
Princess. The last-named, observing that her son appears ill at ease, explains

that she has not come to disturb his merry-making and be a burden to him, but because she must discuss the subject of his marriage, for which purpose she has chosen this day of his coming-of-age.

'Since I am growing old,' the Princess declares, 'I wish you to marry while I am still alive. I can then die in the knowledge that your marriage has brought no disgrace upon our famous line.'

The Prince, although he resents his mother's suggestion and has no pressing desire to marry, is prepared to submit dutifully to her will. He respectfully enquires as to whom she has chosen for his bride.

'I have selected no-one,' she replies, 'since I wish you to choose your bride yourself. To-morrow I am giving a big ball, at which the nobility and their daughters will be present. You must choose from among those maidens the one that pleases you the most, and she shall be your bride.'

Siegfried, seeing that the matter is not quite so serious as he had feared, answers that he will carry out his mother's wishes.

'I have said my say,' declares the Princess, 'and now I shall depart. Make merry and do not allow this matter to weigh upon you.' She exits.

When she has retired, the Prince's friends surround him and he imparts to them the depressing news.

'This means an end to our merry-making,' he laments, 'and farewell to my freedom.'

'The actual event is still some way off,' observes Benno, trying to soothe him. 'It belongs to the future. And, since the immediate prospect is pleasing, why not let us enjoy ourselves while we may.'

'You speak truly,' smiles the Prince.

So the feasting is resumed. The peasants dance in groups or apart. The respected Wolfgang, having again indulged in wine, begins to dance himself but in so ridiculous a manner as to arouse derision. His dancing at an end, Wolfgang begins to plague the peasant girls with his attentions, but they mock the tutor and flee from him. One of the girls has a particular attraction for him and, having declared his passion, he tries to kiss her, but the pert girl eludes his grasp, and, as always happens in ballets, he kisses her swain instead. Wolfgang's bewildered air provokes general laughter.

Night begins to fall and the scene grows darker. One of the guests suggests a dance while holding wine-cups in their hands. They assent to his proposal.

A flock of swans is seen flying in the distance.

'Do you think they are too difficult to hit?' says Benno, pointing to the swans and trying to incite the Prince.

'Of course not,' the Prince replies. 'I should hit the target for sure. Bring me my cross-bow.'

' *Nay, do not heed him,*' reproves Wolfgang, '*the hour is late and it is time to retire.*'

The Prince's expression seems to imply assent. But, as soon as the pacified old man withdraws, Siegfried summons a servant, calls for his cross-bow, and hurries away with Benno in the direction of the flight of the swans.

ACT TWO

Scene. A wild and mountainous country, bounded on all sides by forest. In the distance a lake, on the bank of which to the audience's right is a half-ruined stone building resembling a chapel. It is night and the moon is shining. Over the surface of the lake glides a flock of swans accompanied by cygnets. They swim towards the ruins. The flock is led by a swan bearing a crown on its head.

Enter the Prince and Benno. They appear exhausted.

'*I can go no farther,*' gasps the latter. '*I am too weary. Let us rest awhile, shall we?*'

'*As you will,*' replies Siegfried. '*We have probably come too far from the castle. Doubtless we shall have to pass the night here.*'

'Look!' cries the Prince pointing to the lake. 'That is where the swans are. Quick! Give me my cross-bow!'

Benno hands him the weapon. But, as soon as the Prince aims at the birds, they vanish. *At the same moment the interior of the ruin becomes illumined by some fantastic radiance.*

'They have flown away, what a pity!' laments the Prince. 'But look! What is that!' he continues, drawing Benno's attention to the glowing ruins.

'Strange,' muses Benno, 'the place must be bewitched.'

'Ah, we will look into this at once,' replies the Prince, going towards the ruins. No sooner does he approach them, than on the steps appears a girl dressed in white and wearing a crown of precious stones. The figure is radiant in the moonlight. Amazed, the Prince *and Benno* draw back from the ruins.

Having mournfully shaken her head, the girl asks the Prince:

'Why do you pursue me, noble knight? What harm have I ever done to you?'

In confusion, the Prince replies: 'I did not imagine...I did not expect...'

The girl descends the steps, quietly approaches the Prince, and, having rested her hand on his shoulder, says to him reproachfully:

'The swan you sought to slay was I.'

'You were the swan! But that cannot be!'

'Yes, listen. I am called Odette. My mother was a good fairy, but, ignoring my father's wishes, she fell passionately in love with a noble knight and married him. Alas, he brought her to a sad end and she disappeared. *My father married a second time and thought no more of me. My wicked stepmother, who is a witch, hated and ill-treated me.* But my grandfather took care of me, for he dearly loved my mother. Indeed, he was so distraught at her death and wept so much, that from his tears was formed this lake, *into whose depths he descended and hid me away from all the world. Now, of late, he began to spoil me and gave me full liberty to enjoy myself. So by day my friends and I become transformed into swans and, joyfully cleaving the air with our breasts, we soar almost as high as the sky. And at dusk we dance and play near the old man. But my stepmother does not leave either my friends or myself in peace. (At this moment the hoot of an owl is heard.)*

'Listen! That is a voice of ill omen,' cried Odette, looking about her in alarm. 'Look! There *she* is!' (N.B.—*In all versions today the owl is Rothbart, a male enchanter.*)

On the ruins appears a gigantic owl with gleaming eyes.

'She would have killed me long ago,' continues Odette, '*only my grand-father watches her closely and will not allow her to work her wicked will.* When I marry, the witch will lose the power to harm me. Until then, this crown alone protects me from *her* evil wiles. That is all. My story is soon told.'

'Oh, forgive me, my beautiful one,' pleads the bewildered Prince, falling on his knees.

From the ruins emerge a stream of *young girls and children* who hasten towards the young huntsman, saying that thanks to his foolish pastime he nearly robbed them of their dearest friend.

The Prince *and Benno* are overwhelmed with despair.

'That is enough,' says Odette to her friends. 'You see that he is good and sorry, and that he feels pity for me.'

Quickly the Prince takes his cross-bow and, breaking it, casts it away, saying: '*I swear that henceforth my hand shall never more be raised to slay any living bird.*'

'Calm yourself, Sir Knight, all is forgotten; and now come and share in our pleasures.'

Dancing begins *in which the Prince and Benno take part.* The swans and the cygnets form beautiful groups or dance apart. The Prince is continually at Odette's side. During the dancing he falls madly in love with her and implores her not to reject him (*Pas d'action*). Odette laughs as though to express her doubt of his sincerity.

'You do not believe me!' cries the Prince. 'Oh, cold and cruel Odette!'

'I dare not believe you, noble knight,' retorts Odette. 'I fear that you are simply deceived by your own imagination. To-morrow at the ball that is to be given by your mother, you will see many beautiful young girls. You will fall in love with one of them and soon forget me.'

'O never, I swear it on my knightly honour.'

'Very well then, listen. I shall not conceal from you that I, too, love you. But I am filled with a foreboding that the evil witch may contrive some misfortune for you that will wreck our happiness.'

'I defy the whole world,' challenges Siegfried. 'You shall ever be my one and only true love, and naught that the witch may do shall avail.'

'Very well, to-morrow shall decide our fate. Either you will never see me again or else I shall lay my crown at your feet. But enough, it is time to depart, dawn is approaching. Farewell till to-morrow.' (N.B.—*Odette is much more in command of this situation than she is in contemporary versions.*)

Odette and her friends vanish into the ruins. The sky is flushed with the roseate hue of sunrise. Over the lake glides a flock of swans. Above them hovers a gigantic owl.

(*Curtain*)

ACT THREE

Scene. A magnificent hall in the Princess's castle. Everything is prepared for the festival.

Old Wolfgang is giving his final orders to the servants. The Master of Cere-monies receives and places the guests.

A herald announces the arrival of the Princess and of Prince Siegfried, who enter, accompanied by their courtiers, pages, *and dwarfs*. The noble couple bow graciously to the guests, then take the seats of honour which have been prepared for them. The Master of Ceremonies goes to the Princess and receives the signal for the dances to begin. Guests of both sexes compose different groups. *The dwarfs begin to dance.* The sound of a trumpet announces the arrival of a new guest. The Master of Ceremonies goes forward to greet him and a herald announces their names to the Princess.

Enter the *aged Baron von Stein with his wife and young daughter. They bow respectfully to their hosts, and the daughter, at the Prince's invitation, takes part in the dancing.* Once more the trumpet sounds, and the Master of Ceremonies again performs his office. *New guests arrive.*

The Master of Ceremonies seats the older people, while the young girls are invited by the Princess to dance. After several such arrivals, the Princess summons her son to her side and asks him who among the guests has produced a favourable impression upon him. The Prince sadly replies: 'So far, there is no one who appeals to me, mother.'

The Princess shrugs her shoulders in irritation, *calls Wolfgang*, and angrily imparts to him her son's words. *The tutor tries to persuade his pupil*, but at the same time the trumpet sounds anew, and into the hall comes Rothbart with his daughter, Odile.

At the sight of the newcomer, the Prince is struck by her beauty. Her features remind him of the swan-maiden, Odette. *He signs to his friend, Benno, and asks him:*

'*Do you not think this latest arrival is very much like Odette?*'

'*Well, not to my way of thinking*,' replies Benno. '*You see your Odette everywhere.*' (N.B.—*Benno is not present at the ball in most contemporary versions.*)

The Prince admires Odile's dancing for some time, then himself joins in. *The gratified Princess summons Wolfgang and tells him that it seems as though the latest guest has produced a favourable impression upon her son.*

'Oh, yes,' admits Wolfgang, 'but bear with him a little longer. The Prince is not made of stone, he will fall madly in love with her.'

Meanwhile, the dances continue, during which time the Prince shows a marked preference for Odile, who coquettishly uses her beauty to lure him on. In a mood of infatuation, the Prince kisses Odile's hand, whereupon the Princess and old Rothbart rise and go towards the dancers in the centre of the hall.

'My son,' observes the Princess, 'you may not kiss a lady's hand except she be your affianced bride.'

'I am willing to ask her to be my wife, mother,' replies the Prince.

'What says her father to that?' enquires the Princess.

Von Rothbart triumphantly takes his daughter's hand and places it in that of the young Prince. Immediately the scene grows darker. The hoot of an owl is heard. Rothbart's costume falls from him and he is revealed as a demon. Odile laughs.

A window opens noisily and upon the sill appears a white swan with a crown upon its head. Terrified, the Prince drops Odile's hand and, pressing his hand to his heart, dashes out of the castle hall. General confusion.

(*Curtain*)

ACT FOUR

Scene. Same as Act II. Night.

Odette's friends are awaiting her return. Some are beginning to wonder what has become of her. Overwhelmed with sadness, they try to seek distraction in dancing and by making the cygnets dance too.

Suddenly, Odette enters, *her hair hanging loose down her shoulders from beneath her crown.* She is in tears and filled with despair.

Her friends surround her and ask the reason for her distress.

'He has not kept his troth. He could not support the test.'

Her friends, disgusted, try to soothe Odette, and beg her to dismiss the unfaithful lover from her mind.

'But I love him,' confesses Odette wistfully.

'Poor girl,' sympathises one of her friends. 'Let us away. See, he is coming towards us.'

'He!' cries Odette, in alarm, and she runs towards the ruins. All at once she stops and declares:

'I wish to look on him for the last time.'

'But you will ruin yourself!' protest her companions.

'O, no, I shall take heed. Go away, sisters, and wait for me.'

They all go into the ruins. Thunder is heard, at first distant and rumbling, then coming nearer and nearer. The scene grows darker and from the gathering clouds dart occasional flashes of lightning. The surface of the lake becomes more and more turbulent. At this point Siegfried hurries in, crying:

'Odette! Odette!'

'I am here,' she replies, and he runs towards her.

'Oh, forgive me, dear Odette.'

'It is not in my power to forgive you. Everything is at an end. We look upon each other for the last time.'

The Prince entreats her pardon, but Odette remains unmoved. She gazes fearfully at the boiling lake, and, slipping from Siegfried's embrace, runs towards the ruins. He pursues her, seizes her hand, and despairingly cries:

'No, no. Whether you will or no, you shall remain with me for ever!' *Quickly he snatches the crown from her head and casts it into the storm-tossed lake, which is already overflowing its banks. Overhead flies a hooting owl carrying in its claws the discarded crown of Odette.*

'*What have you done? You have destroyed us both!*' cries Odette. '*I am dying,*' she continues, *falling into the Prince's arms,* and through the rumble of thunder and the noise of the waves is heard the swan's sad last song.

One after another the waves roll over the Prince and Odette, and soon they disappear beneath the water. The storm subsides, with only a faint distant rumbling of thunder. The moon's pale rays pierce through the scattered clouds and on the now calm lake appears a flock of white swans.

The Ballet Scenario: Twentieth Century

A. DIAGHILEV'S BALLETS RUSSES

ALTHOUGH we reproduce at Appendix IV Alexandre Benois's account of the scenario of *Petrouchka* we have been unable to find the actual scenarios of any early Diaghilev ballet. We reproduce, therefore, the scenario of *Parade*, created by Jean Cocteau in 1917, to be one of the first ballets by Massine. With music by Satie and décor by Picasso this signalled the growth of French influence over the later Diaghilev ballet, weakening the dominant Russian influence which Fokine had personified.

Parade was first produced at the Châtelet Theatre, Paris, on 18th May, 1917, with choreography by Massine. To say the least its scenario was brief, written in a style to correspond with the cubist preoccupation of its author and his collaborators.

BALLET RÉALISTE

avec la collaboration de

PICASSO

pour les décors et costumes et de

ERIK SATIE

pour la musique
Représenté au théâtre du Châtelet
en 1917 par la
Compagnie des Ballets Russes de

SERGE DE DIAGHILEW

Chorégraphie de

LÉONIDE MASSINE

d'après les indications plastiques
de l'auteur

Le décor représente les maisons à Paris, un dimanche. Théâtre forain. Trois numéros du Music-Hall servent de Parade.
Prestidigitateur chinois.
Acrobates.
Petite fille américaine.
Trois managers organisent la réclame. Ils se communiquent dans leur langage terrible que la foule prend la parade pour le spectacle intérieur et cherchent grossiérement á le lui faire comprendre.
Personne n'entre.

Après le dernier numéro de la parade, les managers exténués s'écroulent les uns sur les autres.

Le Chinois, les acrobates et la petite fille sortent du théâtre vide. Voyant l'effort suprême et la chute des managers, ils essayent d'expliquer à leur tout que le spectacle se donne à l'intérieur.

N.B.—*La direction se réserve le droit d'intervertir l'ordre des numéros de la parade.*

La chorégraphie de *Parade* a été faite techniquement par Massine d'après les directives de l'auteur. Les gestes de la vie étant, pour la première fois, amplifiés et magnifiés jusqu'à la danse.

B. FRENCH BALLET

Prométhée by Pierre Rhallys. First produced by Les Ballets 1956 de Miskovitch et Lidova at the Festival of Lyon Charbonnières, June 1956.

In France the poet finds recognition as a ballet scenarist. The poet, Pierre Rhallys, has written a number of ballets and may be regarded as a rare example of the professional ballet scenarist. His scenario of *Prométhée* was written for the choreographer, Maurice Béjart, who took Rhallys' idea and adapted it in a number of ways, as choreographers often do. In particular, Béjart devised the final climax of the ballet, the hanging of Prometheus.

Rhallys laid out his scenario for Béjart very clearly in concise sections as follows:—

Prométhée

Book by Pierre Rhallys
Music by Maurice Ohana
Décors and costumes by Bernard Daydé
Choreography by Maurice Béjart

Set: (1) A throne. (2) Some distance behind the throne some posts bearing intertwined ropes. (3) Blocks scattered in a semicircle in the front of the set. (4) In front of steps leading to the throne a support fashioned in wood.

Characters: The Hero—Prometheus
           The Guardian of the Fire
           A Creature
           A Three-headed Monster

1. Arrival of the hero.
2. The Monster appears.
3. Struggle with the monster.
4. The monster is overcome. (The hero drives the monster off the stage.)
5. The hero seeks to climb the steps of the throne upon which the guardian is seated. When the mobile support is turned the hero finds the creature fastened upon the support.
6. He unfastens it and breathes life into it, so that it becomes strong. (It was amorphous and soft.)
7. Leaving the creature fixed like a statue he goes to steal the fire.
C.A.—23

8. The thief gives fire to humanity. (One by one the cubes light up.)

9. After which, last of all, he gives light to the creature.

10. Dazzled by life she dances with him a dance of wonder and love. The dance ends in a pose of union in love, creator and creature.

11. The Guardian of the Fire rises from her throne. Taking the ropes in her hand she descends into the arena.

12. She attacks the hero.

13. Dreadful struggle between the two. (The creature crouches at the side, but centre, of the arena.)

14. The hero is overcome.

15. The Guardian summons her men. They appear. She orders the hero to be hanged.

16. The hero is hanged.

17. The posts are lowered. They are raised again carrying the hero bound with the ropes.

18. The Guardian points at him.

19. The creature lies upon the ground, arms and legs wide in a cross, face towards the hero.

C. ENGLISH BALLET (i). A Scenario

Harlequin in April by John Cranko, with choreography by John Cranko, décor by John Piper and music by Richard Arnell. First produced for the Sadler's Wells Theatre Ballet at the Sadler's Wells Theatre on 8th May, 1951. This is a symbolical ballet of man's life, inspired by lines in T. S. Eliot's *The Waste Land.* The following version of the scenario is the one which was given to the composer, Richard Arnell, to guide his creation of the music. As in all scenarios there are differences between this and the actual production, but they are very slight. Such differences occur when the author's idea is translated into choreography. Some ideas have to be discarded or replaced, usually for practical reasons, e.g. at the end of Act ! Harlequin does *not* mount the Unicorn and he does not leave Pierrot behind. The timing of the dances and many other details were discussed and agreed separately by the collaborators. This is one of the best of Cranko's early scenarios, showing a good use of symbols.

Characters

Pierrot
Harlequin
Columbine
Plants, Unicorns

Prologue

A short fanfare: the curtain rises to reveal the act drop. Pierrot enters with music for song. Introduction as for song. Pierrot draws breath and on cue for note no sound comes. He tries again. And again. In despair and embarrassment, he goes off.

ACT I: April

Spring creatures are seen in a huddle, centre. Enter Pierrot with a watering can and waters them. They stir and breathe a bit. Pierrot waters them again. They stir more violently. Pierrot retires in awe. The 'plants' begin to grow; after a while, Harlequin rises from the centre, his head in the same blossom and cowl headdress. The arms twine around him, but his growth is not stopped by them.

Harlequin stands upright and tries, with his arms lifting slowly outwards, to get his balance. When he falls, the 'plants' catch him and put him on his feet again. Slowly his hands begin an exploration and he taps at them and on his own body, 'discovering' things. Then slowly he starts to walk, guided by the plants. He reaches out for imaginary objects and puts them in his mouth. The hands all move to his mouth as if feeding him.

Pierrot appears with Harlequin's jacket and wistfully tries it on himself. He goes and helps Harlequin on with the coat and gives him his wand. Harlequin snatches off the headdress and stands up strongly in the Harlequin position; light floods down on him. Harlequin's solo. This starts by his thwacking Pierrot so soundly with his wand that Pierrot runs off. Harlequin dances alone.

At end of the solo, Harlequin looks at 'plants', who have been moving blindly across the stage in ones or twos during his solo. He advances to them and they cringe. He is very curious and pokes among them, and finally pulls a young girl from amongst them.

Pas de Deux. The girl is very timid and Harlequin encourages her to dance with him. But she is so slow and fumbling and he so quick and impatient that they constantly get in one another's way. Harlequin touches her bandage, but she shrinks away once or twice. He comforts her, and suddenly whips it off and flings it away. She joins him in a moment of ecstatic dance, but blinded and dizzy with the light, she grows weaker and weaker till she is quite limp.

The other 'plants' appear. Harlequin is puzzled and upset. The plants bear her headdress, slowly they place it on her head. Harlequin draws away. The girl revives. She feels sap running in her veins again.

The 'plants' go off with the characteristic step. For a moment, the girl, a bit apart from the group, seems to remember Harlequin, but the other 'plants' call her and she leaves with them.

Harlequin kicks his own headdress, which lies on the floor. A unicorn charges across the stage. Harlequin sees it and is amazed and delighted by it. He pursues it and captures it, and mounts it. It gallops off with him, leaving Pierrot behind.

Entr'acte

Pierrot comes out to play a tune on the fiddle. Fanfare: he bows to audience, very pleased with himself. He commences to play, but after a few bars, a string snaps. A bit appalled, he starts again (every 4th note is missing), but the string breaks again, etc. etc., till all strings are gone, and once more Pierrot is dumb.

ACT II

The Sky (very mysterious to begin with). Pierrot and Harlequin enter. Pierrot is frightened and won't go on. He tries to make Harlequin turn back, but Harlequin refuses to be afraid. Suddenly a unicorn charges across. Pierrot, overcome by fear, runs away. Harlequin is frightened also. Two unicorns trot on, bearing Columbine, who sits submissively on their backs. They do a short dance, in which she is quite passive and resigned.

Harlequin steals out of his hiding place and declares his love for her. Columbine sees him and she stretches out her arms to him. The unicorns stamp and keep them apart for a bit, but she strokes them and they fall asleep. When they are asleep,

Pas de deux, Harlequin and Columbine, very tender, etc.

The unicorns awake and snatch Columbine away in the middle of an embrace. Harlequin tries to rescue her, but is unable to do so. He draws his sword and stabs one of them, but as it falls two spring up in its place. Follows the battle of the unicorns, mounting in violence. Occasionally Columbine is seen being borne across the stage. The battle mounts in fury. Harlequin is beset on all sides by unicorns. They bear him to the ground and stamp upon him. Columbine is brought in and the unicorns cluster round her, doing homage to her. Exhausted and badly hurt, Harlequin tries to break into the scrum which they form around her. Suddenly, all the unicorns gallop off, leaving behind a scarecrow wearing Columbine's dress and headdress.

Solemnly Harlequin throws himself at the feet of the scarecrow. Pierrot totters to the scarecrow and starts kowtowing grotesquely. Harlequin gets up and sees this pathetic mimicry and in a great rage he throws the scarecrow about the stage. Then he beats Pierrot fiercely. Pierrot exits.

Harlequin weeps and weeps and weeps; and as he does so the earth creatures return, bearing with them the headdress of flowers. Gratefully as an old man goes to death, Harlequin dons the headdress and is encircled by the plants. Slowly he disappears as he came in the beginning.

Pierrot appears, wearing Harlequin's jacket. He is trying vainly and patiently to jump and bound like Harlequin. Curtain.

ENGLISH BALLET (ii). A Scenario

Noctambules, by Kenneth MacMillan, with choreography by Kenneth MacMillan, music by Humphrey Searle and décor by Nicholas Georgiadis. First produced for the Royal Ballet at the Royal Opera House, Covent Garden, London, on 1st March, 1956.

The following version of the scenario is the one accepted by the artistic director, Dame Ninette de Valois. It was changed in a number of ways during production (the magician's assistant, for example did not die) but the general development of the idea remained untouched. This scenario, which was remarkably detailed but left the timing of dances and other matters for discussion in a later, fuller, libretto, was published originally in *The Ballet Annual No. 11* to whose Editors, and to Kenneth Macmillan, we are indebted for its reproduction.

Characters

The Magician	The Veiled Lady	A Rich Young Man	6 Rich Couples
His Assistant	A Soldier	A Poor Girl	6 Poor Couples

Scene I

The curtain rises on a street scene with an entrance to a small theatre, centre. A magician enters wearing an enormous cloak and from beneath this emerges his lady assistant. She dances and then, as if in a trance, follows the magician into the theatre.

Richly dressed people now gather outside, waiting for the performance, amongst them a handsome young man and an elegant soldier. They go in. A faded beauty now enters, entirely covered by a long black veil; she too enters the theatre, and finally a group of poor people.

Scene II

The drop curtain rises to reveal the interior of the theatre with a small stage centre back. The people introduce themselves to each other and then sit waiting for the beginning of the performance. The lady assistant does a dance with a drum, heralding the appearance of the magician. He enters through the curtains and proceeds to hypnotise his assistant. At first she complies with his wishes, but fights against his hypnotic powers and refuses to carry on the performance. The magician gets very angry and throws her to the ground. The crowd rises angrily and, shouting abuse at him, troop off stage. At that moment the magician darkens the stage (during which time the dancers change their clothes and the scenery changes).

Scene III

The stage lightens on some fantastic scenery and the dancers are now in much shorter and lighter costumes. The magician now proceeds to hypnotise all the dancers, and make them move at his will. Then follows:

A general dance for all
A *pas de deux* for the rich young man and poor young girl
A dance for the soldier on an enormous drum
A *pas de cinq* for four boys and the veiled lady

It ends with a general dance in which the magician follows the veiled lady, and finally catching her, disappears with her down a trap-door. The others, waking from the magician's hypnotic power, rush off leaving the poor young girl and rich man. They rather like what has happened to them and move off together, leaving the lady assistant alone on the stage. She, now like a Trilby without her Svengali, or a puppet without its master, is useless without the magician. She does a mad dance with her drum and finally drops dead. The curtain falls.

ENGLISH BALLET (iii). A libretto

A Mirror for Witches, by Andrée Howard with choreography by Andrée Howard, music by Denis ApIvor, scenery by Norman Adams, costumes by Howard and Adams. First produced for the Sadler's Wells Ballet at the Royal Opera House, Covent Garden, London, on 4th March, 1952. This ballet of five scenes and a prologue was based on Esther Forbes's novel of the same name, published in 1928. It has not survived in the repertoire, although it was one of Howard's most powerful works.

At Plate XXXVI we have photographed the first two pages of the choreographer's notes to show the moment at which a scenario can become a detailed libretto to guide the collaborators, especially the composer.

Andrée Howard always prepares her scenarios in this way when the score is specially commissioned. The typewritten timings on the left indicate the length of each section musically after the score was composed. The handwritten timings show the final length after adjustment. Opposite is the choreographer's lighting draft for the corresponding scenes of the ballet.

Characters

A Witch
Doll, her daughter as a child
Bilby, a ship's captain
Hannah, his wife

Doll, their foster child as a young girl
Titus, a young son of the village
The Twins, his sisters
The Stranger

Villagers, Fiends, Warlocks, Priests, Witches, Soldiers,
Peasants, Men, Women, Judge and Councillors

ENGLISH BALLET (iv). A choreographer's notes for his composer

Sir Frederick Ashton gave detailed notes of his requirements to Hans Werner Henze, the composer of *Ondine*. At Plate XXXVII we reproduce an extract from these notes for the opening of Act III, published originally by Clive Barnes in *Dance and Dancers*, January 1960.

ENGLISH BALLET (v). A choreographer's personal notes

A Place in the Desert, by Norman Morrice with choreography by Norman Morrice, music by Carlos Surinach (written originally for a television play *David and Bathsheba*), scenery and costumes by Ralph Koltai. First produced for Ballet Rambert at Sadler's Wells Theatre, London, on 25th July, 1961.

Characters

A Village Elder
His Heir
His Daughter

His Younger Son
A Company Agent

Norman Morrice prepares his ballets on paper in the most detailed manner. The notes at Plate XXXVIII show the first two pages from his note-book for *A Place in the Desert* and are included to illustrate how this particular choreographer prepares himself on paper to meet his dancers. On the left are the opening positions of the dancers on stage. On the right the notes describing their movement. The entire ballet is noted in this way before rehearsal.

D. AMERICAN BALLET. A choreographer's personal notes

Rodeo, or The Courting at Burnt Ranch, by Agnes de Mille with choreography by Agnes de Mille, music by Aaron Copland, scenery by Oliver

Smith, costumes by Kermit Love. First produced at the Metropolitan
Opera House, New York, for the Ballet Russe de Monte Carlo on 16th
October, 1942.

Characters

The Head Wrangler   The Rancher's Daughter
The Champion Roper   The Caller
The Cowgirl
Easterners from Kansas City, Cowhands, Womenfolk

This ballet of three scenes, a first version of which was presented in
London in 1938, marked a turning-point in the development of American
ballet and in the career of its choreographer.

At Plate XXXIX we reproduce neither a scenario nor a libretto, but,
like Norman Morrice's notes above, the actual notes of the musical counts
and movements which this particular choreographer has made for rehearsal. Agnes de Mille, however, prepares notes of this kind usually *after*
she has tested out steps in the rehearsal room. They are for the riding
sequence at the rodeo in the opening scene of the ballet, sequences whose
distinctive movement helped to graft American temperament on to the
vocabulary of classical ballet in America. The Freddie referred to is
Frederick Franklin who created the role of the champion roper. Miss de
Mille herself created the role of the cowgirl.

THE COLLABORATORS AT WORK

The Creation of Petrouchka

IN the autumn of 1910 in St. Petersburg, Alexandre Benois, the artist, received a letter from Diaghilev which he said, 'greatly perturbed me'. So began one of the most fruitful collaborations in ballet, although only a few months earlier Benois had quarrelled with Diaghilev in Paris over the authorship of *Schéhérazade*. He was still not reconciled when the letter arrived.

'Its contents', he wrote in his *Reminiscences of the Russian Ballet*, 'were approximately the following: he did not doubt that my decision was final, and yet, in view of certain *exceptional* circumstances, he addressed me again in the hope that I would forgive the insult I had suffered and once more join my friends. The exceptional circumstances were that, only a few days ago, Stravinsky had composed and played to him a sort of Russian Dance and another piece which he had named *Petrouchka's Cry*, and that both these compositions were, in every sense of the term, works of *genius*. They had both had the idea of using this music for some new ballet, but no story had as yet been devised. They had only conceived the idea of representing the St. Petersburg Carnival and of including in it a performance of Petrouchka, the Russian Punch and Judy show. 'Who else but you', wrote Seriozha, 'could help us in this problem?' Therefore they had decided to apply to me and Seriozha expressed the assurance that I could not *possibly* refuse.

'Seriozha certainly had every foundation for his assurance. Petrouchka, The Russian Guignol or Punch, no less than Harlequin, had been my friend since my earliest childhood. Whenever I heard the loud, nasal cries of the travelling Punch and Judy showman: "Here's Petrouchka! Come, good people, and see the Show!" I would get into a kind of frenzy to see the enchanting performance, which consisted, as did the *balagani* panto-mimes, in the endless tricks of an idle loafer, who ends up by being captured by a hairy devil and dragged off to Hell.

'As to Petrouchka in person, I immediately had the feeling that "it was a duty I owed to my old friend" to immortalise him on the real stage. I was still more tempted by the idea of depicting the Butter Week Fair on the stage, the dear *balagani* which were the great delight of my childhood, and had been the delight of my father before me. The fact that in 1911 the *balagani* had, for some ten years, ceased to exist, made the idea of building a kind of memorial to them still more tempting. They perished under the onslaught led by Prince A. P. Oldenburg[1] against alcoholism (the common

[1] The Prince had perhaps a special dislike to the noisy *balagani* because they took place under the windows of his palace. The *balagani* were transferred from the centre of the town—The Tsaritsin Loug—to the Semeonovsky Place, where they soon ceased to exist.

folk certainly gave themselves up to the Russian Vodka-Bacchus at the Butter Week Fair!).

'Besides the duty I felt I owed to Petrouchka and my wish to "immortalise" the St. Petersburg Carnival, I had yet another reason for accepting Seriozha's offer—I suddenly *saw* how this ballet ought to be presented. It at once became plain that Guignol-Petrouchka screens were not appropriate to a stage performance. A year before we had tried to arrange a similar Petrouchka performance with real people in the Arts Club, but although Dobuzhinsky had put much of his wit into the production, it turned out to be rather absurd and on the dull side. The effect of big grown-up people acting with their heads over the edge of a curtain and little wooden legs dangling below, was more pitiful than funny. The effect on the stage of a real theatre would have been still worse; a ballet would have been entirely out of the question, for what could a ballet artist do if he were not allowed to use his "natural" legs? Once the screens were abolished from the stage, they had naturally to be replaced by a small theatre. The dolls of this theatre would have to come to life without ceasing to be dolls—retaining, so to speak, their doll's nature.

'The dolls should come to life at the command of a magician, and their coming to life should be somehow accompanied by suffering. The greater the contrast between the real, live people and the automatons who had just been given life, the sharper the interest of the action would be. It would be necessary to allot a considerable part of the stage to the mass of real people—the "public" at the fair—while there would only be two dolls, the hero of the play, Petrouchka, and his lady.

'Soon I decided that there should be a third character—the Blackamoor. In the street performances of Petrouchka there was invariably a separate intermezzo, inserted between the acts: two Blackamoors, dressed in velvet and gold, would appear and start unmercifully hitting each other's wooden heads with sticks. I included a similar Blackamoor among my "chief characters". If Petrouchka were to be taken as the personification of the spiritual and suffering side of humanity—or shall we call it the poetical principle?—his lady Columbine would be the incarnation of the eternal feminine; then the gorgeous Blackamoor would serve as the embodiment of everything senselessly attractive, powerfully masculine and undeservedly triumphant. Having once visualised what an interesting collision of contrasted elements must inevitably ensue, how could I refuse Seriozha's proposal that I should help to interpret it as a ballet on the stage? I fully believed what Diaghilev had written when he claimed that the *Russian Dance* and *Petrouchka's Cry* were works of genius, and was still further encouraged. How could I maintain my stubbornness and my attitude of "injured pride"? I gave in and informed Seriozha that I accepted his proposal and had forgiven all grievances; I was once more entirely with him and Stravinsky.

'Several weeks later Seriozha arrived in St. Petersburg. My scheme was accepted with enthusiasm. We met daily in Diaghilev's flat in Zamiatin Lane, where, at the traditional evening tea with *boubliki*, we discussed the "forthcoming" *Petrouchka*. At one time I let loose my imagination and the subject began to swell and fitted ultimately into four, fairly short acts, without any intervals. The first and last acts were to take place at the

Carnival Fair; the two middle ones were to show the interior of the Conjuror's theatre. The puppets that had come to life in the first act, under the magic spell of the Conjuror, were to continue living a real life in their own quarters, where a romance was to begin between them. *Petrouchka's Cry*, which Seriozha now described to me in detail, was to fill the first of the two intimate acts; the second was to be devoted to the Blackamoor. The detailed action had not yet been decided.

'Stravinsky arrived in December on a short visit to his mother and I was at last able to hear the two fragments which had been the "beginning of everything". Igor played them to me in my little dark-blue drawing-room; the piano was my old, fearfully hard Gentach, the same instrument (the poor old fellow had since had his abnormally long tail chopped off) on which Albert used to tell me the story of the little boy caught by the devils. What I now heard surpassed my expectations. The *Russian Dance* proved to be really magic music in which infectious, diabolical reckless-ness alternated with strange digressions into tenderness—then, after a cul-minating paroxysm, came to an abrupt end. As for *Petrouchka's Cry*, having listened to it about three times, I began to discern in it grief, and rage, and love, as well as the helpless despair that dominated it. Stravinsky accepted my comments, and later on this programme, that was constructed *ex post facto*, was worked out by me in full detail.[1]

'Today, when I listen to the music of this second act of *Petrouchka* and watch what the artist is expressing, more or less successfully, in his gestures and mime—*demonstrating* the absolute coordination of action and music—it is difficult even for me to believe that the music was not written to a set programme, instead of the programme being subsequently fitted to the music.

'We continued to collaborate, actively and harmoniously, in the crea-tion of the new ballet, in spite of the fact that we did not meet again till the spring of 1911. Stravinsky went back to Switzerland to live with his family while I remained in St. Petersburg,[2] but we kept up a constant interchange of letters. The subject was acquiring definite shape. The dramatic situation produced by the "hopeless love" of the "poet" Petrouchka in the second act was counter-balanced in the third by the undeserved passion awakened in the Ballerina by the foolish Blackamoor. Their personalities began to take definite shape, and when I heard the music of the "Blackamoor's room", I invented his monologue in all its absurd detail: the playing with the coconut, the coconut's resentment at being chopped open, etc. The Ballerina appears at the moment of the Blackamoor's wild, religious ecstasy before the coconut. At the climax of their love-making, when the enamoured Blackamoor is almost ready

[1] It was then that I imagined the black room where the wicked conjuror imprisons his puppe·—now, alas, fully conscious of its surroundings.

[2] The room I used when working at the composition of the décor and costumes for *Petrouchka* was above the flat occupied by Count Bobrinsky's coachmen, for Count Bobrinsky's house was next door to ours. Unceasing revels and dancing went on there all day long to the sounds of the balalaika and the laughter of gay ladies. At any other time this would have greatly disturbed me, but in the present case all the noise, shouts and stamping only helped to inspire me. It was almost a gift of providence.

to devour his charming visitor, poor Petrouchka, mad with jealousy, rushes in, but, as the curtain falls, the Blackamoor pushes out his ridiculous rival.

'The last part of the third act foretells the final *dénouement*. Similar scenes are supposed to go on inside the tiny theatre, passions grow, and at last the pathetic, luckless lover reaches a fatal end. It was essential to carry the finale outside the intimate surroundings of the previous two acts; to set it among the Carnival crowd, at the fair where, in the first act, the puppets had actually been brought to life. I was delighted with Stravinsky's idea of introducing a party of *riageni*[1] into the street crowd. This was a regular feature of the Russian Carnival, which could not do without such a "devil's diversion". All sorts of "creatures of hell" and even the Devil himself were to appear among these masked visitors. At the climax of the drunken revelling, Petrouchka's cries were to be heard coming from the conjuror's theatre. Petrouchka rushes out into the crowd, trying to escape from his infuriated enemy, but the Blackamoor overtakes him and puts an end to his existence with a blow from his curved sword.

'This was the general plan of the finale, but we only began working it out when Stravinsky and I met again in Rome. The composer reached the height of tragedy in the final few bars expressing Petrouchka's agony, his piteous goodbye to life. To this day I cannot listen to it without the deepest emotion. The very moment of death—when Petrouchka's soul departs to a better world—is expressed in an unusual and very successful way. A broken sob is heard—produced by the throwing on the floor of a tambourine. This "unmusical" sound seems to destroy the spell, to bring the spectator back to "reality". But the drama of the Conjuror who has dared to put a heart and a soul into his toys does not end so simply. Petrouchka turns out to be immortal, and when the old magician disdainfully drags the broken doll along the snow in order to mend it (and again torment it), the "genuine" Petrouchka suddenly appears in miraculous transformation above the little theatre, and the terrified Conjuror drops the doll and turns to flight.

'The finale did not come to Stravinsky at once, and he had to search and use different combinations for it. He finished composing the music only a few weeks before the performance. We were staying at the same hotel in Rome for nearly a month, and every morning I used to hear from my room a confused tangle of sounds, interrupted from time to time by long pauses. This was the maturing of the last bars of the fourth act. . . . When everything was ready, *Petrouchka* was played to Diaghilev and me from beginning to end. Diaghilev was no less delighted with it than I; the only thing he argued about was the "note of interrogation" upon which the ballet score ended. For a long time he would not agree to it, but demanded a more traditional solution—a curious proof of how strongly influenced Diaghilev was by "academic prejudice" even in 1911!'

Translated by Mary Britnieva
Reproduced by permission of the publishers, Putnam & Co. Ltd., of London

[1] *Riageni* were masked revellers, in traditional dress, who, at times of Festival, enjoyed special privileges.—Trans.

THE COMPOSER AT WORK

(i) *The Music of 'Job'*

IT is rare that ballet music is analysed for the benefit of dancers as clearly as the Master of the Queen's Music at the Chapel of the Savoy, Dr. William Cole, F.R.A.M., has analysed Vaughan Williams's score of *Job* for the Royal Academy of Dancing. The following notes on the music of *Job* are based on Dr. Coles' analysis and are included to show the help a composer's score can give to choreographer and dancers.

Job was first produced for the Camargo Society by Ninette de Valois at the Cambridge Theatre, London, on 5th July, 1931 as a Masque for Dancing in eight scenes. The characters were as follows:

Job	The Three Comforters
His Wife	Elihu
His Three Daughters	Satan
His Seven Sons	The Children of God
War, Pestilence and Famine	Sons of the Morning
The Three Messengers	Job's Spiritual Self

Job is one of the great works of the English repertoire, musically and choreographically. Vaughan Williams's music contains colour, atmosphere, clarity of theme and pulse—all the elements a dancer needs.

Dancers should first listen to this score to grasp its conception. Through this study they should try to understand the pastoral, folk and devotional elements which inform de Valois' choreography and ought to underlie the performance. The strongest musical influences are Palestrina, Bach, Holst and, of course, traditional English folk music.

The ballet opens with a pastoral introduction and a sarabande for the Sons of God, suggesting spiritual peace, headed in the score 'Hast thou considered my servant, Job?' Vaughan Williams divided his score into eight scenes, corresponding to the eight engravings to which the scenario reduced Blake's original total of twenty-one engravings.

But Vaughan Williams did not follow all the details of the scenario by Geoffrey Keynes and Gwendolen Raverat. He turned for emotional atmosphere to the biblical story itself, annotating his score with biblical quotations and brief descriptions of the action of the ballet. A glance at the score, therefore, will help a dancer, even though Ninette de Valois' choreography, in its turn, has not followed precisely all Vaughan Williams's instructions. She did not have the resources to match his conception.

The opening pastoral dance to flutes, harps and violas, expresses Job's material prosperity. Vaughan Williams writes in the score that the figures in the dancing should derive from the old tune *Jennie Pluck Pears*.

When the Sons and Daughters have dispersed, leaving Job and his Wife alone, Satan enters unperceived. His music, like that of the whole scene, begins almost from nothing rising to a crescendo just after the Heavens have gradually opened to reveal 'God sitting in Majesty, surrounded by the Sons of God'. Satan watches.

A succession of rising fourths describe 'the line of Angels stretching from Earth to Heaven' (groups of angels rather than a line in the choreography) and a sublime Sarabande for the Sons of God describes the Godhead itself. Majesty and repose are suggested by a repetitive use of two chords often used in the sixteenth century as the amen to psalms. The music starts in A major, then moves to the reposeful G major, C major and F major instead of to the less reposeful sharps which are reserved for Satan when he cries, 'Put forth thy hand now and touch him and all that he hath and he will curse thee to thy face'.

As soon as God has consented to the trial Satan breaks into a triumphant leaping dance which ends with his usurpation of the throne. It is a very difficult dance in counts of four, much syncopated in three time, using instruments like the xylophone to give harsh effects. It begins as Satan's music began for his first entrance, becomes more and more evil as it parodies the plainsong Gloria, 'Glory to God in the highest', and ends with trumpets, trombones and full orchestra as Hell enters (in the music, but not in the choreography) and Satan sits upon the throne. Note that Satan, as Vaughan Williams, and later de Valois, created him, is not an ignoble figure.

So Job's trial begins. The Sons of Job and their wives dance a minuet in the sunlight of Job's prosperity. They hold golden cups which they clash periodically as the cymbals dictate. 'The dance', says Vaughan Williams in his instructions, 'should be formal, statuesque and slightly voluptuous.' So it is in the choreography in the manner of Blake's drawings, with the oboes overlapping woodwind and strings to emphasise these qualities. Suddenly Satan enters. The dance stops. The sons and their wives fall dead.

In Job's dream, which follows, the choreography makes its biggest digression from the musical instructions. Vaughan Williams asks for a stage full of people, a request it was impossible to grant at the time the choreography was created in 1931.

Job stirs uneasily in his sleep (*allegro*). In the music Satan enters (although in the choreography he has been discovered already on stage) to a chromatically descending theme, 'stands over Job and calls up terrifying visions of Plague, Pestilence, Famine, Battle, Murder and Sudden Death, who posture before Job'. This is the crowd the music depicts. They are created in a grimly musical procession. In the choreography, however, we see only war, pestilence and famine.

Then messengers bring tidings to Job of the destruction of all his possessions and the death of his sons and daughters. The funeral cortège of his family passes, but Job still blesses God. (The funeral, in fact, does not pass visibly on stage. The messengers describe it.)

The messengers are followed by 'three wily hypocrites', their hypocrisy exactly defined by oily saxophones. The whole of this sixth scene conjures up an exceptional picture which it is as hard to describe in words as it is in movement. The unreal compassion of the comforters changes suddenly to anger and reproach. The true quality of these men is revealed musically (and can only be revealed in this way) by a suggestion in their anger *motif* of part of Satan's earlier music when he prophesied to God, 'Put forth thy hand now and touch all that he hath and he will curse thee to thy face'.

The use of this *motif* signifies, too, the weakening and collapse of Job's will. When the comforters again offer their hypocritical sympathy, Job stands and curses God: 'Let the day perish wherein I was born'. As Job speaks the music of Satan is heard in the background. Job invokes God, but Heaven opens to show the hosts of Hell, who parody the Sons of God in Scene I. The *motif* from Satan's prophecy sounds once more. Satan reveals himself on the throne; Job cowers and the vision vanishes.

Real comfort comes to Job through 'the young and beautiful Elihu'. 'I am young and ye are very old.' Elihu performs a dance of Youth and Beauty to a violin solo, *andante tranquillo*, recalling the enchanted bird-song of *The Lark Ascending*. A clarinet tune takes up the theme in the middle section. Like the rest of the score Elihu's dance is so full of atmosphere and colour and so well constructed rhythmically that it actually helps the performance. 'I don't have to dance,' said Pirmin Trecu, one of the most musical interpreters of this role, 'the music just lifts me.'

Elihu's qualities help Job to understand his complacent materialism. He regains his spiritual self. The qualities and the change in Job are conveyed clearly in the music. Elihu's violin solo is composed partly of God's theme when he replies to Satan, 'All that he hath is in thy power'. The solo leads into a Pavane of the Sons of the Morning. At first the Pavane is dimly heard as the inner change in Job begins. Then, as Heaven lights up, the dancers are seen to be before God's throne with God seated upon it. Through Elihu Job has conquered Satan and regained himself. Revealed as false, the comforters exit.

When Satan claims the victory, therefore, God banishes him. A triumphant galliard begins, one of the most famous pieces in the ballet, which reflects clearly the influence of Holst's Jupiter movement from *The Planets*. Holst directly helped Vaughan Williams with much of *Job*, showing well how one composer can learn from another and still remain himself.

To the tune of the galliard the Sons of the Morning drive Satan down. At its climax Satan 'falls out of heaven'. There is dancing on earth as in heaven, with a majestic reference in the music to the theme of the Godhead, leading directly to the epilogue. In this we hear again the pastoral theme with which the ballet opened. Job sits, an old and humbled man, in the sunrise of spiritual prosperity surrounded by his family upon whom he bestows his blessing.[1]

Ninette de Valois' choreography splendidly realised Vaughan Williams's inspiration in spite of the small resources at her disposal in 1931. One of the earliest English ballets thus set an example of true collaboration between composer, choreographer, designer, scenarist and dancers.

[1] Dr. Cole further discusses the music of *Job* and other British ballet music in 'Some Reflections on British Ballet Music' in *The Ballet in Britain* (O.U.P. London, 1962.)

APPENDIX VI

THE CHOREOGRAPHER'S TECHNICAL INHERITANCE

PRESENT-DAY vocabularies of classical steps are descended directly from great teachers, such as Cecchetti and Vaganova, and great choreographers like Petipa and Fokine. Less well known are the schools which form the antecedents of these teachers and choreographers. Two are of particular interest. The Romantic Movement rested technically on the teaching of the School of Vestris in Paris; the Classical movement at its height made great use of the teaching of the School of Blasis at Milan.

Very little is known of the School of Vestris, except what is preserved in the work of Bournonville at Copenhagen. More is known of the School of Blasis but little has been published about its technical development, particularly the developments which contributed to the evolution of the Russian School in the last two decades of the nineteenth century.

The importance of these two schools warrants their discussion here. It will help to emphasise the technical inheritance which is common to choreographers and dancers throughout the world of classical ballet.

A. THE SCHOOL OF VESTRIS-BOURNONVILLE

August Bournonville, the great Danish teacher and choreographer, was born in Copenhagen in 1805. He studied dancing first under his father and the Italian ballet-master, Galeotti, in Copenhagen. Then he went to Paris to study under Auguste Vestris, the most renowned teacher of the day. Hence the Bournonville style is virtually the French style of Vestris. Even today one may see this style in Copenhagen carefully preserved in the Bournonville ballets. *Konservatoriet*, the one-act version of a longer earlier ballet, is the nearest thing to the School of Vestris to be seen anywhere on the contemporary stage, a work of pure classical dancing in the old French style.

On stage Bournonville introduced new elements to the School of Vestris, notably *demi-caractère* qualities from folk steps and elements of national dancing. To strengthen this side of his choreography he tended to emphasise those qualities of the teaching of Vestris which would train his dancers most suitably for his ballets, as well as the qualities which specially benefited his own technique as a dancer.

Nevertheless, in the classroom, Bournonville taught nothing but the School of Vestris. This school he imparted to the Danes and to his Swedish pupil, Christian Johansson. Johansson took the method to St. Petersburg where it reinforced the French teaching of Didelot and Petipa and was mingled with the teaching of the Italian School of Milan. Combining with the Russian physique and temperament these two schools became the Russian School brought to Paris and London by Diaghilev.

319

In 1861 Bournonville left Copenhagen for four years. As a kind of guide to his pupils he published in that year *Études chorégraphiques*, stating his principles in a foreword and listing recommended exercises and *enchaînements*. For greater clarity everything, except the French names of the steps, was written in Danish as well as French.

An authoritative analysis of the Bournonville method, based on the *Études chorégraphiques*, was made recently by Erik Bruhn and Lillian Moore in *Bournonville and Ballet Technique* (A. & C. Black, London). The authors translate the foreword in full but refrain from reprinting any of the exercises as fully. Presumably this is because 'the technical part of the book is in a sort of French balletic shorthand, without any detailed explanations, and was obviously intended for people who were already familiar with his way of combining steps and dance phrases'.

We believe it would be interesting, even helpful, to the general reader, as well as to choreographers, teachers and dancers, to read at least some of Bournonville's actual notes for exercises from the *Études chorégraphiques*. Accordingly we reproduce and translate, where necessary, the first set of exercises given for each of his main divisions of a lesson. To these we add in italics a few comments of our own.

But, first, here is the foreword in which Bournonville expounded his philosophy of ballet and art. Choreographers of today might base their own philosophy with advantage on Bournonville's.

'Dancing is an art because it demands vocation, knowledge and talent. Dancing is a fine art because it puts forward an ideal, not only of plastic beauty, but of lyric and dramatic expression.

'The beauty which it seeks to achieve is founded not on vague principles of fashion or fancy, but on firm natural laws.

'The art of mime reflects every aspect of the soul; dancing is fitted especially to express joy and to follow the rhythms of music.

'The aim of art in general and of the theatre in particular is to uplift the soul and to invigorate the spirit. Dancing, then, should be on guard particularly against the too emphatic preference of a spoiled public for effects which are as contrary to good manners and good taste as they are to the real interests of art.

'Joy is strength, rapture a weakness. Noble simplicity will always be beautiful. Display, on the other hand, ultimately becomes boring. Dancing can, with the help of music, rise to the heights of poetry. Equally it can sink to circus tricks through excess of acrobatics. Would-be difficulties are indicated by many experts, whereas the appearance of ease is achieved by a chosen few. The greatest talent is to know how to disguise technique with a quiet orderliness which is the foundation of real grace.

'To maintain this simple grace in the midst of the most tiring movements, this is the great problem of dancing. Such virtuosity can be acquired only through proper exercises designed to develop the qualities and eliminate the weaknesses which everyone, even the greatest talents, has to fight. Such are the choreographic exercises which I offer here to my dear pupils and worthy colleagues, reminding them of the oft-repeated saying that progress and skill depend less on the number of exercises than on their careful use.'

Then follow Bournonville's exercises grouped as for a class and sub-devided into sets, or series. *The full development is discussed in 'Bournonville and Ballet Technique'. He began with the fundamental positions of the body and the arms, and the different attitudes and their variants. Next he listed the principal steps of the classical vocabulary, with their variants. A study of these alone indicates the kind of technical developments which have taken place in the classical vocabulary during the hundred years since the Études was written.*

From the vocabulary Bournonville moved on to actual exercises in the order in which they might be taken in class. The emphasis was all on centre practice. Exercises allotted to the barre were few and limited, a weakness of the school corrected only within the last decade.

Obviously, Bournonville's pupils were supposed to make a selection for their daily practice from the long list he gave them. Line and turn-out do not seem to have received special attention. Batterie, elevation and pirouettes were much stressed, although Bournonville himself was not good at turns. The exercises for pirouettes introduce a great many positions of the body and combinations of these positions requiring much control, rather than the multiple pirouettes performed at speed which the Italian School particularly developed.

The exercises for elevation are divided into slow and quick, presumably large and small, ballon and batterie. They start with the frequent repetition of a very simple movement and build up into choreographic enchaînements. The dancers, Bournonville's material, obviously had strength and control, as well as speed and lightness.

He equipped them with a feeling for music and with a vocabulary which was exceptionally rich for the period. It had much more variety, for example, than the vocabulary of the Italian School suggested in Legnani's notes below. But it did not range as widely as vocabularies today.

Generally, we reproduce here only the first set of exercises (often it appears to be the most elementary) which Bournonville listed for each division of his class. The remarks are Bournonville's, except where our own are indicated in italics.

Positions and Directions

The five fundamental positions:—
(a) l'effacé
(b) le croisé
(c) l'épaulé
(d) en avant, en arrière, de côté
(e) obliquement (en avant ou en arrière)

Arm Positions

(a) Bras-bas
(b) Demi-bras
(c) Bras-droits (à la seconde)
(d) Bras-arrondis (*in front of the chest*)
(e) L'opposition (*in all directions*)
(f) Les deux bras (*above the head*)
(g) La position de la lyre
N.B.—These positions are modified according to the character of the dance and, especially, to suit the position of the head.

C.A.—24

Attitudes

(leg raised or on the ground)

(a) Effacée *(with one or two arms)*
(b) Croisée (,, ,, ,,)
(c) à l'arabesque *(effacée ou croisée)*
(d) à la couronne (,, ,, ,,)
(e) à la lyre (,, ,, ,,)

N.B.—These attitudes are developed and modified, tendues, pliées, on the sole of the foot or on point, according to the imagination of the choreographer. But they ought always to conform to the laws of good taste, guided by feeling for the requirements of the scene.

Pas de temps fondamentaux

Adagio—École ancienne

1ère Série

Demi-coupé à la première: en avant, en arrière
à la cinquième: en avant, en arrière
de côté

Dégagé et coupé-croisé: en avant, en arrière et obliquement

Temps de courante: sur les deux pieds
sur le cou-de-pied

Pas de bourrée: en avant, en arrière, croisé, ouvert, dessous et dessus, balancé

Pas tombé: de côté, en remontant, en descendant.

Pas de menuet: en avant, de côté, en tournant, pas grave.

A second, third and fourth series follow, then a fifth series (Allegretto).

Exercises at the barre

Exercises at the barre are necessary only as far as required without too much fatigue, so as to prepare for the lesson proper. Methods, for forcing the turn-out of the thighs and feet are, in my opinion, far from pretty, even ridiculous, improper, and almost always absolutely useless.

1ère Série

(a) Plié à la 1ère, relevé sur les pointes
(b) ,, ,, relevé à la seconde
(c) ,, ,, et rondejambe, en dehors
(d) ,, ,, en dedans
Changes de main et de pied
Followed by seven more series up to the eighth series.

N.B.—All these exercises are repeated without support.

Exercices d'Adagio

(Études d'Aplomb)

1ère Série

(a) Plié à la 1ère, relevé à la seconde
(b) ,, ,, à la quatrième devant et derrière

(c) Plié à la 1ère, en attitude et dégagé
(d)   „   „   croisé devant et attitude à deux bras
And so through to eight series.

Mouvements à trois temps
1ère Série

(a) Ballotté avec l'assemblé soutenu
(b)   „   avec l'attitude
(c)   „   bras contraire et amenez la jambe
(d)   „   avec plié relevé et tournant
And so through to a third series.

Temps de Pirouettes
1ère Série

(a) Dégagé, echappé et relevé à la seconde
(b)   „   „   „   en attitude
(c)   „   „   „   en rondejambe
(d)   „   „   „   sur le cou-de-pied
(e)   „   „   „   rondejambe
(f)   „   „   „   battements
(g)   „   „   „   arrondi en dehors
(h)   „   „   „   arrondi en dedans
And so through to four series.

Pirouettes
1ère Série (en dehors)

(a) La pirouette à la seconde
(b)   „   en attitude
(c)   „   en rondejambe sur le cou-de-pied
(d)   „   à battements
(e)   „   à rondesjambes
(f)   „   arrondie, devant et derrière
N.B.—For one, two or three days and arranged to match the third series of temps de pirouettes.
And so to a second series (en dedans) 'N.B.—composed to match the fourth series of temps de pirouettes'; *third series* (*jetés*); *fourth series* 'N.B.—applicable to most of the pirouettes mentioned'; *fifth series* (*pirouettes finales*).

N.B.—Virtuosity requires the second part of the pirouette to be doubled in speed and number. Turns on the whole foot are below standard and deserve no merit.

Exercices d'élévation
(Adagio)
1ère Série

(a) Plié à la cinquième. Changement de jambes
(b)   „   „   Attitude, effacée, croisée, allongée
(c)   „   „   Rondesjambes, en dehors et en dedans
And so for two series.

Temps de cou-de-pied
(Allegretto)
(a) Relevez sur les pointes et changez à la 5me.
(b) Assemblé et six changements de jambes précipités
(c) Trois changements précipités et un fondu
(d) Pliez à la 5me, relevez sur une pointe, en attitude, à la seconde, et avec dégagé dans toutes les directions
(e) Coupés sur la pointe (dans toutes les directions) et assemblé
(f) Jetés sur la pointe (dans toutes les directions) et assemblé
(g) Pas de bourrée sur les pointes (trois, cinq, neuf) et assemblé, dessous, dessus, en avant, en arrière et obliquement

Études de Ballon
(à 4 temps)
1ère Série
(a) Un demi-coupé, en avant et assemblé
(b)   ,,   ,,   en arrière et assemblé
(c) Deux demi-coupés et trois assemblés (en avant et en arrière)
(d) Deux glissades et assemblés (dev. et derr.)
(e) Deux ballonés et assemblés (dev. et derr.)
(f)   ,,   ballonés arrondis
(g)   ,,   rondejambes et assemblés arrondis
(h)   ,,   ,,   en dedans et   ,,

And so for two series. 'N.B.—All these enchaînements stop at the fourth repetition', *and thence through twelve series.*

Exercices de taqueté
(à quatre temps)
1ère Série
(a) Trois pas de bourrée dessous et deux emboîtés
(b)   ,,   ,,   ,,   dessus et   ,,   ,,
(c) Coupé-dessous, balloté, bis, quatre, emboîtés
(d)   ,,   en tournant, trois emboîtés et fouetté
(e) Quatre pas de bourrée en tournant, dessus et dessous, assemblé-dessus et six temps de cou-de-pied, finis sur une jambe.
(f) Rondejambes, coupé-dessous, jeté-dessous, bis; deux rondejambes et trois emboîtés.
(g) Glissade à trois pas-dégagés, un battement et changez de pied. Bis. Glissade à trois pas, jeté-lancé, pas de bourrée-dessus en tournant et trois emboîtés.
(h) Pas de bourrée, ouvert à trois pas, un battement, changez de pied. Bis. Deux relevés-changes, plié-fondu et relevé en tournant.
And so through two series which end à trois temps.

Pirouettes Composées

(Adagio)

1ère Série

(a) À la seconde, port de bras et en dedans
(b)   ,,   ,,   ,,   et en attitude
(c) En attitude en dehors, port de bras et renversé
(d) En rondejambe, port de bras et sur le cou-de-pied, terminée en attitude
(e) Sur le cou-de-pied, port de bras et en attitude à la couronne, à la lyre ou à l'arabesque.
(f) à rondejambes, terminée à la seconde, port de bras, en dedans et arrivez à l'attitude allongée, en tous genres.
   2nd series in tempo di marcia.
   3rd series.

Temps battus

(Allegretto)

1ère Série

(a) Deux entrechats à quatre, relevé sur deux pointes
(b)   ,,   ,,   dégagé à demi-hauteur, à la seconde.
(c)   ,,   ,,   dégagé effacé ou croisé-du-pied
(d)   ,,   attitude, effacé ou croisée, en tous genres
   (*N.B.*—(b), (c) et (d) sur le bout de la pointe)
(e) Deux entrechats relevé sur les deux pointes, en tournant
(f)   ,,   ,,   et trois temps de cou-de-pied
   2nd, 3rd, 4th, 5th series
   6th series (Danse d'homme)
   7th series, 8th, 9th and 10th series (*last three all* danse d'homme).
   Bournonville ends the Études *with remarks about the exercises, four pages of wise counsel.*

B. THE SCHOOL OF VESTRIS-BLASIS

In his *Traité de la Danse* (1820) and *The Code of Terpsichore* (1830) Blasis gave a very full account of his theories and teaching methods. These were developed during his direction of the Imperial Academy of Dancing at La Scala from 1837 onwards. No similar account remains of the way these methods evolved under Blasis's successors during the rest of the century, nor do we know all the details of the technical training which made Italian ballerinas the world's leading dancers at that time.

Examining material generously placed at his disposal by the director of the museum at La Scala, Peter Brinson came across records which go some way to fill this gap. An exercise book contained very full details of the weekly cycle of classes given by Caterina Beretta and Cesare Coppini, two principal authorities of the Italian School, to the young Pierina Legnani. The exercises are recorded, apparently, in Legnani's own hand and were probably written down for reference during her first tours abroad. Since the Italian teachers tended to give their pupils cycles of lessons which hardly varied week in week out these notes present a very fair idea of the teaching methods of the School for advanced pupils in the seventies and eighties. They indicate, too, the kind of technique with which one of the greatest of the Italian ballerinas astonished St. Petersburg from 1893–1901. Here they are, complete with her occasional spelling mistakes.

Méthode de Madame Caterina Beretta
copié par (or pour) l'élève Pierina Legnani

Leçon de danse pour le jour de Lundi

No.
1. Exercice à la barre
2. Port des bras simples
3. Grands battements en croix
4. 2 petits battements et un grand d'un côté et de l'autre
5. Exercice au milieu marché
6. Changements du pieds pliés chaques

Adagios

1. Adagio composé
2. Grand fouetté (12 fois)
3. Renverser à la 2nde de 2 tours, puis en attitude le même.

Pirouettes

1. Pirouettes à la 2nde d'un, deux et trois tours
2. Pirouettes sur le cou-de-pied le même
3. Pirouettes en attitude le même

Allegros

1. 8 assemblés arrétes en avant et en arrière puis (*unreadable*) assemblé et deux petits changements
2. Jeté et petits battements, 6 simples et 8 doubles en avant et en arrière
3. Enchaînement des petits battements.
4. Jeté battement rond de jambe en dehors battement rond de jambe en dedans d'un côté et de l'autre.
5. Enchaînement des petits battements sur la pointe
6. Autres enchaînements sur la pointe
7. Rond de jambe pointu (*unreadable*) 4me devant derrière temps de cuisse finir 4me devant, derrière, devant réléver rond de jambe assemblé derrière et entrechat quatre
8. La quadrilles et variations
9. Petits changements des pieds finis grands battements

Leçon de danse pour le jour de Mardi

No.
1. Exercice à la barre
2. Port des bras en 4me positions
3. 8 Grands battements en toutes les positions

4. 2 Grands arretés et 3 de suite
5. Exercice au milieu avec l'adagio
6. Changements des pieds pliés de suite

Adagios

1. Développé à la 2nde, puis avec 2 tours, puis un tour lentement
2. La même chose en attitude
3. Relévés en face, avant, derrière et tour

Pirouettes

1. Pirouettes à la 2nde en dehors passer à l'arabesque en tournant
2. Un, deux et trois tours sur le cou-de-pied en 4me position
3. Pirouette en attitude en dedans et passer à l'arabesque

Allegros

1. 16 Assemblés de suite en avant et en arrière puis assemblé et deux petites changements.
2. Brisé et pas de bourré en avant puis glissé brisé derrière sur une jambe jeté et pas de bourré en dessous
3. Échappé sur les pointes de deux tours sur la pointe
4. La même chose en attitude
5. Cabriole en attitude retomber 4me devant et 2 tours renverser en attitude
6. Échappé et 3 rélévés sur la pointe en attitude
7. La même chose à la 2nde et touts rélévés
8. Enchaînement des échappés (Variation)
9. Petits changements des pied finis grands battements

Leçon de danse pour le jour de Mercredi

No.
1. Exercice à la barre
2. Port des bras sur les pointes
3. Grands battements de travers avec les bras en positions
4. Grands battements à la rond-de-jambe
5. Exercice au milieu tout d'un coté (les battements à terre en croix)—*this may belong below*
6. Entrechat quatre et changement des pieds finis deux (*or* puis deux battement à terre en croix)

Adagios

1.
2. } Compositions et enchainements
3.

Pirouettes

1. Couppé temps de cuisse et 2 tours attitude en déhor tour des 4 fois
2. Couppé temps de cuisse et deux tours sur le cou de pied la? taille? très pliés et avec les bras

3. Coupé fouetté 2 tours en attitude dedans pas de bourrée tour de reins deux fois coupé temps de cuisse assemblé rond de jambe en l'air et 3 sur le cou de pied

Allegros

1. Enchainements des assemblés
2. Second enchainement
3. ⎫
4. ⎪
5. ⎬ Touts enchainements de ballon
6. ⎪
7. ⎪
8. ⎭
9. Petits changements des pieds, puis grands battements

Leçon de danse pour le jour de jeudi

No.
1. Exercice à la barre
2. Port de bras marches
3. Grands battements pointu en touts positions
4. 6 grands battements de suite d'un coté et de l'autre
5. Exercice au milieu avec l'adagios
6. Changements des pieds sur les pointes

Adagios

1. 2 Grands changements, 2 tours en dehor renverser à la 2nd.
2. La même chose en attitude
3. Grand port des bras (*unreadable*) arabesque en tournant temps de cuisse en avant, en arrière, en avant entrechat 5 et jété

Pirouettes

1. Pirouette en déhors faisant petits rond de jambes assemblé et un tour en l'air
2. 2 tours en déhors et en dedans sur le cou de pied de suite 4 fois, puis 3 tours.
3. Pirouette à la seconde en dedans pas de bourré passer à la seconde déhors toujours en tournant et 3 tours sur le cou de pied

Allegros

1. Assemblé et entrechat quatre puis assemblé et petits changements
2. 8 jeté tres haute et 16 petits en avant et en arrière
3. 8 Sissones battus en diagonale d'un coté et de l'autre
4. Entrechat 5 en tournant d'un coté et de l'autre
5. 2 Brisés sur une jambe brisé et pas de bourrée
6. Grand fouetté et ballotté
7. Rélévé sur les pointes et entrechat six
8. Enchainements des grands fouettés
9. Petits changements puis grands battements

Leçon de danse pour le jour de Vendredi

1. Exercice à la barre
2. Port des bras simples
3. Grands battements en croix
4. Grands battements à la 2nde arretés chaqu'un
5. Exercice au milieu marché
6. Plier beaucoup et rond de jambe en l'air

Adagios

1. 2 tours developpé a la 2nde appuyer deux fois changer la jambe et 2 tours à la renversée
2. Fouetté et ballonné 12 fois
3. Developpé à la 2nde passer a l'arabesque tourner doucement et puis toujours plus vite et finir très lent

Pirouettes

1. Pirouette a la 2nde en dedans et passer à l'arabesque
2. Grand pirouette sur la cuisse finir 4eme derrière grand rond de jambe très lent finir à la 2nde.
3. 3 tours sur le cou de pied appuyer
4. 5eme avant et un tour en l'air

Allegros

1. Assemblé et grand temps levé puis assemblé et 2 petits changements
2. Cabriole en attitude passer 4eme devant et poser sur la pointe attitude
4. Jeté en avant et cabriole 6 fois grand échappé sauté temps levé appuyer et grand jeté en tournant finis avec tour de reins
5. Coupé et cabriole en arrière de suite en diagonale
6. 2 pas de bourrés en dessous gargouillarde en dedans pas de bourré brisé pas de bourrée entrechat 4 et échappé sur les pointes
7. Grands fouettés en tournant sur les pointes très lent
8. Grands jetés très bas au tour du salon
9. Petits changements finis grands battements

Leçon de danse pour le jour de Samedi

1. Exercice à la barre
2. Port des bras à 4eme position
3. 8 grands battements en toutes positions avec les bras
4. 3 grands battements et un rond de jambe
5. Exercice au milieu en tournant
6. Plier entrechat six et entrechat quatre

Adagios

1. Deux tours developpé à la second fouetté en dehors et en dedans
2. Developpé à la 2nde descendre avec la taille retourner à place et 2 tours en attitude en dehors

3. Rond de jambe en dehors 2 fois, petits battements 2 fois passer attitude et 2 tours lentements

Pirouettes

1. Pirouette à la 2nde en déhors passer attitude tour de reins et pas de bourrée
2. Pirouettes a la seconde et serrer sur le cou de pied
3. 3 tours sur la cuisse et finir à l'arabesque très bas

Allegros

1. Assemblé et 3 relevés sur une jambe puis assemblé et 2 petits changes
2. Pas de bourré en dessus et cabriole en attitude
3. Brisé cabriole entrechat 4 ouvert et entrechat 3
4. Pas de bourré en tournant en dehors brisé pas de bourré et finir la tour et brisé en face
5. 4 Brisés sur une jambe puis en tournant brisé fouetté et 2 brisés derrière
6. Enchainement des rond des jambes
7. Toutes enchainements des réléves sur les pointes très vite
8. Toutes des galoppes au tour du salon
9. Petits changements puis grands battements sur la pointe

Méthode de M. Cesare Coppini
copié par (or pour) l'élève Pierina Legnani

Leçon de danse pour le jour de Lundi

1. Exercice à la barre *normal*
2. Port des bras simples
3. Exercice au milieu
4. 16 grands battements en avant et 16 en arrière
5. Changements des pieds sur les pointes

Grands temps d'adagios

1. Grand coupé
2. Developpé en tournant en toutes positions
3. Grand fouetté ballotté a la (*unreadable*)

Pirouettes

1. Temps de preparations pirouettes (en face)
2. Pirouette de 3 tours en dehors sur le cou de pied
3. Pirouette d'un tour à la 2nde et casser deux sur le cou de pied

Allegros

1. Assemblé soutenus puis de suite
2. 3 petits battements et deux ballonées
3. Coupé et rond de jambe sauté
4. Ronds des jambes en l'air très hauts
5. Arabesques et posés sur la pointe
6. 2 Échappés sur les pointes et 2 tours sur le cou de pied

7. Une variation
8. Changements des pieds 16 hauts et 48 petits

Leçon de danse pour le jour de Mardi

1. Exercice à la barre *composé*
2. Plier en première position
3. Ports des bras composés
4. Exercice au milieu
5. Rélévés sur les pointes en Ier position

Grands temps d'adagio

1. Developpés en face en toutes positions puis grand rond de jambe
2. Rélévé rond de jambe et fouetté en face et en tournant en dehors et en dedan
3. 2 tours renverser à la 2nde d'un coté et de l'autre

Pirouettes

1. Pirouette à la 2nde en dehors rélévé et 2 tours attitude en dedans
2. 3 tour à la 2nde en dehors 2 ronds de jambes (*unreadable*) tour et fouetté en face finir à l'arabesque derrière
3. 3 tours à la 2nde en dehors et relever sur la pointe en face

Allegros

1. 3 assemblés et un brisé
2. Cabrioles composés en avant et en arrière
3. Brisé et cabriole à la 2nde très haut
4. 2 jeté en dessous en tournant assemblé et rond de jambe 3 fois (lentement) et tour des reins
5. Entré des pas de bourrés
6. Pirouettes d'un tour sur la pointe très vite
7. Une variation
8. Changements des pieds 16 très hauts puis entrechat quatre et entrechat trois

Leçon de danse pour le jour de Mercredi

1. Exercice à la barre *normale*
2. Port des bras marchés
3. Exercice au milieu
4. Grands battements sur la $\frac{1}{2}$ pointe
5. Échappés sur les pointes

Grands temps d'adagios

1. Développé à l'arabesque 4eme devant fouetté développé à la 2nde fouetté développé 4eme derrière puis deux tours en dedans sur le cou de pied finir 4eme devant pointu
2. Relevés en face et en tournant en dehors et en dedans

Pirouettes

1. Les quatre pirouettes en dedans

2. 3 tours à la 2nde en dehors puis fouetté en face et s'en tournant
3. Exercice des pirouettes sur le cou de pied

Allegro

1. Assemblé 2 changements et 2 assembles de suite
2. Grands jeté très hauts d'un coté et de l'autre
3. Jeté battements en avant et en arrière
4. Coupé et 3 ronds de jambes en tournant en dehors et en dedans
5. Grand fouetté Ballotté sauté à la Blasis
6. Un developpé en face et un en tournant sur la pointe d'un coté et de l'autre
7. Une variation
8. 2 changements des pieds et un tour sur la pointe d'un coté et de l'autre

Leçon de danse pour le jour de jeudi

1. Exercice à la barre *composé*
2. Plier en 1ere position
3. Port des bras composés
4. Exercice au milieu
5. Changements des pieds sur les pointes

Grands temps d'adagios

1. 2 tours developpé 4eme devant fouetté puis 2 tour attitude dehors
2. Grand fouetté ballotté à la Blasis
3. Pas-de-Chaconne

Pirouettes

1. Pirouette à la 2nde en dehors puis relever un tour sur la pointe en pliant les jambes
2. 3 tours à la 2nde passer en attitude 3 tours, tour de reins et pas de bourré
3. 3 tours sur le cou de pied 2 ronds de jambes sauté en face assemblé derrière et entrechat quatre

Allegros

1. Assemblé et temps levé battu
2. Jeté et entrechat 5 d'un coté et de l'autre en avant et en arrière
3. (*Unreadable*) ronds des jambes retombés rélévés sur la pointe
3. ? ronds des jambes retombés rélévés sur la pointe
4. Coupé fouettés deux fois, chassé très grand de coté et 2 grands jétés derrière
5. Brisé pris avec préparation et entrechat 6 puis le quatre des brisés
6. Un echappé sur les pointes et 2 petits changements 2 fois puis 6 changements de suite le tout sur les pointes
7. Une variation
8. Changements des pieds 16 pliés et 32 vite petits

Leçon de danse pour le jour de Vendredi

1. Exercice à la barre *Normale*
2. Ports des bras simples

3. Exercice au milieu
4. Grands battements sur les pointes
5. Réléves sur les pointes en Iere position

Grands temps d'adagios

1. Arabesques et posés
2. Adagio composé
3. Glissé devant un tour à l'arabesque fouetté en tournant en dedans attitude fouetté en tournant arabesque croisée et 2 tours renversé à la seconde

Pirouettes

1. Pirouette à la 2nde en dedans et passer à l'arabesque toujours en tournant
2. 3 tours sur le cou de pied finir à l'arabesque derrière glissé cabriole jeté attitude en tournant et pas de bourrée
3. Grands renversés finir à l'arabesque reguillère

Allegros

1. Assemblé et entrechat 4
2. Jeté et 3 temps élévés sur la pointe très lentement
3. Cabriole brisé sisonne et entrechat cinque
4. Coupé rond des jambes assemblé et grand rond des jambes en l'air
5. Entrechat quatre et entrechat six
6. Temps de cuisse et entrechat 6 en diagonale
7. Une variation
8. Changements des pieds 16 hauts et 32 petits

Leçon de danse pour le jour de samedi

1. Exercice à la barre composé
2. Plier en 1ère position
3. Ports des bras composés
4. Exercice au milieu (marché)
5. Echappés sur les pointes

Grands temps d'adagios

1. 2 tours developpé 4eme devant plier relever un tour en dedans attitude plier relever un tour arabesque puis 2 tours renverser
2. Grands attitudes composée en dehors
3. Jete derrière, tour attitude en dedans 2 fois puis renversé à la 2nde contre temps, temps de cuisse et 2 pas de chat

Pirouettes

1. 3 tours en dehors à la 2nde et un grand rond de jambe finis à la 2nde sur la demie pointe
2. Grande pirouette sur la cuisse passer attitude renversé et pas de bourré
3. Grands pirouette à la 2nde et rélévér 3 fois sur la pointe la 4eme la $\frac{1}{2}$ pointe pliant la jambe attitude renversé et pas de bourré

Allegro

1. Assemblé 2 petits changements et 2 temps de cuisse
2. Coupé rond de jambe, 2 en face et 3 en tournant
3. Brisés sur une jambe en dessou et en dessus d'un coté et de l'autre
4. Grand fouetté sauté temps de cuisse et jeté en avant
5. Enchainements de vigueur
6. 2 Developpés d'un tour sur la pointe à la 2nde et 2 tours sur le cou de pied
7. Variation
8. Changements des pieds 16 petits, 16 sur les pointes, 16 pliés, 16 tres hauts

Notes by Peggy van Praagh

The picture presented is of a girl of great determination, character and energy. One presumes the notes are in her own hand because the writing is the same for both teachers and the title suggests this. Even the grammar and spelling errors suggest a pupil.

Barre—it is unfortunate that there are no details of the *Barre* work. Presumably, a set *barre* was used which was the same every day.

Port de bras: There seem to have been a series of these, *simples*, *marchés* etc. but not many variations.

Centre Pliés: In 1st position only.

Centre Work—like the whole class, always seems to finish with *changements* or a small *sauté* step.

Point shoes must have been worn throughout as exercises at the end of the first section are sometimes done *sur la pointe*, and there is no mention of special *pointe* steps.

Adage—Seems to vary between
    (a) short simple movements repeated many times (e.g. Beretta's second exercise for Monday.)
    (b) composed adage (i.e. invented?)
    (c) Set adage, presumably from Blasis, but used only by Coppini.
    (d) Slow (presumably) turning movements.

Pirouettes—Since a whole section is devoted to these, they were obviously very important. Legnani's virtuosity in pirouettes was one of her qualities which impressed the Russians. Pirouettes, singly and in series in various positions, were practised every day.

Many *renversés* were used also. These are used very rarely today in the West.

Allegro—Very limited number of steps used in very simple combinations. 1st exercise invariably includes *assemblés*. Many *ronds des jambes* are used and beaten steps. Many *changements* always finish each class.

General—The shape of the class is very similar to that in use today, except that there are more pirouettes given as a separate study.

Combinations appear simpler throughout with a stress on repetition of particular movements, and slow tempi. This would be inclined to give strength and control but would build more muscle, and would require a less alert intellect than is demanded today.

Some adage and enchaînements are very similar to those of Cecchetti, but there is less variety and not the daily grouping of steps in allegro which he set out.

There is no mention of Directions of the Body (e.g. *croisé*, *effacé*, etc. and no *épaulement*) although it seems likely that these were used, even though not named. It was Cecchetti who classified the eight directions of the body.

THE PRESERVATION OF BALLETS: FILM

BESIDES preservation in dancers' memories, critical records, notation and film records, stage ballets are increasingly being produced in special film versions for cinema and television. These film versions are not the same as filmed records of a stage production. They require enormous preparation involving reinterpretation of the choreography and, often, cuts or changes in the action.

Because these film versions are likely to increase and exert a growing influence over audiences, if not over choreographers, we reproduce below two sections from the script and camera script prepared by Margaret Dale for her film version of *Giselle* on B.B.C. television in 1958, with Nadia Nerina of the Royal Ballet as Giselle, partnered by Nicolai Fadeyechev of the Bolshoi Ballet as Albrecht. The pages illustrate the detailed preparation, rearrangement and rehearsal required and are also a tribute to the remarkably high standard of the B.B.C.'s ballet productions, for which Miss Dale is generally responsible.

Both sections cover the early moments of the ballet from Albrecht's first appearance to Giselle's first appearance. Section one is the script; section two the corresponding camera instructions.

Section 1: Script

Change of music No. 2. Prince comes out of cottage door on right.
CUT to closer shot of Prince as he mimes reference to his peasant disguise. Pan him over to Giselle's cottage door. He listens at the door.
CUT to 2-shot Prince, foreground, back to cam. (Fig. 11.) Wilfred comes out of Prince's cottage rather anxious. Says that no good will come of this. Prince won't listen, takes him by the shoulders in a friendly way and says he is quite safe in his disguise. He turns and looks again at Giselle's cottage door, with his back to Wilfred. Wilfred slowly and reluctantly exits up-stage right.
CUT to close shot Prince (reverse angle? or back view, or side view). He knocks on cottage door and then hides himself by side of cottage. N.B.—Possible see Giselle pass window first looking out (Music to fill up).
(*Allegro moto de danse*)
CUT to close shot door as it opens. Giselle is framed in doorway for an instant. She looks young and radiant.
CUT to long shot. As she dances round looking for whoever knocked.
CUT to mid-shot on mime about knocking.
CUT to long shot as she runs around again (reverse angle shot as she faces up-stage?) and for *ballotté* step, and for *attitude* listening step. See Prince in background still beside the side of her cottage. He blows her kisses while she holds the *attitudes*.

CUT to medium-close-up Giselle—she guesses who it is and is both
    excited and nervous.
CUT to long shot. She goes over to Prince's cottage and looks in *window*. It
    is plain that she is in love with the man she associates with that cottage.

Section 2: Cameras

CAMS	VISION	SOUND
On change of music		
(7) CUT CAM 2 Tight L.S. Albrecht. He comes out of Woodman's cottage door. Pan him to Giselle's cottage. See Wilfred.	Wilfred.	
(8) CUT CAM 1 C.S. Giselle's cottage door. Albrecht listens at door.		
(9) CUT CAM 2 L. 2-shot Albrecht and Wil- fred, as Albrecht comes to Cam.		
(10) CUT CAM 1 M.S. Albrecht		
(11) CUT CAM 2 M.L. 2-shot Albrecht and Wilfred as they come to Cam. Albrecht says he is in love with Giselle.	Albrecht tells Wilfred he loves Giselle.	
(12) CUT CAM 3 2-shot Albrecht and Wilfred. Wilfred tries to stop Albrecht but he tells him to go.	Tells Wilfred to go.	
(13) CUT CAM 1 Med. L.S. Albrecht. See him knock on Giselle's cottage door.	Knocking.	
(14) CUT CAM 2 L.S. Giselle's cottage. See Albrecht hiding.	Hiding.	
(15) CUT CAM 5 (14°) C.S. Giselle's cottage door, as it opens see Giselle. As she dances		
(16) CUT CAM 2 (28°) L.S. Giselle.	Giselle comes out of cottage.	
(17) CUT CAM 1 (24°) Tight L.S. Giselle *ballottés*.	*Ballottés*.	

*Note—Abbreviations: L.S.=Long Shot; C.S.=Close Shot; M.S.=Medium
            Shot, and so on.*

C.A.—25

THE TRAINING OF CHOREOGRAPHERS

A. *The Soviet Choreographer*

AFTER the Second World War the growth of ballet throughout the countries of the Soviet Union and its allies required special measures for training choreographers and choreographic teachers. Accordingly, in 1946, a four-year course was established at the Lunacharsky State Theatrical Institute in Moscow, and a department for training teachers of choreography was established at the Leningrad State Conservatoire. This marked the beginning of higher education for ballet in the U.S.S.R.

The following description of the course and its development in Moscow was given by A. V. Shatin, dean of the Institute's Choreographic Department, at an All-Union choreographic conference in Moscow in 1960. It has been translated by Eleanor Fox, summarised by us and combined with information gained from a visit to the department.

At the conference two viewpoints emerged on the problem of the organisational training basis. One group considered that the department should be founded as an independent higher educational institution. The second group held that it would be more valuable to open the department organisationally based on an already established higher educational establishment, the latter already possessing considerable experience in the training of various specialists. The latter viewpoint won since the Ministry of Higher Education decided to make the ballet-masters' department part of the Institute in Moscow.

The first group of students numbered 12—representing the R.S.F.S.R., Tadjikistan, Uzbekistan, Turkmenia, Latvia, Estonia and the Ukraine. Seven of the first intake are today recognised as leading people in their chosen field and have won governmental awards and decorations.

In the fourteen years of the department's existence 79 pupils in all have been accepted and have completed the course; since the second intake, students from Eastern Europe have been accepted.

What is the background of the students accepted for the course and what specialised training have they already had before enrolment? As a rule, the students have already been selected in their own localities and been put forward by Republican Ministries of Culture as people socially (from society's standpoint) and artistically suitable for such further training. They are almost always ballet dancers who want to be choreographers. A condition of acceptance for the course is almost without exception a complete secondary specialist education and at least two years' practical work in a theatre or ensemble. Of the 58 Soviet students, 45 had the necessary qualifications. They had completed their studies at Moscow, Leningrad, Kiev and other institutions or in choreographic studios in those areas without training schools. The remaining 13 were accepted from national dance ensembles, the circus, etc.

The Institute worked out a system of entrance examinations and a methodology for them which made it possible to learn in advance something of the capacities of the potential entrants and made it possible, too, accurately to assess the value of admitting them.

Nowadays, the Institute does its best to get to know the potential candidates for entry long before the actual entrance examinations and this has undoubtedly improved the work of the entrance examining boards, reducing to a minimum the margin of possible error, though errors do occur.

The actual *syllabus* for the ballet-masters has undergone many changes in detail over the years, while retaining its overall features. It needs to be stressed how complex and multiform is the knowledge required of a ballet-master and that these requirements must naturally be taken into account when planning the course.

The ballet-masters at the Institute take the full drama theatre producer's course plus a considerable additional course related to choreographic work. Particular attention is devoted to those subjects which deal with musical education—theory and history of music, pianoforte, etc. The main aspects of this work are covered by the subject titled 'Study of the Ballet Keyboard'. This latter has been extensively developed after its establishment by the senior conductor A. D. Tseitlin. The subject is of such interest that an increasing number of young composers working on ballet music like to attend these lessons.

The special lecture cycle entitled 'Composition of the Dance' includes the following sub-headings—composition of the classical dance, composition of the folk dance on the stage, and composition of the historical dance, from all of which it may be seen that study of such subjects gets the students into the habit of preparing choreographic work with limited artistic means, while dealing with many aspects of the choreographer's art.

'Production' and 'Mounting a Production' are two other main headings for subjects studied. The subject title 'The Art of the Ballet Master' is central to the whole of the subject matter taught. This subject is divided into theoretical and practical. Of late years the creative side of this subject, involving the student in the preparation of an independent production, has grown enormously. The number of productions the student has to prepare during his study course has increased. Such productions increase in complexity and length, beginning with excerpts and finishing at the end of the course with the student's preparation of an entire production.

Students study a number of established choreographic masterpieces, such as *Swan Lake*, *Giselle* and others, but the main attention of the work with the students is given to their own independent study and their training as capable, creative ballet-masters able to make big demands of themselves.

Alongside the general teaching carried out under the direction of trained teachers, students have a considerable number of hours of individual tuition with their tutors and individual lessons with pianists so that they can prepare their practical work.

The students are fortunate in being able to work out their productions with the young dancers of the Bolshoi and other theatres. This exchange of creative experience often leads ballet theatre personnel to take an interest in the Institute's external studies courses of all kinds and sometimes in the ballet-master's course. An example of this is furnished by the acceptance this year (1960) of Yuri Zhdanov, Honoured Artist of the R.S.F.S.R., for the first year of the ballet-master's course. He helped to stage some of the student work as far back as the early years of the department's work.

The great interest shown by established ballet dancers in the Institute's external courses leads one to the view that it would do well to consider establishing these external courses rather more firmly and taking them out of their experimental stage. The time also appears to have come to consider the establishment of some form of assistance to professional ballet-masters of great practical experience who want to extend their knowledge. They come from the ranks of directors of amateur dance groups, from folk dance theatres and national dance ensembles.

The department is considering expansion of its work and to this end has appointed three ballet-masters as assistants. Those who teach the special subject come directly within the purview of the Chair of Choreography, headed by Professor R. V. Zakharov. The Chair staff is working on new syllabus material, some research is in progress and it is hoped that several books will be published shortly.

The first 12 students, who graduated in 1950, are all working, as are some of the 45 Soviet students who have graduated so far in the leading ballet companies and dance groups of the country and 14 of them are chief ballet-masters.

Twenty national (non-Russian) ballet productions have been staged by the students, including two which were the diploma (final qualifying examination) work of the students concerned and which won Stalin Prizes. It is interesting to see the national ballets gradually emerging from the use of nothing but historical subject-matter.

In addition to ballet-master's work a number of the Institute's graduates have prepared and had accepted successful ballet librettos and many have won high government awards and recognition. The press is very good about reviewing their productions.

At the time of writing this report (1960) there are 37 students and 3 post-graduate students studying in the ballet-master's department and these include, in addition to Soviet students, those from France, Yugoslavia, China and East European countries.

Students are helping to run amateur ballet groups and give dance recitals in factories and on farms. Many third- and fourth-year students are responsible for acting as assistants or even chief ballet-masters in the production of a variety of short and full-length ballets.

Syllabus Notes. The syllabus of the department's course on 'The Art of Choreography' may be summarised as follows:

First Cycle. Composition of Choreography. This begins by using limited material. Some folk dances of the Soviet Union are studied, for example, and students are then taught how to compose using these steps— called folk stage dance. Compositions are based later on the classical dance, on historical dances such as those of the sixteenth century, and on 'dances of everyday life' from the first half of the twentieth century. This first section also includes production, staging and ballet design taught, not in isolation, but separately and then interrelated.

Second Cycle. Principles of Musical Theory. A very large subject, including all kinds of music, this is taught in parallel with the history of music. It includes some attention to composition and much study of ballet music and musical dramaturgy. The student is taught to understand the ideas in music in order to comprehend musical form and meaning.

Final subject in this section is the study and playing of the piano in order to help student's appreciation of music.

Focussed, of course, on choreography, all these subjects are taught all the time throughout the four years of the course in the department. The syllabus for each of the four years, therefore, seems on paper to be always the same, but is not really so because the emphasis is varied, e.g.

1st Year. Emphasis may be on content and plot.
2nd Year. Emphasis perhaps on music with much attention given to time factor.
3rd Year. Emphasis on stage space.
4th Year. Methods of work. Creation of choreographic images and characterisation. The element of mime and acting in choreography.

Each year becomes gradually more complicated and more intense. At the end of the year the student must fulfil certain tests, as follows:

1st Year. Show proper understanding of music and produce a scene of seven minutes, based on folk dance, which creates, develops and resolves a situation. The scene must include a solo, *pas de deux* and crowd scene. Usually these scenes are quite original.
2nd Year. The same, but can use a basis of classical dance so that the resources are wider.
3rd Year. (a) Student prepares the first act of a full-length ballet, thinking of it as a full-length ballet with characters conceived accordingly.
  (b) Preparation of dances for an opera.
4th Year. Student works out a full-length ballet. It is impossible for the examiners to be shown the whole of this so significant fragments are shown indicating the development of characters and the climaxes.

The student also has to perform two exercises in the creation of character.
  (a) 4 students (e.g.) chose four birds and had to show the image of the bird's type rather than its physical manifestation.
  (b) Students had to be able to portray in choreography well-known roles such as Violetta and other operatic characters.

If the student passes the full four-year course he spends the first six months of the fifth year taking stock of what he has learned and gathering it all in to a theory for himself. The final six months are spent preparing a whole production in a professional theatre. For this graduation task the student often returns home to his own theatre. He may use a subject chosen for him or he may choose his own subject. Sometimes his designer and composer also use the ballet to fulfil the graduation tasks of their own courses so that all three collaborators hope to graduate through the ballet.

For physical material throughout the course the students use fellow students and/or young Bolshoi dancers.

B. *The British Choreographer*

No regular course of choreographic training yet exists in Britain. Opportunities for initial experience are confined to choreographic

performances sponsored by the Royal Ballet, occasional student performances by various schools, and the performances of the Sunday Ballet Club.
We believe that a proper study course would be invaluable, not only
for potential choreographers but also for potential *répétiteurs* charged
with the reproduction of a choreographer's work.

Ideally, such a course should last two or three years. To meet current
British needs and conditions, however, we propose an initial short course
of six months. This should be subsidised and should be under the direction
of someone with university qualifications, familiar with the fine arts, but
not necessarily a dancer. If this were so the assistant director should be a
dancer/choreographer/teacher fully qualified to conduct the craft aspects
of choreographic training. It does not matter, in fact, which of these two
persons is nominally in charge of the course so long as the direction is a
partnership between craft training and the wider aesthetic training which
a university mind can contribute. Intellectually, the course should be of
university standard.

We envisage three terms of seven weeks each, divided by two holidays,
each of one week. There should be not more than twelve students,
experienced dancers, preferably six men, six women.

Instruction would be given by visiting lecturers, practitioners in their
own field, and by individual tuition or discussion seminars conducted by
the resident staff. The resident staff would be small, consisting, at least, of a
Director, assistant director, classical dance teacher, musical director/pianist
and secretary. Minimum accommodation and equipment required would
be one rehearsal room with *barre*, mirrors, piano, tape recorder and record
player; one lecture room with tables, chairs, blackboard, projection screen,
slide projector, film projector and, of course, appropriate books and
note-books.

If possible, the course should be full-time. If it has to be part-time its
length would need to be extended proportionately. It should seek to
collaborate with drama and music schools, particularly in its composition
classes.

Generally speaking the mornings would be devoted to dance classes,
including a study of various dance vocabularies, and to practical work,
including rehearsals of student compositions. The afternoons would be
devoted to theoretical study including individual tutorials or seminars and
visits to museums, art classes and so on. The evenings would be free with
special arrangements made for visits to appropriate concerts, plays and
ballet performances.

Assuming instruction periods of 1½ hours each, two such periods can be
provided each morning and afternoon. This allows seventy periods of
theoretical instruction and seventy practical periods in each term, although
practical work would receive a greater share of time in the third term in
view of the advanced nature of the compositions.

We propose the following syllabus:

TERM I

History of Choreography. From the Ballet de Cour to 1830, including social
history, period dances and deportment.

History of Music. 17th–early 19th centuries. Principles of music. Elementary musical theory and eurhythmics. Use of music by choreographers of the period. Harmony.

History of Stage Design. 17th–early 19th centuries, including history of costume.

Daily Class, including study of contemporary dance vocabularies.

Elementary Dance Composition. Theory of space. Directions of the body. Composition of a solo or *pas de deux* in period, classical or free techniques. Stage-craft.

Composition of Libretti. Analysis of existing libretti. Elements of dramatic construction. Choreographic treatment of themes.

TERM 2

History of Choreography. 1830–1900 including social history, period and national dances, classical mime, deportment. Study and analysis of established repertoire.

History of Music. 1830–1900. Principles of music. Elementary musical theory and harmony. Use of music by choreographers of the period.

History of Stage Design. 1830–1900, including history of costume and stage lighting. Influence of costume on choreography.

Daily Class, including study of contemporary dance vocabularies. Eurhythmics.

Intermediate Dance Composition. Stage-craft. Composition of group dances to existing music, using a maximum of six dancers with one week for rehearsals. Preparation of advanced compositions, including the commissioning of a score from a student composer.

Composition of Libretti. Original compositions by students analysed and discussed in seminars.

TERM 3

History of Choreography. Idioms of the 20th century. Choreographers of the 20th century. Study and analysis of established repertoire.

History of Music. Composers of the 20th century. Principles of collaboration between choreographers and composers. Preparation of music for rehearsal.

History of Stage Design. Designers of the 20th century. Principles of collaboration between designers and choreographers. Contemporary lighting and stage production.

Daily Class, including study of contemporary dance vocabularies.

Advanced Dance Composition. Ballets to commissioned scores for eight to twelve dancers with an outline of design, costumes and lighting plot. Staging of successful ballets in collaboration with established workshop organisations.

THE EDUCATION OF CRITICS AND AUDIENCES.
THE UNIVERSITY CONTRIBUTION

THE most effective way to extend critical and audience appreciation of choreography is to create works which appeal to the public because they are truthful, human and well constructed. Every art, however, has its conventions and its important works from the past. Full enjoyment of an art comes only from understanding its history and creative problems.

Critics play a significant part in the day-to-day transmission of this understanding. But the most powerful and lasting impression is made by agencies which can educate critics and audiences alike. Of these agencies, which include the schools, the most important are the universities.

Universities can help by providing internal and external courses.

Internal Courses

Since no academic post yet exists in Britain to study the history or aesthetics of choreography a beginning could be made by allied departments of drama, music or the fine arts.

An annual course of eight or more lectures on the history or aesthetics of choreography, delivered under the guidance of such departments, might be made available to members of a particular university, or even to members of the university and the public in the manner of the Slade lectures at Oxford. This would provide an introduction to students who might contemplate ballet criticism as a career.

In time, of course, such lectures would need to widen their scope in order to give a proper grounding in music and theatre design to students seriously wishing to undertake ballet criticism. Potential ballet critics should certainly study dance notation in order to acquire a knowledge of the classical vocabulary.

The art of ballet is sufficiently established in Britain to justify at least one university in providing an annual course of such lectures. The quality of ballet criticism greatly depends upon such help.

External Courses

The help which universities can give is discussed at greater length in *The Ballet in Britain*, edited by Peter Brinson (Oxford University Press, 1962). Here it can be seen that a number of university extra-mural departments, notably those of Oxford, Cambridge and London, have arranged several series of lectures on aspects of ballet. There is no doubt that such courses are a principal means of raising audience appreciation.

What is needed now is for such courses to take on a more regular aspect offering, say, a course of lectures over two, three or four years leading to an examination for a certificate or diploma similar to the Extension Diploma in Music History awarded by the Extra-Mural Department of London University. This is designed for non-professional students and requires no previous academic qualifications. Its purpose is 'to encourage students to undertake continuous and systematic study of a high standard in the history of music'. The Diploma requires four years' study, each year's work consisting of twenty-four lecture meetings, the writing of essays, and private reading and listening to music. There is an examination at the end of each year and a general examination at the end of the course. The years may be taken in any order (though the chronological is preferable), except that the fourth year of the syllabus must be the student's final year. For each year four works are prescribed for special study.

It is not difficult to see how such a scheme could be adapted to a study of ballet, or the benefits which could follow from the establishment of a similar Diploma Course in Ballet History and Aesthetics.

Ideally, any such course in ballet history and aesthetics should be run in association with the Royal Ballet, Royal Ballet School or Royal Academy of Dancing. It should be possible to ask the help of these organisations when practical demonstrations are needed. It would be particularly satisfactory if certificate courses taught by university extra-mural departments (as distinct from occasional courses of lectures) were to be agreed with the Royal Academy of Dancing leading at the end to an Academy, rather than a university, certificate. This would establish national standards and a national certificate which could be attractive to the general evening student as well as being of value to anyone hoping to become a critic.

This course should include in its syllabus: history of choreography, history of music and history of costume and stage design, all from the *ballet de cour* to the present day; principles of music and elementary musical theory, including use of music by choreographers of each period; principles of dance composition and study of the contemporary repertoire; the history, composition and analysis of ballet libretti; history of ballet criticism and the technical literature of choreography; history of dance notation; principles of stage lighting and production; elementary aesthetics; general history of the British theatre; theories and development of free or modern dancing; principles of British national dancing and of the more important foreign national dances. Regular written work should be demanded in the form of essays or critical exercises.

GLOSSARY OF BALLETS

THE following glossary of the principal ballets mentioned in our text is based, with permission of the author and publishers, on Mr. G. B. L. Wilson's *A Dictionary of Ballet*, first published by Penguin Books Ltd., in 1957, then in a new and revised edition by Cassell & Co. Ltd., London, in 1961. We have varied or enlarged the entries to suit our purpose and added many ballets omitted from the *Dictionary*, usually because they have been created since 1957, in descriptions we have written ourselves following the style laid down by Mr. Wilson. For these we have sometimes referred to *A Dictionary of Modern Ballet*, published in Britain by Methuen and Co. in 1959. Our most frequent abbreviations are:

> Am. American; B. Ballet; b. born; C.Gdn. Royal Opera House, Covent Garden; ch. choreography; chor. choreographer, choreographed; Co. Company; cost. costumes; déc. décor; f.p. first produced; m. music; Met. Op. Metropolitan Opera House, New York; N.Y. City B. New York City Ballet; Op. Opera House; R. Royal; R.B. Royal Ballet, London; sc. scene, scenes, scenery; S.Wells B. Sadler's Wells Ballet; Th. Theatre, Théâtre.

A

ADAM ZERO, ballet 1 act, book Michael Benthall, ch. Helpmann, m. Bliss, déc. Furse, f.p. S. Wells B., C.Gdn., 10.4.1946 (Helpmann, June Brae, Gillian Lynne, Paltenghi). The life cycle of Man symbolised in the creation of a ballet.

AFTERNOON OF A FAUN, ballet 1 act, ch. Robbins, m. Debussy, déc. J. Rosenthal, f.p. N.Y. City B., City Center, N.Y., 14.5.1953 (Leclercq, Moncion). A ballet of mood for two dancers, set in a ballet studio.

AGE OF ANXIETY, ballet based on W. H. Auden's poem, ch. J. Robbins, m. Bernstein, déc. O. Smith, f.p. N.Y. City B., City Center, N.Y., 26.2.1950 (Leclercq, Bolender, Robbins, Moncion).

AGON, (1) ballet 1 act, ch. Balanchine, m. Stravinsky, lighting Nananne Porebor, f.p. N.Y. City B., City Center, N.Y., 1.12.1957 (Diana Adams, Melissa Hayden, Arthur Mitchell). (2) ch. MacMillan, déc. Georgiadis, f.p. R.B., C.Gdn., 20.8.1958 (Linden, Blair). Choreographically intricate work of abstract dance set to an equally complicated score.

ALGUES, LES (Seaweed), ballet 4 sc., ch. Charrat, m. Bernard, book and déc. Castelli, f.p. Charrat's Co., Th. des Ch.-Élysées, Paris, 20.4.1953 (Charrat, van Dijk). This powerful ballet of a lunatic asylum was one of the first to make use of *musique concrète*.

ANNABEL LEE, ballet with sung words (Edgar Allan Poe), ch. Skibine, m. Schiffmann, déc. Delfau, f.p. De Cuevas Co., Deauville, 26.8.1951 (Marjorie Tallchief, Skibine).

ANTIGONE, ballet 1 act, ch. Cranko, m. Theodorakis, déc. Tamayo, f.p. R.B., C.Gdn., 19.10.1959. Free adaptation of Sophocles' tragedy.

APOLLON MUSAGÈTE, (1) ballet 2 sc., book and m. Stravinsky, ch. Adolph Bolm, f.p. Library of Congress, Washington, 27.4.1928 (Bolm, Ruth Page, Berenice Holmes, Elise Reiman). (2) ballet 2 sc., m. Stravinsky, ch. Balanchine, déc. Bauchant, f.p. Diaghilev's Co., Th. Sarah Bernhardt, Paris, 12.6.1928 (Lifar, Nikitina, Tchernicheva, Doubrovska), and subsequently by the Am. B., déc. S. Chaney, Met. Op., 27.4.1937, and, as *Apollo* by Ballet Theatre, déc. Tchelitchev, f.p. Met. Op., 25.4.1943 (Eglevsky, Zorina, Kaye, Hightower), and again for the Paris Opéra, 21.5.1947, déc. A. Delfau (Kalioujny, Maria Tallchief, Jacqueline Moreau, Denise Bourgeois).
   The birth, upbringing and apotheosis of the god, Apollo. Balanchine's version for Diaghilev marked one of the first appearances of a neo-classic style of choreography.

APPARITIONS, ballet in prologue, 3 sc. and epilogue, book Lambert (from the theme of Berlioz's *Symphonie Fantastique*), ch. Ashton, m. Liszt (orch. Jacob), déc. Beaton, f.p. S. Wells B., S. Wells Th., London, 11.2.1936 (Helpmann, Fonteyn, Turner). A poet takes refuge in dreams and dies in despair.

APRÈS-MIDI D'UN FAUNE, L', ballet 1 act, ch. Nijinsky, m. Debussy's setting for Mallarmé's poem, déc. Bakst, f.p. Diaghilev's Co., Th. de Châtelet, Paris, 29.5.1912. Nijinsky is generally credited with having conceived book and choreography though Stravinsky has stated that the theme was Diaghilev's later modified by Bakst.

AURORA'S WEDDING, suite of dances from the last act of *The Sleeping Beauty* with some additions. Ch. Petipa, m. Tchaikovsky, cost. from Benois's *Pavillon d'Armide*, déc. Bakst. f.p. Diaghilev's Co., Paris Opéra, 18.5.1922 (Trefilova, Vladimiroff). This divertissement was all that remained from the 1921 production of *The Sleeping Princess*. It is in the repertoire of several companies.

B

BAISER DE LA FÉE, LE, ballet in 4 sc., based on Hans Andersen's *The Ice Maiden*, m. Stravinsky. This ballet is in the repertoire of many companies. The first version was ch. Nijinska, déc. Benois presented by Ida Rubenstein Co., Paris Opéra, 27.11.1928. Ashton ch. a version for S. Wells B., déc. Fedorovitch, 26.11.1935. The version referred to in this book is that ch. by MacMillan, déc. Rowell, f.p. 12.4.1960, R.B., C.Gdn.

BAL, LE, ballet, book B. Kochno. (1) ch. Balanchine, m. Rieti, déc. Chirico, f.p. Diaghilev's Co., Monte Carlo, 7.5.1929. Revived ch. Massine, Monte Carlo, 1935. A masked ball in costume inspired by architecture. The décor and costume dominated the work and hindered the choreography. (2) ch. Jooss, m. Rieti, déc. Heckroth, f.p. Ballets Jooss, Essen, Nov. 1930.

BALLET COMIQUE DE LA REINE, spectacle of dancing, singing and music staged by Balthasar de Beaujoyeux (lyrics La Chesnaye, m. de Beaulieu and Thibault de Courville, déc. Jacques Patin), f.p. Palais-Bourbon, Paris, 15.10.1581, for the betrothal of Marguerite de Lorraine to the Duc de Joyeuse. This work, based on the ideas evolved by de Baïf, an account of which was printed and circulated to the principal European courts, contributed greatly to the development of the court ballet in France and the Masque in England. It is often held to have been the first ballet, although there were earlier productions of a similar style in Italy, descended from the dinner-ballet of the fifteenth century and other entertainments.

BALLET DE LA JEUNESSE, LE, divertissement consisting of *entrée de ballet* and sung recitative between the acts of a play by Dancourt, ch. Beauchamps, m. Michel–Richard de Lalande, déc. and cost. by Jean Bérain. Cast included Duchesse de Bourbon (La Jeunesse), and nobles such as Comte de Briaux, the Marquis de Châteauneuf and professionals such as Beauchamps, Pécour, Ballon, Mlle de la Fontaine.

BALLET IMPERIAL, ballet, ch. Balanchine, m. 2nd piano concerto of Tchaikovsky, déc. Doboujinski, f.p. Am. B., Hunter College, N.Y., 29.5.1941 (Marie-Jeanne, Caccialanza, Dollar). Frequently revived, notably with déc. Berman, S. Wells B., C.Gdn., 5.4.1950 (Fonteyn, Grey, Somes, Field). Ballet of pure dancing, a choreographic interpretation of the music.

BARN DANCE, ballet in 1 act, ch. Catherine Littlefield, m. Guion, Powell and Gottschalk, déc. A. and S. Pinto, f.p. Littlefield B., Philadelphia, 23.4.1937.

BAYADÈRE, LA, ballet, ch. Petipa, m. Minkus, f.p. St. Petersburg, 23.1.1877. A shortened version is still in the Soviet repertoire.

BEAUTY AND THE BEAST, ballet, ch. Cranko, m. Ravel, déc· Margaret Kaye, f.p. S. Wells Th. B. at S. Wells Th., 20.12.1949 (Patricia Miller, David Poole). A *pas de deux*, inspired by the famous fairy tale.

BICHES, LES, ballet, 1 act, ch. Nijinska, m. Poulenc, déc. Laurencin, f.p. Diaghilev's Co., Th. de Monte Carlo, 6.1.1924 (Nemchinova, Tchernicheva, Woizikovsky, Vilzak). In England this work is known as *The House Party*. It was in the repertoire of Markova-Dolin Co. (1937) and the de Cuevas B. (1947). Parody on the smart life of the twenties.

BIG CITY, THE, ballet in 3 scenes, ch. Jooss, m. Tansman, déc. Heckroth, f.p. Ballets Jooss, Opera House, Cologne, 21.11.1932. An evocation of life in the big city and its evils.

BILLY THE KID, ballet, 1 act, book Lincoln Kirstein, based on life of Wm. Bonney, Am. outlaw of nineteenth century, ch. Eugene Loring, m. Aaron Copland, déc. Jared French, f.p. B. Caravan, Chicago Op., 16.10.1938 (Loring, Marie-Jeanne, Christensen). Considered by some to be the first really American ballet.

BIRTHDAY OFFERING, ballet in neo-classic idiom for 25th Anniversary Performance of S. Wells Ballet, ch. Ashton, m. Glazounov, déc. Levasseur, f.p. C.Gdn., 5.5.1956 (Fonteyn, Somes, Grey, Chatfield,

Elvin, Blair, Jackson, Doyle, Beriosova, Ashbridge, Nerina, Grant, Fifield, Shaw). A divertissement of virtuoso dancing.

BLACK CROOK, THE, extravaganza, book C. M. Barras, ch. David Costa, f.p. Niblo's Garden, N.Y., 12.9.1866. It ran for some sixteen months and was revived again and again over a period of years. Perhaps the forerunner of the modern musical.

BLOOD WEDDING, ballet 1 act, ch. Rodrigues, m. ApIvor, déc. Isabel Lambert, f.p. S. Wells Th. B., 5.6.1953 (Fifield, Poole, Trecu). An adaptation of the play by Lorca.

BONNE-BOUCHE, ballet 3 sc., ch. Cranko, m. Oldham, déc. Osbert Lancaster, f.p. S. Wells B., C.Gdn., 4.4.1952 (May, Clayden, Shaw, Hart, Grant). A farce and burlesque of Edwardian Kensington.

BOURRÉE FANTASQUE, ballet 1 act, ch. Balanchine, m. Chabrier, cost. Karinska, f.p. N.Y. City B., City Center, 1.12.1949 (Leclercq, Maria Tallchief, Janet Reed). Ballet of pure dancing with a fantastic twist and touches of humour. Reproduced for Festival B., at Royal Festival Hall, London, 18.8.60.

BURROW, THE, ballet 1 act, ch. MacMillan, m. Frank Martin, déc. Georgiadis, f.p. R.B., C.Gdn., 2.1.1958 (Heaton, Seymour, Britton). The tensions of a group of people hiding from the secret police.

C

CARMEN, ballet 5 sc., ch. Petit, m. Bizet, déc. Clavé, f.p. B. de Paris, Princess Th., London, 21.2.1949 (Jeanmaire, Petit, Perrault, Hamilton). A translation of the opera into ballet.

CARNAVAL, LE, ballet 1 act, ch. Fokine, m. Schumann, déc. Bakst, f.p. Diaghilev's Co. in its final version at Teater des Westens, Berlin, 20.5.1910 (Karsavina, Pilts, Nijinsky). An earlier performance had been given that year at a charity performance in St. Petersburg, at which Leontiev had taken the role of Harlequin, and including Cecchetti, Nijinska, Karsavina, Fokine. The Soviet ballet-master V. Bourmeister has also produced a ballet to this music at the Stanislavsky Th., Moscow. In the repertoire of many companies.

CASSE-NOISETTE. See NUTCRACKER.

CATERINA, OU LA FILLE DU BANDIT, ballet 3 acts, 5 sc., ch. Perrot, m. Pugni, déc. Marshall, f.p. Her Majesty's Th., London, 3.3.1846 (Grahn, Perrot). This ballet, about an incident in the life of Salvator Rosa, remained in the St. Petersburg repertoire for many years.

CHATTE, LA, ballet 1 act, ch. Balanchine, m. Sauguet, déc. Gabo and Pevsner, f.p. Diaghilev's Co., Monte Carlo, 30.4.1927 (Spessivtseva, Lifar). Based on an Aesop fable. The scenery was of talc.

CHECKMATE, ballet 1 sc. and a prologue, ch. de Valois, book and m. Bliss, déc. E. McKnight Kauffer, f.p. S. Wells B., Th. des Ch.-Élysées, Paris, 15.6.1937 (Brae, May, Turner, Helpmann). A game of chess between Love and Death. One of de Valois' best ballets, always popular with Continental audiences. The original costumes and décor were lost in Holland during the German invasion.

CHOPINIANA (*Les Sylphides*), ballet 1 act, ch. Fokine, m. Chopin, déc. Benois, f.p. outside Russia by Diaghilev's Co., Th. de Châtelet, Paris, 2.6.1909 (Pavlova, Karsavina, Baldina, Nijinsky). The first performance of *Chopiniana*, in the form subsequently renamed by Diaghilev *Les Sylphides*, was given at a charity performance at the Maryinsky Th., St. Petersburg, 8.3.1908 (Preobrajenska, Pavlova, Karsavina, Nijinsky). On 7.2.1907 Fokine had presented a ballet *Chopiniana* at a charity performance. This was set to a suite of Chopin pieces of that name, orchestrated by Glazunov, and was a series of scenes in national costume. One of these scenes was a *pas de deux* to the valse, danced by Oboukhoff and Pavlova, who wore the long white tutu of *La Sylphide*. From this dance came the conception the following year of *Chopiniana* as a ballet blanc.

Les Sylphides is a romantic composition, classical in form, but the four variations and the *pas de deux*, set between the ensemble dances with which the ballet opens and ends, merge into each other without the stilted choreographic joinery of the old classical ballets. It is a ballet of mood—there is no plot, but pure interpretation of the music into terms of movement, and to this extent it must be regarded as a forerunner of the symphonic ballet. The faultless technique and plasticity of movement, which it demands of soloists and *corps de ballet* alike, make *Les Sylphides* one of the hardest tests of a company. Several other settings have been used for the ballet, notably one inspired by a painting of Corot, but the original décor of Benois, with its ruined monastery, remains the best. The ballet is in the repertoire of many companies and Fokine himself revived it many times with slight changes in choreography but without enhancing the beauty of his original version. *Les Sylphides*, with various modifications, is given by some companies under the original title of *Chopiniana*.

CHOREARTIUM, ballet 4 parts, ch. Massine, m. Brahms's 4th Symphony, déc. Terechkovich and Lourie, f.p. de Basil Co., Alhambra, London, 24.10.1933 (Baronova, Danilova, Riabouchinska, Verchinina, Jasinski, Lichine, Petroff, Shabelevski). This was Massine's second symphonic ballet, one of sombre mood.

CINDERELLA, ballet based on Perràult's fairy story, 3 acts, ch. Ashton, m. Prokofieff, déc. Malcles, f.p. S. Wells B., C.Gdn., 23.12.1948 (Shearer, Somes). Fonteyn was prevented by illness from appearing in the first performance of the ballet but has since danced the role many times. The music was first created for a production at the Bolshoi Th., Moscow, 15.11.1945, ch. Zakharoff, déc. Williams (Ulanova, Gabovich). A year later the ballet was produced at the Kirov Th., Leningrad, ch. Sergeyev.

CLÉOPÂTRE, ballet in 1 act, ch. Fokine, m. Arensky and others, déc. Bakst, f.p. Diaghilev's Co., Châtelet Th., Paris, 2.6.1909 (Rubinstein, Pavlova). This ballet, under the title *Une Nuit d'Égypte*, had originally been produced at a children's matinée in St. Petersburg, 21.3.1908.

COMUS, ballet 2 sc., ch. Helpmann, m. Purcell, déc. Messel, f.p. S. Wells B., New Th., London, 14.1.1942 (Fonteyn, Helpmann). Based on Milton's Masque (of 1634, m. Lawes), this was Helpmann's first work for S. Wells B. and included the speaking of two passages from the poem, later omitted.

CONCERTO BAROCCO, ballet, ch. Balanchine, m. Bach's Double Violin Concerto in D Minor, déc. Berman, f.p. Am. B., 29.5.1941, Hunter College Playhouse, N.Y. (Marie-Jeanne, Dollar). In the repertoire of several companies, usually in practice dress. Ballet of pure dancing.

CONCERTO DE GRIEG, pas de deux with a solo piano, ch. Charrat, m. Grieg, f.p. Ballets de France de Janine Charrat, 1954 (Charrat, Van Dijk).

CONFLICTS, ballet in 1 act, ch. Norman Morrice, m. Ernest Bloch (Quintet for piano and strings). Realisation Ralph Koltai, f.p. B. Rambert, S. Wells Th., 23.7.1962. Ballet about a choreographer's relationships with his dancers.

CONSERVATOIRE, LA or KONSERVATORIET (in Danish 'Conservatoriet eller et Avisfrieri'), ballet in 1 act arranged by H. Lander and V. Borchsenius in 1941 from ch. Bournonville, m. Paulli, f.p. Royal Th., Copenhagen, 6.5.1849, and never out of the repertoire. Incidents during a ballet class.

CONTES RUSSES, LES, ballet, ch. Massine, m. Liadov, déc. Larionov, f.p. Diaghilev's Co., Th. du Châtelet, Paris, 11.5.1917 (Tchernicheva, Sokolova, Woizikovsky). Suite based on Russian folk-lore.

COPPÉLIA ou LA FILLE AUX YEUX D'ÉMAIL, ballet 3 acts, book Nuitter and Saint-Léon from a tale by Hoffman, ch. Saint-Léon, m. Delibes, déc. Cambon, Despléchin, Lavastre, cost. Lormier, f.p. Paris Opéra, 25.5.1870 (Bozzacchi, Fiocre, Dauty). One of the most popular of ballets and the most successful of those marking the return of the ballet d'action after the decline of the romantic movement. First presented in London 8.11.1884 at the Empire Th. arranged by M. Bertrand, the maître de ballet, cost. Chasemore (Alice Holt, W. Warde), a one-act version. Full ballet first presented at Empire Th., 14.5.1906 (Genée). The ballet, largely in its original form, is still in the repertoire of the Paris Opéra, where the tradition of playing Frantz by a girl has been maintained until recently. Also in the repertoire of many other companies but with revised choreography and in some cases only Act II is given. The last act is in the form of a divertissement. The S. Wells B. has a version by Ivanov and Cecchetti reproduced by Sergueeff, f.p. in a two-act version at S. Wells Th., 21.3.1933 (Lopokova—later de Valois, Stanley Judson, Hedley Briggs), and it remains in the repertoire with the third act added. The Royal Danish B. have danced it in a two-act version since 1896 (version of Glasemann and Beck, present version by Lander).

COQ D'OR, LE, ballet 1 act, ch. Fokine, m. Rimsky-Korsakov, déc. Goncharova, f.p. Diaghilev's Co., Paris Opéra, 24.5.1914 (Karsavina, Bulgakov, Cecchetti). In the original version there was a cast of singers but these were not employed in the de Basil Co. version of 1937. A Russian fairy tale.

CUPID OUT OF HIS HUMOUR, ballet in seventeenth-century style, ch. Skeaping, m. Purcell, déc. from old Swedish designs, f.p. Royal

Swedish B., Drottningholm Palace Th., 14.6.1956 (von Rosen, Holmgren).

CYGNE, LE (*The Dying Swan*), solo dance to music by Saint-Saëns (from *Le Carnaval des Animaux*) arranged by Fokine for Pavlova in 1905 at a concert in St. Petersburg. It was Pavlova's most famous dance. The costume was by Bakst.

CYRANO DE BERGERAC, ballet 3 acts, ch. Petit, m. Marius Constant, déc. Basarte, cost. Yves Saint-Laurent, f.p. Petit Co., Th. de l'Alhambra, 17.4.1959 (Petit, Jeanmaire, Tessa Beaumont, Lucien Mars, José Ferran). The Rostand story.

CZERNYANA, ballet, ch. Frank Staff, m. Czerny, déc. Eve Swinstead-Smith, f.p. B. Rambert, Duchess Th., London, 5.12.1939 (Sally Gilmour, France, Clayden, Gore, Staff, Kersley). When the ballet was revived in 1943 some dances were omitted and replaced by dances from *Czerny 2* (same collaborators, 15.5.1941, Arts Th., London). A witty satirical suite of various types of ballet with some brilliantly inventive dancing.

D

DAME AUX CAMÉLIAS, LA, ballet 2 acts, ch. T. Gsovsky, m. Sauguet, f.p. Berlin Festival, 30.9.1957 (Chauviré).

DANSES CONCERTANTES, ballet, ch. MacMillan, m. Stravinsky, déc. Georgiadis, f.p. S. Wells Th. B., S. Wells Th., 18.1.1955 (Lane, Britton, Poole). Suite of dances.

DANTE SONATA, ballet 1 act, ch. Ashton, m. Liszt (*D'après une lecture de Dante*), déc. Fedorovitch after Flaxman, f.p. S. Wells B., 23.1.1940 (Fonteyn, May, Somes, Helpmann). A powerful ballet in the modern idiom inspired by the fall of Poland. Children of Light and Darkness as the Souls in Purgatory struggling for redemption. Danced barefooted.

DAPHNIS AND CHLOE, ballet 3 sc. (1) ch. Fokine, m. Ravel, déc. Bakst, f.p. Diaghilev's Co., Châtelet Th., Paris, 8.6.1912 (Karsavina, Nijinsky). (2) ch. Ashton, déc. Craxton, f.p. S. Wells B., C.Gdn., 5.4.1951 (Fonteyn, Somes).

DARK ELEGIES, ballet 2 sc., ch. Tudor, m. Mahler's *Kindertotenlieder* (sung), déc. Nadia Benois, f.p. B. Rambert, Duchess Th., London, 19.2.1937 (Maude Lloyd, van Praagh, de Mille, Gore, Laing). The mourning of a fishing village. The singer sits on the stage.

DEMOISELLES DE LA NUIT, LES, ballet 3 sc., ch. Petit, m. Françaix, déc. Fini, f.p. B. de Paris, Th. Marigny, 21.5.1948 (Fonteyn, Petit). A ballet about cats.

DIVERSIONS, ballet, ch. MacMillan, m. 'Music for Strings' by Sir Arthur Bliss, déc. and cost. Philip Prowse, f.p. R.B., C.Gdn., 15.9.1961 (Beriosova, Macleary, Lane, Usher). Plotless ballet.

DONALD OF THE BURTHENS, ballet in 2 sc., ch. Massine, m. Ian Whyte, déc. Robert Colquhoun and Robert Macbryde, f.p. S. Wells B., C.Gdn., 12.12.1951. Libretto based on a Scottish legend, and ch. based on Scottish dancing.

DON JUAN, ballet 3 sc., ch. Angiolini, m. Gluck, f.p. Vienna, 17.10.1761.

DON QUICHOTTE, ballet in 4 acts and 8 sc., ch. Petipa, m. Minkus, f.p. Bolshoi Th., Moscow, 26.12.1869. A revised version by the same chor. was presented at St. Petersburg two years later and it was again revived in 1902 in Moscow by A. Gorsky—a version revised by Zakharoff which is still in the Soviet repertoire. In 1962 the Polish choreographer, Witold Borkowski, reproduced this version for the Ballet Rambert with designs by Voytek, the first time the full ballet had been seen in Britain. A shortened version with ch. L. Novikoff, was given by the Pavlova Company. Excerpts have also been presented by the Am. Ballet Th. The theme, taken from the novel by Cervantes, had tempted many earlier chors. incl. Noverre, Didelot, Milon and Paul Taglioni. The Petipa version contains a number of fine classical *soli* and *pas de deux*. The Grand Pas de Deux from *Don Quichotte*, often given as a divertissement, is usually the version by Oboukhoff.

E

ÉCHELLE, L', ballet by Milko Sparemblek, ch. Dick Sanders, déc. François Geneau, m. Zdenko Turjak, f.p. Les Ballets 1956 de Miskovitch et Lidova at Festival de Lyon-Charbonnières June 1956 (Mayer, Vassili Sulich, Milko Sparemblek). Three interpretations of one murder.

ELEKTRA, ballet, ch. Helpmann, m. Arnold, déc. Boyd, f.p. R.B., C.Gdn., 26.3.1963 (Nerina, Blair). Ballet based on the Greek tragedy.

ESMÉRALDA, LA, ballet 3 acts, 5 sc., ch. Perrot, m. Pugni, déc. Grieve, cost. Copère, f.p. Her Majesty's Th. London, 9.3.1844 (Grisi, Perrot, Saint-Léon, Frassi, Gosselin, Coulon). Based on Hugo's *Notre-Dame de Paris*, it is still in the repertoire in Russia. First danced in Russia by Elssler in 1848. Also in repertoire of Festival Ballet, with original ch. by Beriozoff, déc. Nicola Benois, f.p. Festival Hall, London, 15.7.1954 (Krassovska, Gilpin, Briansky, Wright, Dolin, Beckett). The first ballet on this theme was Antonio Monticini's *Esmeralda,* f.p. Scala, Milan, 1839.

ÉTUDE, ballet 1 act, ch. Lander, m. Czerny, arr. Riisager, déc. Nordgreen, f.p. R. Danish B., Copenhagen, 15.1.1942 (Margot Lander, Brenan, Jensen). Under the title *Études* Lander mounted it for the Paris Opéra, 19.11.1952 (Bardin, Renault, Kalioujny), and for the Festival B., R. Festival Hall, London, 8.8.1955 (Toni Lander, Gilpin, Polajenko, Dolin). A ballet of crescendo and accelerando showing the progress and technique of the dancer.

EUNICE, ballet, ch. Fokine, m. Stcherbatchev, f.p. Maryinsky Th., St. Petersburg, 10.2.1907 (M. Kschessinskaya, Pavlova, R. A. Gerdt). The theme was based on one of the episodes of Sienkiewicz's *Quo Vadis*.

EXCELSIOR, ballet in 12 sc., ch. Manzotti, m. Marenco, déc. Edel, f.p. La Scala, Milan, 11.1.1881 (Vergani, Montenara), and in 1885 at Her Majesty's Th., London (Limido, Cecchetti). In praise of technical progress.

F

FAÇADE, ballet 1 act, ch. Ashton, m. Walton (originally written as an accompaniment to poems of Edith Sitwell), déc. John Armstrong. One of the wittiest of Ashton's ballets, this work was originally created for the Camargo Soc. at the Cambridge Th., London, 26.4.1931, and included immediately afterwards in the repertoire of the B. Rambert. When the ballet was added to those regularly performed by the Vic-Wells B. in 1935 a new number was included, and when revived by the S. Wells B. in July 1940 further numbers were added and fresh déc. and cost. (also by Armstrong) were introduced. This latter version was one subsequently given by the S. Wells Th. B. In the original production by the Camargo Soc. Lydia Lopokova danced the Milkmaid and also the Tango, Markova the Polka, and Ashton the Dago.

FACSIMILE, ballet, ch. Robbins, m. Bernstein, déc. Smith, cost. Charaff, f.p. Ballet Theatre, Broadway Th., N.Y., 24.10.1946 (Kaye, Robbins, Kriza). A flirtation on a beach, but deals also with the modern problem of what man shall do with his time.

FALL RIVER LEGEND, ballet, ch. de Mille, m. Gould, sc. Smith, cost. White, f.p. Ballet Th., Met. Op., N.Y., 22.4.1948 (Alonso, Bentley). This ballet, of the story of Lizzie Borden the murderer, is de Mille's masterpiece and provides one of the great dramatic roles in ballet—a role since associated with Nora Kaye.

FANCY FREE, ballet 1 act, ch. Robbins, m. Bernstein, sc. Smith, cost. Love, f.p. Ballet Th., Met. Op., N.Y., 18.4.1944 (Laing, Kriza, Robbins, Janet Reed, Muriel Bentley, Shirley Eckl). Am. B. of manners in a humorous vein, with slick timing and clever use of contemporary dance-hall styles wedded to classical technique. It was Robbins's first ballet and tells of three sailors and two girls. It inspired a musical and a film *On the Town*.

FANFARE, ballet, ch. Robbins, m. Britten (*Young Person's Guide to the Orchestra*), déc. Sharaff, f.p. N.Y. City B., City Center, N.Y., 2.6.1953 (Hounsey, Jillana, Larsson, Bolender, d'Amboise, Bigelow, Bliss). This was Robbins's tribute to Elizabeth II, performed on Coronation night. The dancers represent the various orchestral instruments.

FEMMES DE BONNE HUMEUR, LES (*The Good Humoured Ladies*), ballet 1 act, ch. Massine, m. D. Scarlatti, déc. Bakst, f.p. Diaghilev's Co., Teatro Costanza, Rome, 12.4.1917 (Lopokova, Idzikovski, Cecchetti). Based on Goldoni's comedy.

FÊTE ÉTRANGE, LA, ballet, book R. Crichton after Fournier's *Le Grand Meaulnes*, ch. Howard, m. Fauré, déc. Fedorovitch, f.p. London B., Arts Th., London, 23.5.1940 (Lloyd, Staff, Paltenghi). Now in repertoire of Royal Ballet. A sensitive ballet of mood, in which a country boy falls in love with the young châtelaine on the eve of her marriage. Two songs are sung in it by a singer off stage.

FILLE DU DANUBE, LA, ballet in 2 acts, 4 sc., ch. F. Taglioni, m. Adam, déc. Despléchin, f.p. Paris Opéra, 21.9.1836 (Taglioni, Mazilier). Romantic ballet in which a mortal falls in love with the spirit of a girl who has drowned herself.

FILLE MAL GARDÉE, LA or VAIN PRECAUTIONS, ballet 2 acts, ch. Dauberval, m. by various composers, f.p. Bordeaux 1789 (Mlle Théodore as Lise). One of the oldest ballets in the modern repertoire, it was danced by the Pavlova Co., the Mordkin Co., B.Th., de Cuevas Co., etc., and is also in the repertoire of Soviet companies. Nowadays different music is used. It was one of the first ballets to be based on the life of the people, thus breaking away from the pre-French Revolution tradition of the mythological ballet. The music was rewritten by Hérold in the 1820s when Aumer produced it. In 1864 new music by Hertel was used, and in 1882 it was re-staged by Petipa and Ivanov, using Hertel's score with additions by Delibes, Minkus, Pugni, Drigo and Rubenstein.

A new two-act version with ch. Ashton, m. Hérold arr. Lanchbery, and déc. Lancaster was f.p. by R.B. at C.Gdn., on 28.1.60, and has become one of the greatest successes of the British repertoire. It includes a mime scene from Petipa's version, reproduced by Tamara Karsavina.

FIREBIRD. See Oiseau de Feu, L'.

FLORE ET ZÉPHYRE, ballet 1 act, ch. Didelot, m. Bossi, déc. Liparotti, f.p. Kings Th., London, 7.7.1796 (Hilligsberg, Rose, Parisot, Didelot). This, one of the greatest of Didelot's works, was the first to use a flying ballet. Taglioni made her début in it in London, Kings Th., 1830.

FORAINS, LES, ballet 1 sc. by Kochno, ch. Petit, m. H. Sauguet, déc. Bérard, f.p. B. des Ch.-Élysées, Paris, 2.3.1945 (Pagava, Petit). This was one of Petit's most pleasing works, showing the efforts of a travelling circus and its pathetic departure.

FOUNTAIN OF BAKHCHISERAI, THE, ballet 4 acts, ch. Zakharoff, m. Asafiev, déc. Khodasevitch, f.p. Kirov Th., Leningrad, 22.9.1934 (Ulanova). Pushkin's poem. One of the most important Soviet ballets, performed all over the U.S.S.R. in various versions.

FOUR SEASONS, THE (Les Quatres Saisons), ballet 1 act, ch. Perrot, f.p. Her Majesty's Th., London, 13.6.1848 (Grisi, Rosati, Cerrito, the younger Taglioni). This ballet appears to have resembled in execution and intention the famous Pas de Quatre of Perrot.

FOUR TEMPERAMENTS, THE, ch. Balanchine, m. Hindemith, déc. Seligmann, f.p. Ballet Society N.Y., 20.11.1946. A Balanchine masterpiece. Music illuminated by dancing.

FUGITIVE, THE, ballet in 1 act, ch. Howard, m. L. Salzedo, book and déc. H. Stevenson, f.p. B. Rambert, Royal County Th., Bedford, 16.11.1944 (Gilmour, McClelland, Gore).

G

GAIETÉ PARISIENNE, ballet in 1 act, book and déc. G. de Beaumont, ch. Massine, m. Offenbach and Rosenthal, f.p. Ballet Russe de Monte Carlo, Monte Carlo, 5.4.1938 (Tarakanova, Massine, Youskevitch).

GALA PERFORMANCE, ballet in 2 sc., ch. Tudor, m. Prokofieff, déc. Stevenson, f.p. London B., Toynbee Hall, London, 5.12.1938 (van Praagh, Lloyd, Larsen). A comic ballet; a skit on the pre-Fokine style.

GISELLE, ou LES WILIS, ballet 2 acts, book by Gautier and Saint-Georges, ch. Coralli and Perrot, m. Adam and some numbers by Burgmüller, déc. Ciceri, f.p. Paris Opéra, 28.6.1841 (Carlotta Grisi, Lucien Petipa, with Adèle Dumilâtre as Myrthe). This, the greatest of the Romantic ballets, was inspired by a passage in Heine's De l'Allemagne describing the tradition that betrothed girls who have died before their wedding day return, as Wilis, to dance in the misty moonlight. In the first act Giselle, a country girl, kills herself with a sword on discovering that her lover, Albrecht, has deceived her. In the second act she rises from her grave and dances with the Wilis, saving her lover from them. The ballet makes the greatest demands on the dramatic powers of the dancer (in Act I) and on her technique and sensitivity (in Act II): consequently it has always been the touchstone by which ballerinas have been judged for over 100 years, and the ballet which all wish to interpret. It was first produced in London in 1842 (Grisi).

GLI STRELIZZI, mimodrama 6 acts, book and ch. Viganò, m. various arr. Viganò, déc. Alessandro Sanquirico, f.p. Teatro la Fenice, Venice, 1809. Staged in the grand manner; a story of national struggle in the Russia of Peter the Great.

GODS GO A-BEGGING, THE, or LES DIEUX MENDIANTS. There have been a number of ballets of this name using Handel's music (arranged as a suite by Beecham) notably: (1) book Boris Kochno, ch. Balanchine, déc. Bakst, f.p. Diaghilev's Co., His Majesty's Th., London, 16.7.1928 (Danilova, Woizikovsky); (2) same book, ch. de Valois, déc. H. Stevenson, f.p. S. Wells B., S. Wells Th., 21.2.1956 (Elizabeth Miller, William Chappell); two gods in disguise amuse themselves among mortals at a pastoral picnic in the manner of Watteau.

GREEN TABLE, THE, ballet in 8 sc., ch. Jooss, m. Cohen, déc. Heckroth, f.p. Th. des Ch.-Elysées, Paris, 3.7.1932 (Jooss, Uthoff, Pescht, Lisa Czobel). This ballet won the first prize in the first competition organised by the Archives Internationales de la Danse and brought fame to Kurt Jooss, whose finest work it remains. It is a satire inspired by the First World War. The Green Table is that at which politicians meet to decide the fate of mankind.

H

HAMLET, ballet 1 sc., ch. Helpmann, m. Tchaikovsky, déc. Hurry (his first work for the theatre), f.p. S. Wells B., New Th., London, 19.5.1942 (Fonteyn, Franca, Helpmann, Paltenghi). This mime drama deals with the thoughts which flit across the brain of the dying Hamlet. Nijinska also chor. a *Hamlet* at the Paris Opéra, 1934 (her own Co.), m. Liszt, déc. Annenkoff (Nijinska as Hamlet, Chanova as Ophelia). T. Gsovsky made another version at Städtische Oper, Berlin, 1954 (m. Blacher).

HARLEQUIN IN APRIL, ballet, prologue, 2 acts and epilogue, ch. Cranko, m. Arnell, déc. Piper (inspired by fire at Theatre Royal, Hanley, where the company lost much scenery and costumes), f.p. S. Wells Th. B., 8.5.1951 (Miller, Holden, Blair). A symbolical ballet of man's life. The title taken from some lines of T. S. Eliot's *The Waste Land*. (See Appendix III c (i).)

HAROLD IN ITALY, ch. Massine, m. Berlioz, déc. Lamotte, f.p. Ballet Russe de Monte Carlo, Boston, 14.10.1954 (Danielian, Borowska, Chouteau).

HARVEST ACCORDING, THE, ballet 1 act, ch. de Mille, m. Virgil Thomson, dec. Lemuel Ayers, f.p. Ballet Th., 1.10.1952 (Gemze de

Lappe, Kelly Brown, Ruth Ann Koesun). Inspired by Walt Whitman's lines 'Life, life is the tillage, and death is the harvest according'. In three parts: childhood, games, war as seen through a woman's eyes. Music based on American folksong, old hymns and modern songs.

HAUNTED BALLROOM, THE, ballet 1 act 3 sc., ch. de Valois, m. Geoffrey Toye, déc. Motley, f.p. Vic-Wells Ballet, S. Wells Th., 3.5.1933 (Markova, Appleyard, Helpmann). A nobleman is destroyed by the spirits of his ancestors.

HAZAÑA, dance drama in 1 act, ch. Norman Morrice, m. Carlos Surinach, déc. Ralph Koltai, f.p. B. Rambert, S. Wells Th., 26.5.1959 (June Sandbrook, Morrice, Gillian Martlew). Set in a South American village on the eve of a religious festival, a story of one man's Hazaña (Achievement).

HOMAGE TO THE QUEEN, ballet 1 act, ch. Ashton, m. Arnold, déc. Messel, f.p. S. Wells B., C.Gdn., 2.6.1953 (Fonteyn, Grey, Elvin, Nerina, Somes, Field, Hart, Rassine), f.p. for the Coronation of Elizabeth II, and has since remained in the repertoire.

HOROSCOPE, ballet 1 act, ch. Ashton, m. Constant Lambert, déc. Fedorovitch, f.p. S. Wells B., S. Wells Th., 27.1.1938 (Fonteyn, Somes). Young lovers ruled by the signs of the zodiac. Michael Somes made his first success in this ballet.

HOUSE OF BIRDS, ballet, ch. MacMillan, m. Mompou, déc. Georgiadis, f.p. S. Wells Th. B., S. Wells Th., 25.5.1955 (Tempest, Lane, Poole). Revived R.B., C.Gdn., 6.6.63, with new choreographic and musical ending.

I

ICARE, ballet 1 act, ch. Lifar, rhythms by Lifar orchestrated by Szyfer, déc. Larthe, f.p. Paris Opéra, 9.7.1935 (Lifar). This ballet has no music, only sounds emitted by percussion and other instruments. Legend of Icarus.

IDYLLE, ballet 1 act, ch. Skibine, m. Serrette, déc. Camble, f.p. de Cuevas Co., Empire Th., Paris, 2.1.1954 (Marjorie Tallchief, Skibine, Skouratoff). A charming ballet about horses in a field.

INTERPLAY, ballet 1 sc., ch. Robbins, m. Morton Gould, déc. Carl Kent, f.p. Concert Varieties, Ziegfield Th., N.Y., 1.6.1945 (Janet Reed, John Kriza, Robbins). In repertoire B.Th. (déc. O. Smith, cost. I. Sharraff) since 17.10.1945, and N.Y. City B. This ballet in the modern Am. idiom has greatly influenced continental choreographers.

INVITATION, THE, ch. MacMillan, m. Matyas Seiber, déc. Georgiadis, f.p. R.B., New Th., Oxford, 10.11.60 (Seymour, Heaton, Gable, Doyle). At a house party in the country a boy and a girl are seduced with tragic consequences for the girl.

J

JARDIN AUX LILAS (*Lilac Garden*), ballet 1 act, ch. Tudor, m. Chausson, déc. Stevenson, f.p. B. Rambert, Mercury Th., London, 26.1.1936 (Maude Lloyd, van Praagh, N. Laing). Revived by B.Th. N.Y., 1940, and N.Y. City B. 1951. Using a small number of characters, Tudor, in a manner reminiscent of Proust, has succeeded in conjuring up their emotional strain under the restraint of social convention. Also in repertoire of National B. of Canada 1954.

JEUNE HOMME ET LA MORT, LE, ballet 2 sc. by Cocteau, ch. Petit and Cocteau, m. Bach, déc. Wakhevitch, f.p. B. des Champs-Élysées, Paris, 25.6.1946 (Nathalie Philippart, Jean Babilée). The ballet was originally rehearsed to jazz music, but eventually the conductor, Girard, suggested the use of Bach's 'Grand Passacaglia', played three times. It is one of the most notable ballets of our times (a *pas de deux*) and has been called 'a *Spectre de la Rose* of our epoch'.

JEUX, ballet, ch. Nijinsky, m. Debussy, déc. Bakst, f.p. Diaghilev's Co., Th. des Ch.-Élysées, Paris, 15.5.1913 (Karsavina, Shollar, Nijinsky). This was the first Diaghilev ballet in contemporary dress and setting. The dancers were dressed as tennis players at a tennis party.

JEUX D'ENFANTS, ballet 1 act, ch. Massine, m. Bizet, déc. J. Miro, f.p. de Basil Co., Monte Carlo, 14.4.1932 (Riabouchinska, Toumanova, Baronova, Lichine). A ballet of children's toys in Miro's surrealist nursery, its creation was bound up with the débuts of the 'baby ballerinas' Riabouchinska and Toumanova.

JOB, a masque for dancing in 8 sc., book Geoffrey Keynes (after Blake), ch. de Valois, m. Vaughan Williams, déc. Gwen Raverat, f.p. Camargo Soc., Cambridge Th., London, 5.7.1931 (Dolin as Satan). The scenario and score had been offered to and declined by Diaghilev. It was taken into the repertoire of the Vic-Wells B., 22.9.1931. In 1948 new déc. was designed by John Piper.

L

LADY AND THE FOOL, THE, ballet, ch. Cranko, m. Verdi-Mackerras, déc. Beer, f.p. S. Wells Th. B., New Th., Oxford, 25.2.1954 (Miller, MacMillan, Mosaval). A noble lady rejects her fine life and suitors in favour of a poor clown. This ballet was revised in 1955 and taken into the S. Wells repertoire at Covent Garden (f.p. C.Gdn., 9.6.1955, Grey, Chatfield, Powell).

LADY INTO FOX, ballet 3 sc., ch. Andrée Howard, m. Honegger, déc. Nadia Benois, f.p. Ballet Club, Mercury Th., London, 15.5.1939 (Sally Gilmour, Boyd). Based on David Garnett's novel, the story of a girl who changes into a fox. The role is one by which Sally Gilmour will always be remembered.

LILAC GARDEN. See JARDIN AUX LILAS.

LOUP, LE, ballet 1 act, ch. Petit, m. Dutilleux, déc. Carzou, f.p. B. de Paris, Empire Th., Paris, 17.3.1953 (Violette Verdy, Petit). A girl falls in love with a wolf and they are hunted to death. Remarkable for its interpretation by Verdy as the girl and Petit as the wolf, and for Carzou's forest décor.

LOVES OF MARS AND VENUS, THE, the earliest recorded *ballet d'action* and therefore a milestone in the history of ballet. 'A dramatick entertainment of dancing attempted in imitation of the pantomimes of the Ancient Greeks and Romans.' Ch. John Weaver, m. Henry Symonds, déc. not known, f.p. Drury Lane, 2.3.1717. This remarkable production by England's first important choreographer undoubtedly influenced the later development of the *ballet d'action* in France. Dupré senior, one of the finest French dancers of the period, took the role of Mars; Mrs. Santlow, a talented English dancer, danced Venus; and Weaver himself appeared in the character role of Vulcan.

M

MAM'ZELLE ANGOT, ballet 3 sc., based on the opera by Lecocq, ch. Massine, m. Lecocq, déc. Doboujinski, f.p. B.Th., Met. Op., N.Y., 10.10.1943 (Massine, Nora Kaye, Eglevsky, Hightower). Re-created by Massine for S. Wells B., C.Gdn., 26.11.1947, déc. Derain (Grant, Fonteyn, Somes, Shearer).

MARGUERITE AND ARMAND, ballet, ch. Ashton, m. Liszt, orch. Searle, déc. Beaton, f.p. R.B., C.Gdn., 12.3.1963 (Fonteyn, Nureyev, Somes). Based on the Dumas tale.

MASQUES, LES, ballet 1 act, ch. Ashton, m. Poulenc, déc. Federovitch, f.p. B. Rambert, Mercury Th., London, 5.3.1933 (Markova, Argyle, Ashton, Gore).

MEDEA, ballet, ch. Cullberg, m. Bartok, déc. Granstrom, f.p. Swedish Ballet, Prince's Th., London, 12.2.1951 (von Rosen, J. Mengarelli). Mounted by Royal Swedish B., Stockholm, 11.4.1953 (same cast), and by N.Y. City B., N.Y., 26.11.1958 (Hayden, Verdy, d'Amboise).

MÉDÉE ET JASON, ballet, ch. Noverre, m. Rodolphe, f.p. Stuttgart, 11.2.1763 (Nancy, G. Vestris). One of Noverre's greatest *ballets d'action*, the scenario is reproduced in Appendix I B.

MERMAID, ballet 4 sc., ch. Andrée Howard and Susan Salaman, m. Ravel, déc. Howard, f.p. Ballet Club, Mercury Th., London, 4.3.1934 (Argyle, Chappell, Elizabeth Schooling). The Hans Andersen tale.

MIRACLE IN THE GORBALS, ballet 1 act, book Michael Benthall, ch. Helpmann, m. Bliss, déc. Burra, f.p. S. Wells B., Princes Th., London, 26.10.1944 (Helpmann, Clayden, Paltenghi, Franca). Christ returns to the slums of Glasgow and is martyred again.

MIRAGES, LES, ballet, ch. Lifar, m. Sauguet, déc. Cassandre, f.p. Paris Opéra, 15.12.1947 (Chauviré, Bardin, Dynalix, Lafon, Renault). This ballet was prepared in 1944 but not performed until Lifar was reinstated at the Opéra in 1947. One of Lifar's best works and one of Chauviré's finest roles.

MIRROR FOR WITCHES, ballet, prologue and 5 sc., based on a novel by Esther Forbes, ch. Howard, m. ApIvor, déc. Adams, cost. Howard and Adams, f.p. S. Wells B., C.Gdn., 4.3.1952 (Heaton, Farron, Edwards, Hart, Chatfield). A ballet remarkable for its dramatic impact, especially in the performances of Julia Farron and Anne Heaton. (See Appendix III c iii.)

MISS JULIE, ballet, book by A. Fridericia based on Strindberg's play, ch. Cullberg, m. Rangström, déc. Fridericia, f.p. Riksteatern, Stockholm, 1.3.1950 (von Rosen, Mengarelli). When performed by Royal

Swedish B., Stockholm, 7.9.1950, and in London, 1951, déc. Erixson. Taken into repertoire of Ballet Theatre and Royal Danish B. 1958.

MOON REINDEER, ballet, ch. Cullberg, m. Riisager, déc. Falk, f.p. Royal Danish B., Copenhagen, 22.11.1957 (Vangsaa, Kronstam, Björnsson), and by Royal Swedish B., Stockholm, 31.1.1959 (Orlando, Selling), and Ballet Th., New York, Oct. 1961 (Serrano, Fernandez). A Lapland legend of a girl who becomes a reindeer.

MOVES, ballet in 5 pts., ch. Robbins, *a ballet in silence about relationships*. No décor or music, f.p. Ballets: U.S.A. for Festival of Two Worlds, Spoleto, Italy, June 1958, this work had an enormous success on the company's European tour a year later.

N

NAPOLI, ballet in 3 acts, ch. Bournonville, m. Paulli, Halsted, Gade and Lumbye, déc. Christensen, f.p. Royal Th., Copenhagen, 29.3.1842 (Bournonville, Fjelsted, Stramboe). A condensed version mounted by H. Lander for Festival B., London, in 1954 (Toni Lander, Briansky).

N.Y. EXPORT: OP JAZZ, ballet in 5 pts., ch. Robbins, m. Robert Prince, déc. Ben Shahn, cost. Shahn and Florence Klotz, f.p. Ballets: U.S.A., Festival of Two Worlds, Spoleto, Italy, June 1958. A ballet based on 'the kinds of movements, complexities of rhythms, relationships and qualities of atmosphere found in today's social dances of young people in America'. The work captures the moods of young Americans to a remarkable degree.

NIGHT AND SILENCE, THE, ballet, ch. Gore, m. Bach, arr. Mackerras, déc. R. Wilson, f.p. Edinburgh International Festival, Empire Th., Edinburgh, 25.8.1958 (Hinton, Poole). An outstanding ballet for two dancers, about jealousy.

NOCES, LES, ballet 4 sc., ch. Nijinska, m. Stravinsky, déc. Goncharova, f.p. Diaghilev's Co., Th. Gaîté Lyrique, Paris, 14.8.1923 (Doubrovska). There was a chorus, with wailing and chanting, and two grand pianos on the stage (with four pianists), with percussion. In England the four pianists were Auric, Poulenc, Rieti and Dukelsky—each one of whom had written a ballet for Diaghilev. In the controversy which followed in the English press H. G. Wells wrote a vigorous support of the ballet in *The Times*.

NOCTAMBULES, ballet, ch. MacMillan, m. H. Searle, déc. Georgiadis, f.p. S. Wells B., C.Gdn., 1.3.1956 (Nerina, Lane, Linden, Edwards). In a back-street variety theatre a hypnotist is duped by his own magic. The ballet provided Maryon Lane with one of her best roles as the hypnotist's assistant. (See Appendix III c (ii).)

NOCTURNE, ballet 1 act, book E. Sackville-West, ch. Ashton, m. Delius (*Paris*), déc. Fedorovitch, f.p. S. Wells B., S. Wells Th., 10.11.1936 (Fonteyn, Brae, Helpmann, Ashton). An outstanding ballet of atmosphere, one of Ashton's best.

NUTCRACKER, THE, OR CASSE-NOISETTE, ballet 2 acts and 3 sc., based on the tale by Hoffman, ch. Ivanov, m. Tchaikovsky, déc. Botcharov and Ivanov, f.p. Maryinsky Th., St. Petersburg, 6.12.1892 (dell-Era, Gerdt, Legat, Preobrajenska, Kyasht). Petipa was prevented by illness from carrying out this work and it fell to his assistant Ivanov. The ballet was revived in its entirety in a version by Sergueeff for the S. Wells B., S. Wells Th., 30.1.1934 (Markova, Judson), and twice for Festival Ballet—first in 1950 in a version by Beriozoff (Markova, Dolin), then in 1958 in a version by Lichine (Krassovska, Gilpin). Balanchine mounted the complete ballet for the N.Y. City B., 2.2.1954 (Tallchief, Magallanes). The last act is a divertissement 'The Kingdom of the Sweets' and is in the repertoire of many companies.

O

ODE, ballet 2 acts, ch. Massine, m. Nabokov, déc. Tchelitchev, f.p. Diaghilev's Co., Th. Sarah Bernhardt, Paris, 6.6.1928 (Beliamina, Lifar). The dancers were intertwined with ropes, and use was made of flashing lights and cinema projections. One of the first abstract ballets.

OISEAU DE FEU, L' (*Firebird*), ballet 3 sc., ch. Fokine, m. Stravinsky, déc. and cost. (except those for the Firebird and the Tsarevna designed by Bakst) Golovine, f.p. Diaghilev's Co., Paris Opéra, 25.6.1910 (Karsavina, Fokine). The first ballet-composition by Stravinsky for Diaghilev, the theme is a medley of Russian fairy tales and provided Karsavina with one of her great roles. A new version with ch. Balanchine and déc. Chagall was made for the N.Y. City B., 27.11.1949 (Maria Tallchief, Moncion). In 1945, Bolm presented a version (déc. Chagall) for Ballet Theatre (Markova). The ballet was revived by the S. Wells B. for the 25th anniversary of Diaghilev's death by Grigorieff and Tchernicheva, Empire Th., Edinburgh, 23.8.1954 (Fonteyn, Somes), déc. Goncharova (her 1926 version). A new version, ch. Lifar, déc. Wakhevitch, was mounted at the Paris Opéra, 7.4.1954 (Vyroubova, Algaroff).

ONDINE, (1) ballet in 6 sc., ch. Perrot, m. Pugni, déc. Grieve, f.p. Her Majesty's Th., London, 22.6.1843 (Cerrito, Perrot). This ballet contained one of Cerrito's most celebrated solos, the *pas de l'ombre* in which she dances with her shadow. (2) ballet in 3 acts, ch. Ashton, m. Hans Werner Henze, déc. de Nobili, f.p. R.B., C.Gdn., 27.10.1959 (Fonteyn, Somes, Farron, Grant). Freely adapted from the story by the German romantic writer, La Motte Fouqué, the scenario bears little similarity to Perrot's scenario but gives to Fonteyn, as Perrot's did to Cerrito, one of her finest roles. (See Appendix III C (iv).)

ON STAGE!, ballet 1 act, ch. Michael Kidd, m. dello Joio, déc. O. Smith, cost. A. Colt, f.p. B. Theatre, Boston, Mass., 4.10.1945 (Janet Reed, Nora Kaye, Kriza, Kidd). A tender ballet on a young girl's first rehearsal with a ballet company.

ORPHÉE, choreographic drama in 3 acts, 8 sc., ch. Béjart, *musique concrète* Pierre Henry, déc. Rudolph Kühner, f.p. Ballets des Béjarts, 13.3.1959, Th. des Ch.-Élysées, Paris. The Orpheus legend in modern terms. The first three-act ballet to *musique concrète*.

OTHELLO, (1) ballet in 5 acts, book and ch. Viganò, m. various, déc. Sanquirico, f.p. Teatro alla Scala, Milan, 6.2.1818. Scenario follows closely the play by Shakespeare. (2) ch. Chabukiani, m. Machavariani, f.p. Tbilisi Theatre of Opera and Ballet, 1957.

OUR LADY'S JUGGLER, ballet, ch. Andrée Howard and S. Salaman, m. Respighi, déc. A. Howard and S. Salaman, f.p. B. Rambert, Mercury Th., London, 29.10.1933 (Howard, Gore, Morfield).

OUVERTURE, ballet to a theme from Proust, ch. Jack Carter, m. Bloch, déc. McDowell, f.p. Ballet Workshop, 1952.

P

PALAIS DE CRISTAL, ballet 4 movements, ch. Balanchine, m. Bizet (Symphony), déc. Fini, f.p. Paris Opéra, 28.7.1947 (Darsonval, Touma-nova, Kalioujny, Ritz). This ballet was later danced by Ballet Society at N.Y. City Center, without déc. on 22.3.1948 under the title *Symphony in C* (Maria Tallchief, Leclercq, Magallanes, Moncion), and was taken into the repertoire of the Royal Danish B. in this form in 1953.

PARADE, ballet 1 act, book Cocteau, ch. Massine, m. Satie, déc. Picasso, f.p. Diaghilev's Co., Châtelet Th., Paris, 18.5.1917 (Lopokova, Massine). A cubist ballet, 'one of the works that changed the face of modern ballet'. The scenario is reproduced in Appendix III A.

PAS D'ACIER, LE, ballet 1 act, ch. Massine, m. Prokofieff, déc. Iakoulov, f.p. Diaghilev's Co., Th. Sarah Bernhardt, Paris, 8.6.1927 (Tcherni-cheva, Lifar). Glorification of the factory. A constructivist ballet. At the end the décor began to move like machines.

PAS DE QUATRE, LE, divertissement by Jules Perrot, m. Pugni, f.p. Her Majesty's Th., London, 12.7.1845, with Marie Taglioni, Carlotta Grisi, Fanny Cerrito and Lucile Grahn, which caused a sensation, for never before had the four greatest dancers of the time appeared together. The event has been recorded in one of the most beautiful lithographs of the period by A. E. Chalon. The idea of the ballet was Lumley's and he had to use all his diplomacy to avoid a quarrel between the dancers. It was performed three times only in 1845 (Queen Victoria and the Prince Consort attended the second performance), and marked the high point of the romantic movement in ballet. In its elevation of the ballerina alone it also expressed the fatal weakness of romanticism which came near to destroying ballet in Western Europe. A revival to the original music (orchestrated Leighton Lucas) with ch. Keith Lester has been produced by a number of companies, but better known is a further revival by Anton Dolin, very popular in the repertoire of Festival Ballet and several other companies.

PAST RECALLED. See OUVERTURE. *Ouverture* was renamed *Past recalled* when this ballet was staged for B. Rambert in 1953.

PATINEURS, LES, ballet ch. Ashton, m. Meyerbeer (from *Le Prophète* and *L'Étoile du nord*), déc. Chappell, f.p. S. Wells B., 16.2.1937 (Fon-teyn, Helpmann, Turner). Taken into repertoire of Ballet Th., N.Y., 1946, with déc. Beaton. A skating ballet, using the classical technique in its full virtuosity.

PAVILLON D'ARMIDE, LE, ballet 1 act, 3 sc., book and déc. Benois, ch. Fokine, m. Tcherepnin, f.p. Maryinsky Th., St. Petersburg, 25.11.1907 (Pavlova, Nijinsky, Gerdt). This was Benois' first ballet and was also danced on the first night of Diaghilev's first season in Paris

(Châtelet Th., 19.5.1909, Karalli, Nijinsky, Mordkin). Gobelins tapestries come to life. Based on Gautier's story *Omphale*.

PÉRI, LA, a *pas de deux*, ch. Ashton, m. Dukas, déc. Chappell, f.p. Ballet Club, Mercury Th., London, 16.2.1931 (Markova, Ashton). Ashton ch. a further version for Fonteyn and Somes at C.Gdn., 15.2.1956, déc. Hitchens, cost. Levasseur. Other ballets on this theme have been created, namely, a two-act version at Paris Opéra, 17.7.1843, another there with Pavlova 1921 and a Lifar version at Monte Carlo in 1946. The décor for the version at Covent Garden in 1956 met with disapproval and was redesigned by Levasseur in 1957.

PERSEPHONE, ballet, 3 sc., ch. Frederick Ashton, m. Stravinsky, déc. and cost. Nico Ghika, f.p. R.B., C.Gdn., 12.12.61. Realisation of the melodrama by Gide in speech, song and dance originally commissioned by Ida Rubinstein and performed at the Paris Opéra 1934. On that occasion ch. by Kurt Jooss.

PETER AND THE WOLF, ballet to Prokofieff's music, ch. Staff, déc. Sheppard, f.p. B. Rambert, Arts Th., Cambridge, 1.5.1950 (Lulu Dukes, France, Gilmour, Kersley). A narrator unfolds the story.

PETITS RIENS, LES, (1) ch. Noverre, m. Mozart, f.p. Acad. Royale (Opéra), Paris, 11.6.1778 (Guimard, Dauberval). Noverre commissioned Mozart for the music for this ballet, the score of which was not discovered until 1872 in the library of the Opéra. It was revived at the Opéra-Comique in 1912. (2) ch. Ashton, m. Mozart, déc. Chappell, for B. Rambert, Mercury Th., 10.3.1928 (Rambert, Argyle, Turner, Ashton). (3) ch. de Valois, m. Mozart, déc. Smyth, f.p. Old Vic, London, 13.12.1928. It was the first ballet produced by de Valois for the Old Vic, and it was also the first ballet in the first programme given by the Vic-Wells B., S. Wells Th., 5.5.1931.

PETROUCHKA, ballet 4 sc., ch. Fokine, m. Stravinsky, déc. Benois, f.p. Diaghilev's Co., Th. du Châtelet, Paris, 13.6.1911 (Karsavina, Orloff, Nijinsky, Cecchetti). One of Fokine's great masterpieces with a brilliant score by Stravinsky, this ballet is in repertoire of many large companies today. The emotions of puppets.

PIÈGE DE LUMIÈRE, ballet 3 sc., ch. Taras, m. Damase, déc. Labisse, cost. Levasseur, f.p. de Cuevas B., Empire Th., Paris, 23.12.1952 (Hightower, Golovine, Skouratoff). Fantasy of escaped convicts who catch butterflies in a forest.

PILLAR OF FIRE, ballet 2 sc., ch. Tudor, m. Schönberg (*Verklärte Nacht*), déc. Mielziner, f.p. Ballet Th., Met. Op., N.Y., 8.4.1942 (Nora Kaye, Chase, Lyon, Tudor). Tudor's first major work in the U.S.A. and his masterpiece. Nora Kaye's interpretation of the leading role established her as one of the greatest dramatic dancers in contemporary ballet.

PINEAPPLE POLL, ballet 3 sc., ch. Cranko, m. Sullivan (arr. Mackerras), déc. Osbert Lancaster, f.p. S. Wells Th. B., 13.4.1951 (Fifield, Claire, O'Reilly, Poole, Blair). Also in repertoire of Australian B. It is inspired by W. S. Gilbert's Bab Ballad *The Bumboat Woman's Story*.

PLACE IN THE DESERT, A, ch. Norman Morrice, m. Carlos Surinach, déc. and cost. Ralph Koltai, f.p. B. Rambert, S. Wells Th., 25.6.61. The building of a dam in the desert and the effect of this on the builders and the local inhabitants. (See Appendix III c (v).)

PLANETS, THE, ballet, ch. Tudor, m. Holst, déc. Stevenson, f.p. B. Rambert, Mercury Th., London, 28.10.1934 (Argyle, Laing, Lloyd). Suite of dances to Holst's *The Planets*.

POLOVTSIAN DANCES FROM PRINCE IGOR, ballet 1 act, ch. Fokine, m. Borodin, déc. Roerich, f.p. Diaghilev's Co., Th. de Châtelet, Paris, 19.5.1909 (Fedorova, Smirnova, Bolm). This ballet, one of Fokine's best (and his own favourite), came as a revelation to a public accustomed to the conventional ballets of the period. It also, more than any other, helped to restore the male dancer to the stage in Western Europe where for several decades he had been but a porteur, all male parts being taken by a *danseuse en travestie*. The ballet is in the repertoire of many contemporary companies.

PRÉSAGES, LES, ballet in 4 parts, ch. Massine, m. Tchaikovsky's 5th Symphony, déc. Masson, f.p. de Basil Co., Monte Carlo, 13.4.1933 (Baronova, Verchinina, Riabouchinska, Lichine, Woizikovsky). Massine's first symphonic ballet, it tells of Man's conflict with his Destiny.

PRINCE OF THE PAGODAS, THE, ballet 3 acts, ch. Cranko, m. Britten, déc. Piper, cost. Healey, f.p. S. Wells B., C.Gdn., 1.1.1957 (Beriosova, Farron, Blair, Edwards). A fairy story. Since produced at Munich (ch. Alan Carter) and by Cranko himself at Stuttgart.

PRISONER OF THE CAUCASUS, THE, (1) ballet based on Pushkin's poem: 4 acts, ch. Didelot, m. Cavos, f.p. Bolshoi Th., St. Petersburg, 27.1.1823 (Istomina, Goltz). One of Didelot's best ballets in Russia. (2) ch. Lavrovsky, m. Asafiev, f.p. Leningrad, Maly Opera Th., 1938.

PRISONERS, THE, ballet, ch. Darrell, m. Bartok, déc. B. Kay, f.p. Western Th. B., Dartington Hall, Devon, 24.6.1957 (Musitz, Salt, Sunde). Two prisoners escape and quarrel over a woman.

PRISONNIER DU CAUCASE, LE, ballet ch. Skibine, m. Khatchaturian, déc. Doboujinsky, f.p. de Cuevas Co., Th. de l'Empire, Paris, 1951 (Skibine, Marjorie Tallchief). Pushkin's Poem.

PRODIGAL SON, THE (1) ballet 3 sc., ch. Balanchine, m. Prokofieff, déc. Roualt, f.p. Diaghilev's Co., Th. Sarah Bernhardt, Paris, 21.5.1929 (Lifar, Doubrovska). Revived for N.Y. City B., 23.2.1950 (Robbins, Mounsey). (2) ch. Lichine, same m. and déc., f.p. de Basil Co., Sydney, 30.12.1938 (Lichine, Osato). (3) ch. Jooss, same m., déc. Heckroth, f.p. Essen, 1931. (4) ch. Jooss, m. Cohen, déc. Bouchène, f.p. Ballets Jooss, Prince's Th., Bristol, Oct. 1939. (5) ch. Kramer, m. Alfven, déc. Lindström, f.p. R. Swedish B., Royal Opera, Stockholm, 1957. Based on five biblical paintings from Dalarna, this is Ivo Kramer's most successful work and one of the first truly Swedish ballets of international quality.

PROMÉTHÉE, French ballet, book by Pierre Rhallys, ch. Maurice Béjart, m. Maurice Ohana, déc. and cost. B. Daydé, f.p. Les Ballets 1956 de Miskovitch et Lidova, Festival de Lyon Charbonnières, June 1956. (See Appendix III B.)

PROMETHEUS, ch. Viganò, m. Beethoven, f.p. Vienna, 1801. Notable among Viganò's ballets because this was one of the few occasions he had music specially commissioned.

PROSPECT BEFORE US, THE, ballet 7 sc., ch. de Valois, m. Boyce, déc. Furse, f.p. S. Wells B., 4.7.1940 (May, Honer, Helpmann, Ashton, Newman). Based on a Rowlandson print of the name, it depicts the rivalry between the Kings Th. and the Panthéon, London, in 1789.

PULCINELLA, ballet 1 act, ch. Massine, m. Pergolesi-Stravinsky, déc. Picasso, f.p. Diaghilev's Co., Paris Opéra, 15.5.1920 (Karsavina, Massine). A *commedia dell' arte* ballet and one of the best creations of Massine's early period.

Q

QARRTSILUNI, ballet 1 act, ch. Lander, m. Riisager, déc. Johansen, f.p. Royal Th., Copenhagen, 21.2.1942 (Larsen). An Eskimo priest's ritual dance to welcome the breaking through of the sun after winter.

QUATUOR, book and ch. Milko Sparemblek, m. Raffaello de Banfield, déc. Dupont, f.p. Les Ballets 1956 de Miskovitch et Lidova, Festival de Lyon Charbonnières June 1956 (Meyer, Carrié, Sparemblek, Sulich). Four beings in front of a wall of solitude—Friendship—Discovery of Love—Ties which hinder—Alone we are weak—Quartet.

R

RAKE'S PROGRESS, THE, ballet 6 sc., ch. de Valois, m. Gavin Gordon, déc. Whistler, f.p. S. Wells B., S. Wells Th., London, 20.5.1935 (Gore, Markova). The ballet is based on the Hogarth paintings.

RAYMONDA, ballet 3 acts, 4 sc., ch. Petipa, m. Glazunov, déc. Allegri, Ivanov, Lambini, f.p. Maryinsky Th., St. Petersburg, 19.1.1898 (Legnani, Preobrajenska, Gerdt). This ballet is still in the repertoire of the Soviet Ballet and has been revived in Europe and America. Ballet of medieval Hungary.

RENDEZVOUS, LES, ballet 1 act, ch. Ashton, m. Auber (ballet music in *L'Enfant Prodigue*), déc. Chappell, f.p. S. Wells B., S. Wells Th., 5.12.1933 (Markova, Idzikovski). A lightly linked suite of dances.

RIO GRANDE, ballet, ch. Ashton, m. Lambert, déc. Burra, f.p. Camargo Soc. under title *A Day in a Spanish Port* (Markova). Revised in 1935 with Fonteyn dancing the Creole Girl, her first important role. The ballet uses a solo piano, solo alto and a chorus. Freely adapted from Sacheverell Sitwell's poem.

RITE OF SPRING, THE, ballet, ch. MacMillan, déc. and cost. Sydney Nolan, m. Stravinsky, f.p. R.B., C.Gdn., 3.5.1962. MacMillan's version of *Le Sacre du Printemps* (see below).

RODEO, ballet 3 sc., ch. De Mille, m. Copland, déc. Smith, cost. Love, f.p. Ballet Russe de Monte Carlo, Met. Op., N.Y., 16.10.1942 (Mladova, Franklin, De Mille). This ballet introduces an American square dance with a caller. (See Appendix III D.)

ROMEO AND JULIET, ballet (1) ch. Galeotti, m. Schall, f.p. R. Danish B., Copenhagen, 2.4.1811 (Schall and Antoine Bournonville). (2) 1 act, ch. Nijinska-Balanchine, m. Constant Lambert, déc. Miro and Ernst, f.p. Diaghilev's Co., Monte Carlo, 4.5.1926 (Karsavina, Lifar). The music was the first to be commissioned by Diaghilev from an English composer. The ballet was not a straightforward telling of the story but was styled a rehearsal, without scenery, in two parts. (3) 3 acts, ch. Lavrovsky, m. Prokofieff, déc. Peter Williams, f.p. Kirov Th., Leningrad, 11.1.1940 (Ulanova, Sergueeff). (4) 1 act, ch. Tudor, m. Delius, déc. Berman, f.p. Ballet Th., Met. Op., N.Y., 6.4.1943 (Markova, Hugh Laing). (5) 1 act, ch. Lifar, m. Tchaikovsky, f.p. Nouveau B. de Monte Carlo 1946 and at Paris Opéra (déc. Moulène), 13.4.1949 (Chauviré, Lifar). (6) 1 act, ch. Bartholin, m. Tchaikovsky, déc. Pedersen, f.p. R. Danish B., Copenhagen, 8.12.1950 (Vangsaa, Bruhn). Bartholin originally produced this ballet for the Ballets de la Jeunesse, Paris, 1937 (Moulin, Bartholin). (7) ch. Parlic, m. Prokofieff, déc. Gedrinsky, cost. Kostincer-Bregovac, f.p. Zagreb Opera, June 1949 (Roje, Lhotka). (8) 3 acts, ch. Ashton, m. Prokofieff, déc. Rice, f.p. R. Danish B., Copenhagen, 19.5.1955 (Vangsaa, Kronstam). (9) 2 acts, ch. Lifar, m. Prokofieff, déc. Wakhevitch, f.p. Paris Opera, 28.12.1955 (Daydé, Renault).

RUSES D'AMOUR, ballet 1 act, ch. Petipa, m. Glazunov, f.p. Hermitage Th., St. Petersburg, 29.1.1900 (Legnani, Gerdt). In the style of a Watteau painting.

S

SACRE DU PRINTEMPS, LE, ballet 2 acts, ch. Nijinsky, m. Stravinsky, déc. Roerich, f.p. Diaghilev's Co., Th. des Ch.-Élysées, Paris, 29.5.1913 (Piltz). There was an uproar at the first performance and it was only danced six times. In October 1920 it was given again at the same theatre and with the same décor, but ch. Massine, with Sokolova as the chief dancer. In 1930 Martha Graham danced this version at the Met. Op., N.Y. Primitive ritual in which a Chosen Maiden is sacrificed as a fertility offering.

SAILOR'S RETURN, THE, ballet 6 sc., ch. Howard, m. Oldham, déc. Howard, f.p. B. Rambert, S. Wells Th., London, 2.6.1947 (Gilmour, Gore, Gilpin). Based on David Garnett's novel of the same name.

SCHÉHÉRAZADE, ballet 1 act, ch. Fokine, m. Rimsky-Korsakov, déc. Bakst, f.p. Diaghilev's Co., Paris Opéra, 4.6.1910 (Ida Rubenstein, Bulgakov, Nijinsky, Cecchetti). This ballet caused a furore at the time of its production and was the most sensational of all Diaghilev's early productions, partly because of its sensuous theme, and the dancing of Nijinsky, and partly because of the entirely new type of déc., with its brilliant masses of colour, which caused a gasp of admiration and surprise when the curtain rose. This déc. greatly influenced the art of interior decoration and the fashions of the period. The critics argued and disagreed among themselves over the use of the music and the cutting of one of the four movements.

SEA CHANGE, ballet 1 act, ch. Cranko, m. Sibelius (En Saga), déc. Piper, f.p. Gaiety Th., Dublin, 18.7.1949 (O'Reilly, Hogan, Shore, Zullig). Tragedy of fisher-folk bereaved by a shipwreck.

SERENADE, ballet 1 act, ch. Balanchine, m. Tchaikovsky (Serenade for Strings), déc. Lurçat, f.p. Sch. of Am. Ballet, Hartford, 6.12.1934. Its first official performance was by American Ballet, 1.3.1935, at Adelphi Th., N.Y. (Anchutina, Boris, Caccialanza, Mullowney, Dollar, Laskey). With various changes of cost. this has been danced by many companies and was mounted at the Paris Opéra, 30.4.1947. Ballet of pure dancing.

SEVENTH SYMPHONY, ballet 4 parts, ch. Massine, m. Beethoven, déc. Bérard, f.p. de Basil Co., Monte Carlo, 5.5.1938 (Markova, Franklin, Youskevitch). Massine's least successful symphonic ballet.

SHADOW, THE, ballet 1 sc., ch. Cranko, m. Dohnányi, déc. Piper, f.p. S. Wells B., C.Gdn., 3.3.1953 (Beriosova, Lindsey, Chatfield, Shaw, Ashbridge). Romantic theme of a man torn between two loves, and afflicted by nameless fears.

SIMPLE SYMPHONY, ballet, ch. Gore, m. Britten, déc. R. Wilson, f.p. B. Rambert, Th. Royal, Bristol, 29.11.1944 (Gilmour, Gore). A gay frolic on the beach.

SLAUGHTER ON TENTH AVENUE, ballet, ch. Balanchine, m. Rodgers, cost. Sharaff, déc. Mielziner, f.p. in the revue *On Your Toes*, Imp. Th., N.Y., 11.4.1936 (Geva, Vilan, Bolger). The ballet formed part of the story of the revue, but is important in itself as one of the earliest appearances of Balanchine and the classical vocabulary on the popular stage.

SLEEPING BEAUTY, THE (*The Sleeping Princess, La Belle au bois dormant*), ballet 4 acts, 5 sc., ch. Petipa, m. Tchaikovsky, déc. Levogt, Botcharov, Shishlov, Ivanov, cost. Vsevolojsky, f.p. Maryinsky Th., St. Petersburg, 15.1.1890 (Carlotta Brianza, Paul Gerdt, with Cecchetti as Carabosse, Marie Petipa as Lilac Fairy, Cecchetti and V. Nikitina as Blue Birds). In 1921 Diaghilev revived the ballet, reproduced by Sergueeff using the Stepanoff Notation, Alhambra Th., London, 2.11.1921 (Spessivtseva, Vladimiroff, Carlotta Brianza as Carabosse, Lopokova as Lilac Fairy, Idzikovski and Lopokova as Blue Birds). The Lilac Fairy was also danced by Nijinska who chor. the hunting dances and part of last act. Déc. Bakst and a fortune lavished on the production in anticipation of a long run. It was withdrawn after a run of three months at great financial loss. The audience, used to short one-act ballets, was not ready for the revival of a classical ballet. Revived S. Wells Th., 2.2.1939 (Fonteyn, Helpmann, Brae, Honer and Turner), déc. Nadia Benois, ch., Sergueeff. With déc. Messel it was again revived by S. Wells B. to reopen Covent Garden after the war (Fonteyn, Helpmann, who also played Carabosse, Grey, May and Massine). Sergueeff also revived it for International B. Co.

SNOW MAIDEN, THE, ballet in 3 acts, ch. Bourmeister, m. Tchaikovsky, déc. Yuri Pimenov and Gennady Epishin. Full f.p. London's Festival B., Royal Festival Hall, London, 17.7.1961. Based on the fairy tale.

SOLEIL DE NUIT, LE, ballet, ch. Massine, m. Rimsky-Korsakov, déc. Larionov, f.p. Diaghilev's Co., Grand Th., Geneva, 20.12.1915 (Massine). This was Massine's first ballet and Larionov's first work for Diaghilev. Russian folk dances.

SOMNAMBULISM, ballet, ch. MacMillan, m. Kenton, f.p. Sunday Choreographers, S. Wells Th., 1.2.1953 (Lane, MacMillan, Poole). Revised version f.p. S. Wells Th. B., 29.5.1956 (Heaton, Hill, Britton). MacMillan's first ballet.

SPARTACUS, ballet in 4 acts, ch. Yakobson, m. Khatchaturian, déc. Khodasievitch, f.p. Kirov Th., Leningrad, 27.12.1956 (Shelest, Makarou). The rebellion of Roman slaves in 73 B.C.

SPECTRE DE LA ROSE, LE, ballet 1 sc., ch. Fokine, m. Weber, déc. Bakst, f.p. Diaghilev's Co., Monte Carlo, 19.4.1911 (Karsavina, Nijinsky). This romantic *pas de deux* was suggested by J. L. Vaudoyer who had been inspired by a poem of Gautier.

STARS AND STRIPES, ballet, ch. Balanchine, m. Sousa, déc. Hays, cost. Karinska, f.p. N.Y. City B., City Center, N.Y., 17.1.1958 (Allegra Kent, Hayden, Adams, d'Amboise). Patriotic humour in military costume.

STONE FLOWER, THE, (1) ch. Muller, m. Fridlander, f.p. Sverdlovsk Opera & Ballet Th., 1947. (2) ch. Lavrovsky, m. Prokofieff, déc. Starshentsky, f.p. Bolshoi Th., Moscow, 1954 (Plisetskaya, Chorokhova, Yermolayeff, Koren, Preobrazhensky). (3) ch. Grigorovich, m. Prokofieff, déc. Virsaladze, f.p. Kirov Th., Leningrad 1957.

SUITE EN BLANC, ballet, ch. Lifar, m. Lalo (from the ballet *Namouna*), f.p. Paris Opéra, 23.7.1943 (Darsonval, Schwarz, Chauviré, Dynalix, Lifar, Ritz, Fenonjois). This is a ballet blanc with no décor, and displays all the company. A version, under the title *Noir et Blanc*, was danced by the Nouveau B. de Monte Carlo and by de Cuevas Co.

SWAN LAKE, ballet 4 acts, book by Begitchev and Geltser, (1) ch. J. Reisinger, m. Tchaikovsky, déc. Shangin, etc., f.p. Bolshoi Th., Moscow, 4.3.1877 (Karpakova, Gillert II). (2) Revised at Maryinsky Th., St. Petersburg, 27.1.1895, ch. Petipa–Ivanov, m. Tchaikovsky, déc. Botcharov and Levogt (Legnani, Gerdt). In 1901 revived by Gorsky in Moscow, etc., f.p. England 16.5.1910 at the London Hippodrome with Preobrajenska and in France by Diaghilev's Co., Monte Carlo, 13.4.1912 (Kchessinska), f.p. America, 19.12.1911, Met. Op., N.Y. (Geltser). Reproduced by Sergueeff for the Vic-Wells B. in 4 acts at S. Wells Th., 20.11.1934, déc. Stevenson (Markova, Helpmann). Countless later productions and many versions in many countries.

SYLPHIDE, LA, ballet 2 acts, book A. Nourrit, ch. Filippo Taglioni, m. Schneitzhoffer, déc. Ciceri, cost. Lormier, f.p. Paris Opéra, 12.3.1832 (Marie Taglioni, Noblet, Mazilier, and Mme Élie as the Sorceress). This work, by its success, launched the Romantic era in ballet and confirmed the preference of the public for romantic themes in place of the old classical themes. The Scottish setting, with its theme of a supernatural being falling in love with a mortal, epitomised the Romantic movement in literature. The costume created for Taglioni, with its tight-fitting bodice, leaving neck and shoulders bare, and its white muslin bell-shaped skirt, coming midway between knee and ankle, rapidly became the accepted costume for the danseuse in the Romantic ballet. In this ballet also dancing on *pointes* first fully established itself. The ballet was first performed (by Taglioni) in London, 26.7.1832 (C.Gdn.), St.

Petersburg, 18.9.1837 (Maryinsky Th.), Milan, 29.5.1841 (La Scala). It has been revived for the B. des Ch.-Élysées, ch. Gsovsky, déc. Serebriakoff, cost. Bérard, Paris, 15.6.1945 (Vyroubova, Petit). It has been in the repertoire of the Royal Danish B., ch. Bournonville after F. Taglioni, m. Lovenskjold, since 28.11.1836 (Lucile Grahn, Bournonville). Lander mounted a version of this for the de Cuevas Co., Empire Th., Paris, 9.12.1953 (Hightower, Golovine), déc. B. Daydé. The ballet entered the British repertoire for the first time when the Swedish ballerina Elsa-Marianne von Rosen, and her husband Allan Fridericia, the Danish producer and critic, produced a revised version of the Bournonville ballet for Ballet Rambert at the S. Wells Th., 20.7.1960.

SYLPHIDES, LES. *See* CHOPINIANA.

SYLVIA, OU LA NYMPHE DE DIANE, (1) ballet, 3 acts, 4 sc., book Barbier and Reinach, ch. Mérante, m. Delibes, déc. Cheret, Rubé, Chaperon, cost. Lacoste, f.p. Paris Opéra, 14.6.1876 (Sangalli, Marquet, Sanlaville, Mérante). The ballet was revived at the Opéra in 1919 (by Staats), 1941 (Lifar), and 1946 (Aveline), and was then principally associated there with the dancer, Lycette Darsonval. In London a production at the Empire Th. was staged by C. Wilhelm and Fred Farren, 18.5.1911 (Kyasht, P. Bedells, Unity More, Mossetti, Farren). (2) ballet, 3 acts, ch. Ashton, m. Delibes, déc. Ironsides, f.p. S. Wells B., C.Gdn., 3.9.1952 (Fonteyn, Somes, Hart, Grant, Farron). The story follows the original Paris version with slight alterations. As a result of difficulties put in his way when he attempted to stage *Sylvia* at the Maryinsky Th., St. Petersburg, in 1900, Diaghilev resigned from the staff of the Imperial Theatres. Ivanov was working on a revival of the ballet when he died in 1901.

SYMPHONIC VARIATIONS, ballet 1 act, ch. Ashton, m. César Franck, déc. Fedorovitch, f.p. S. Wells B., C.Gdn., 24.4.1946 (Fonteyn, Shearer, May, Somes, Denton, Shaw). A purely abstract ballet for six dancers, one of Ashton's most successful.

SYMPHONIE FANTASTIQUE, ballet 5 sc., ch. Massine, m. Berlioz, déc. Bérard, f.p. de Basil's Co., C.Gdn., 24.7.1936 (Massine, Toumanova). The story is that of Berlioz's *Fantastic Symphony*.

SYMPHONY, ballet 1 act, ch. MacMillan, m. Shostakovitch, déc. Yolanda Sonnabend, f.p. R.B., C.Gdn., 15.2.1963 (Seymour, MacLeary, Parkinson, Doyle). A plotless ballet.

SYMPHONY FOR FUN, ballet, ch. Charnley, m. Don Gillis, déc. Lingwood, f.p. Festival B., Festival Hall, London, 1.9.1952. (Rossana, Landa, Gilpin). Exactly described by its title, the ballet combines young people's dance styles with classical and modern steps.

SYMPHONY IN C. *See* PALAIS DE CRISTAL.

T

TARAS BULBA, (1) ballet 3 acts, 5 sc., ch. Lopokov, m. Soloviev-Sedoy, f.p. Kirov Th., Leningrad, 1940 (Dudinskaya, Chaboukiani). Based on Gogol's novel about medieval Ukraine and the Cossacks. (2) new production, ch. Fenster, f.p. Kirov Th., 1955.

THEME AND VARIATIONS, ballet, ch. Balanchine, m. Tchaikovsky, déc. and cost. Woodman Thompson, f.p. Am. Ballet Th., N.Y. City Center, 26.11.1947. Described by John Martin of the *N.Y. Times* as 'a Kind of glorified epitome of Petipa . . . a brilliant medium for pure choreographic abstraction'.

THREE CORNERED HAT, THE. *See* Tricorne, Le.

TITANI, I, ballet in 6 acts, book and ch. Viganò, m. various, déc. Sanquirico, Teatro alla Scala, Milan, 11.10.1819. Detailed story of the ancient Gods.

TRAIN BLEU, LE, ballet 1 act, by Cocteau, ch. Nijinska, m. Milhaud, déc. Laurens, curtain Picasso, f.p. Diaghilev's Co., Th. des. Ch.-Élysées, Paris, 20.6.1924 (Nijinska, Sokolova, Dolin, Woizikovski). A ballet inspired by Dolin's acrobatic dancing and never given again after he left the Co.

TRICORNE, LE, ballet 1 act, ch. Massine, m. de Falla, déc. Picasso, f.p. Diaghilev's Co., Alhambra Th., London, 22.7.1919 (Karsavina, Massine). One of Massine's greatest ballets and now in the repertoire of many companies. Revived for S. Wells B., C.Gdn., 6.2.1947 (Fonteyn, Massine). Important for its blending of the classical vocabulary with national (in this case, Spanish) dancing.

TRUMPET CONCERTO, ch. Balanchine, m. Haydn, déc. Kernot, f.p. S. Wells Th. B., S. Wells Th., 19.9.1950 (Beriosova, Blair). Ballet of pure dancing.

TULIP OF HARLEM, THE, ballet in 3 acts, 4 sc., ch. Ivanov, m. Schell, f.p. Maryinsky Th., St. Petersburg, 4.10.1887 (Bessonne, Legat, Gerdt). In this ballet Bessonne turned fourteen fouettés, but when Legnani danced the role in 1893 she turned thirty-two, the first time this feat had been performed in Russia.

TWO BROTHERS, ballet, ch. Norman Morrice, m. Dohnányi, déc. Ralph Koltai, f.p. B. Rambert, S. Wells Th., 15.9.1958 (Martlew, Chesworth, Morrice). Love of two brothers, rivals for same woman. Morrice's first ballet, remarkable for its dramatic quality and its evocation of the street world of young adolescents today.

U

UNDERTOW, ballet 1 act, ch. Tudor, m. W. Schuman, déc. Breinin, f.p. Ballet Th., Met. Op., N.Y., 10.4.1945 (Laing, Alonso, Adams). Symbolic ballet of the birth of man and his emotions.

V

VALENTINE'S EVE, ballet, ch. Ashton, m. Ravel, déc. Fedorovitch, f.p. B. Rambert, Duke of York's Th., London, 4.2.1935. A ballet, strong in atmosphere, in which, said Lionel Bradley, 'Ashton matched the mood of Ravel's various "valse" by the qualities of his characters', the poet, the coquette, and so on.

VALSES NOBLES ET SENTIMENTALES, ballet 1 act, ch. Ashton, m. Ravel, déc. Fedorovitch, f.p. S. Wells Th. B., 1.10.1947 (Heaton). Ballet of pure dancing.

VENEZIANA, ballet 1 act, ch. Howard, m. Donizetti (arr. ApIvor), déc. Fedorovitch, f.p. S. Wells B., C.Gdn., 9.4.1953 (Elvin, Powell). Carnival in Venice. Fedorovitch's last décor.

W

WEDDING BOUQUET, A, ballet 1 act, ch. Ashton, m. and déc. Lord Berners, f.p. S. Wells B., 27.4.1937 (Honer, Fonteyn, Helpmann, Farron, de Valois). The ballet is accompanied by verses of Gertrude Stein; at first these were sung by a chorus but later were spoken by Constant Lambert. Ninette de Valois (as Webster, the Maid) danced for the last time as a member of the Co. in this ballet.

WEST SIDE STORY, a musical in 2 acts based on a conception of Jerome Robbins, book Arthur Laurents, m. Leonard Bernstein, lyrics, Stephen Sondheim, ch., prod. and dir. Robbins, déc. Smith, cost. Sharraff, f.p. Winter Gdn. Th., N.Y., 26.9.1957 (Larry Kent, Carol Lawrence, Chita Rivera), f.p. Her Majesty's Th., London, 12.12.1958 (Don McKay, Marlys Watters, Chita Rivera). A modern Romeo and Juliet story on New York's West Side, notable for the success with which it combines all the elements of theatre—music, décor, lighting, speech, song, acting and dancing—on a basis of choreographic movement.

WHIMS OF CUPID AND THE BALLET MASTER, THE, ballet, ch. Galeotti, m. Jens Lolle, f.p. Royal Th., Copenhagen, 1786. The oldest existing ballet in any repertoire and still performed by The Royal Danish Ballet. Now performed with déc. by Pederson. Lander mounted it at Paris Opéra 27.2.1952, déc. Chapelain-Midi. Comic ballet introducing many national *pas de deux* and ending with a general mélange.

WITCH BOY, THE, ballet, ch. Jack Carter, m. Salzedo, déc. McDowell, f.p. Festival Ballet, Festival Hall, London, 15.7.1958 (John Gilpin, Anita Landa, Dolin, Kenneth Sudell). Free adaptation of the Dark of the Moon legend of Barbara Allen. Carter's best-known work and one of the best new works commissioned by Festival Ballet.

SUGGESTIONS FOR FURTHER STUDY

MOST of the books in the list below have contributed in one way or another to our own study of choreography and we gladly acknowledge their help. Many of the older books are important source material available only in national libraries or archives. More recent publications can be obtained from local libraries, or bought in the bookshops.

Amberg, George: *Ballet* (New York, 1949).
Appia, Adolphe: *Die Musik und die Inscenierung* (Munich, 1899).
Arbeau, Thoinot: *Orchésographie* (Langres, 1588, trans. Beaumont, London, 1925).
Aubert, Charles: *L'Art mimique* (Paris, 1901).
Authors various: *Les Ballets suédois* (Paris, 1931).

Baron, A.: *Lettres et entretiens sur la danse* (Paris, 1824).
Beaumont, Cyril: *Complete Book of Ballets* (London, 1937).
   The Diaghilev Ballet in London (London, 1940).
   Supplement to the Complete Book of Ballets (London, 1942).
   The Ballet Called Giselle (London, 1944).
   Ballet Design: Past and Present (London, 1946).
   The Ballet Called Swan Lake (London, 1952).
   Ballets of Today (London, 1954).
   Ballets Past and Present (London, 1955).
Beaumont and Idzikowski: *A Manual of the Theory and Practice of Classical Theatrical Dancing* (Revised Edition, London, 1955).
Benois, Alexandre: *Reminiscences of the Russian Ballet* (London, 1941).
   Memoirs (London, 1960).
Bjurström, Per: *Giacomo Torelli and Baroque Stage Design* (Stockholm, 1961).
Blasis, Carlo: *Traité élémentaire théorique et pratique de l'art de la danse* (Milan, 1820).
   The Code of Terpsichore (London, 1830).
   Notes Upon Dancing (London, 1847).
Bogdanov–Berezovsky: *Ulanova and the Development of Soviet Ballet* (London, 1952).
Boigne, Charles de: *Les Petits Mystères de l'Opéra* (Paris, 1857).
Borisoglebsky, M.: *Materials for a History of the Russian Ballet* (Leningrad, 1938).
Bournonville, August: *Mid Teaterliv* (Copenhagen, 1848).
   Études chorégraphiques (Copenhagen, 1861).
Bradley, Lionel: *Sixteen Years of Ballet Rambert* (London, 1946).

Brinson, Peter (Ed.): *The Ballet in Britain* (London, 1962).
Bruhn and Moore: *Bournonville and Ballet Technique* (London, 1961).
Buckle, Richard (Ed.): *Memoirs of Lydia Sokolova* (London, 1960).

Capon, Gaston: *Les Vestris* (Paris, 1908).
Caroso, Fabritio: *Il ballerino* (Milan, 1581).
Carrieri, Raffaele: *La danza in Italia 1500–1900* (Milan, 1946).
Castil Blaze: *La Danse et les ballets depuis Bacchus jusqu'à Mlle Taglioni* (Paris, 1852).
Cellarius: *La Danse des salons* (Paris, 1847).
Chauviré, Yvette: *Je suis ballerine* (Paris, 1960).
Chujoy, Anatole (Ed.): *The Dance Encyclopaedia* (New York, 1949).
 The New York City Ballet (New York, 1955).
Clarke, Mary: *The Sadler's Wells Ballet* (London, 1955).
 Dancers of Mercury (London, 1962).
Cooper, Martin: *French Music* (London, 1951).
Copland, Aaron: *Copland on Music* (London, 1961).
Craig, Edward Gordon: *On the Art of the Theatre* (London, 1911).

Dacier, Émile: *Une Danseuse de l'Opèra sous Louis XV: Mlle Sallé* (Paris, 1909).
Desrat, G.: *Dictionnaire de la danse* (Paris, 1895).
Duncan, Isadora: *My Life* (London, 1928).

Evans, Edwin: *Music and the Dance* (London, 1948).

Feuillet, Raoul: *Chorégraphie ou l'art d'écrire la danse* (Paris, 1701).
Fokine and Chujoy: *Fokine: Memoirs of a Ballet Master* (Boston, 1961).
Fridericia, Allan: *Harald Lander og hans Balleter* (Copenhagen, 1951).

Gallini, Giovanni-Andrea: *A Treatise on the Art of Dancing* (London, 1765).
Gautier, Théophile: *The Romantic Ballet* (trans. Beaumont, London, 1932).
 Voyage en Russie (Paris, 1858).
Gilder and Freedley: *Theatre Collections in Libraries and Museums* (London 1936).
Grigoriev, Serge: *The Diaghilev Ballet* (London, 1953).
Guest, Ivor: *The Ballet of the Second Empire 1858–70* (London, 1953).
 The Romantic Ballet in Britain (London, 1954).
 The Ballet of the Second Empire 1847–58 (London, 1955).
 Victorian Ballet Girl (London, 1957).
 Adeline Genée (London, 1958).
Guest, Ivor (Ed.): *La Fille mal gardée* (London, 1960).

Haskell, Arnold: *Ballet* (London, 1938).
 Diaghilev (London, 1953).
Hood, Robin: *Svensk Ballet* (Stockholm, 1952).
Horst and Russell: *Modern Dance Forms* (San Francisco, 1961).
Humphrey, Doris: *The Art of Making Dances* (New York, 1959).

Jelgerhuis, J.: *Theoretische Lessen over de Gesticulatie en Mimiek* (Amsterdam, 1827).

Karsavina, Tamara: *Theatre Street* (London, 1930).
  Ballet Technique (London, 1956).
Kirstein, Lincoln: *Blast at Ballet* (New York, 1938).
Kirstein, Stuart, Dyer and Balanchine: *The Classic Ballet* (London, 1953).
Kochno, Boris: *Le Ballet* (Paris, 1954).
Kragh-Jacobsen, Svend: *Royal Danish Ballet* (Copenhagen, 1955).
Krasovskaya, Vera: *The Russian Ballet Theatre* (Leningrad and Moscow, 1958).
  The Russian Ballet Theatre from its Origin to the Middle of the Nineteenth Century (Moscow, 1959).

Lambert, Constant: *Music Ho!* (London, 1934).
Lambranzi, Gregorio: *New and Curious School for Theatrical Dancing* (Nuremberg, 1716, trans. Derra de Moroda, London, 1928).
Lanchbery and Guest: *The Scores of La Fille mal gardée. Theatre Research*, Vol. III, Nos. 1 and 2 (London, 1961).
Lauze, F. de: *Apologie de la danse* (Paris, 1623, trans. Joan Wildeblood, London, 1952).
Lawson, Joan: *Classical Ballet* (London, 1960).
Legat, Nicholas: *The Story of the Russian School* (London, 1932).
Levinson, André: *The Russian Ballet* (Berlin, 1926).
  Marie Taglioni 1804-1884 (Paris, 1929).
  La Danse d'aujourd'hui (Paris, 1929).
Lynham, Deryck: *The Chevalier Noverre* (London, 1950).

Magriel, Paul (Ed.): *Isadora Duncan* (London, 1948).
Martin, John: *The Modern Dance* (New York, 1933).
Mille, Agnes de: *Dance to the Piper* (Boston, 1951).
Moore, Lillian (Ed.): *Russian Ballet Master. The Memoirs of Marius Petipa* (London, 1958).

Negri, Cesare: *Nuove inventioni di balli* (Milan, 1604).
Noverre, Jean George: *Lettres sur la danse et les ballets* (St. Petersburg, 1803, trans. Beaumont, London, 1951).
  Lettres sur les arts imitatifs en général et sur la danse en particulier (Paris, 1807).
Nuitter, Charles: *Costumes des Ballets du Roy* (Paris, 1885).

Pemberton, E.: *An Essay for the further improvement of dancing* (London, 1711).
Playford, John: *The English Dancing Master* (London, 1651).
Propert, W. A.: *The Russian Ballet in Western Europe 1909-1920* (London, 1921).
  The Russian Ballet 1921-1929 (London, 1931).
Prunières, Henri: *Le Ballet de cour en France* (Paris, 1914).

Rameau, Pierre: *Le Maître à danser* (Paris, 1725, trans. Beaumont, London, 1931).
Rebling, E.: *Een Eeuw Danskunst in Nederland* (Amsterdam, 1950).
Reggiano, Carlo: *Vita ed opera di Viganò* (Milan, 1838).
Rootzen, Kajsa: *Den Svenska Baletten* (Stockholm, 1945).

Sachs, Kurt: *World History of the Dance* (New York, 1937).
Saint-Léon, Arthur: *La Sténochorégraphie* (Paris, 1852).
Scholes, Percy: *The Oxford Companion to Music*, 9th Edition (London, 1955).
Sharp, Cecil, and Oppé, Paul: *The Dance: An Historical Survey* (London, 1924).
Slonimsky Yuri: *Masters of the Russian Ballet* (Moscow, 1937).
  Didelot (Leningrad and Moscow, 1958).
Sonrel, Pierre: *Traité de scénographie* (Paris, 1943).
Sparger, Celia: *Anatomy and Ballet* (London, 1949).
  Ballet Physique (London, 1958).
Stanislavsky, Constantin: *My Life in Art* (Moscow, 1924; London, 1948).
  An Actor Prepares (trans. Magarshack, London, 1936).
Stravinsky and Craft: *Conversations with Igor Stravinsky* (London, 1959).

Tchaikovsky, Modeste: *The Life and Letters of Peter Ilyich Tchaikovsky* (London, 1906).
Terpis, Max: *Tanz und Tänzer* (Zürich, 1946).
Terry, Walter: *The Dance in America* (New York, 1956).
Tomlinson, Kellom: *The Art of Dancing* (London, 1735).

Vaganova, Agrippina: *Basic Principles of Classical Ballet* (trans. Chujoy, London, 1948).
Valois, Ninette de: *Invitation to the Ballet* (London, 1937).
van Praagh, Peggy: *How I Became a Ballet Dancer* (London, 1954).

Weaver, John: *Essay Towards an History of Dancing* (London, 1712).
  Anatomical and Mechanical Lectures upon Dancing (London, 1721).
Welsford, Enid: *The Court Masque* (Cambridge, 1927).
Williams, Ralph Vaughan: *National Music* (London, 1934).
Wilson, G. B. L.: *A Dictionary of Ballet* (London, 1957 and 1961).
Wood, Melusine: *Advanced Historical Dances* (London, 1960).
Worsthorne, S. T.: *Venetian Opera in the Seventeenth Century* (Oxford, 1954).

Zakharov, Rostislav: *The Art of the Ballet Master* (Moscow, 1954).

Ballet Annual (London, 1946 onwards).
Enciclopedia dello Spettacolo (Rome, 1954–62).

INDEX

by Vera Brinson